RANSOM KIDNAPPING IN ITALY

Crime, Memory, and Violence

For over thirty years, modern Italy was plagued by ransom kidnappings perpetrated by bandits and organized crime syndicates. Nearly 700 men, women, and children were abducted from across the country between the late 1960s and the late 1990s, held hostage by members of the Sardinian banditry, Cosa Nostra, and the 'Ndrangheta. Subjected to harsh captivities and psychological abuse, the victims spent months and even years in isolation while law enforcement and the state struggled to find them.

Ransom Kidnapping in Italy examines this Italian criminal phenomenon. Alessandra Montalbano argues that abduction is a key vantage point from which to understand modern Italy: it troubled the law, terrified society, ignited juridical and parliamentary debates, and mobilized citizens. Bringing together archival and media materials with the victims' accounts and diverse forms of cultural response, the book examines ransom kidnapping through the lenses of historiography, law, literary criticism, trauma studies, phenomenology, and political philosophy. *Ransom Kidnapping in Italy* traces how and at what price Italians became aware of living in a country that was being blackmailed by criminal organizations that arguably jeopardized the nation even more than terrorism.

(Toronto Italian Studies)

ALESSANDRA MONTALBANO is an associate professor of Italian at the University of Alabama.

Ransom Kidnapping in Italy

Crime, Memory, and Violence

ALESSANDRA MONTALBANO

UNIVERSITY OF TORONTO PRESS
Toronto Buffalo London

© University of Toronto Press 2024
Toronto Buffalo London
utorontopress.com
Printed and bound by CPI Group (UK) Ltd, Croydon, CR0 4YY

ISBN 978-1-4875-4683-0 (cloth)   ISBN 978-1-4875-4687-8 (EPUB)
ISBN 978-1-4875-4684-7 (paper)   ISBN 978-1-4875-4688-5 (PDF)

Toronto Italian Studies

Library and Archives Canada Cataloguing in Publication

Title: Ransom kidnapping in Italy : crime, memory, and violence /
   Alessandra Montalbano.
Names: Montalbano, Alessandra, author.
Series: Toronto Italian studies.
Description: Series statement: Toronto Italian studies |
   Includes bibliographical references and index.
Identifiers: Canadiana (print) 20230521258 | Canadiana (ebook)
   20230521339 | ISBN 9781487546830 (cloth) |
   ISBN 9781487546847 (paper) | ISBN 9781487546885 (PDF) |
   ISBN 9781487546878 (EPUB)
Subjects: LCSH: Kidnapping – Italy – History – 20th century. |
   LCSH: Ransom – Italy – History – 20th century. |
   LCSH: Organized crime – Italy – History – 20th century.
Classification: LCC HV6604.I8 M66 2024 | DDC 364.15/40945 – dc23

Cover design: Liz Harasymczuk
Cover image: Detail of the *Statue of Saint Peter* (*San Pietro*, 1708–13) inside the Basilica of St. John Lateran in Rome, Italy. Sculpture by Pierre-Étienne Monnot. Photo by Massimo Merlini via Getty Images.

We wish to acknowledge the land on which the University of Toronto Press operates. This land is the traditional territory of the Wendat, the Anishnaabeg, the Haudenosaunee, the Métis, and the Mississaugas of the Credit First Nation.

This book has been published with the assistance of the University of Alabama.

University of Toronto Press acknowledges the financial support of the Government of Canada, the Canada Council for the Arts, and the Ontario Arts Council, an agency of the Government of Ontario, for its publishing activities.

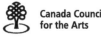

To Simonetta Camuffo and Agostino Montalbano

Contents

List of Illustrations   ix

Acknowledgments   xi

Introduction   3

1 Italy's Extraterritorialities: Tracing the History of Ransom Kidnapping   16

2 The Kidnapping of the Golden Hippy   40

3 The Day Cristina's Body Was Found   67

4 Troubling the Rule of Law   97

5 Trauma and Language in the Kidnapping Victim Memoir   128

6 The Anatomy of Captivity   167

Conclusion   198

Notes   207

Bibliography   253

Index   275

Illustrations

2.1 First Polaroid of Aldo Moro (19 March 1978)   41
2.2 Second Polaroid of Aldo Moro (21 April 1978)   41
2.3 Polaroid of Paul Getty III, *Corriere della Sera*, 23 November 1973   62
3.1 Cristina Mazzotti, *Corriere della Sera*, 2 September 1975   74
4.1 Angela Casella in Calabria, 1989   116
4.2 "La marcia dei rapiti" in Rome   120
4.3 Appeal for Farouk Kassam   125
4.4 The white sheets for Farouk   127
6.1 Luigi Rossi di Montelera enters his cell   180
6.2 Luigi Rossi di Montelera's cell   180

Acknowledgments

This book would not have been possible without the generosity of the people and institutions that supported me during my research and writing. I am thankful to the exceptional scholars that have been my mentors at New York University and have guided me ever since. I am indebted to Ruth Ben-Ghiat for reading every page of my manuscript, for her invaluable feedback and thoughtful perspective, and for continuing to be an intellectual inspiration. I am thankful to David Forgacs for his stimulating comments and especially for his thoughtful response to the case study on the Getty abduction that I presented at the Columbia Seminar of Modern Italian Studies in 2018. It is also my pleasure to thank Virginia Cox for encouraging me to pursue this project from its earliest days and Stefano Albertini for his complete support during my years at NYU. My deep thanks go also to my mentor at the University of Verona, Adriana Cavarero, for her intellectual generosity, passion, and creativity, for all the conversations I have been lucky to have with her about political philosophy, and for the doors she literally and figuratively opened to me.

Numerous friends and colleagues helped me bring this project to its final shape. I am indebted to Paola Bonifazio, Jonathan Mullins, and the members of the Works in Progress Seminar at the Department of Modern Languages and Classics at the University of Alabama, including Fabio Battista, Matthew Feminella, Micah McKay, Claudia Romanelli, Kelly Shannon-Henderson, Gina Stamm, and William Worden, for offering detailed and valuable feedback on different chapters of the manuscript. Additional thanks for feedback, suggestions, and support are due to Silvia Benso, Amy Boylan, Shane Butler, Antonio Calcagno, Patrizia Dogliani, Guido Foa, Elisabetta Girardi, Ernest Ialongo, Paula Landerreche Cardillo, Filippo La Porta, Douglas Lightfoot, Nicoletta Marini-Maio, Sara Miglietti, Marie-Anne Matard-Bonucci, Tricia

McElroy, Leslie Morgan, Ellen Nerenberg, Robin Pickering-Iazzi, Leonardo Proietti, Eugenio Refini, Dana Renga, Elvira Roncalli, Beatrice Sica, Benedetta Tobagi, Cheryl Toman, and David Ward.

I thank Melissa Swain for her editorial work and express my special thanks to Annamarie Lisko for her insights and skill in helping me edit the final version of the book. I am also grateful to my editor at the University of Toronto Press, Mark Thompson, my managing editor, Mary Lui, and my copy editor, Barbie Halaby. The two anonymous reviewers' detailed and thoughtful comments have strengthened the quality of this book.

The generous support of the University of Alabama, Loyola University Maryland, and the American Philosophical Society made possible the archival research necessary for this study. Thanks are also due to the staff at the Archivio e Biblioteca della Camera dei Deputati; Biblioteca del Senato; Biblioteca Nazionale Centrale di Firenze; Biblioteca Nazionale Centrale di Roma; Centro di Documentazione Cultura della Legalità Democratica di Firenze; Discoteca di Stato; Museo del Risorgimento Torino; and RAI Archives in Rome, Florence, and Turin. I also thank La Fondazione Corriere della Sera for supplying images taken from their historical archives.

I acknowledge the permission to reproduce portions of this book that have previously appeared in print. Portions of chapter 1 appeared in "Ransom Kidnapping: The Anonymous Underworld of the Italian Republic," *Modern Italy* 21, no. 1 (February 2016): 35–49, https://doi.org/10.1017/mit.2015.3, and sections of chapter 6 appeared in "Snatched from the World: The Phenomenology of Captivity in Italian Ransom Kidnapping," *Modern Language Notes* 132, no. 1 (January 2017): 204–22, https://doi.org/10.1353/mln.2017.0010.

My most special thanks go to my wife, Jessica Goethals, who knows more about kidnapping in Italy than she would have ever wanted. A superb scholar, excellent baker, and perfect travel companion, Jess not only made this book possible by reading every single draft and supporting me along the way, she made our life full of love, adventures, and laughter. My stepfather Giorgio Bisotto offered continuous support and hospitality, while my sister Sabrina Montalbano and my niece Viola Grassi made my trips to Italy so special. Finally, this book is dedicated to my mother, Simonetta Camuffo, and my father, Agostino Montalbano, for having always encouraged me to follow my passions and for all their love.

RANSOM KIDNAPPING IN ITALY

Introduction

"They bind me like a dog, like any beast that you want to keep captive," Carla Ovazza states in her memoir, *Cinque ciliege rosse: Una notte lunga trentacinque giorni* (Five red cherries: A thirty-five-day-long night).[1] Ovazza was abducted by the 'Ndrangheta (the Calabrian Mafia) in Turin in 1975 and held hostage in a farmstead in Piedmont for over a month, chained, blindfolded, and terrified by her persecutors, who demanded a five billion lire ransom from her family. She was liberated after the Ovazzas paid hundreds of millions of lire. Two years later, she published the account of her ordeal to mobilize public opinion and politicians against what she called a "market for human flesh."[2] Her abduction was part of a phenomenon that in the 1970s became daily news in Italy and lasted for three decades, with nearly 700 people abducted across the country. Linked to Sardinian banditry, Cosa Nostra ("Our Thing," the Sicilian Mafia), and especially the 'Ndrangheta, kidnapping was a crime that dehumanized its victims and horrified their families and society in order to obtain money. Although the violence perpetrated by banditry and organized crime reached a national scale and marked the country's identity and memories, ransom kidnapping is today a phenomenon largely overshadowed by the violence and the political abductions inflicted by ideological domestic terrorism for which the 1970s are mostly remembered.

For those who know something about the kidnappings of those years, Aldo Moro is the name that comes to mind. Moro, the former prime minister and president of the Christian Democratic Party (DC), was snatched and killed in 1978 by the Marxist-Leninist terrorist group the Red Brigades (BR). On the morning of 16 March, Moro and his police escort were driving on Via Fani in Rome when a commando of the BR blocked their cars and opened fire. The bodyguards were killed, and Moro was taken hostage. He spent fifty-five days in the "prigione del popolo" (the people's prison), as the BR called the hiding spot, during which time he was subjected to a "trial" by his warders and wrote letters to his family, his colleagues, and even the pope, asking them to save his life.[3] Some of his letters were published by the press, who followed the development of Moro's detention as if the country itself were a hostage of terrorism. The Italian government refused to negotiate with the BR, and on 9 May his perpetrators executed Moro. They left his body in the trunk of a red car parked in the heart of Rome.[4]

The Moro affair is the event that most marked the history of the Italian Republic, in a way comparable for an American reader to the assassination of President John F. Kennedy in 1963. However, unlike Kennedy's assassination, Moro's kidnapping was not a single shocking occurrence but the peak of the Italian season of terrorism remembered today as the *anni di piombo* (Years of Lead, 1969–c. 1983). Beginning in 1970, the BR (the most prominent of the far-left terrorist groups active in the country, such as Prima Linea and the Nuclei Armati Proletari) embraced violence and turned the political protests first held by workers and students into an anti-capitalism armed struggle with revolutionary objectives.[5] Abductions, *gambizzazioni* (kneecapping), and killings were daily actions for which the BR claimed credit by leaving behind messages featuring their well-known five-pointed star insignia. Their targets were individuals considered symbols of the economic and power systems, such as factory leaders and administrators, politicians, judges, and journalists. It is certainly not difficult to understand why 1970s Italy is associated with terrorism. Although the expression *anni di piombo* is commonly associated with the violence of the far left, far-right terrorists were also very active. Indeed, scholars consider the first event of the Years of Lead to be the 1969 Piazza Fontana bombing in Milan (seventeen dead, eighty-eight wounded), which was planned by neofascists.[6] Far-right terrorists used bombs to randomly kill a large number of people without ever claiming responsibility for their operations (a technique called *stragismo*, slaughter tactics).[7] Their goal was to create panic within society in order to destabilize the country, influence elections (fear usually results in a more conservative vote), and impose law and order through a more authoritarian regime.[8] The Moro kidnapping and murder remain emblematic of these highly controversial and bloody years.

A Statistical Overview

Today Italian bookstores dedicate entire sections to the terrorism of the Years of Lead and the Moro affair, which are, not surprisingly, at the centre of scholarly investigations and critiques.[9] However, abductions were not exclusively a tool of terrorists. Although the most famous kidnapping was political or, better, ideological, less than thirty abductions were carried out for political motives.[10] According to the Ministero dell'Interno (Ministry of the Interior), between January 1969 and February 1998, there were in contrast 672 cases of ransom kidnapping in Italy linked to Sardinian banditry and organized crime.[11] As some of these cases involved more than one victim, the number of people kidnapped reached 694, of which 564 were men and 130 women.[12] The highest incidence was in 1977 (before the Moro abduction), with seventy-five cases. Other peaks were hit in 1975 (62 cases), 1979 (66), and 1982 (51). Kidnappings occurred with the greatest frequency between the mid-1970s and the mid-1980s, when bandits and 'ndranghetisti were active at the same time. Between 1975 and 1984, there were 471 cases with 489 victims. Thus 70 per cent of all kidnappings occurred in this period – that is, during the Years of Lead. The year 1985 marked the beginning of a decline in the phenomenon, which decreased even further after 1991 due to the 'Ndrangheta's new policy towards the crime and to anti-Mafia activism.[13] Of Italy's twenty regions, the only ones in which there were no kidnappings were Valle d'Aosta, Friuli Venezia Giulia, and Molise. In contrast, the most hard-hit regions were Lombardy (158 cases), Calabria (128), and Sardinia (107). Of the victims, eighty-one never returned home, and of these the bodies of fifty-three were never found. Of all the people kidnapped in these years, only ninety-three were freed by the police. In the majority of cases (511), investigations nevertheless obtained positive outcomes that brought about the arrests of 3,302 criminals.[14] While it is not possible to calculate the total proceeds from the ransoms, the sum likely reaches hundreds of billions of lire (the presumed average ransom in the period between 1969 and 1990 was almost 500 million lire).

Originating in the Sardinian mountains of Barbagia and gaining national dissemination at the hand of the 'Ndrangheta (responsible, in addition to those in Calabria, for the vast majority of the abductions perpetrated in Lombardy and all over the peninsula), ransom kidnapping captured public attention and brought the problem of crime to the doorsteps and television sets of Italian citizens. The effects of the violence linked to banditry and criminal syndicates were not secondary; they affected the civic life of the country to the point that many Italians adopted security measures, such as requesting gun licences, hiring bodyguards, and even leaving the country.[15] Former prime minister Silvio Berlusconi and France's former first lady Carla Bruni, born and raised in Italy, both told journalists that in the 1970s kidnapping forced them and their families to live abroad.[16] While terrorists were making history by forging the 1970s and the early 1980s into the Years of Lead, bandits, *mafiosi*, and especially the *'ndranghetisti* were transforming Italy into the European country of ransom kidnapping. In *I sequestri di persona a scopo di estorsione* (Kidnappings for ransom, 1984), which analyses the years 1968–83, Salvatore Luberto and Antonio Manganelli compared the Italian data with that available from other European nations. Italy, it turned out, was the one in which the phenomenon was the most widespread for the longest period of time, a sad record to hold.[17] For this reason, the historian Enzo Ciconte defined kidnapping as an "Italian offence."[18]

The Years of Ransom Kidnapping

Terrorism is not the only factor overshadowing the violence that made Italy nationally exposed to, and therefore aware of, its domestic organized crime. Another factor is that the way we generally think about the Mafia (at least until recently) is shaped more by fiction and imagination than by facts and historiography. The 1969 novel *The Godfather* and its 1972 cinematographic adaptation, for example, as well as the internationally known 1984 Italian television series *La piovra* (*The Octopus*), made the Italian Mafia coincide with the Sicilian Mafia and even with a Sicilian mentality, culture, and identity.[19] Italy, in reality, is the homeland of three main Mafias, each originating in the nineteenth century and rooted in three different regions: the Camorra in Campania, Cosa Nostra in Sicily, and the 'Ndrangheta in Calabria.[20] Of the three, the Camorra and Cosa Nostra existed before the Italian Unification (1861), while early evidence of the existence of the 'Ndrangheta comes from the 1880s. Settled in the poorest region of the peninsula, the 'Ndrangheta is today the most powerful Mafia in Italy. While all three criminal syndicates are active on a global scale, the 'Ndrangheta is the one with the highest number of colonies outside its regional headquarters.[21] However, among the Italian Mafias, the Calabrian one remains the least "famous." The 'Ndrangheta lacks the same cultural mediation that Cosa Nostra, and more recently the Camorra, has received through literature, film, and TV series.[22] Roberto Saviano's bestseller *Gomorra* is probably the most familiar example.[23] A non-fiction book that resembles a journalistic investigation into the global black market controlled by the violent Neapolitan Camorra, *Gomorra* was published in Italy in 2006, printed in more than fifty countries, and adapted to both a cinematographic representation and a fictional television series that instantly became international successes.[24]

Historians also recognize the role that fiction and especially *omertà*, the silence that surrounds and protects the Mafia, play in shaping collective imagination and knowledge. However, they identify in a specific historical event the moment in which the real nature of organized crime emerged: the 1980s maxi-trial against Cosa Nostra. Mafia boss Tommaso Buscetta's revelations on the structure of the Sicilian Mafia to Judge Giovanni Falcone offered a detailed picture of the organization, its military essence, its rituals of initiation, and the different roles of its affiliates. In short, the possibility of writing the history of the Mafia began with the confession of one of the first Mafia *pentiti* (defectors) in Italy.[25] The subsequent shocking assassinations by Cosa Nostra of Falcone in May 1992 and of his colleague and friend Judge Paolo Borsellino in July of the same year – both by bombs that also killed their bodyguards and brought Italy's memory back to the *stragismo* of far-right terrorism – are considered the moment in which the country realized that the Mafia was not a Sicilian but rather a national issue and was frighteningly more powerful than the state.[26]

Yet, if a history of organized crime depends on the available accounts of its affiliates, the histories of its impact do not. Indeed, the kidnapping phenomenon had already exposed the entire country to the presence of organized crime within Italian territory and democracy. The syndicate responsible for the 1992 *stragi di mafia* (Mafia massacres), the *corleonesi*, was the same whose former boss Luciano Leggio (called Liggio) began the abduction season in the north in 1972 and became a nationally well-known figure after being arrested in 1974 in Milan.[27] Moreover, ransom kidnapping made the country especially aware of the 'Ndrangheta. Perhaps more difficult to investigate and study than Cosa Nostra – the *'ndranghetisti* generally belong to the same nuclear families and are therefore less inclined to speak – the Calabrian Mafia was known for decades by the Italians to be responsible for the kidnappings of hundreds of people. *Lettere a San Luca: L'Italia scrive al "paese dei sequestri"* (Letters to San Luca: Italy writes to "the village of ransom kidnappings"), a 1990 collection of letters written by Italians and addressed to the mayor, the priest, and the administrators of San Luca – a village in Aspromonte, the epicentre of abduction and headquarters of the 'Ndrangheta – is an example of how the region of Calabria became associated with its organized crime and subjected to criticism that equated its inhabitants with criminals.[28] In the same year, however, as we shall see in chapter 4, a movement of solidarity that involved the families of the victims, the people of Calabria, and engaged citizens from all over the country united to fight against ransom kidnapping and free the Aspromonte. The ordeals of the kidnapped people, their

8 Ransom Kidnapping in Italy

kin, communities, and cities, as well as the responses of judges, politicians, and intellectuals, offer a narrative that gives the 'Ndrangheta a much less "unknown" and marginal role in twenty-first-century Italy and instead portrays it as a Mafia eager to control capitalism and kill judges decades earlier than the Camorra depicted by Saviano and the frightening Cosa Nostra. Ransom kidnapping, this book argues, was the means by which banditry and especially organized crime empowered and modernized themselves and extended their activities across the country and beyond. Seen through the lens of abduction, the 1970s are not only the years of terrorism. They are also, and not less importantly, the years in which Italians became aware of organized crime as a domestic and national threat. Indeed, by the year 1978, when Moro was abducted and killed, Italy had already witnessed hundreds of ransom kidnappings and would do so for two additional decades until the late 1990s.

Ransom Kidnapping in Italy thus tackles two deeply rooted beliefs about violence in the second half of twentieth-century Italy: that at the national level violence only coincided with terrorism; and that Mafia violence was only perpetrated among its own syndicates in the south. If the first belief is the result of how we remember the 1970s, the second is the outcome of how we forgot them. In early 2010, for instance, the mayor and the prefect of Milan, Lombardy, publicly asserted that in their region there was no Mafia.[29] Yet, among all the Italian regions, between 1969 and 1998 Lombardy had the highest number of abductions perpetrated by organized crime, a clear indicator that the Mafia has been there for decades. During the Years of Lead, indeed, ransom kidnapping became a veritable industry across the country. For its main perpetrators, abducting was a means of accumulating capital to invest in both licit and illicit business (as we shall see in chapter 1). Bandits, *mafiosi*, and *'ndranghetisti*, unlike the BR, never claimed responsibility for their actions. Abduction was not for them a symbolic strike against power or a financial tool to sponsor subversive projects (as it was for the BR). It was instead a business with which to grow and create other businesses. Visibility and publicity were, conversely, the enemy of banditry and organized crime, which did not have any revolutionary intent and wanted to remain anonymous. This secrecy brought the media to initially identify the abductors under the general name of *anonima sequestri* (anonymous kidnapping) – a label still used today to talk about the kidnapping phenomenon. They believed that behind the crime existed a sole and impenetrable organization moved by masterminds above suspicion.[30] *Anonima sequestri* was later used with the adjectives *Sarda* (Sardinian) or *Calabrese* (Calabrian) to specify the matrix of the kidnapping cases in the news, but it was also followed by the acronym *S.p.A.* (*società per azioni*, joint-stock company), which emphasized the unknown and suspicious identity of the abductors, like that of anonymous financial investors. Employed by journalists to suggest that professionals could have been involved in the abduction business, this acronym remarkably captured the nature of the syndicates behind ransom kidnapping. While leftist terrorism opposed capitalism, banditry and organized crime instead made use of it to accumulate and launder money. The 'Ndrangheta in particular was able to exploit the country's ongoing economic transformation to become today one of the strongest and richest criminal organizations on earth.

The Effects of Ransom Kidnapping

This is the first book to examine the impact that abduction had on Italian civic life, politics, and media. By bringing together archival materials with the testimony of the victims and cultural productions, this study explores the violence of kidnapping and its legacy and, just as importantly, reconstructs from an interdisciplinary framework the memory of a crime that shaped the collective imagination, perception, and future of the Italian Republic. Despite its extended and extreme social and political consequences, there have been no studies of the kidnapping phenomenon to date. The existing Mafia and criminological studies exclusively consider abducting in terms of the kidnappers' agency – that is, their criminal intent, economic objectives, or networks. Victimological studies (a branch of criminology) frames the victims' ordeals through psychological or psychoanalytical lenses. Yet histories of Mafia syndicates and criminological inquiries are narrow in scope, leaving unexplored the magnitude and broader social significance of ransom kidnapping as a phenomenon that plagued Italy for over thirty years. What was the impact of being exposed to the violence of ransom kidnapping on society, blackmailed families, and vulnerable hostages? How did the Italian state handle the presence in its territory of extra powers such as banditry and especially organized crime?

By widening the analysis to media, parliamentary, public, and testimonial narratives of abduction, *Ransom Kidnapping in Italy* shifts perspective to look at the crime through its effects: public critique, social awareness, trauma, and disembodiment. Merging a historical-juridical examination of kidnapping with theoretical lenses from the fields of literary theory, trauma studies, phenomenology, and political philosophy, this book considers not merely the facts and the perpetrators but also the experience of captivity and its literary depiction, as well as media and visual representations of the phenomenon. I analyse the violence of ransom kidnapping through, for example, a theoretical frame that puts at the centre of the analysis bodily vulnerability and perception. To do so, I use Adriana Cavarero's reflections on contemporary violence and the figure of the *inerme* (helpless) to examine the horrific materials to which Italians were exposed by the media, such as the Polaroid photos of the hostages in captivity and the testimonial accounts of the survivors.[31] I also use Maurice Merleau-Ponty's phenomenology of perception to examine the mediation of kidnapping's violence by television newscasts, the language of the testimonial narratives, and the experience of disembodiment that the kidnapped people suffered during their confinement.[32]

It is especially through the stories of kidnappings, and thus through the power that the philosopher Hannah Arendt recognizes in storytelling, that this book allows its reader to bear witness to the trauma that ransom kidnapping represented for the hostages and for Italy. The kidnapped people were suddenly attacked and ripped from their social and familial contexts, without any subsequent possibility for communication. Hidden in unknown places, whether caves or holes in the ground, they disappeared from their lives. From the first moment of the assault, a victim's body was deprived of perception: beaten, immobilized, blindfolded, and disoriented. Isolated from the rest of the world, and completely under the control of their warders, the abducted lived highly traumatic ordeals that lasted anywhere from a few weeks to several years. They were men and women, adults and children alike. Hundreds of families were forced to collect money and drive up and down Italy following kidnappers' instructions and claims. Police and army helicopters flying over the peninsula's mountain territories in search of hidden hostages created a new view of the Italian landscape in the media. It became clear to the public that Italy's territory included distant, impenetrable, and unreachable zones in which people could disappear.

The testimonial narratives of the ransom kidnapping survivors possess the perceptual frame that permits the imagining of an otherwise unimaginable ordeal for those who never experienced it. However, as we see in chapter 5, for Carla Ovazza, Luigi Rossi di Montelera, Donatella Tesi Mosca, Dante Belardinelli, and Giuseppe Soffiantini, writing a memoir was a way to bear witness to their own ordeals. As Cathy Caruth emphasizes in her pivotal book *Unclaimed Experience: Trauma, Narrative, and History*, trauma is "an event that is experienced too soon, too unexpectedly, to be fully known and is therefore not available to consciousness until it imposes itself again, repeatedly, in the nightmares and repetitive actions of the survivors."[33] All the kidnapped victims describe in detail their assault because it is the most unexpected and sudden moment of their abduction. "A traumatic experience is not fully assimilated as it occurs," Caruth continues, which explains why writing a memoir can be for the survivors an attempt to assimilate this experience and to make the "not known" something known.[34] Yet the kidnapping memoir opens a unique window on the chain of traumatic experiences that abduction provokes, on the terrifying isolation of captivity, and on the dangerous bond between hostage and warder. Testimonial narratives, I argue, give to the authors/survivors a viewpoint that they lacked while inside their hiding places with their traumatized ego. Through their accounts the kidnapped victims return to their hostage self with the reader as a witness.

In this book I also explore ransom kidnapping as a collective traumatic experience. Sociologist Jeffrey C. Alexander calls "cultural trauma" a concept of trauma as a process, a construction, or a mediation for which it becomes a collective experience, even if the traumatic event is lived by a group or a minority.[35] Media, public speakers, civic organizers, and survivors, for example, can be agents of the process that constructs cultural trauma. Ransom kidnapping, this study demonstrates, was a violent phenomenon that shaped the Italian imagination and became a collective experience. The abductions of Paul Getty III in 1973 and Cristina Mazzotti in 1975, analysed in chapters 2 and 3, respectively, are perfect examples of how this crime captured national attention and made the trauma of ransom kidnapping collective. These two stories, and especially the analysis of Cristina Mazzotti's ordeal, show that the 'Ndrangheta traumatized Italy with ransom kidnapping before the Red Brigades did with the 1978 political abduction of Aldo Moro. The kidnapping and death of Cristina Mazzotti shocked the country and initiated the political debate about the negotiations that became central during Aldo Moro's captivity. The expression "hard line" (*linea dura*), commonly associated with the state's refusal to negotiate with terrorists to liberate Moro, was initially used by some judges and politicians in the aftermath of Mazzotti's death to convince the public that in order to stop the unbearable growth of ransom kidnappings in Italy, the state had to prevent the victims' families from paying the ransom by freezing their assets. When Moro was abducted, as we shall see in chapter 4, Italy was already the European country with the highest number of ransom kidnappings, and Moro's request to negotiate with his kidnappers was not just the result of his unbearable situation; it also reflected the doubts about the hard line that he held even before being kidnapped himself.

The stories this book tells are also stories of resistance against the violence of ransom kidnapping and critiques against a state often

12   Ransom Kidnapping in Italy

perceived as incapable of fighting organized crime. The creation of the Cristina Mazzotti Foundation in the 1970s; the 1988 protests in Turin to free seven-year-old Marco Fiora, held hostage by the 'Ndrangheta in Aspromonte for seventeen months; Angela Casella's trip to Calabria in 1989 to obtain the solidarity of the local women and mobilize the region to liberate her eighteen-year-old son Cesare after more than two years; and, among others, the 1990 *marcia dei rapiti* (the march of the kidnapped people) in Rome to demand that political institutions liberate Aspromonte and end abduction all demonstrate that to remember the phenomenon of ransom kidnapping also means to remember the anti-kidnapping and anti-Mafia movements. By protesting against the kidnappers and the state, this civic engagement made the crime too visible and too risky for the 'Ndrangheta to continue – as its *pentiti* affiliates confessed.[36]

Book Synopsis

Six chapters and a conclusion unite archival materials with victims' memoirs and other cultural representations, retracing the kidnapping stories that created the national narrative of the phenomenon. The study passes chronologically and geographically through the origins, spread, and development of ransom kidnapping and thematically through civic, political, and ontological analyses. Not simply a study of organized crime, this book brings back to memory a forgotten chapter of modern Italy and demonstrates that the spectre of ransom kidnapping permeated late twentieth-century collective identity and imagination. The book shows that the most prominent intellectuals, novelists, and directors of the period – Italo Calvino, Natalia Ginzburg, Alberto Moravia, Vittorio De Seta, and Ettore Scola, among others – thought through questions of violence by pointing to the kidnapping phenomenon as one of the most troubling threats of the century. Even in today's literature, as we shall see in the conclusion through the analysis of Elena Ferrante's bestseller *L'amica geniale* (*My Brilliant Friend*, 2011), abduction is an unbearable evil deeply rooted in the Italian imagination. *Ransom Kidnapping in Italy* traces how and at what price Italians became aware of living in a country blackmailed by criminal organizations that jeopardized democracy even more than did terrorism.

Chapter 1, "Italy's Extraterritorialities: Tracing the History of Ransom Kidnapping," offers a historical and cultural reconstruction of kidnapping that examines its three main roots: Sardinian banditry, Sicilian Mafia, and Calabrian 'Ndrangheta. Through an analysis of parliamentary and trial documents, the chapter traces the different periods and development of the phenomenon as well as the distinct uses that bandits and organized crime made of it. In addition to archival materials, cultural representations and scholarly investigations are examined in order to grapple with the variety of ways in which kidnappers were depicted. A comparative and diachronic exploration counters the notion of abducting as an archaic phenomenon and instead – without negating continuities with the past – demonstrates its modernity. Deconstructing a common social class approach to the crime, it instead sees kidnapping as the result of the presence in Italy of powers other than the state capable of controlling entire territories of the country. Finally, by exploring the assassinations by the 'Ndrangheta of Francesco Ferlaino in Calabria (1977) and Bruno Caccia in Piedmont (1980), judges close to dismantling the ransom kidnapping network, this chapter demonstrates that organized crime represented a threat to the state and used violence and corruption to obstruct the regular functioning of democracy.

Chapter 2, "The Kidnapping of the Golden Hippy," is a case study on the abduction of Paul Getty III by the 'Ndrangheta in 1973. The first kidnapping of its kind, the seizure became a true media sensation, not least because its victim was an American teenager and the grandson of the then richest man in the world. His abduction marked a new and torrential phase in organized crime that led the 'Ndrangheta to create a "kidnapping industry." Getty was indeed the first of the many hostages abducted outside of Calabria and brought to the mountains of Aspromonte, the southern part of the region, which became for the Italians an impenetrable territory where people could disappear. This chapter analyses the media representation of young Getty and his family, the use of newspapers and Polaroid photography by the kidnappers, and the public debate that followed the hostage's ear mutilation. By approaching the ransom kidnapping phenomenon through a case study, the chapter allows the reader to observe how the country became aware of the existence and threat of the 'Ndrangheta and to explore the origins of the national narrative on ransom kidnapping. The Getty abduction shocked the country and the world and pushed Italian intellectuals such as the novelist Alberto Moravia to analyse the horrifying wave of violence by criminal syndicates.

Chapter 3, "The Day Cristina's Body Was Found," examines the impact that the abduction and murder of eighteen-year-old Cristina Mazzotti by the 'Ndrangheta in 1975 had on Italy's identity and memory. Cristina's body was found two months after her abduction in a garbage dump in Piedmont. Of the hundreds of kidnapping episodes that occurred in the country, Cristina's was perceived as a true national traumatic event. Through the analysis of civic responses and media

14   Ransom Kidnapping in Italy

reactions to her death, the chapter sheds light on how her abduction changed the debate on negotiations, law, and organized crime and how it shaped representations of ransom kidnapping and violence in Italy. Based on newspaper and public television archival research, this chapter explores symbols, objects, and rhetorical codes that mapped the crime in the collective imagination of the 1970s. The Mazzotti kidnapping became the counterpoint of the Getty abduction and the case that made ransom kidnapping an Italian phenomenon. These two case studies allow us to trace the public discourse on criminal violence and ransom kidnapping that shaped the Years of Lead and anticipated the Moro affair.

Chapter 4, "Troubling the Rule of Law," examines the twenty-year-long debate on whether the state should allow victims' families to negotiate with criminals. Through analysis of the legal literature on kidnapping, the chapter traces the legislative process that in 1991 led Italy to enact a law that froze victims' assets. The media representation of the institutions and their response to the crime; the reaction of public opinion; and civic engagement as a critique of the state will all be discussed. Starting from the political answer to the Mazzotti kidnapping and murder, passing to the impact that the Moro abduction had on the redefinition of the crime, and arriving at the second kidnapping crisis of the late 1980s and early 1990s, this study examines the evolution of Italy's reaction to kidnapping from an initial horror and dismay to a participatory solidarity expressed towards the victims and their relatives. By examining the cases that most mobilized families, communities, and associations to the point of creating an anti-kidnapping movement, the chapter demonstrates that ransom kidnapping was not simply a crime but rather a violent phenomenon that meddled in the relationship between the state and its constituents. This investigation elucidates the legal and political debate over terrorist and ransom kidnapping as one about the state itself and shows that the country's active citizenry was the key factor that led organized crime and banditry to stop abducting.

Chapter 5, "Trauma and Language in the Kidnapping Victim Memoir," examines the testimonial book through the lens of literary theory and trauma studies. Without the victims' self-narratives, it would not be possible to frame ransom kidnapping at both political and relational levels. The memoirs of the victims are in fact the testimony of the hostages of the Italian underworld, and their agency stems from a desire and duty to make visible a reality that was otherwise invisible in media, legal, and victimological narratives. By analysing the language and rhetoric of these accounts, and especially the impact of the isolation of captivity on the traumatic bond between the kidnapped and their warders, this chapter identifies the different confessional narratives of the victims as a form of resistance against the power of the abductors and as a way to return to society. The chapter concludes by mapping the witness borne by these memoirs on public discourse and civic awareness.

Chapter 6, "The Anatomy of Captivity," looks at the crime beyond the financial scope of the abductors. Through Maurice Merleau-Ponty's ontology of the flesh and Adriana Cavarero's ontology of vulnerability, the chapter analyses captivity as an experience of disembodiment. I argue that the sensorial deprivation imposed by confinement prevented the victims not only from perceiving the world outside – and therefore from being able to localize their hiding place – but also from being exposed (from being visible, audible, etc.) to the world. Without the reflexivity of perception, through which one is present to oneself as an embodied subject (sentient and sensible), victims became disembodied consciousnesses, meaning that they could not situate their body in a topological space. Chained, the hostages also completely depended on their persecutors and occupied the position that Cavarero calls the *inerme*. If infancy is the condition in which a human being is at the same time vulnerable and helpless, the circumstance of the kidnapped people was therefore a forced return to that primal condition.

Abducting became an ontological crime that, in the words of its victims, like those of Ovazza quoted earlier, reduced the hostages to animals in chains. *Ransom Kidnapping in Italy* provides a new perspective on the violence in Italy during the second half of the twentieth century, and it does so by exploring the broader social and human impact of Italy being the European country of ransom kidnapping. In addition to writing a missing chapter of contemporary Italy, this book offers an original interpretation of the memory and experience of ransom kidnapping through the analysis of the unfolding narrative in media and political discourses. By focusing on what was visible on television, the press, and the accounts of the victims – images that are still present in the mind of every Italian who lived through that time – this study explores what the country learned and knew about a crime that revealed the unscrupulous cruelty and nature of domestic criminal syndicates capable of abducting and traumatizing men, women, and children for profit.

Chapter One

Italy's Extraterritorialities:
Tracing the History of Ransom Kidnapping

It is not surprising that in 1973 the prominent novelist Alberto Moravia might have mistakenly believed that Paul Getty III's kidnapping – the first abduction of its kind to bring international attention to this Italian phenomenon – was linked to banditry rather than to organized crime.[1] Up until the early 1970s, newspapers and media broadcasts told Italians that the vast majority of ransom kidnappings in the country were connected to Sardinian banditry. Italians were therefore accustomed to imagining kidnappers as bandits. The news, a lack of knowledge about the 'Ndrangheta, and the history of brigandage in Calabria (a reality similar to that of banditry in Sardinia) led Moravia to conflate the figure of the bandit and the *'ndranghetisti* responsible for Getty's abduction.[2] Yet organized crime and Sardinian banditry – that is, the two main perpetrators of ransom kidnapping in Italy – gave rise to distinct models of abduction that, as we shall see in this chapter, greatly differed in duration, structure, purpose, and effects.

While Moravia's misinterpretation is explained by early journalistic narratives of kidnapping, his horrified conclusion that Getty's ear mutilation was indicative of a sociological mutation of banditry finds its perceptual frame in early 1950s cultural anthropology. Moravia was particularly familiar with Franco Cagnetta's fieldwork on bandits and pastoral communities in Orgosolo, Sardinia, at the heart of Barbagia – the island's mountain region. In 1954, in fact, *Nuovi Argomenti* (New topics), a journal directed by Moravia himself, dedicated an entire issue to Cagnetta's pioneering study, which firmly criticized law enforcement's colonialist attitude towards the local population.[3] As a result, the Minister of the Interior, Mario Scelba, denounced both Cagnetta and Moravia for "defamation of the armed forces" and "publication of news intended to disturb public order."[4] The journal *Nuovi Argomenti* was temporarily shut down.

In spite of (or perhaps because of) this censorship, Cagnetta's work had a strong impact on public opinion, historiography, and cinema. The acclaimed historian Eric Hobsbawm cites Cagnetta's work in his well-known analysis of social bandits and rebels, for example, while Vittorio De Seta's anthropological film *Banditi a Orgosolo* (*Bandits of Orgosolo*) – inspired by Cagnetta's work – won the Premio Opera Prima at the 1961 Venice Biennale.[5] Unlike in his 1958 nostalgic short documentaries on the pastoral Sardinia, in *Banditi a Orgosolo* De Seta denounces the state's policy and the unbearable living conditions that were turning the island's shepherds into bandits.[6] Although it took two decades for Cagnetta's complete study on Orgosolo to come out in Italy after its initial banning, his book was first published in French in 1963 under the title *Bandits d'Orgosolo* and with a preface written by Moravia.[7] Crime on the island, writes Moravia, is the effect of the colonialist attitude of the Italian state towards Orgosolo. Certainly the state cannot match Cagnetta's ethnographic competence, he observes, but it especially lacks the "human sympathy" and "pietas" of his work, that is, "the only attitude that should be kept towards the past."[8] Notably, what strikes Moravia is Cagnetta's scientific but at the same time "poetic" way of relating to "archaic" societies and the past – something that he had encountered previously in Claude Lévi-Strauss's anthropological study of Amazonia.[9]

Moravia's horror at the 1973 mutilation of Getty's ear is therefore a reaction to the downfall of a long-standing belief both in banditry as a resistance against state and police injustices and in the bandit as a Robin Hood figure. However, in Moravia's public commentary on Getty's ordeal, ransom kidnapping went from being in itself a shocking event to a tool with which to examine his own historical moment. Between 1973 and 1976, he published four articles and a short story on this subject.[10] In a 1974 article celebrating the referendum on divorce, for example, Moravia employed the term "kidnapping" as an antonym for democracy and modernity. After sarcastically presenting ransom kidnapping as Italian society's way of balancing out the existence of tax dodgers, or the recent political abduction of a judge, Mario Sossi, by the BR as a way of counteracting the excessive use of censorship by the judiciary, Moravia depicts the referendum as an "antidote" to what he calls the "kidnapping society" – that is, "the society in which, thanks to abuses and crimes of all sorts, an equilibrium establishes itself."[11] This, continues Moravia, "is not a modern and democratic society ... but rather a much more traditional and antiquated kind of society, which lately has increasingly surfaced in our country."[12] It is striking that Moravia looks at one of the most significant referenda of the Italian Republic through the lens of kidnapping, but even more so is the fact that he applies the term "kidnapping" to society and not to a crime. In his view, the referendum is an antidote because it shows Italians the power of the vote. By voting out the ineffective political establishment, Italians can "drive back the kidnapping society" that they have allowed to take hold.[13]

However, what is increasingly evident in Moravia's articles is the impact that ransom kidnapping had on his view of the past and of archaic Italy. While in his 1963 preface to Cagnetta's book he declares sympathy and pietas to be the only possible attitude towards the past, in his 1970s analysis of abduction, the past turns into the thing that haunts society, democracy, and modernity. No longer the downfall of a previous conception of banditry, kidnapping is now for Moravia an old legacy that prevents the country from moving forward. In his 1976 "Pasolini or the Myth of Peasant Culture," kidnapping is something that proves wrong his good friend and acclaimed poet, writer, and film director Pier Paolo Pasolini – a fervent defender of Italy's disappearing agropastoral culture.[14] Written a year after Pasolini's death, Moravia's article reads, "It was pointless for me to tell him, for example, that Italy's ills did not really come from industrialization and consumerism but from the secular decay of his beloved peasant culture; what he used to call mass criminality, that is, the mafia, the kidnappings, the robberies … was instead the criminality of poorly and insufficiently urbanized peasants."[15] The poetic approach to the past that Moravia recognized in anthropologists like Cagnetta and Lévi-Strauss shifts, in his conversations with Pasolini, into a literary myth, a golden age that appeals to nostalgic audiences, while in the real country Mafia and kidnappings – products of the past and a secular cultural decay – prevent Italy from becoming a modern country.

This chapter draws the opposite conclusion than Moravia – that is, ransom kidnapping, even if not new, was not a legacy of Italy's past but rather a modern phenomenon. Yet Moravia's articles are notable because they show the impact that abductions linked to both banditry and organized crime had on Italian intellectuals and their cultural analysis before the most well-known and best-remembered kidnapping, that of Aldo Moro by leftist terrorists in 1978. In other words, ransom more so than political kidnapping offered Moravia a lens through which to frame his time. Although his personal opinions on the phenomenon led him to reject peasant culture, the anthropological perspective he initially embraced was similarly adopted by those in charge of investigating the crime in Sardinia. The relationship between the state and the pastoral communities that anthropology emphasizes is in fact at the centre of criminological and parliamentary studies of abductions on the island. The same anthropological gaze, however, was never used to examine the ransom kidnappings conducted by Cosa Nostra and the 'Ndrangheta – a clear indication of cultural and social diversity among kidnappers that Moravia erased. By looking at ransom kidnapping as a three-decade-long phenomenon, this chapter offers a comparative study of Sardinian, Sicilian, and Calabrian kidnappings that underscores the relationship between local and national criminal contexts, as well as between regional communities and the state's economic, legal, and political reach (or, at times, lack thereof). This chapter shows that ransom kidnapping was not merely an "Italian crime" but was rather a specific tool through which banditry and criminal organizations alike accessed the wealth produced by the national economic transformation and converted the country's less industrialized and more isolated areas into profitable places of business.

While they both made use of abductions to access this wealth, their scopes were notably different. If the evolution of ransom kidnappings in Italy occurred in such a way that bandits came in contact with other criminal organizations capable of laundering dirty ransom money, they nevertheless did not invest this money in illegal activities like the drug and arms trafficking that constituted the Sicilian Mafia's and the 'Ndrangheta's springboard into the international sphere.[16] Rather, the bandits invested in construction, building dwellings in the towns of Barbagia. In other words, this type of criminality remained more provincial in scope.

Within the Mafia only one branch – the *corleonesi* – performed abductions in Sicily and on the mainland during the first half of the 1970s. Conversely, within the 'Ndrangheta numerous *cosche* actively engaged in kidnapping at both regional and national levels from 1970 up to the early 1990s. Therefore, the pervasiveness and the duration of kidnapping is far more pronounced with the 'Ndrangheta than in other branches of organized crime. While the Mafia did not transport victims to Sicily, hundreds of hostages were brought to Calabria from all over the country – in particular from Lombardy – and we can understand why journalists and public opinion identified the 'Ndrangheta (together with Sardinian banditry) as the *anonima sequestri* (anonymous kidnappers). Likewise, the financial impact that the abductions had on the 'Ndrangheta cannot be compared with the impact they had on the Mafia. The ransoms from kidnapping in fact radically changed the former, helping the *'ndrine* (families of the 'Ndrangheta) become entrepreneurs capable of taking advantage of public investments in the 1970s and, by the beginning of the 1990s, of becoming leaders in international drug trafficking.

20 Ransom Kidnapping in Italy

By examining the 'Ndrangheta's killings of Judges Francesco Ferlaino in Catanzaro (1977) and Bruno Caccia in Turin (1980), both engaged in fighting the syndicate's kidnapping business, this chapter also sheds a new light onto the memory of these two cities where the most important trials against far-right and far-left terrorism, respectively, took place. In addition to signifying the threats of terrorism, this chapter argues, Turin and Catanzaro demonstrate that an 'Ndrangheta specialized in ransom kidnapping endangered the rule of law and democracy through corruption and violence against judicial power. Neither symbolic nor ideological, as it was for terrorism, the killing of judges was for the 'Ndrangheta a matter of convenience and anticipated Cosa Nostra's 1992 shocking assassinations of judges Giovanni Falcone and Paolo Borsellino.

The chapter thus not only provides a full picture of Italian ransom kidnapping in the second half of the twentieth century but also offers a comparative perspective on the country's most violent decades. By pinpointing kidnapping's roots and the evolution of abductions, we will observe how and why organized crime branched out across the country and for years constricted its citizens, whom the state ultimately failed to protect.[17]

Sardinian Ransom Kidnapping

In the Italian Republic, kidnapping for ransom started in Sardinia, where banditry gave rise to a specific model of abductions that criminologists call pastoral kidnapping. Between 1966 and 1968, we find thirty-three cases on the island. The phenomenon caused great alarm throughout the entire country to the point that in October 1969, the parliament instituted a Commissione parlamentare d'inchiesta sui fenomeni di criminalità in Sardegna. On 29 March 1972, the committee's president, Senator Giuseppe Medici, submitted to the chambers a report that defined kidnapping as a modern variant on the island's traditional rural brand of criminality:

The crime characteristic of Sardinia belongs to its pastoral world, which has its centre in Barbagia ... it is not that there is no crime in the city ... but in Barbagia and in the nearby countryside, there exists a typical crime, whose deep roots must be sought in the nomadic pastoral world that produces it. As long as that nomadic pastoral world – which we will call *barbaricino* in order to better define its characters – exists, the crime of its bandits will also exist: a crime that is a product of that world just as the Mafia of the fiefs flourished in the large Sicilian estates.[18]

The committee therefore asserted a correlation between Sardinian crime and the crime characteristic of its internal area, the Barbagia, long a land of brigandage. Ransom kidnapping was thus a modern crime perpetrated by traditional Sardinian banditry. Kidnapping's newness corresponded not to the novelty of the crime, which in the case of Sardinia had ancient roots going back to the fifteenth century, but instead to the fact that it had become a "dominant crime."[19] Indeed, between 1950 and 1971, eighty kidnappings were carried òut on the island. To the committee, the crime appeared to be a reaction to the region's industrialization and economic transformation in those same years. To the greater availability of wealth and to the new consumerist lifestyle models corresponded just as many new reasons to commit crimes. Nevertheless, as Nereide Rudas and Pietro Marongiu later noted, "kidnapping ... is not reducible to a simple origin of *pauperism* but rather more complex and dialectic interactive processes."[20] The Medici report was of the same opinion, with two documents illustrating that the most well-known figures of Sardinian banditry came from well-to-do shepherding families.[21] If poverty cannot be considered the direct cause of banditry, Sardinia's economic structure nevertheless remains crucial to understanding pastoral kidnapping. It was between the world of the Barbagia, founded on the precariousness of its nomadic shepherds, and the modern development of the island that the bandits found both the support and the resources with which to enrich themselves.

The committee's insistence on the region's socio-economic situation had three objectives: to suggest that the state intervene by means other than the force that had been adopted theretofore and that had proven unsuitable for resolving the question of banditry;[22] to push Sardinia's internal areas out from the isolation that criminologists had singled out as facilitating crime;[23] and to alter the lifestyle of the nomadic shepherd in order to avoid the danger of *latitanza* (abscondence or fugitiveness) that, as we shall see, constituted a fundamental source of manpower in the kidnappings.[24] The Medici report deemed it necessary to transition from a nomadic to a settled form of shepherding because the former produced a sociocultural environment in which such crimes could exist. The so-called *barbaricina* (of Barbagia) culture was in fact considered the ideological baggage of banditry and therefore the origin of Sardinian extortion kidnapping: life in the Barbagia communities was based on their own laws and customs, handed down for centuries, which contrasted starkly with the legal code of the Italian state. Several anthropologists have identified egalitarianism (that is, the just distribution of scarce resources), vendetta, and envy to be among the guiding principles of this archaic society.[25] Stealing was considered "taking" by the shepherds, and killing in response to a suffered offence was a "duty." Many of the behaviours judged to be criminal by the official state power were therefore not only accepted according to the *barbaricina* cultural norms but in fact represented archaic methods for returning to social order. Among the typical crimes in the nomadic pastoral world, those most perpetrated were destruction of property, extortion, livestock theft (*abigeato*, or rustling), and kidnapping. Observing these trends, the Anti-Mafia Parliamentary Committee noted that on the one hand, kidnapping perfected the pervasive phenomenon of blackmail and, on the other – and more importantly – offered a progressive "substitution" for rustling. In the *barbaricina* culture there was no ethical distinction between the theft of sheep and the abduction of men.[26] This lack of distinction is reflected in the saying "men do not bleat," common among shepherds and indicative of how it was easier for them to hide the owner of a flock and to keep him from speaking than to hide the flock itself – not to mention the greater gains that the ransom for a person represented.[27]

However, the most serious criminal problem in Sardinia was *latitanza* (fugitiveness from justice). In 1967, there were officially 139 clandestine outlaws.[28] Indicted by the state, these men were considered bandits by Italian society but not by their *barbaricine* communities of origin, which instead protected them from investigations by the police and magistracy. Furthermore, these communities helped fugitives withstand a difficult life hidden among the mountains of Barbagia, the territories of which were more accessible to the wandering shepherds who belonged to that environment than to forces of order. These bandits therefore enjoyed the support of their villages, and they often came to be mythologized and celebrated as heroes capable of epitomizing to the highest degree *balentìa*,[29] the foremost value of that world, denoting the courage and strength of an ideal masculinity. Among the most renowned bandits of this era, Pasquale Tandeddu and Graziano Mesina[30] were famed as elusive outlaws and encircled by a romantic aura that made them appear more like symbols than men.[31] It was often around these charismatic and economically well-off figures that the bands responsible for numerous kidnappings formed. The Medici report held *latitanza* to be "the natural school for banditry," and it identified the slowness of the Italian legal proceedings, as well as the marked contrast between the laws of the state and the *barbaricino* code, as a cause of the phenomenon. Shepherds suspected of criminal behaviour were routinely subjected to a preventive imprisonment that could last even for years before a definite sentence was reached, one that often established the innocence of the accused. This process meant the economic ruin of the shepherds, since they had to abandon their flocks. Mistrust of the legal system and its time frames thus brought many to choose the life of the *latitante* and dedicate themselves to the holding of hostages, thereby becoming bandits.[32]

In their more recent and in-depth criminological study, Pietro Marongiu and Francesco Paribello frame the Sardinian matrix of kidnapping within the broad time span between 1966 and 1997. According to these two scholars, it is necessary to subdivide the abductions occurring in the region into "at least two fundamental subtypes, called *internal* and *external kidnapping* respectively."[33] In the internal kidnapping – the traditional criminal manifestation of the agropastoral areas of "internal" Sardinia – offenders and victims belonged to the same geographical, social, and cultural space. This subtype, predominant until the mid-1970s, has been numerically exceeded by the external, evolutionary form of the traditional type, in which the victims are above all entrepreneurs and professionals of urban origin rather than local farmers and landowners, often natives of continental Italy and at times foreigners.[34] Analysing the temporal distribution of the 143 kidnappings that took place between 1966 and 1997, Marongiu and Paribello demonstrate that 50 per cent are concentrated in two five-year blocks. Between 1966 and 1970, forty kidnappings took place in Sardinia, of which twenty-four were internal and sixteen were external. In the five years between 1976 and 1980, the kidnappings numbered thirty-three, of which nine were internal and twenty-four external. The most important detail emerging from these data is that even if the identity of the victims changed during the evolution of the crime, that of the kidnappers did not. This is clear from the fact that no matter where they were picked up, the hostages were released mainly in the district of Nuoro, in Barbagia, the geographical origins of the crime's authors.[35] Far from scaling back following the 1969 parliamentary investigation, in the subsequent ten years banditry spread, striking with greater frequency urban and tourist centres of the island, whose inhabitants represented the possibility of accessing greater amounts of wealth. The expanding radius of captures signalled a radical change in the crime on multiple levels. With regard to the hostages, the duration of their imprisonment lengthened notably as a result of the vast sums asked of their families, who found it difficult to procure the money. The bandits – ever more inclined to obtain the material privileges they saw in their victims and less and less serving as symbols of the values of *barbaricina* culture – progressively lost the approval of the pastoral community, which now expressed an "inert" and merely "economic" solidarity with the bandits that was linked to the "advantages induced by the flow of riches that arrived

24 Ransom Kidnapping in Italy

in the community through kidnapping."[36] For this reason, as well as the elevated risks and the difficult profits that kidnapping by then represented, the phenomenon completely dried up after a last flare-up in 1991–5, which with ten kidnappings saw Sardinia surpass every other region of Italy.

As a conclusion to this discussion of pastoral kidnapping, we must consider a few final aspects that distinguish this form from the organized crime matrices, including the provisional nature and structure of banditry as well as the use to which the profits were put. While the Sardinian criminals were connected horizontally and formed bands that dissolved at the end of each kidnapping, the *'ndrine* that specialized in the crime were internally hierarchized, always remained the same, and thus over time became true professionals, as we shall see. Moreover, bandits, unlike *mafiosi* and *'ndranghetisti*, invested the ransom money in real estate but not in drug trafficking. Finally, the "Sardinian-Tuscan" postscript of kidnapping's pastoral origins should not be forgotten. The emigration of *barbaricini* shepherds recreated on the mainland the sociocultural conditions that protected bandits: in the mountainous territories of Tuscany, Lazio, and part of Emilia-Romagna, abductions took place until the end of the 1990s.[37] Moreover, numerous Sardinian shepherds, having emigrated, took part in kidnappings with Mafia roots, assuming secondary roles.

However, the highest number of abductions performed by banditry happened in Sardinia, where the phenomenon remained linked to its pastoral roots. As the Anti-Mafia Parliamentary Committee and criminologists highlight, though, kidnapping was not merely a result of the *barbaricina* culture but was the consequence of its clash both with economic development on the island and with the state, which was largely responsible for turning shepherds into bandits and for the isolation of the Barbagia. Banditry therefore exposes the presence in the Italian Republic of an entire area excluded from progress and in contrast with the modern state. The well-to-do figures of banditry (and those who could benefit from money laundering) transformed the precariousness of the Barbagia into a business. The same happened in another mountainous area of the country, the Calabrian Aspromonte. Unlike Sardinian banditry in Barbagia, though, the 'Ndrangheta held complete territorial control over Aspromonte.

Organized Crime and Ransom Kidnapping

Whereas Sardinian banditry remained a localized phenomenon in terms of both scope and impact, the Sicilian Mafia and the Calabrian

'Ndrangheta enacted ransom kidnapping on a national scale. Of these two criminal organizations, the 'Ndrangheta took the lead in developing what would become a kidnapping industry. In this section, we will first explore how and why the Mafia performed abductions before analysing the 'Ndrangheta ransom matrix. Finally, we will examine the impact that these two criminal organizations had on ransom kidnapping and, conversely, that ransom kidnapping had on them.

The Mafia Root

For the Sicilian Mafia, ransom kidnapping was a means of acquiring both capital and power. However, within the Mafia only the Corleone branch dedicated itself to this crime, and only in the first half of the 1970s. The *corleonesi* were active both in Sicily and on the mainland, especially in Lazio, Piedmont, and Lombardy. After a few kidnappings on the island, they moved their activity to the north, where they abducted the entrepreneur Pietro Torielli Jr. in Lombardy on 18 December 1972 and snatched Luigi Rossi di Montelera in Turin, Piedmont, on 14 November 1973. Of the defendants convicted by the tribunal and Milan's court of appeals, the powerful boss Luciano Liggio, a fugitive in the Lombard capital shielded by both Mafia affiliates and members of the state, was called the "organizer and leader" of the band responsible for the crimes.[38] The Sicilian season of abductions in the mainland ended after Liggio's arrest in 1974. Even if brief, though, this period marked the beginning of a long series of ransom kidnappings in the industrialized areas of the country and allowed the Mafia to create connections and collaborations with other national and international criminal organizations – such as the Calabrian 'Ndrangheta and the French Marseillais clan – with whom Liggio performed several abductions.[39]

The brevity of the Mafia root phase is attributable to several factors, at both the regional and the national level. Sicily, unlike Sardinia and Calabria, was not a centre for kidnapping in the Italian Republic because the Cosa Nostra regional commission banned the practice within the island in February 1975. This prohibition has been interpreted in diverse ways that are not necessarily mutually exclusive. Historian John Dickie sees kidnapping and its forbiddance in terms of power struggles between Mafia branches. The Corleone branch – whose bosses were noted figures like Salvatore Riina, the aforementioned Liggio, and Bernardo Provenzano – was responsible for three strategic abductions on the island (those of Pino Vassallo, Luciano Cassina, and Luigi Corleo) between 1971 and 1975. By kidnapping key figures of the Sicilian upper class close to and protected by Mafia leaders such as the La Barbera brothers, Tano Badalamenti, and Stefano Bontate, the *corleonesi* proved both the weakness of these other bosses' territorial control and the rise of their own power. It was in response to this power grab, Dickie suggests, that the Sicilian Mafia adopted a ban on kidnapping that was "a tactical move as well as a practical one: it was aimed at the *corleonesi*, and intended to isolate them within Cosa Nostra."[40]

Voices from within the Mafia, on the other hand, suggest that the ban was an act of consensus taken to protect the organization's social position and authority. Tommaso Buscetta, the powerful boss from Palermo who became a police cooperator, explained that the prohibition was a question of convenience.[41] The Mafia bosses worried about attracting the attention of the police and public opinion to the island, which would have impeded the development of other, more lucrative criminal activities, as well as losing the support of the Sicilians who might have disapproved of a crime as odious as kidnapping. Buscetta's interpretation of the ban shows us that the Mafia, unlike the 'Ndrangheta, decided against using kidnapping as a means of territorial control.

Another factor in the Mafia's resistance to kidnapping in its own territory is that *mafiosi* had already developed different ways to access the capital of the region's richest social classes. Journalist Ottavio Rossani – author of *L'industria dei sequestri* – asks with bitter irony: "Who to kidnap, if almost all the powerful people, the holders of economic power, were connected to Mafia and political power?"[42] On the problem of the dearth of potential victims, the criminologists Salvatore Luberto and Antonio Manganelli further observe that the island's entrepreneurial and commercial sectors, general targets for kidnapping elsewhere, were compelled to pay the Mafia in order to conduct their activities, which probably immunized them from other forms of extortion.[43]

Outside of Sicily, the 1996 Commissione parlamentare d'inchiesta sul fenomeno della mafia e sulle altre associazioni criminali identifies three main factors that compelled the Mafia to halt kidnapping on a national scale. First, after initially having accumulated financial capital, the Sicilians invested in drug and arms trafficking. Compared to these other illegal businesses, in fact, abduction was not a profitable activity, nor was it as quick. The second factor was that the Sicilian Mafia lacked an available territory that would permit it to continue to kidnap. By contrast with the approach taken by the 'Ndrangheta in Calabria, as explored later, the Cosa Nostra committee's ban on kidnapping effectively prevented the Mafia from keeping hostages in their home territory of Sicily. The third determining factor is linked to the different models of settlement that the Sicilian *mafiosi* and the Calabrian *'ndranghetisti* developed in central and northern Italy, to which we now turn.

Luberto and Manganelli highlight what can be taken as a decisive reason for why the Mafia moved the kidnapping business off the island and what made possible the expansion of the crime – especially its Calabrian matrix – into the economically rich regions of central and northern Italy. The state's 1965 anti-Mafia law, which compelled convicted criminals to resettle far from their regions of provenance, "created numerous mafia hotbeds in a large part of the national territory and especially in the north."[44] Thus it is possible to understand how, from 1974 onwards, "the geography of the crime was completely upset,"[45] not only encompassing Sardinia, Calabria, and Sicily but also involving a large part of Italy, and Lombardy in particular. "It would be arbitrary and ungenerous," in the assessment of the two criminologists, to attribute the diffusion of kidnapping "to the imposing emigratory flow from the south and the islands towards the more industrialized regions."[46] The crime was in fact spread throughout the country by criminals and particularly by those who were forced to leave their own regions. The anti-Mafia law (which of course included the 'Ndrangheta as well) had disparate impacts on the Sicilian and the Calabrian criminal organizations. Compelled to abandon their places of origin, the Calabrian *'ndranghetisti*, unlike the Sicilian *mafiosi*, moved their families into the forced residences and thereby recreated their networks in the north: "By sending to the north parts of the *cosche* [Mafia clans] that established themselves there permanently, Calabrian Mafiosi were able to create real *enclaves*. This conscious choice of the 'Ndrangheta allowed it to create – in the heart of the industrial triangle and amid the full economic boom – a real control of the territory, a Mafia dominion of town squares, streets, portions of villages and neighbourhoods in cities such as Turin and Milan or in municipalities of the Torinese and Milanese outer belts."[47] If the presence of Sicilian criminals in the north did not have a territorial characteristic, the *'ndranghetisti* established themselves permanently, colonizing those territories in which they were constrained to move. In short, the 'Ndrangheta was able to export from its native region not only crime, as the Mafia did, but also an operating model that took control of the territory away from the state and entrusted it to the *locali* of the *'ndrine* (urban businesses or rural farms that became true meeting places for 'Ndrangheta families).[48] In this way, the Calabrian criminal organization could create colonies that represented Calabria – and in particular the Aspromonte – throughout the Italian state. In the next section we will see how the network established between the *'ndrine* settled in the north and the *cosche* in Calabria was the key factor that allowed the 'Ndrangheta to create a perfect kidnapping machine.

28   Ransom Kidnapping in Italy

The 'Ndrangheta Root

The 'Ndrangheta is the criminal organization that had the strongest impact on the phenomenon of ransom kidnapping and the one which was the most impacted by it. With its *'ndrine* scattered across the country, the group essentially blackmailed Italy for more than twenty years until deciding to stop the practice in the early 1990s. Through this criminal activity, the 'Ndrangheta became famous throughout the nation (and beyond) and was identified as the Mafia of kidnapping. Unlike the Sardinian banditry and the Sicilian Mafia, the 'Ndrangheta made use of abduction as a strategic tool of territorial control, to solidify the network between the *'ndrine* in Calabria and those settled outside the region and to demonstrate power. After a first kidnapping committed in Calabria on 26 August 1970,[49] the *'ndranghetisti* operated uninterrupted in this sphere until 1991, performing 128 kidnappings in the region and numerous cases on a national scale. Lacking a committee at the time that decided matters for all of the clans (*cosche*) in a manner akin to that in Sicily, the Calabrian organization did not have a univocal line of conduct. In the first period of kidnappings, many *'ndrine* were involved in the phenomenon.[50] This changed profoundly after the second half of the 1970s, when a handful of 'Ndrangheta families took over the business.

In the early 1970s, while the more traditional *cosche* resolutely resisted this type of moneymaking activity, due in part to the perceived dishonour that the kidnapping of women and children brought to the Honoured Society (Onorata Società),[51] numerous *'ndrine* that belonged to the younger generations rejected the ideology of the patriarchs and subverted their authority, becoming active abductors. As the magistrate Nicola Gratteri and the historian Antonio Nicaso aver, "kidnappings were a pretext and contributed to creating a vortex in the bosom of the 'Ndrangheta" that resulted in the "first Mafia war" (1975–9), considered a generational clash between the old and new bosses.[52] Antonio Macrì and Mico Tripodo, declared opponents of the kidnappings and respected supporters of a certain kind of Mafia "morality," were assassinated by younger *cosche*, of which the Piromalli of the Gioia Tauro plain, the Strangio of San Luca, the Barbaro of Platì, and the Ietto of Natile di Careri – *'ndrine* of unscrupulous kidnappers – were all allies.[53] Ciconte also noted the ideological conflicts between the various 'Ndrangheta families like, for example, that in 1978 between the De Stefanos and the Mammolitis. The boss of the 'Ndrangheta in Reggio Calabria, Paolo De Stefano, proclaimed himself completely against the kidnappings, while in the provinces the Mammolitis – responsible for the 1973 abduction of Paul Getty III – continued undeterred in their activity.[54] In the following years, the 'Ndrangheta not only learned how to perfectly perform abductions but was also the criminal organization that transformed kidnapping into a perfect industry, able to capture hundreds of hostages and earn money for thousands of collaborators.

However, we cannot understand how or why ransom kidnapping became what it did by looking exclusively at the development of this crime as the result of a "moral shift" within the 'Ndrangheta. We also need to consider the economic transformation of Calabria and its impact on the different *cosche*. The public prosecutor of Locri – a hotbed of kidnapping – Carlo Macrì highlighted the connection between the Calabrian economy in the 1970s and the escalation of abductions.[55] According to Macrì, at that time the region was divided into three macro zones – the city of Reggio Calabria, the Tyrrhenian area, and the Ionian area – to which corresponded three distinct economies, respectively: an urban tertiary economy; a developed and quite rich agricultural economy; and a combination of pastoral, poor agricultural, and small tertiary economies. The 'Ndrangheta was present in all of these zones, but it was in the Tyrrhenian and Ionian areas that ransom kidnapping became the crime that, for different reasons and in different periods, financed the local *'ndrine*. The capital accumulated with the abductions allowed the *cosche* of the Gioia Tauro plain (in the Tyrrhenian area) to go from being "a Mafia that exercised its domination parasitically mostly through extortions"[56] to being entrepreneurs and drug traffickers.

The occasion for this transformation came when, as a consequence of the 1970 Reggio revolt that broke out when Catanzaro and not Reggio was named the region's capital, the Italian state decided to support Calabria through a massive public investment project, the construction of an iron and steel centre and a port in Gioia Tauro (the so-called Colombo package).[57] The 'Ndrangheta used the money extorted from the victims' families to acquire "trucks, lorries, excavators, and gave life to the formation of Mafia companies in the construction industry that participated in the competition for public contracts."[58] In other words, kidnapping allowed the *'ndranghetisti* to seize the state's investments in Calabria. The *'ndrine* immersed into the licit market the illicit capital obtained from ransoms, thus contributing to their transformation into entrepreneurs capable of controlling both public investments and the construction market in the territory of Calabria.[59] Moreover, the powerful *cosche* of the Gioia Tauro plain (Piromalli and Mammoliti) used ransom kidnapping as a means of accumulating money to then invest in different and more profitable crimes, such as drug and weapons trafficking. As active kidnappers between 1970 and 1980, they performed extremely remunerative abductions at the national level – especially in

30 Ransom Kidnapping in Italy

Lazio, Piedmont, and Lombardy – and, with the kidnapping of Paul Getty III in 1973, opened the season in which Calabria became Italy's hiding place. Nevertheless, the *cosche* of the Gioia Tauro plain were allied with the *'ndrine* of the Ionian zone, whose members, we shall see, were the true professionals of ransom kidnapping.

The 'Ndrangheta of the Ionian area was strongly connected to the 'Ndrangheta families settled in the north, became the centre and organizer of the kidnapping business, and gained complete control over the Aspromonte. This zone was the poorest in the region and the one in which criminal kidnapping remained present for the longest period (up to the 1990s). The local *'ndrine* had been active at the regional level since the beginning of the 1970s, performing abductions that targeted small business owners, professors, lawyers, doctors, and often pharmacists. The judicial response to this early 1970s phase of kidnapping in Calabria was very weak and coincided with the removal of criminals from the region[60] that, as seen, had the side effect of both exporting and re-rooting the 'Ndrangheta all over the country. As a result, in the second half of the 1970s a close collaboration developed between the *'ndrine* of Calabria and those in the rich regions of northern Italy.

The revelations made by two *'ndranghetisti* who became police cooperators – Antonio Zagari and Saverio Morabito – helped the magistrates of Milan understand the 'Ndrangheta's operating model.[61] While the *'ndrine* settled in the north handled the capture of the victims (who were more well-to-do and accessible than their southern counterparts) and their transport to Aspromonte, where they would be hidden, the 'Ndrangheta families in Calabria oversaw the imprisonment, the ransom payment negotiations, and the liberation of the hostages. This explains the birth of a monopoly over extortion kidnapping. The *cosche* of Locride, and especially those of the Aspromonte triangle – Platì, San Luca, Natile di Careri – became the most active, given the suitability of their locations for the hiding and keeping of hostages.[62] The Calabrian mountains, geographically very similar to those of the Barbagia in Sardinia and therefore impenetrable to those who did not know them well – were rich in "natural prisons" in which hostages were confined for interminable periods. Carlo Celadon, a nineteen-year-old boy from Vicenza (Veneto) kidnapped on 25 January 1988 and released 5 May 1990, was held chained in the caves of Aspromonte for 831 days. In the same period the eighteen-year-old Cesare Casella of Pavia (Lombardy), seized 18 January 1988 and freed on 30 January 1990, was hidden in the area for 743 days.[63] The 'Ndrangheta from the Locride did not spare children from the same treatment. In 1987, seven-year-old Marco Fiora from Piedmont was confined in Aspromonte for seventeen months. When his kidnappers released him, Marco could barely walk.[64]

Kidnapping provided a source of income to economically marginalized inhabitants of the area that "received" kidnapping victims, which reinforced the 'Ndrangheta's hold on the territory and provided the syndicate with a power base. The *'ndranghetisti* were able to foster a consensus about the crime in Aspromonte, thanks to the production of "a particular economy linked to the material administration of the kidnappings."[65] The *'ndrine* entrusted the care of the hostages to the numerous *latitanti* present in the vicinity, as well as to shepherds and their young affiliates, which kept costs low and provided income to the area. At the end of the 1980s, the Commissione parlamentare d'inchiesta sul fenomeno della mafia e sulle altre associazioni criminali, asking why the 'Ndrangheta abductions continued even though the criminal organization had for some time dedicated itself to much more lucrative crimes, responded:

> As many prosecutions against followers make clear, the custody of the hostage allows very poor shepherds to make about twenty million lire per year while maintaining their own jobs. The main benefit to the masterminds is probably not directly economic in nature. Aspromonte connects the Ionian and Tyrrhenian seas, that is, the top of North Africa and the Middle East with Naples, Rome, and Genoa, the heart of Italy and the door to Europe. Through kidnapping, the masterminds therefore guarantee an annual income to an extensive network of followers and in so doing receive consent, loyalty, and, above all, the control of an essential territory for their more profitable activities.[66]

For the 'Ndrangheta, kidnapping was an endeavour that went beyond the earnings that the extortions guaranteed for their bosses. Rather, it appeared to be, in the words of the committee, a system that guaranteed the inhabitants of Aspromonte an economic advantage through which the bosses obtained territorial control, via the local population itself, over the Mediterranean crossroads, which were also a stronghold of the Calabrian criminal organization. This extraterritoriality of Aspromonte had a strong political valence, given that with it the 'Ndrangheta made the state appear incapable of liberating the hostages everyone knew were imprisoned in those caves.[67] Rendering the mountains of Calabria inaccessible to the forces of law and order meant demonstrating the inviolability of the territories around San Luca, a town in which all of the leaders of the *'ndrine* and their affiliates from around the world met annually. The impenetrability of Aspromonte therefore symbolized the invulnerability of the 'Ndrangheta itself.[68] Anything but the rural and pastoral criminals that they wished to depict themselves as, the *'ndrine* – wearing the masks of kidnappers and pocketing the ransom monies – experienced a radical modernization that carried them into the 1990s as renowned in international crime in narcotics and at the cutting edge of money laundering.

The year 1991 drew the organized crime matrix of kidnappings to a close. The phenomenon wound down for several reasons. Motivated in part by a law freezing the assets of hostages' families (see chapter 4), drawn up that very year, the decision to end the kidnappings was one of convenience for the 'Ndrangheta. The year 1991 coincided with the end of the "second Mafia war" (1984–91), which caused nearly seven hundred deaths over seven years. The long trail of blood was the consequence of the conflicts that arose between different *'ndrine* of Calabria (as well as some in northern Italy) over important contracts and territorial control. The war concluded with a *pax mafiosa* that more than anything else was "a non-aggression pact,"[69] allowing the 'Ndrangheta to concentrate fully on the international narcotics trade in which it had that year become the undisputed leader. One fundamental aspect of the truce was the creation of a committee charged with the direction of the Calabrian Mafia. In addition to putting an end to the feud between 'Ndrangheta families, the committee "decided to put an end to ransom kidnapping."[70] A consensus thus emerged in 1991 as the 'Ndrangheta – engaged on other criminal fronts – decided to prohibit a crime that had by then become too expensive and too visible.

A comparison between Cosa Nostra and 'Ndrangheta kidnapping practices leads to the following conclusions. Among the Sicilian Mafia, only the *corleonesi* carried out ransom kidnappings, and almost exclusively in the first half of the 1970s, without bringing hostages abducted in other regions to Sicily. In contrast, in the 1970s, the collaboration between the *'ndrine* in the Tyrrhenian area and in the Ionian area and those settled in central and northern Italy gave rise to an extremely well-organized network. This development transformed a rural regional crime into a modern national factory that over the following decade the *cosche* of the Aspromonte triangle improved even further, becoming the largest owners of this business.[71] Moreover, ransom kidnapping was for both the Sicilian and the Calabrian criminal organizations a means of acquiring capital to invest in other, more lucrative activities such as drug trafficking, of which the 'Ndrangheta became in the 1990s a global leader. Finally, the crime also played a different role at a political level. In Sicily, kidnapping became a means of negotiating power within the organization. After having marked an internal generational clash within the *cosche* in the late 1970s, ransom kidnapping represented for the 'Ndrangheta the means by which to assert a complete territorial control over the Aspromonte and to shape an image of itself as unscrupulous and impenetrable.

Before concluding our comparison of Italy's ransom kidnappers, we must consider two violent events that show not only what ransom kidnapping meant for the 'Ndrangheta but how this crime impacted its relationship with the state. The violence the 'Ndrangheta used against the judiciary during the Years of Lead sheds different light on the decade that Italy remembers for terrorism. Rather than connecting the 'Ndrangheta of kidnapping to a past brigandage, this exceptional use of violence, as we shall see, anticipated future Mafia attacks against the magistracy.

Excellent Cadavers

During the Years of Lead, Turin and Catanzaro, the capitals of Piedmont and Calabria, respectively, held sensitive trials against leftist (red) and right-wing (black) terrorism: the Turin Trial against the leaders of the Red Brigades, and the Catanzaro Trial against neo-fascist terrorists responsible for the Piazza Fontana bombing (Milan, 12 December 1969). The latter was assigned to Catanzaro for reasons of public order.[72] The aftermath of the Piazza Fontana bombing sparked a chain of violent episodes and marked the beginning of the "strategy of tension," that is, the use of massacres by black terrorism and deviant powers to destabilize the country and push for a more authoritarian regime.[73] Although the bombing's masterminds were acquitted on account of the lack of evidence – due to an initial sidetracking of the investigations – the long Catanzaro Trial opened an upsetting window onto subversive plots in Italy. Televised by RAI (Italian public television), this trial showed that involved in the bombing were not just terrorists but the Italian secret service and politicians as well.[74] In Turin, a city where red terrorism was particularly active, the trial against the Red Brigades provoked several high-profile assassinations meant to stop the prosecution.[75] The revolution of the proletariat, the BR's leaders loudly claimed in court, could not be sentenced by the bourgeois state. These violent intimidations made it almost impossible for Turin to find citizens willing to participate as jury members in the trial, which was, indeed, postponed twice.[76]

In the history of the Italian Republic, Turin and Catanzaro therefore signify two threatening moments for democracy. This is so for the contents of their trials – the origins of terrorism in the country – but also, and perhaps especially, because they exemplify an attempt to obstruct the course of justice and undermine the rule of law. Yet, if we look at their courthouses today, we see that the Years of Lead connected these two cities for reasons other than terrorism. The current courthouses of Catanzaro and Turin are named after Francesco Ferlaino and Bruno Caccia, respectively, both judges and 'Ndrangheta's "excellent cadavers" – that is, high-profile Mafia victims.[77] Ferlaino, state attorney general at the Catanzaro Court of Appeals, was killed in Lamezia Terme-Nicastro on 3 July 1975 and was Calabria's very first excellent cadaver. Caccia, state attorney general, was killed in Turin on 26 June 1983, the first and only judge murdered in northern Italy by any organized crime syndicate.[78] The killing of a judge by the 'Ndrangheta is rare because it attracts unwanted public attention. At the time of their assassinations, Ferlaino and Caccia both were investigating ransom kidnappings. The magnitude and visibility of the trials against terrorism – although of unquestionable historical importance – risk obscuring a past that, in addition to pinpointing the presence of the 'Ndrangheta from Calabria to Piedmont, shows its use of violence against the state and its threat to democracy.

Ferlaino and Caccia were eliminated because they were inconvenient judges. Their work hindered the plans of a rapidly expanding 'Ndrangheta. Ferlaino's killers remain officially unknown to this day. Giacomo Lauro, a former 'Ndrangheta high-ranking affiliate who in the 1990s collaborated with justice, said that Ferlaino was murdered because he "opposed the degeneration of the Masonic structure from a licit to an illicit body."[79] Between the late 1960s and the 1970s, the 'Ndrangheta introduced a new rank called *Santa* (Holy).[80] Unlike the other affiliates, a *santista* was allowed to take part in Masonic lodges. The purpose was for the 'Ndrangheta to create and control networks of politicians, judges, and entrepreneurs that belonged to Freemasonry in order to have access to public contracts and money in exchange for guaranteed votes and favours.[81] Ferlaino, himself a Mason according to Lauro, opposed this infiltration. Judges and scholars do not deny Lauro's explanation.[82] However, we must acknowledge that the trial of the suspected murderers – acquitted for lack of evidence – ascribed the Ferlaino murder to names involved in ransom kidnappings. Of the three men accused, the mastermind was believed to be Antonio Giacobbe – Cristina Mazzotti's kidnapper. Ferlaino was killed in Calabria three days after Cristina was abducted in Lombardy. He had recently investigated Giacobbe's clan and was about to send the boss to a forced resettlement (*soggiorno obbligato*). National media depicted Ferlaino as the prosecutor of the *anonima sequestri* and hated by the Calabrian

Mafia because he was close to discovering the connection between all the kidnappings in the region and throughout Italy.[83] The suspected assassins were two fugitives from justice: Pino Scriva and Antonio Scopelliti. The latter had been previously involved in the abduction of Giuseppe Calì (Calabria, 1974), a case that Ferlaino investigated and for which Scopelliti was sent to jail. Both Scriva and Scopelliti escaped from different prisons a few months before Ferlaino's death.[84] While they were *latitanti* (fugitives) in the mountains of Calabria – argued the prosecutor – Giacobbe hired them to kill the magistrate.[85] Lauro's revelations, the trial, and the new *Santa* rank show that the *'ndrine* devoted to abducting reshaped the 'Ndrangheta's relationship to economic and political powers. Although the 'Ndrangheta sought to portray itself as rural and linked to the past, the media depicted the syndicate responsible for the killing of a judge as "the mafia with clean shoes" which "lives by contraband and abductions," connecting the Mafia of kidnapping to an entrepreneurial, modern economy.[86]

The first excellent cadaver in Calabria displayed the strength of the 'Ndrangheta to the nation. Killed at his doorstep in broad daylight by two *colpi di lupara* (a sawed-off shotgun used in Mafia assasinations), Ferlaino was executed as an example meant to warn his colleagues and successors. Journalists linked the murder to an upcoming large trial in Calabria for nine ransom kidnappings with more than thirty plaintiffs.[87] However, it was the response of the High Council of the Judiciary that amplified the alarm. After a short enquiry into Ferlaino's death by three delegates sent from Rome to Catanzaro, the High Council ordered a large investigation of the judiciary in the region.[88] It was the first and only time in post-war Italy that this independent institution launched an investigation of this nature, the purpose of which was to clarify the relationship between the judicial system in Calabria and the 'Ndrangheta. It was not just the murder of a judge eliminated while probing the *'ndrine* active in the province of Catanzaro and the Ionic coast to come under scrutiny. What concerned the High Council were the numerous acquittals, the unclear ways the trials were assigned to judges, and the frequent furloughs obtained by prisoners – to name just a few matters.[89] Strikingly, the death of Ferlaino in Calabria provoked the High Council to go after prosecutors rather than persecutors. In other words, the effect of the exceptional use of violence against the judiciary by the 'Ndrangheta was to shine a light on its consolidated power of corruption. Although the investigation never took place, its mediatic echo lasted for months, while doubts about the correct functioning of justice in the region lingered for years.[90]

36   Ransom Kidnapping in Italy

Whereas no one was found guilty of the Ferlaino murder in Calabria, the Caccia assassination in Piedmont was attributed to the boss of the Clan dei Calabresi ('Ndrangheta), Domenico Belfiore. The night of 26 June 1983, Caccia was shot and killed while walking his dog on his street. It was national Election Day. Caccia was known as the judge who in 1975 put the Red Brigades' leaders on trial. In 1980, he became state attorney general of Turin and oversaw the most troubled judicial cases of the time concerning politicians involved in illicit business and bribes. Among his investigations, one concerned money laundering. Like Ferlaino in Calabria, Caccia tried to dismantle the kidnapping network by following the ransom money. The targets were the casinos of Sanremo and Saint Vincent, where money from kidnappings conducted in Piedmont was laundered. Caccia also investigated doctors working at Turin's prison hospital clinic. Members of organized crime, it turned out, were using corruption to obtain the medical diagnoses needed to avoid imprisonment. The BR were at first believed to be Caccia's executioners, a belief based on false accusations received by newspapers and RAI television in the days following the shooting. Red and black terrorist groups nevertheless distanced themselves from the murder.[91] But the assassination demonstrated that the violence of the Years of Lead in Turin extended beyond terrorism. While the Red Brigades and Prima Linea – both red terrorist organizations that Caccia prosecuted – were threatening Turin's civic life, two criminal syndicates were dominating its underworld. These were the Clan dei Catanesi (Sicilian Mafia), in control of the city's drug trafficking, and the aforementioned Clan dei Calabresi, specializing in ransom kidnappings and connected to the *'ndrine* of the Ionic coast. By undertaking different crimes, the Catanesi and Calabresi occupied the same territory without becoming enemies. Moreover, they occasionally cooperated and shared hitmen. Yet it was the collaboration of the Catanesi and their boss Francesco Miano that allowed the secret service to identify the Calabresi boss Belfiore as the mastermind of Caccia's murder.[92] The result of this collaboration was not just Belfiore's life sentence. It was the end of the long bond between the Mafia and the 'Ndrangheta in Turin.

The trial for the 1983 murder began in May 1989, and the final verdict was pronounced in March 1992 – meaning that it took the Italian legal system nine years to sentence the mastermind behind the assassination of a state attorney.[93] According to the sentence, Caccia was killed because he was incorruptible. Furthermore, his impeccable behaviour and the way he led the state attorney's office in Turin obstructed the availability of other judges who had "dangerous relationships" with members of organized crime. In short, Caccia was killed because he

Italy's Extraterritorialities 37

was preventing the 'Ndrangheta from extending and consolidating its influence within the city's judicial system.[94] Remarkably, in Piedmont, as in Calabria, the assassination of an attorney general brought to the surface a grey zone in which judges, politicians, entrepreneurs, and the 'Ndrangheta overlapped. While in Calabria Ferlaino's assassination was staged according to Mafia rituals to send a clear message, as seen before, in Turin Caccia's murder was hidden amid the national election and ongoing terrorism to distract the public. The goal was to replace the attorney general of Turin – a strategic city for money laundering – with someone open to collusion. What the Ferlaino and Caccia Courthouses remind us is that in the Years of Lead, the kidnapping industry connected the *'ndrine* of Calabria to those widespread throughout the country and extended the 'Ndrangheta's judicial, political, and economic control beyond its regional borders. While Italy was mourning Cristina Mazzotti and the others who never returned home, their persecutors were killing inconvenient judges and cultivating useful relationships.[95] Although the media depicted the abductors and their violence as a presence alien to the country, as we will see in chapter 2, their business was already intersecting with sectors of society willing to collaborate with horrifying kidnapping syndicates.

Conclusion

The sympathy that bandits received from local and even national public opinion in the 1960s turned to disdain when the violence they used against their hostages became visible. If the famed songwriter and singer Fabrizio De André, kidnapped in Sardinia in 1979, could still publicly forgive his warders – but not the masterminds – after six harsh months spent in Supramonte, Barbagia,[96] the same narrative no longer existed by the time bandits cut off part of the ear of a seven-year-old boy, Farouk Kassam, to obtain a ransom in 1992.[97] Understanding kidnapping is not a matter of dropping anthropology and condemning the past, as the novelist Moravia did, but rather of framing it as a modern phenomenon. It is true that the crime was not new to Sardinia, Sicily, or Calabria, but between the late 1960s and the 1990s, kidnapping became both a reaction to and a means of modernization. The criminological literature available on Sardinia insists on the relation between the increase in abductions and the industrial development of the island. They were simultaneous processes – one the side effect of the other – in a region where the presence of the state was lacking and troubled. It would therefore be misleading to frame the phenomenon as a legacy of a past still present in modern Italy. This also applies to the Calabrian matrix of the crime. As observed, though, pastoral kidnapping has been investigated by scholars from different angles that shed light on the socio-economic dynamics of this phenomenon. However, the analysis of magistrates and historians and the revelations made by police cooperators show how for the 'Ndrangheta abductions represented a means of accessing the wealth of industrialized Italy and, in addition, a way to innovate and modernize itself. As a result, the Calabrian 'Ndrangheta, unlike Sardinian banditry and the Mafia, was able to use the season of abductions to establish political and economic networks and to widen their future horizons. Today, while banditry has more or less disappeared, the 'Ndrangheta is one of the most powerful criminal organizations in the world. Ransom kidnapping helped make this transformation possible.

The expression "kidnap industry" is in fact not merely a "colorful term coined in journalistic circles,"[98] a "journalistic cliché,"[99] or Moravia's term to indicate a social banditry subjected to capitalism.[100] It is also a term that criminologists, magistrates, historians, and parliamentary committees used to frame the dimension of the crime and especially how it was organized. In terms of numbers, the years between 1975 and 1984 were those in which this industry was particularly productive, given that 70 per cent of the abductions happened when Sardinian bandits, the Sicilian Mafia, and the Calabrian 'Ndrangheta were active kidnappers at the same time. In terms of structure, though, it is more appropriate to label ransom kidnapping as an industry in relation to the 'Ndrangheta. The 'Ndrangheta was able to create a perfect machine in which a small number of clans commissioned specific tasks to different *'ndrine* inside and outside the region and created an entire economy based on ransoms. The underworld of the 'Ndrangheta involved thousands of collaborators at all levels: from the warders and the transporters of the hostages to the bankers who laundered the money. This does not mean that Sardinian bandits or the Sicilian Mafia were amateurs in this business. Bandits and *mafiosi* were both able to perfectly organize lucrative and long abductions as well. For the reasons examined here, the Mafia decided to dedicate less time to this kind of crime. Unlike the 'Ndrangheta, Sardinian banditry did not create a large structured system because at the end of each kidnapping the bands dissolved. In other words, banditry was not a criminal organization and lacked the horizon of other illicit investments such as drug dealing. Moreover, even if bandits performed abductions on the mainland, the Sardinian pastoral matrix never reached the national dimension that the 'Ndrangheta matrix achieved. While the Barbagia became the "natural prison" of Sardinia, Aspromonte became the "natural prison" of Italy. This different proportion was not only linked to the difficulty of transporting hostages onto an island. It was also, as this chapter highlights, the expression of two different models of criminal kidnapping – a pastoral kidnapping and a kidnapping industry – and their correlate challenges to the state.

Nearly thirty years of abductions in the second half of the twentieth century do more than just tell us about an "Italian offence"; they also open a window onto modern Italian history. Italy was a country (and in part still is) in which the state had neither a complete territorial control nor the monopoly of force, and where the price of its economic development was extremely high for hundreds of its citizens, who, snatched from their world, lived unbearable ordeals in the underworld of the Italian Republic.

Chapter Two

The Kidnapping of the Golden Hippy

The two most iconic images of kidnapping in modern Italy are the proof-of-life Polaroid photographs of Aldo Moro taken in 1978 by the left-wing terrorist group the Red Brigades, who abducted and then murdered the former prime minister after fifty-five days of captivity (figures 2.1 and 2.2). In the black-and-white images, a dishevelled-looking Moro gazes directly at the camera, as he is seated against the backdrop of a Red Brigades banner; in one of the images, he is seen holding up a copy of the national daily newspaper *La Repubblica*, its headline asking, "Moro assassinato?" (Has Moro been assassinated?). Moro was kidnapped in Rome on 16 March 1978.[1] On 9 May, his body was found inside the trunk of a red car left by the terrorists on the Roman street Via Caetani. During his abduction, the Italian government decided to adopt a hard line and refused to negotiate with the Red Brigades, who were demanding the release of their comrades then in prison. The two Polaroids originally appeared in the news while Moro was a hostage, as proof that he was still alive.[2] Since then, they have been reproduced and shown innumerable times and in different formats by media, films, documentaries, books, comics, theatre, and exhibitions, reappearing over time and becoming part of the iconography that frames the Italian 1970s as the *anni di piombo* (Years of Lead).[3] While historical and traumatic, Moro's abduction belongs to a relatively small number of high-profile kidnappings performed by political terrorists. Indeed, of the more than five hundred abductions committed in the country between 1969 and 1982, fewer than thirty had ideological roots. Rather, the vast majority of kidnappings were committed for ransom by banditry and organized crime.

Terrorists were not the only kidnappers to use Polaroid photography to expose their hostages in the media. On 22 November 1973, the Roman daily *Il Tempo* published five Polaroids taken by the 'Ndrangheta to

Figure 2.1. First Polaroid of Aldo Moro (19 March 1978)

Figure 2.2. Second Polaroid of Aldo Moro (21 April 1978)

prove to the world that they had snatched Paul Getty III. Abducted for ransom by the Calabrian Mafia on 10 July 1973, Getty was the sixteen-year-old grandson of Paul Getty, the owner and founder of the Getty Oil Company, who was known to be the richest man in the world. During the kidnapping, Getty Sr. refused to negotiate with the criminals and famously proclaimed, "I have fourteen other grandchildren and if I pay one penny now, I'll have fourteen other kidnapped grandchildren."[4] As a result of this refusal, the kidnappers sent a plastic envelope containing Getty's right ear, a lock of hair, and two letters to the Roman newspaper *Il Messaggero* in October of that year; a month later, they sent Polaroids of the mutilation to *Il Tempo*. Getty was released on 15 December after his family paid a ransom of nearly $3 million.

The Italian scholar Marco Belpoliti has observed that Polaroid photography was not used by the Red Brigades simply as a means of evidence, a quality that the medium of photography in general possesses.[5] As demonstrated by the work of Andy Warhol, Polaroid images have identification and advertisement effects. Belpoliti argues that the terrorists used these effects to publicize themselves and affect audiences. In short, they made an advertisement out of the Moro kidnapping in order to attract new potential members.[6] Organized crime also used the Polaroid camera to shape public opinion – the technology was particularly useful because it did not require external development and printing.[7] Yet the photos of Getty are very different than those produced by the

Red Brigades. Unlike Moro, Getty is not facing the camera. Although rich and visible, he was not a symbol for his abductors, who, unlike the terrorists, did not claim responsibility for the kidnapping by framing their hostage with their name or logo. They wanted to remain anonymous. In these photos, Getty is seen inside a cave, and his profile – showing his mutilated ear – faces the camera. If the Red Brigades used Polaroid pictures of their hostages to invite others to join an ideological cause from the *prigione del popolo* (the people's prison), as they called their kidnapping hideouts, the *anonima sequestri* (anonymous kidnapping syndicate) deployed the same technology to demonstrate what happens when the ransom money is not paid. The 'Ndrangheta used the Polaroid for shock advertising, not propaganda.

The Getty kidnapping is perhaps the best-remembered kidnapping from this period in Italy for reasons that go beyond the hostage's high profile. If the Moro case made history, the Getty abduction possessed all the elements of a perfect story: the richest and stingiest man in the world, a mother who negotiated alone in a foreign country, a suspicious teenager nobody trusted, and a gruesome turning point. As a matter of fact, in 1973, Getty's kidnapping was at first believed by the Italian media and even by some of his family members to be a hoax. Even after many years, a film, *All the Money in the World* (2017) by Ridley Scott, and a TV series, *Trust* (2018), written by Simon Beaufoy, could still spark a heated debate about the kidnapping's authenticity.[8] Scott and Beaufoy offer two different narratives of young Getty's ordeal. The film, the screenplay of which was written by David Scarpa, portrays Getty as a kidnap victim.[9] In contrast, the TV series suggests that Getty staged his own abduction and then unwittingly became the victim of a crime syndicate. After *All the Money in the World* came out, Michael Mammoliti, an Italian American actor and the nephew of the powerful 'Ndrangheta boss Saverio Mammoliti, claimed in an interview with *Variety* that the film did not tell the truth, that Getty in reality took part in his abduction, and that Scarpa's screenplay disrespectfully depicted his uncle as only an amateur gangster.[10] However, it has largely been in reaction to the narrative in *Trust* that English-language magazines and newspapers have written abundantly on the subject, especially after Paul Getty III's sister Ariadne Getty threatened to sue the production.[11] In addition to sharing continuity with the past by reconstructing the same dichotomy of "hoax or kidnapping?" in the media, both these cultural mediations leave Italy in the background as if it were the ideal stage for their tales. For Scarpa and Beaufoy, the Italian setting is just one of the elements that made the Getty case appealing; both productions present the country through

The lens of cultural stereotypes and, more importantly, overlook Italian narratives and public discourse about the abduction. In stark contrast, Getty's story and the Polaroids of his mutilation shaped the imagination of the country far beyond their fictional potential by making the nation aware of the existence of the 'Ndrangheta and its horrifying violence.

The Abduction

At the time of his kidnapping, Paul was living in Rome with his mother, Gail Harris Getty Jeffries, and his siblings. His parents were divorced, and his father, Paul Getty II, was living in London. In 1971, Getty II's wife Talitha Pol Getty had died from a heroin overdose in his apartment in Rome, after which he refused to return to Italy in order to avoid legal investigations. His son was the first hostage to be abducted by the 'Ndrangheta outside of Calabria and to be brought into the mountains of Aspromonte, the southern part of the region, where he was hidden in caves and huts for more than five months. Getty's captivity was extremely harsh. He suffered from physical deprivation, psychological abuse, and the ear mutilation. In a long interview published by the magazine *Rolling Stone* in May 1974, a few months after his abduction, Getty entrusted the vivid account of his ordeal to the journalist Joe Eszterhas. His story was one of the first published testimonies on the condition of the kidnapped hostages in Italy. "It is a story told most starkly by a boy's ear," opens Eszterhas, who warns the reader that Getty knows that "some people will always view him as a monstrous charlatan, the teenager who plotted his own kidnap[ping] and supervised his own mutilation to rob his own grandfather."[12] After letting Getty introduce himself as an "awful snot" and as "very rude," Eszterhas describes the teen's life in Rome surrounded by women and artists (Andy Warhol, Paul Morrissey, Jack Nicholson, Faye Dunaway, Roman Polanski, and Mick Jagger), his relationship with his grandfather and family, and his refusal to get involved with politics.

However, when Getty begins to talk about his captivity, Eszterhas gives space to the young man's words, which he reports in first person. The story shifts from biography to testimony. Getty describes the capture, the transfers from one hideout to another, the meals, the letters, and the kidnappers' behaviour. Throughout the ordeal, Getty was blindfolded or his abductors wore masks, since recognizing them would have been a death sentence. Never allowed to see their faces, Getty instead stared at photographs of people published in the magazines that he was occasionally given. He reread their pages hundreds

44   Ransom Kidnapping in Italy

of times. He was sporadically allowed to listen to a radio that broadcast the news about his kidnapping. Yet the constraints of the hut in which he spent fifty days of his captivity were unbearable:

> I felt myself going nuts. I had to force myself to do something. Anything. Or I'd just sit back and start crying. So, it became the biggest thing for me each day to put a scratch on a single rock. That scratch, on that ugly bare rock, was my whole, whole routine. My calendar. The only record that a person named Paul Getty was alive ... even though he was chained up like somebody's pet animal.[13]

In that hut, Getty started to lose his sense of time and to emotionally overreact to simple things, such as feeling intense joy when he found extra food in his feeding can. His testimony becomes an increasingly intimate account of himself and of what the isolation brought him to do. "I was like a little kid playing with his sandcastles on the beach," he states after describing being allowed to draw in the sand with a stick. When the abductors gave him watercolours to paint rocks, he recounts painting and repainting his own face. Being exposed only to masks made him feel invisible. He used a spoon to try to see his face, but the effect was a distorted and scary perception. He completely lacked any bodily care, which caused him to experience an instinctive physical self-preservation:

> Or when they wouldn't take me to the stream and my hands got dirty somehow, I'd lick them. At least it was something to do and I really felt my hands clean from my own saliva. I started collecting my fingernails. Biting them off whenever they grew a little bit. Keeping the bitten-off nails in a matchbox, counting the nails and looking at my fingers each day to see if they'd grown any. Then biting them off again.

By confessing the most unimaginable actions that he performed, Getty depicts hostages' need to reach a bodily reflexivity that the extreme condition of isolation from the world radically interrupts, making the abducted disappear. In his account, the captivity of ransom kidnapping is an imposed confinement designed to dismantle the victims themselves:

> They were watching me get destroy [sic] physically and mentally and only after a while did I realize what bastards they were. Because they just watched day after day. I think it's almost easier to kill a person than destroy him that way. Watch him lick himself and collect his own nails.

The only spectators to his regression and his being reduced to an animal in chains were the persecutors who caused it. When his kidnappers moved him to the next hideout – the cave visible in the five Polaroids – Getty says that "the worst kind of solitary confinement" began and, with it, the first threats of mutilation. Following his liberation, Getty found it difficult to talk about his abductors and his brutal experience. His warders terrified him in order to prevent him from talking to the police about his ordeal and from revealing any elements that would identify the perpetrators and their hiding places. Nevertheless, he testified in person at the trial of his kidnappers.

With the abduction of Paul Getty's grandson, the 'Ndrangheta showed its power to the world and became for the next twenty years the organized crime group specializing in ransom kidnapping. Certainly in 1973 Italy could not foresee the kidnapping industry that the 'Ndrangheta would later establish throughout the country. Yet the fact that this abduction was not even perceived as a starting point of a new phase of this crime is due to popular and media narratives of young Getty's kidnapping. In the first interview that Getty gave after his ordeal, to Italian television's Mimmo Scarano in 1974, it is particularly striking to observe the attitude of the journalist, who repeatedly asks questions about Getty's life that have nothing to do with his kidnapping.[14] Shot in Getty's art studio in Via Gregoriana in Rome and broadcast by RAI, this long video radically differs from the account published the same year by the American magazine *Rolling Stone*. Scarano asks Getty approximately seventy questions; the first on the abduction is around the fifty-second. He talks to the teenager in an unusually formal way – that is, using the third person *lei* with such a young interlocutor. Although fluent in Italian, Getty is more reticent than in the *Rolling Stone* piece. Scarano opens the interview by asking, "Have you ever thought about what to do when you grow up?" – a "funny" question to ask in this case, he adds, in an ironic allusion to his interviewee's familial wealth.[15] By repeatedly inquiring about Getty's projects, the answers to which he does not take at all seriously, the journalist clearly aims to frame him as an immature and indolent future billionaire. Aside from his explicitly condescending tone, Scarano's interview has an implicit purpose. In addition to asking about his coming inheritance and the advantages of being a Getty in the business world, he scrutinizes his current financial status, his income, and his ability to pay the expensive rent for his studio. In so doing, he casts a shadow on the economic sources of Getty's enterprises, as if there were an unspoken connection between his abduction and his business.

46   Ransom Kidnapping in Italy

The Italian journalist's scepticism is not only monetary but also moralistic and political in nature. Scarano inquires whether Getty considers himself mature, if he is happy, if he plans to have a family and children, and what a normal life is according to him. He also asks if he identifies as a hippy, a label given to him by the press. After mentioning a protest in which Getty supposedly participated, he asks what Getty thinks about Patricia Hearst, the young American who at that time was still believed to have staged her own kidnapping and joined a political terrorist group.[16] Scarano does not mention her abduction directly, but he challenges Getty by claiming that if her parents would have sent her to work at the age of fifteen, she probably would not have wasted time with the revolution. The first question about his kidnapping arrives after the umpteenth one about his life goals: "Did the abduction help you mature?" There is an educational and even pedantic approach to how Scarano views the Getty abduction, as if the kidnapping was a lesson to be learned by the teenager. "What did you learn?" is in fact a question that follows, while his ordeal becomes in Scarano's language an "adventure" that perhaps changed his personality.[17] Unlike in the American magazine, in this RAI interview Getty cannot give an account of his captivity, which remains unimaginable for its Italian audience. Certainly, personal safety is one of the factors that prevented him from talking about his months in Aspromonte on national public television. However, the confrontational attitude of his interlocutor discouraged testimony. When Getty carefully names what the kidnapping left in his memory and taught him by choosing the words "vacuum," "hate," and "caution," for example, Scarano remains dissatisfied with the answers and abruptly changes the subject to the moment of his capture and the fact that his abduction was initially believed to be a hoax.

The sound and the editing of the RAI interview likewise suggest Getty's guilt by including dramatic noir music in the scenes inside his studio and a video of Italian women hanging out the laundry in a working-class building as a visual background to his voice. The daily life of simple and good Italian people is contrasted with the unimaginable life of the Getty family. The intentional effect of this narrative is to prevent the TV spectators from identifying with Getty, who, ambiguously presented as potentially the guilty party and not the victim, cannot elicit empathy. While Getty talks about normal life, for example, the audience sees black-and-white images of men at work, such as a butcher slicing an animal (perhaps not an appropriate choice for this interview) and a barber, and three women pushing strollers on a crowded street. The camera zooms out, and spectators can see buildings, roofs, working-class suburbs, and blocks of social housing, alluding to the multitude of ordinary people that live by their work, in contrast with the single voice of Getty. Echoing a Franciscan ethical narrative of poverty, more than proposing a sociological analysis of class conflicts, the visual rhetoric of this RAI interview uses a style inspired by neorealism to frame Italy as the authentically innocent one.

The Paul Getty visible to the reader of *Rolling Stone* and the one visible to the audience of RAI are radically different. If the written testimony portrays him as a hostage in Aspromonte, Italian TV frames him as a pretentious dandy inside a rich palace in Rome. Moreover, if his published words open a window onto his traumatic memory, the camera's close-ups fix on his facial expressions, waiting for a wrong answer. Yet the real striking difference between the two interviews is that Scarano, unlike Eszterhas, does not ask Getty any questions about the mutilation and only brings up Getty's abductors to ask whether they were ever nice to him and if he still hates "these individuals."[18] A month after his release, the names of his kidnappers were already publicly known, and the men were under investigation. Among the criminals arrested were powerful 'Ndrangheta bosses. Instead of putting the Italian audience in front of the new reality of the country, the national television crafted a reassuring image of Italy as threatened by a potential hoax more than by organized crime.

The Trial

The trial of Getty's kidnappers began on 12 May 1976 and ended on 29 July, after two and a half months of hearings and more than two years of investigation. The trial took place in Lagonegro, a small town in Basilicata, the region to the north of Calabria, where Getty was released on 15 December 1973. Of the nine men accused of taking part in his abduction – all of them originally from Calabria but some of them then living in Rome – only Giuseppe Lamanna and Antonio Mancuso were sentenced, to sixteen and eight years of imprisonment, respectively. The other seven were acquitted of the charge of kidnapping due to insufficient evidence. They were nevertheless sentenced for other crimes, such as drug trafficking, weapon possession, and criminal conspiracy.

The Lagonegro trial was the result of two separate and parallel investigations that overlapped in January 1974. The first, conducted by public prosecutors in Rome, was an investigation of narcotics trafficking in the capital. By pretending to be drug dealers, officers of the American Drug Enforcement Administration (DEA) were able to infiltrate a criminal syndicate dedicated to drug trafficking in Italy and beyond, and in April 1973 (three months before Getty's abduction), they almost

48 Ransom Kidnapping in Italy

concluded a sting operation against Saverio Mammoliti, a Calabrian fugitive from justice, in Piazzale Clodio in Rome. Although the sting was not successful, the collaboration with the DEA enabled prosecutors to identify members of the Mammoliti clan operating in the Eternal City. The second investigation was that of the Getty kidnapping conducted by the public prosecutors of Lagonegro. The intersection of these two investigations became publicly known on 17 January 1974, when the Italian police simultaneously arrested eight people in Rome, Piedmont, and Calabria, most suspected of being involved in both the abduction and the narcotics dealing. One key piece of evidence was the money found in Giuseppe Lamanna's apartment in Rome, searched by the Roman police in charge of the drug investigation, which was identified as part of the ransom money paid by James Fletcher Chace, Getty Sr.'s emissary, to Paul's kidnappers in Calabria.[19] Lamanna was part of the Mammoliti 'Ndrangheta clan, whose boss Saverio was considered responsible for the Getty abduction.

By the time of the 1974 RAI Getty interview, this news was well known, and the 'Ndrangheta became the subject of social and political concern at the national level. The most widely circulated Italian newspaper, *Corriere della Sera*, published nine articles over three days (17–19 January 1974) about the two investigations, with full pages dedicated to the details and backgrounds of the suspects.[20] Throughout January, one to two articles about the case were published daily; many appeared in February and March, and several came out every month until 27 March 1976 – two years later – when the *Corriere* announced the date of the Lagonegro trial. The reporting of that time clearly shows that the Getty abduction made the 'Ndrangheta visible to the nation. Far from being the innocent place portrayed by RAI, in January 1974 Italy became known in the press as a country involved in an international narcotics ring and the target of an FBI investigation into the origins of drugs sold in the United States, as well as a land where kidnappers were being arrested all along the peninsula. Saverio Mammoliti, the only suspect to have evaded arrest, embodied this new reality. Yet it was the arrest of Girolamo Piromalli in March 1974 that would show the country the real power of the new Mafia.

Over the course of the two-year investigation, both Mammoliti and Piromalli distinguished themselves among those accused in the Getty abduction. Mammoliti was the only suspect to evade trial. Strikingly, in September 1975, while still a fugitive from justice and wanted by the police, Carabinieri (military police corps), and FBI, he got married in a church close to his hometown in Calabria. The news reached the press and became publicly known throughout Italy.[21] It was clearly a symbolic action through which Mammoliti showed that, the presence of prosecutors notwithstanding, Calabria remained his territory. Whereas Mammoliti evaded prosecution, Piromalli was the only suspect in the Getty abduction granted probation. The Italian Minister of the Interior, Paolo Emilio Taviani, reacted to this news by condemning the magistracy for being too soft on criminals, saying, "It means that rather than having one abduction a week, as has recently been the case, we will have one a day."[22] Piromalli received probation in November 1974 for health reasons, but a year later he was arrested for drug dealing by the same prosecutor in charge of the Getty case.[23]

The Lagonegro trial confirmed and emphasized the power of Mammoliti and Piromalli beyond their acquittals for insufficient evidence. Followed daily for months by the national press, the trial featured the absence of the fugitive Mammoliti and the long-awaited hearing of Piromalli. A 20 May 1976 article in the *Corriere* by Roberto Martinelli frames the entrance in court of Piromalli (with three bodyguards and four lawyers) as that of an authority for whom every defendant stood up in silence as a sign of respect. The article also reports that in response to Piromalli's request not to have photographers present, the judge not only agreed but also specified that this was a special concession never before granted to a defendant. Instead of taking a critical view of the judge's response, the journalist underscores, "Even justice knows how to distinguish between bosses and grunts."[24] It is remarkable that a main national newspaper depicts Italian justice as obsequious towards the 'Ndrangheta. Martinelli's fascination with Piromalli is even more noteworthy. In addition to describing him in detail (hair, clothes, sunglasses, and movements), he compares him to Luciano Liggio, the powerful Sicilian Mafia boss, and, in so doing, clearly aims to elevate the 'Ndrangheta to the level of Cosa Nostra (the more well-known Sicilian organized crime syndicate). Yet the fact that Martinelli casts Piromalli's appearance at the trial as a "kept promise" demonstrates the charm that Mafia power held for the media. How could an Italian reporter put a recognized boss of the 'Ndrangheta above the law to the point of considering his mandatory hearing in court to be a personal promise? The journalist's article clearly participates in the Mafia cult of personality and even dismisses the evidence collected by the prosecutors – two bills from the Getty ransom found in Piromalli's possession – as a rookie mistake that the boss would never have made.

The belief that the Getty kidnapping was – at least in its initial phase – a hoax was part of the prosecutors' investigation and one of the main arguments constructed by Piromalli's, Lamanna's, and other defendants' lawyers. Yet the final verdict of the Lagonegro trial completely

50 Ransom Kidnapping in Italy

acquitted Getty himself of any responsibility. The second trial of his kidnappers that took place in 1977 at the Court of Appeals of Potenza, Basilicata, reached the same conclusion, which was also confirmed by the Court of Cassation in 1980. Paul Getty III's was a kidnapping for ransom according to Italian justice, and his abductors were members of the 'Ndrangheta. Getty collaborated with the prosecutors during the investigations in early 1974 and went to Calabria to identify the hideouts where he had been held hostage. At the initial Lagonegro trial, he – together with his mother – brought a civil lawsuit against his kidnappers. But the hearing became a test to prove his innocence. The judge asked him questions about his lack of emotions during captivity and if he had a clear conscience. An article in the *Corriere* reported verbatim the dialogue between the judge and Getty, who is described as being surprised and unable to understand what his emotions had to do with the trial of his kidnappers. However, it was the defendants' lawyers' decision to include Getty's private nude Polaroids of him and his wife – published without their permission by an Italian magazine – that left Getty incredulous.[25] At Lagonegro, the lawyers openly tried to depict him as leading a lascivious lifestyle, as if that would prove his lack of innocence. The accusations against Getty were mostly connected to his personality, to the testimony of a friend who said Getty once mentioned staging an abduction, and to the defence's assumption that the first two letters that his mother received during his captivity were signed not by him but instead probably by a woman. Gail Getty herself was questioned about her financial status and her husband's and father-in-law's doubts about the kidnapping.

Despite his early fascination with the Mafia, the journalist Martinelli later called the acquittals of Piromalli and Mammoliti a "Waterloo" of the Italian justice system.[26] If the media surrounding the trial in Lagonegro characterized the Calabrian 'Ndrangheta as being stronger than the Italian state, this defeat was made even worse when the Court of Appeals of Potenza reduced the sentences of the other men found guilty in the first trial.[27] Yet, even without a final verdict convicting the Piromalli-Mammoliti clan, eleven years later the national chief of police, Rinaldo Coronas, could officially declare, in a summit about crime in Rome and Lazio, that without a doubt the 1973 kidnapping of Getty "was a milestone in the development of the Mafia from Reggio Calabria's criminal activity."[28] Coronas's words demonstrate that the legal narrative of the Getty abduction had definitively dropped any suspicions of a hoax. Scholars of the 'Ndrangheta also recognize in this case of ransom kidnapping the beginning of a new season for the Calabrian Mafia.[29] Even recent Italian media accounts, connected mostly to Getty's death in 2011 and to the 2017 release of *All the Money in the World*, depict this abduction as a crucial event of the 1970s and point to the ear mutilation as the fact that silences any doubts about its nature. It is significant that Getty's is among the few kidnappings mentioned by RAI's *Il giorno e la storia* (Today in history), a broadcast that succinctly lists the most memorable events that occurred on that day in history – an indication that today national television considers the Getty ordeal a key moment in modern Italy.

There is still a forgotten public debate, the discussion of which not only restores the memory of this specific kidnapping but also reveals a new narrative of violence in 1970s Italy. The contrast between the 1974 *Rolling Stone* and RAI television interviews shows two visions of Getty in the media right after his abduction, while the journalistic accounts of the investigations and the initial trial demonstrate both the high level of media interest in the Mafia and the fact that the legal narrative put an end to the hoax hypothesis. We now turn, however, to analyse the popular beliefs and media representations that caused suspicions of a hoax to spread in the first place during Getty's captivity. A 2003 episode of the RAI broadcast *La storia siamo noi* (We are history) on the abduction showed part of a previous RAI interview with Getty dating from the first day of the 1976 Lagonegro trial.[30] The journalist began the interview by emphatically saying, "Paul Getty III – it could be the name of an emperor. What do you consider yourself? A hereditary prince, a playboy, or a poor boy persecuted by wealth?" He continued with questions and bitter jokes that implied a sort of culpability on Getty's part as the "spoiled" scion of a billionaire family who "refuses to collaborate."[31] With a cynical laugh and in a low voice, Getty tried to answer by saying that he was nothing of the kind and left. This interview clearly recalls the 1974 RAI interview in Rome already discussed, but its context is very different. RAI television is here filming in an Italian courtroom. No longer depicted as a dandy playing free inside a rich palace, Paul Getty is seen sitting on a chair surrounded by four bodyguards provided to him by the Italian state. By going to Lagonegro, his life was indeed in danger.[32] Remarkably, even before the judge began the hearing, an Italian journalist was already questioning Getty in the court's waiting room.

No longer aggressive towards the figure of Getty, the present-day *La storia siamo noi* recognizes and articulates this lack of empathy for the young victim, highlighting the accusative attitude of the journalist. The contemporary broadcaster explains this absence of empathy towards the wealthy Getty as a consequence of the suffering of Italian society at large, which in 1973 – the year of the abduction – was enduring an

52 Ransom Kidnapping in Italy

economic crisis. However, I would argue that this economic approach oversimplifies the impact that Getty's abduction had on Italian public debate at the time and furthermore risks framing the phenomenon of ransom kidnapping as the result of class struggle. On the contrary, the kidnappers were not Robin Hoods that took money from the rich to give to the poor. They were powerful criminals who, in the case of the 'Ndrangheta, invested the money they obtained into other criminal activities such as drug trafficking. If the journalist in the 1976 Lagonegro interview could talk to a mutilated victim of Mafia violence in that way, what were the popular and media discourses about his abduction while he was still held hostage? As we shall see, national, ideological, and gender identities shaped the narratives of the Getty abduction in the news as much as, if not more than, the unreachable economic status he embodied. It is from this perspective that the rest of this chapter looks at Getty's captivity apart from his testimony and beyond the walls of a courthouse. Together with gossip and paparazzi depictions of the well-off teenager that characterized Getty in the minds of most Italians, media narratives of his ordeal reveal the anxiety of a society that was slowly becoming aware of the horrific and violent threat that organized crime posed to their country. Despite national television's attempt to cast Italy as innocent, in those years the country was starting to produce what today is considered one of the most powerful organized crime syndicates in the world. Ransom kidnapping was its first means and Getty its first sensational victim.

Getty in the News

Getty's abduction naturally had an international echo and was covered by media all over the world. However, *Il Messaggero* and *Il Tempo* were the two local Roman newspapers that most impacted the narrative of his kidnapping by both interpreting and shaping public opinion. They are especially interesting to our analysis because their pages became a space for the negotiation between the 'Ndrangheta and Getty's mother. As previously noted, Gail Getty, unlike her ex-husband, was living in Rome when her son was kidnapped. Fluent in Italian, she spoke with journalists and held press conferences in her apartment. She often used *Il Messaggero* to reach out to the abductors during those times when they were not communicating with her. Moreover, the kidnappers chose to send Getty's mutilated ear and proof that the hostage was in their hands (and in danger) to *Il Messaggero* and *Il Tempo*, respectively. Finally, these two newspapers are from the same city where the sixteen-year-old Getty was living before his kidnapping. From the moment of his abduction and until his liberation, the columns of *Il Messaggero* and *Il Tempo* were filled with friends, characters, women, stories, and turns of events that always had something new to reveal about the mysteriously missing Getty. In other words, Rome and Getty's life there became the object of their journalistic enquiry. In the pages of these papers we can therefore observe an intertwining of discourses: the columnists' narratives, the mother's appeals, and the kidnappers' messages.

Neither the journalists nor the reading public could know what the hostage Getty was going through. Yet ransom kidnapping was not an unknown phenomenon in Italy. During the months of his abduction, for example, the news reported at least four additional cases of kidnapping in the country: three for ransom and one for political purposes.[33] Nevertheless, the news of Getty's kidnapping was not initially believed. *Il Tempo* and *Il Messaggero*, as well as other prominent newspapers such as *Corriere della Sera*, reported that Getty's girlfriend and friends told police that he had once mentioned that faking an abduction would solve his economic woes.[34] In another version of this rumour, the idea of a simulated kidnapping originated with his friends but upset Getty.[35] In short, when the newspapers began covering this kidnapping, suspicions about its veracity predominated.[36] This doubt persisted in media narratives for all five months of the abduction and was not firmly put to rest even when the kidnappers authenticated the crime by sending the horrifying proof that they had the hostage.

Ambiguity became the narrative strategy of *Il Tempo*. A conservative newspaper, *Il Tempo* announced on the front page of its 13 July issue that Getty was missing and "perhaps abducted."[37] Their reporting was not quite accurate, given that they said Getty had been missing for fourteen days, while in reality he had been kidnapped only three days before, on 10 July. Nevertheless, it is interesting to note how *Il Tempo* introduced Getty to its audience: "The grandson of the richest man in the world is seventeen years old and a far-left activist."[38] Getty had in fact been arrested once for taking part in a political demonstration in Rome that turned violent. It was, however, an isolated incident, and Getty denied his participation.

The next day, *Il Tempo* published a photo of the young Getty with long hair in a front-page article stating that the police were investigating the hippies of Rome while they waited for a second message from the kidnappers. "Kidnappers" is here placed in quotation marks. The journalist also defines the hippies' philosophy as "randagia" (stray), alluding to them as dogs. At this point the abductors had already contacted Getty's mother by phone and instructed her to collect the ransom money. Gail Getty and her Italian lawyer Giovanni Jacovoni, who assisted her in the negotiation with the kidnappers for the duration of the abduction, had no doubt about the seriousness of Paul's kidnapping. However, the internal pages of the same issue of *Il Tempo* put the strategy of ambiguity into action. With three different articles, the news about this kidnapping occupied the entire crime section of the paper. Getty was portrayed in two large photos that framed him as a sort of dandy/queer and as the boy next door. The captions of these photos said, respectively, "Paul Getty III in a curious pose as a model" and "Paul Getty III in a recent photo as 'the good boy.'"[39]

In the first days of his abduction, the columns of *Il Tempo* literally created a character out of Getty. An eccentric figure, "l'hippy d'oro" (the golden hippy) was not trustworthy. Everything and everyone around him was presented with suspicion. Reading the news as reported by *Il Tempo* is like reading the making of a story in which the characters take shape day-by-day. Their personalities and identities are constructed through the description of their habits, bodies, houses, and bohemian lifestyle, which are presented as if they were important details about the abduction. In other words, *Il Tempo* put Getty and his world under investigation for months without asking who his abductors were. For this reason, the unusual approach his kidnappers took to ransom negotiations was perceived as a sign of inauthenticity rather than the signal of a new stage in the phenomenon of ransom kidnapping. For example, the kidnappers sent two letters written by the hostage two and six days after his abduction. The first was sent to Getty's friend, a painter with whom he sometimes lived in Trastevere, the hippy part of Rome. The second was sent to his German girlfriend Martine. The fact that these two letters were not sent to his mother, the "overly dramatic" tone in which they were written, and the long silence that followed them, were interpreted by *Il Tempo* as confirmation that the kidnapping was a hoax.[40]

In reality, the long silence after the initial contact with the family would later become a common technique used by the 'Ndrangheta. It was not safe for the kidnappers to communicate via mail with the families. They had to travel to different cities to send their messages without being discovered. Moreover, this pause put psychological pressure on the blackmailed families while giving them time to collect the enormous sums that the kidnappers began to request. The five-month-long abduction of Getty was the first in a series of this kind of protracted kidnapping in which the victim was captured in the north and brought to Aspromonte, where the 'Ndrangheta had the territorial control that allowed the kidnappers to hide hostages for up to two years.

The media could not foresee the future rise of the 'Ndrangheta. Nevertheless, we can observe that the kind of questions *Il Tempo* was raising in the mind of its readers, while informing them about the two letters Getty wrote from his hiding place, were not "What happened to him?" or "Who are his kidnappers?" but rather "What are we, as readers, reading? Is this for real?" This question (what are we reading?) also became a narrative strategy. The ambiguity in the pages of *Il Tempo* is the effect of the different genres its journalists used when writing about Getty. The story was constructed as a *giallo* (noir or detective story), defined as a drama, presented as tragedy, or even framed as gossip depending on the emerging details, such as the fake news that Getty was seen on a yacht in Corsica with a blond actress.[41] When a so-called friend of Getty's falsely claimed that the kidnapping was a ruse organized by Getty himself to produce a film about his abduction, *Il Tempo* called its readers the "spectators" of his kidnapping, suggesting that what they were reading was the script of a film.[42]

This survey of 1973 news begins to explain why the journalist of the 1976 Lagonegro interview was so aggressive with Getty, to the point of accusing him of not "collaborating" – a word used with interrogated criminals, not interviewed victims. The pages of *Il Tempo* show us that during his kidnapping the media discourse depicted Getty as a potential criminal. The narrative of *Il Messaggero*, though with a less tabloid newspaper style than *Il Tempo* and with a less conservative approach towards hippy and bohemian Rome, was not that different. Both newspapers more than once published lists of reasons why the abduction could be *Vero o Falso* (True or False).[43] *Il Messaggero* perhaps did not use ambiguity as an explicit narrative tool, but it doubted Getty's kidnapping until the very end and even insinuated that the family's lawyer was already at work to keep him from going to jail.[44]

Before looking at how the kidnappers made use of these two newspapers, there is an additional narrative that we must observe: the depiction of Gail Getty. Her figure, I would argue, allows us to identify another discourse that also had the effect of preventing empathy in the readers. This media discourse did not depict just the mother of Paul Getty but rather his *American* mother. This is to say that the narratives that both *Il Tempo* and *Il Messaggero* used in their pages intertwined national and gender identities. *Il Tempo* introduced Gail Getty to its audience by describing her apartment as "a six-room penthouse furnished in sumptuous American style."[45] She was "wrapped in a silk dressing gown," and she had "bags under her eyes from her anguished, sleepless night."[46] Most of the articles in both newspapers described her body and outfits, but the second article *Il Tempo*

56 Ransom Kidnapping in Italy

published about her went even further when it wrote that she was wearing a red blouse that framed her "free breasts" and jeans that shaped her "tapered legs."[47] With this sexually objectifying language, the journalist was not only narrating Gail as a woman, rather than a mother in pain, but he was also identifying her as an American woman who, unlike her Italian counterparts, did not use a bra and wore jeans.

Depending on what was happening in the negotiations, Gail was described as rational and in control or desperate because the Getty family did not want to give her the ransom money. Regardless, she was often presented as a mother who was not completely a mother – that is, she was not acting like an Italian mother would have acted in her place. She went to the movie theatre and was not at home when "the two little German twins" brought Paul's letter to her. She was not taking good care of her home, even if this was understandable. She was not crying enough or did not express the "right" sentiment. As noted earlier, Gail used *Il Messaggero* to negotiate the ransom with the kidnappers (she used the real estate ads section to tell them the sums she had ready) or to call for their attention with public appeals. *Il Messaggero* was the newspaper to which the 'Ndrangheta sent Paul's right ear. Although some of the journalists were supportive, after Paul's liberation one of them (Mario Pandolfo) wrote that Gail Getty "was a brave woman who faced this experience with courage, without any tears, and with calm, and that for this reason she aroused distrust within the Italian audience."[48] Not even after the liberation, he wrote, was she capable of allowing herself to feel the sentiments of "a mother and a woman." The column ends with the words of her Italian lawyer, who, saying that he was moved because Paul had asked his mother to thank him for everything he had done for them, spoke – the journalist declares – "like a good Italian."[49] The stereotypes of the *italiani brava gente* and the Mediterranean people as warmer than Anglo-Saxons are here in play. Ironically, this is an article about an American teenager liberated in Italy after his mother negotiated for five months with his Italian kidnappers. In the narratives of the Roman newspapers as well as in the popular imagination, Gail Getty was a mother from the outside and her son the spoiled offspring of a cruel family too cold and not Italian enough to pay the ransom.

The 'Ndrangheta and the News

According to the media, one sign that the Getty abduction was not real was the kidnappers' threats to mutilate the hostage. In their initial calls,

The criminals said they would send Getty's finger to his mother if the family refused to pay. They later added even more severe threats of bodily mutilation. *Il Tempo* and *Il Messaggero* mocked these threats as if they were an exaggeration written by Getty and his friends, who were incapable of negotiating like professional kidnappers. Some journalists even analysed the messages Gail Getty received by showing what a real and serious abductor would have done instead.[50] In short, they put themselves in the position of a kidnapper as if it were a respectable profession.

The media were wrong. In November 1973, *Il Messaggero*, the newspaper that Gail used to communicate with the kidnappers, received a plastic envelope with a lock of Paul's hair and his right ear inside. The paper immediately published the news and showed the evidence to its audience. The envelope arrived after a delay of three weeks, thanks to a strike of the Italian postal service. It became difficult for doctors to analyse the ear because too much time had passed. According to the kidnappers, though, the delay was because *Il Messaggero* hesitated to publish the news about the mutilation, not wanting to horrify the public. As a result, the 'Ndrangheta called the editorial board of *Il Tempo* and gave them directions for where to find proof that the hair and the ear *Il Messaggero* had received were in fact Getty's. These were the five Polaroid images and a letter that the 'Ndrangheta – this time avoiding the Italian mail service – hid along a highway. The criminals had decided that *Il Tempo* was the right newspaper to use for the horrifying visibility they were seeking.

Il Messaggero reacted to the mail received from the kidnappers by blaming the Getty family and the terrible grandfather who did not take the kidnapping seriously. The title on its front page read "Familyless."[51] One journalist wrote that the kidnappers decided to negotiate with them because they were more reliable than the Getty family. The newspaper also blamed the kidnappers for not having been believable up to then, and it began to use the specialized language of doctors to talk about the mutilation. For the first time, it also asked who the kidnappers were, with an investigative approach. However, if on the one hand *Il Messaggero* was presenting its narrative as rational, professional, and trustworthy, on the other hand it continued to question the authenticity of the Getty abduction, as reflected in the article title "Is it his or not? Is it from a living or a dead man?"[52]

The day after printing the Polaroids that authenticated the mutilation, *Il Tempo* published a full-page spread called "Photo Chronicle of a Night Adventure" which visually described how the journalists found the proof left by the criminals along the highway.[53] By using

58 Ransom Kidnapping in Italy

photography as a narrative tool, *Il Tempo* adopted the same means that the kidnappers used to affect public opinion. However, the 'Ndrangheta's shocking advertisement of the abduction was not just another narrative genre, and its horrifying effect contrasts with *Il Tempo*'s sensationalistic "fotoromanzo" (photo story).

Il Tempo's and *Il Messaggero*'s narratives did not drastically change after the mail they received, to the point that *Il Tempo* described the letter found with the photos as full of "huge mistakes," like "those of a foreigner who ... has devoted very little time to study."[54] Still exemplifying this concern over veracity, though taken from the opposite perspective, another column sought to demonstrate the authenticity of the Polaroids by having a makeup artist cut off the ear of a mannequin that looked like Getty and taking a photo of it to show through photography that a fake mutilation would have been easily recognizable.[55] The message seemed to be that if a professional makeup artist cannot simulate a mutilation, neither can the abductors. Again, *Il Tempo* used photography to prove the validity of the images sent by the kidnappers and, in so doing, emulated the communicative strategies of the 'Ndrangheta. Yet, and in line with the paper's style, the effect of this photography was an ambiguous and gruesome spectacle.

The manner in which the kidnappers conducted the negotiation with the Getty family was not simply the result of Getty Sr.'s refusal to pay the ransom money. His famous statement about having fourteen grandchildren, all of them potential targets of criminals, was continually reported by the media in and outside of Italy. Paul Getty Sr. did not want to create a precedent that could jeopardize his immense fortune. Both *All the Money in the World* and *Trust* well emphasize this point and depict Getty Sr.'s personality as pathologically avaricious. However, if the figure of the terrible grandfather provided the motivation for the mutilation, it could not illuminate the kidnappers' choice of Roman newspapers for the negotiation. The media narrative about him, for example, had the opposite effect on the audience than that about the young Getty and his mother. It created empathy towards the hostage and therefore put pressure on the family. The news reported on letters written by middle school students imploring the old man to pay, as well as on a fundraiser spontaneously held by people to collect the ransom money. It was the prevalent doubt about the kidnapping, even after the mutilation, that pushed the 'Ndrangheta to affect public opinion. By choosing *Il Messaggero* and *Il Tempo* to shock the family and the public, the kidnappers wished to take control of the most prolific discourse that was denying the kidnapping.

The Mutilation

The 1973 mutilation of Getty and the numerous other abductions starting to fill the crime news section of every Italian newspaper that same year had a strong impact on the public discourse, which began to recognize kidnapping as a vast national phenomenon rather than a sporadic or regional crime. This is reflected in the article "L'orecchio di Getty e l'industria del sequestro" (Getty's ear and the kidnapping industry), published by the noted Italian writer Alberto Moravia on the front page of *Corriere della Sera* on 25 November 1973. What is striking about this column is that the full meaning of the title is only clear after one reads the article. The word *industria* (industry), used first by journalists in the 1970s to emphasize the dimension of the crime and later by criminologists to label the abductions operated specifically by the 'Ndrangheta, acquires a different connotation in Moravia's analysis.[56] For the author, Getty's ear "seems to provoke a greater horror than the many cadavers with which, today as well as yesterday, the stories of kidnappings are full."[57] By trying to explain why an ear provokes more horror than a cadaver, Moravia contrasts the gestures of cutting and sending a body part with those of killing – that is, he looks at the intentionality of the kidnappers' actions. Unlike killing, which, he says, can appear as "an act of desperate barbarity," sending a perfectly cut ear "reveals the existence of a plan, however cruel, that is, the presence of a positive element – reason – applied to the crime."[58] Moravia recognizes in the horror the dawning of an awareness that he defines as a "sociological consciousness."[59] It is from this sociological perspective that we should read the term "industry" in the title.

Moravia sees Getty's ear as the horrifying sign of a mutation: that of an ancient banditry, which is no longer the expression of the "fracture" between economic powers and the working class and the poor. Getty's kidnappers are the result of this mutation. They are, according to Moravia, the heirs of the traditional bandits. Although erroneous (the perpetrator of Getty's ordeal was the 'Ndrangheta, not bandits), Moravia's article offers an original perspective on the phenomenon of ransom kidnapping in Italy that contrasts with the view of the abductions as the result of a class struggle: "The bandits of the past were, essentially, 'different'; those of today, just as essentially, are instead 'alike.' Which is the equivalent of saying that the ethics of consumption, of profit, of hedonism at all costs could not in the end but include crime as well."[60] Moravia's interpretation of kidnapping is subtler than the generic observation about a 1973 crisis proposed by today's media, such as the broadcast *La storia siamo noi*. It also contrasts with the representation of a poor Italy made up of good and hard-working people that provided the visual backdrop to the 1974 Getty interview. In his use of the term "essentially," Moravia recalls Pier Paolo Pasolini's thesis of the anthropological transformation of the Italian proletariat as an effect of capitalism and its values. In the same way, the ancient banditry that had opposed economic powers because it was "different" disappeared, and a new and homogenized one established itself. To put it differently, Moravia sees Getty's mutilation as a sign of social class assimilation rather than social class struggle.

The title of Moravia's article and its meaning become clear under this sociological light. Kidnapping is an industry because banditry is no longer the agent of desperate barbarity (killing) but rather the agent of calculated planning (mutilation). This industry is the unexpected expression of an assimilated banditry that appropriated the ideology of power: "It is therefore the similarity of the method that scares, not the diversity. It frightens because it contains a critique, a doubt, a suspicion about the validity of the method itself. This explains why to the horror of public opinion over the cruelty of the bandits there is added a dark and worried disapproval of the grandfather who affirms that he does not want to pay the ransom money."[61] The horror provoked by Getty's severed ear reflects how far the ethics of hedonism and consumerism can go – that is, it can include a crime that interprets its cruelty at the highest levels. Moravia's use of *industria* implies a shared methodology between capitalism and crime. However original, the sociological interpretation offered by Moravia presumes (incorrectly) to know who his kidnappers were and risks seeing the horror of the mutilation in Getty Sr.'s stinginess rather than in the 'Ndrangheta's hostage.

The Hostage Exposed

My analysis of the Getty abduction began with the photographs, to which it now returns. By comparing the Polaroids of Getty and Moro through the lens of Belpoliti's work, I argue that, although to very different ends, both the Red Brigades and the 'Ndrangheta made use of the technology of the Polaroid camera to seek advertisement in the media. Exploring the narratives cast by the newspapers and their role in the ransom negotiations helps explain why the 'Ndrangheta sought shock advertising. By doubting Getty, the media doubted his kidnappers' seriousness and their very existence. Moreover, Moravia's article puts at its centre Getty's ear without telling its story or relating it to the victim. Rather, the article envisioned the severed flesh as an image of his grandfather's avarice and his kidnappers' determination. His cut ear no longer belonged to his body but instead stood for something else. What is horrifying in the photos taken by the 'Ndrangheta is that they show the absence of the ear in the hostage's profile. Getty's ear in flesh needed the Polaroid camera to become – for the world external to the cave – his body again.

When *Il Messaggero* published the news about the mail it received, it also published a photo (taken by one of its photographers) of a transparent plastic envelope through which it was possible to see the ear. Yet it could have been any ear; rather than proving that Getty was kidnapped, it became the terrifying object of media speculation. The *Corriere* published the news of the mail received by the *Messaggero* but without such a photograph. It instead published in its 23 November 1973 issue one of the Polaroids taken by the kidnappers and found by *Il Tempo*. This is the image that I next analyse for both its quality and its content (figure 2.3).

To look at the Getty abduction through photography allows us to contrast the popular and media discourses with the visibility of the hostage exposed by the 'Ndrangheta, as we shall see. As noted earlier, after the mutilation and its authentication, the narratives of *Il Messaggero* and *Il Tempo* were still depicting Paul and Gail Getty as characters. National and gender identities were the usual lenses through which these newspapers approached the hostage's letters and his mother's reactions. Strikingly, the sole national newspaper to report the news of Getty's captivity without fictionalization or sensationalism was the communist *L'Unità*. With an accurate account, this newspaper did not take a hostile position against the Getty family nor give an ideological explanation for the crime. However, the words "kidnapping" and "kidnappers" often appeared in English in its columns. This choice clearly marked the identity of the victim and his family as foreign and emphasized the fact that this kidnapping, unlike the others that were happening in Italy, was international news.

In addition to Moravia's article, the *Corriere* reacted to the mutilation and the photographs of Getty with columns written by some of its most prestigious pens. Its pages increasingly depicted ransom kidnapping as a destabilizing phenomenon that made the country's inhabitants feel vulnerable, as exemplified by Giampaolo Pansa's article "Defenceless Before the Kidnapping Industry" and Francesco Alberoni's "Just Like in the Middle Ages."[62] Even if the *Corriere* sporadically doubted the abduction of Getty, its discourse turned analytical when needed and never sexualized Gail Getty. However, its chronicle sometimes bordered on fiction as, for example, in Alberto Bevilacqua's "This Is the Story of Paul Getty III," in which the author gives a breathtaking

Figure 2.3. Polaroid of Paul Getty III, *Corriere della Sera*, 23 November 1973. The author thanks La Fondazione Corriere della Sera for the historical archive material.

account of the abduction by dividing his column into five chapters as if it were a novel.[63]

By comparing the two snapshots of Moro taken by the Red Brigades in 1978 (figures 2.1 and 2.2), Belpoliti argues in his 2018 monograph that

> If the intention of the Red Brigades was to photograph a hostage (and it is in the first photo), in this second snapshot Moro's gaze nullifies any intention and reaches us. What does he want to tell us? Nothing more than an affirmation of a presence, his *here I am*. Perhaps it is for this *being here* communicated by his dissymmetric gaze that this photograph keeps signifying. It puts a hole into the thickness of history, that History which those who took this image believed that they were writing, or rewriting, with an act of strength. Of all the accumulation of pain, suffering, and mad plans that subtend and follow this act, the only thing that seems to me still significant is the gaze of Aldo Moro.[64]

This passage is enlightening not because the photos of Moro and Getty can be seen as similar, but rather because of the way in which Belpoliti looks at an iconic image of a hostage in 1970s Italy. He looks at this image for what it communicates to us beyond the intentionality of the photographers. I recognize in Belpoliti's approach what Susie Linfield means in her book *The Cruel Radiance* (2010) when she states that in the digital age we are experts "at distancing ourselves from photographs" and that "what we have lost is the capacity to *respond* to photographs, especially those of political violence, as citizens who seek to learn something useful from them and connect to others through them."[65] In the previous passage, Belpoliti responds to the photo and connects with Moro. Moreover, in contrast with theoretical approaches that see voyeurism or exploitation in the photography of violence, Linfield proposes what we might call a perceptual criticism, that is, a way of looking at photographs that uses "emotion as an inspiration to analysis."[66] The photos of Getty were sent by his kidnappers to provoke horror. Yet what is horrifying about them goes beyond the intention of the photographers.

In his 1973 *Corriere* article, Moravia gave a sociological interpretation of Getty's mutilation. In his analysis of the reason why an ear provokes more horror than a cadaver, he linked the horror to the kidnappers' premeditated gesture. Cutting is more horrifying than killing, and it reveals a plan whose ideology is not different from that of economic powers. With the philosopher Adriana Cavarero and her approach to horror, and in contrast with Moravia, I shift the focus from the agent of violence to the *inerme* (helpless) hostage. Comparing cutting and killing

64   Ransom Kidnapping in Italy

in her book *Orrorismo* (*Horrorism*), Cavarero also recognizes the first as more horrifying. However, what horrifies about a violence "that labors at slicing" is not the intention but rather the effect.[67] It is the visibility of the violence embodied in the helpless victim and not the gesture of the agent. In the Getty photo, the cruel radiance we perceive is this effect. What we see when we look at the photo is the absence of his ear. However, as Belpoliti notices in the Moro Polaroid, it is not the intentionality of the photographer that ultimately signifies the photo. We, in fact, do not perceive an intention but its effect, that is, what the photo provokes. Linfield states that photography offers an "immediate, viscerally emotional connection to the world."[68] If we look at the Getty Polaroid beyond the shock advertising that his kidnappers sought by putting at its centre the absence of his ear (their gesture) and we move our gaze to his eyes, the effect of the violence becomes even more visible. Being exposed to the world as mutilated – that is, experiencing his disfigured visibility in front of the Polaroid camera – horrified Getty. The horror of the photograph is in his eyes. Getty in this image is not only the helpless hostage used by his perpetrators to petrify his family and the world with their violence. He is a hostage who perceives the horror. When we look at this photograph, we do not see him; we see *with* him. The Getty Polaroid contrasts with the popular and media narratives of his abduction because it allows us to relate empathically to a victim of the 'Ndrangheta mutilated in a cave of the Aspromonte in 1970s Italy.

Coda

The distinct lack of empathy for Getty was more than just the result of the economic crisis that struck Italy in 1973. It was the effect of common beliefs and media discourses about his abduction that, through national, ideological, and gender stereotypes, expressed the anxieties of living in a country where ransom kidnapping was becoming daily news. The otherness of the eccentric Paul and his divorced American mother – in a Catholic country where divorce was actively under debate – became a way of distancing the reality of Italy through gossip-style and accusatory narratives. Those same narratives shaped the arguments of the 'Ndrangheta and its lawyers at the Lagonegro trial. As we saw, however, suspicions of a hoax were silenced by the courts. Popular discourse also eventually dropped the hoax rumours, as demonstrated by an enquiry into ransom kidnapping in Lazio conducted more than ten years after the Getty abduction by the State Attorney's Office of Rome. In a questionnaire presented to the public, one query asked respondents to name kidnapped victims and why they were memorable. Despite there having been numerous subsequent kidnappings in the region, Getty was listed as number six (following more recent or then-current victims) and his mutilation given as the reason why the abduction was still remembered. A decade after his ordeal, the local imagination thus framed Paul Getty as a victim.

Although RAI had tried to create a reassuring picture of Italy in its interviews with Getty, during and after his abduction the perception of the country, as well as public debates on the crime, drastically changed. While RAI was broadcasting these interviews, it was also, and inevitably, spreading the news about the realities of Aspromonte. The reading of the sentencing at the Lagonegro trial, for example, was televised. Yet it was the view from the helicopters flying over the mountains of Calabria that forever changed the way Italians envisioned the landscape of their country. This new aerial perspective, which also included the mountains of Sardinia and Tuscany, is the perceptual correlate of a different narrative of violence in 1970s Italy and beyond.

Another striking aspect emerging from the Getty case is that the immediate reaction to the first images of a hostage in an anonymous cave and to the first mutilation in ransom kidnapping (of which there would be several) was to condemn the cruelty of the kidnappers and the avarice of Getty Sr. There was initially no discussion about the crime as extortion or about its consequences. The 1973 media was, in short, a pre–Aldo Moro media. Moravia is not the only author that – from the pages of the *Corriere* – equates economic powers and crime at the ethical level. In his article "Cruelty and Avarice," Carlo Laurenzi does so as well: "And if it is true that the grandfather does not pay in order to 'deter blackmail in principle' and to serve civilization in this way, well then his blind, puritan determination matches (not to say exceeds) the nefariousness of the kidnappers."[69] In his view, Getty Sr. is even worse than the kidnappers. My aim is not to defend the senior Getty and his position but rather to observe how kidnapping was articulated before the abduction of Moro. Negotiations were not even under discussion. By 1978, Laurenzi's sentiment would have been problematic at the very least. The position he quotes Getty as taking would become the same one that the Italian state took with the Red Brigades during the fifty-five days of the Moro kidnapping. It is true that political and criminal kidnappings have different targets and blackmail the state or private citizens, respectively, with consequences that are not comparable in nature. However, we do not have to wait until 1978 to see the first concerns and concrete legal reactions to the phenomenon of kidnapping as related to the problem of negotiations. Getty's story opened a public and legal discourse on this subject that would take centre stage for the next twenty years, until the crime came to an end in the late 1990s.

Finally, it is the ordeal that Getty lived in Aspromonte that most shows us the violence of kidnapping. The aftermath of that experience was extremely difficult for Getty, who a few years after his liberation suffered from a stroke caused by an overdose of alcohol and drugs that left him paralysed and unable to speak for the rest of his life, until he died in 2011 at the age of fifty-four. Although inaccessible to most Italians, the detailed account in English of his captivity in the 1974 *Rolling Stone* article makes visible and bears witness to the inhuman condition of kidnapped hostages. If the Getty abduction opens questions on kidnapping at national, social, and political levels, his words warn us that a new narrative of thirty years of violence in modern Italy would not be possible without the perspective of the victims' testimony. In the years that followed his account, other kidnapped hostages published memoirs of their ordeals, which became accessible to an Italian audience. Their language, trauma, and experience are at the heart of chapters 5 and 6, which, unlike the RAI journalist in 1974, listen to the words of the victims and shed light on why "vacuum," "hate," and "caution" – carefully chosen by Getty in his interview – are embodied effects of the violence inflicted by criminal kidnapping.

Chapter Three

The Day Cristina's Body Was Found

When Alvin Shuster, the *New York Times* correspondent in Rome, wrote an article on 12 September 1975 entitled "Italians' Apathy Over Kidnappings Is Shaken by Girl's Murder,"[1] two years had passed since the Getty abduction became a media sensation. That same year, forty-five people had already been snatched in the country. "Of all the kidnapping episodes in Italy in recent months," reads the first paragraph of Shuster's piece, "none has so shocked Italians as that of Cristina Mazzotti, an eighteen-year-old high school student who was kidnapped and murdered even though her family paid a ransom of more than $1 million."[2] It is not surprising that the *New York Times* would report on the abduction and murder of the young Cristina Mazzotti in the form of news about the Italians' unusual response to this recurring crime. Her story became the one with which Italy identified the most and the one that turned ransom kidnapping into a collective tragedy.

Cristina Mazzotti was abducted the night of 30 June 1975, in Eupilio, a small village close to Como, Lombardy, where she was spending the summer in her family's house after the end of the academic year.[3] The daughter of a grain dealer, she was attending the *liceo classico* Carducci in Milan, where she was living with her parents in a rented apartment. The night of her abduction, she was returning home with two friends, Emanuela Luisari and Carlo Galli, when masked and armed men suddenly blocked their car, forced them into the back seat, and drove them away. After a few miles, the abductors forced Cristina to follow them into another car and left Emanuela and Carlo bound and gagged. It was the first time that a young girl had been kidnapped for ransom in Italy. As soon as they were able to free themselves, Emanuela and Carlo sought help at the nearest house. Through their accounts, which were published in the national press, Italians witnessed the trauma of Cristina vanishing into thin air.[4] Italian society's emotional involvement in

68 Ransom Kidnapping in Italy

her kidnapping and in the ordeal of her family is evident in the photos of her funeral. More than 25,000 people went to Eupilio, a village of only 2,000 inhabitants, to pay their final respects to Cristina and to support her family. Her body had been found in a garbage dump near Novara, Piedmont, on 1 September 1975, two months after her abduction. According to the investigators, Cristina was killed by an overdose of sedatives. The exact date of her death remains unknown.

Official documents, criminological analyses, and Mafia historical studies illuminate the magnitude of ransom kidnapping in Italy in terms of numbers, duration, and origins, but they do not allow us to observe the public reaction to and the collective imagination about abductions – that is, what the phenomenon was *for* Italy. It is in fact not just the phenomenon's socio-economic and geographical roots that make it distinctly Italian but also the way in which kidnapping entered into the language and narrative of the country.[5] What Shuster reported in the *Times* in the summer of 1975 was more than a shaken apathy towards a crime that had become a daily routine. The abduction and death of Cristina Mazzotti made Italians view ransom kidnapping as a major event rather than as a series of isolated news stories. Cristina's ordeal was perceived by the country as a new reality with which they had to grapple. The bodily mutilation of Paul Getty III in Calabria in 1973 had certainly been a horrifying novelty. Yet it was the tragic discovery of Cristina's corpse that generated the narratives that made Italian society aware of its coexistence with the underworld of kidnapping. Through an analysis of the press coverage of her abduction, the public response to her death, and the impact of the Mazzottis' ordeal on television and collective imagination, this chapter offers an approach to 1970s Italy that – by looking at violence from a non-ideological perspective – repositions that decade as the one in which organized crime horrified the Italian Republic.[6]

The Girl Next Door

In public discourse and imagination, the Mazzotti abduction represented a story antithetical to the Getty kidnapping. Unlike the young Paul, Cristina did not belong to a famous family, never got into any trouble, and never appeared in the news for political or other reasons prior to her capture. Although she was living in Milan, she was depicted in the media as a girl from a small town who dreamed of becoming a doctor. The opposite of eccentric or foreign, Cristina was Italy's girl next door. The day after her body was found, Enzo Biagi, an acclaimed journalist, wrote a poignant article in *Corriere della Sera* whose headline,

"Cristina, an Existence Like Many Others," captures how her ordeal concerned everyone.[7] Framed by newspapers as true and traumatic from the start, the media accounts of Mazzotti's abduction show that in the two years since the Getty abduction, journalists had drastically changed their expectations regarding kidnapping and kidnappers. The kidnappers' initial silence following the abduction, which had fuelled media scepticism about Gail Getty's negotiations with her son's captors, is no longer a cause for suspicion about the authenticity of the crime. Rather, it was understood by the press and its audience alike to be a proven technique. At the end of his article about Cristina's capture, for example, Arnaldo Giuliani states in *Corriere della Sera*, "The strategy of kidnapping has a fixed script that does not open itself up to many variations. The Mazzottis live next to the phone, by now for hours. But the anguished silence of the ringtone is part of the cruel rule of the game: to keep the hostage's family dangling at the extreme limit of their mental endurance."[8]

In the case of Cristina, the whole country waited with her family for the kidnappers' calls, especially after her father, Elios Mazzotti, paid the ransom without hesitation. Depicted by the media as the antithesis of the stingy Paul Getty Sr., Elios Mazzotti embodied the values of the Italian family ready to sacrifice everything in order to save their daughter's life. Even Paul's and Cristina's friends were portrayed as inverses of each other. While Paul's companions were supposedly suspicious and ambiguous individuals, Cristina's were trustworthy. A few days after she was captured, for example, the press broke the silence requested by the Mazzottis in order to give her friends the opportunity to inform the kidnappers about the real economic status of the family.[9] Of the five billion lire that the abductors demanded for the ransom, Elios Mazzotti was able to pay little more than one billion.

The media attention on Cristina's story shed light on the numerous hostages, especially from Lombardy, who never returned home and whose families lost contact with the abductors after having partially paid the ransom demanded. While Cristina was still a hostage, an alarming fact was becoming evident in the news: the national targets of kidnapping were no longer just extremely well-off families. Analysing this matter in the *Corriere* on 11 July 1975, the prominent journalist Giulio Nascimbeni talks about an "incurable plague of kidnappings" and underscores that "next to the big heist (that today is named Giuseppe D'Amico, the Roman ship owner, and yesterday was named Getty Junior or Alemagna or Rossi di Montelera or Bulgari), we are witnessing an increasing series of minor hits."[10] He explains why there existed a "disproportion between the act of kidnapping and the financial

70   Ransom Kidnapping in Italy

means of the abducted."[11] He first points out that Italy's economic elite had started to defend itself by adopting precautions such as sending their children abroad; surrounding themselves with bodyguards; and acquiring Dobermans, a symbol of power, as guard dogs. However, for Nascimbeni the discrepancy is more likely the result of the spread of abduction due to imitation. In contrast with the "reassuring image" of an existing *anonima sequestri* (anonymous kidnappings) that operated as a central organization, he states that professional kidnappers had become a model for low-level criminals. This imitation made society "defenceless and exposed to a process of potential decimation."[12]

Nascimbeni's alarmism is noteworthy because it depicts kidnapping as a contagion not just because it created victims but also – and perhaps more importantly – because it created amateur kidnappers. One gets the impression from his analysis that in 1970s Italy the crime of abduction was perceived as potentially capable of turning society into Thomas Hobbes's state of nature, in which man is a wolf to man (*homo homini lupus*).[13] Yet Nascimbeni's article adopts another useful lens, namely, his attention to kidnapped children's trauma in order to depict ransom kidnapping beyond an economic perspective. As we all witness a loss of innocence in those children, who will never forget the trauma of having been abducted, he argues, so too do we witness a collective loss of innocence with the kidnapped who never return home. Addressing the unsolved cases in Lombardy, he asks where the victims are and calls the situation endured by their families an "inhumane odyssey," in which they are forced to spend "day after day, night after night, waiting for the phone to ring, for at least a sign of pietas to come, for the tenacious hope to have some comfort."[14] In these cases the innocence lost is that "of work, study, the daily life of a family, under the unknown of a silence that is like a spectre."[15] Emotional and psychological in nature, the loss that kidnapping imposes on the families is not just monetary and, most of all, concerns the country as a whole. Clearly in the words of Nascimbeni, Italy in 1975 appears to be hunted by anonymous kidnappers.

Contagious and frightening, this crime was undermining the country's civic life. However, Italian society also began to mobilize against it. After the Mazzotti family received a letter in which Cristina implored them to pay the ransom, a committee of citizens from Erba (a village close to Eupilio) sent the president of the Italian Republic, Giovanni Leone, a petition in which they asked for his intervention:

> To the President of the Republic: The following citizens, concerned about the spread of criminality, particularly regarding ransom kidnapping, which is most likely connected to the concentration in the region

of numerous compulsory residents, request your intervention in order to promote by means of constitutional forms measures capable of definitively tackling this serious problem. The undersigned also express the anguish and grief of the families of the kidnapped who find themselves economically unable to comply with the absurd demands of the criminals, in order to request your urgent intervention so as to spare others this sad and destructive experience.[16]

Published in the *Corriere*, the text demonstrates the strong impact the Mazzottis' ordeal had on their local community, which recognized the absurdity of the kidnappers' request compared to the family's effective wealth. Yet the most striking aspect of this petition is that it represents perhaps one of the first collective and political actions taken against the violence of organized crime in northern Italy. It is the voice of the people of Lombardy who, aware that they were exposed to the consequences of the forced resettlement of dangerous *mafiosi* in their region by the state, spoke up to reach Rome. The opposite of *omertà* (the code of silence through which the Mafia cements its power), the citizens' petition denounces the escalation of crime in the north, sympathizes with the victims and their families, and asks for urgent protection by the highest office of the state.

The Mazzotti family did not just receive the support of their local community. They captivated the attention of the national media, which made public their vulnerable and powerless situation. The columns of the *Corriere* – to stay on the pages of a main national newspaper – depict Cristina's parents as prostrate with grief. The paper's readers came to know these parents and other family members, such as Cristina's siblings and uncles, who were involved in the communication with her abductors and engaged in appeals to stir public awareness. The media operated a kind of familiarization of the Mazzotti abduction, meaning that they attempted to impact public discourse about ransom kidnapping by making the audience participate in the drama through the perspective of the family involved. For example, the *Corriere* called Cristina by the pet name "Cricri" used by her relatives. However, if at an emotional level the Mazzottis became the "anguished Italian family" desperate over the abduction of their beloved child, at the civic level they became an exemplary family. The Mazzottis did not just make their private grief public. They fought kidnapping as a public issue. They became, as the journalist and writer Corrado Stajano would later describe them in his essay "Il sequestro di Cristina" (Cristina's kidnapping), "active victims."[17]

72 Ransom Kidnapping in Italy

Stajano's expression allows us to envision the double role that the Mazzotti family played for Italian civil society. They were recognized as victims in a country often depicted by national and international media as cynically indifferent towards the ordeals of the kidnapped and their kin and were looked up to as engaged citizens despite the paralysing grief they were experiencing. Indicative of their engagement, and contrasting with the passivity often associated with victims, is an article that Elios Mazzotti himself wrote for the *Corriere* on 17 July 1975, during his daughter's captivity. It is striking to see the first page of the main national newspaper become the platform for a private citizen – who could not pay the ransom demanded by his daughter's abductors – to speak out. It is symptomatic of an emergency. Mazzotti's appeal is particularly interesting because it is not addressed to Cristina's kidnappers but rather to his fellow Italians. In the title, "I Am Going to Talk to You About Kidnapping Now That My Daughter Has Been Abducted," Mazzotti situates himself in relation to his audience by stressing that he will speak publicly about the crime from a perspective that he is personally living.[18] If his experience gave him the authority with which to speak, he also felt compelled to shape the ongoing debate about ransom kidnapping.

In a short editorial introduction, the *Corriere* expresses its admiration for Mazzotti's article, which takes on "with almost calm and very civil words the general subject of violence and kidnappings."[19] Mazzotti's article is indeed impressive for both its content and its tone. Its most noteworthy element, though, is its political meaning. By speaking from his completely helpless position, Mazzotti urges Italians to not remain indifferent and dissuades them from believing those narratives that frame kidnappings abstractly, as if they were the fatalistic consequence of human beings' evil nature. By using language that resembles the widespread Marxist critique of capitalism and exploitation (with which the wealthy hostages were often identified), he instead encourages the readers to consider the abductions as alarming economic and social threats to be fought against collectively. He depicts kidnapping as the greatest form of reification because it reduces the life of a person to merchandise, but also because it detaches money from any production and instead relates it "to the defence of an innocent victim, the sense of family, and sentiments."[20] Like Nascimbeni, Mazzotti sheds light on abduction as a form of violence that menaces the innocence of Italy's civic life. Yet, for Mazzotti, kidnappings threaten the rule of law as well. The danger of this kind of violence is not just its diffusion, which according to Nascimbeni would eventually pit everyone against everyone else. It is also the lack of trust it generates towards the police and the state, which can deteriorate into "voluntary and spontaneous forms of defence": "Against this unfortunate perspective, whoever wishes to defend democratic institutions and the rule of law, and with them his or her own security, must know how to take a stand because the rampant phenomenon of criminality can only be totally and definitively defeated through moral awareness and democratic engagement."[21] Not only does Mazzotti's *Corriere* article denounce the phenomenon of ransom kidnapping. It also shows the country how to resist it. With the example of his local community of Erba in mind, Mazzotti calls on every Italian to take up active citizenship. His article, and the *Corriere*'s decision to publish it, demonstrates that the violence linked to organized crime was perceived as a political matter. A threat to the democratic institutions of the country, he warns, this criminal violence could be defeated only through an engaged civil society. It is striking to read such a topical argument on a page written in Italy in 1975 by the father of a kidnap victim. The idea that the rule of law must be protected and, especially, supported by a culture of legality and commitment is the backbone of the anti-Mafia movement that arose after the killing of judges Giovanni Falcone and Paolo Borsellino by Cosa Nostra in 1992, nearly twenty years after Cristina's kidnapping. The Mazzottis' engagement would continue even after Cristina's death, through the Cristina Mazzotti Foundation, which her father created in her memory. Dedicated to the study of crime prevention and victim trauma, the mission of this foundation – based on memory, testimony, and social awareness – evokes the resistance that anti-Mafia associations perform today.[22]

The Discovery of the Body

When Cristina's body was found on 1 September 1975, the news shocked Italy – not only because of its gravity but also because the country was expecting the imminent announcement of her liberation (figure 3.1). In early August, the *Corriere* revealed that a ransom had been paid and the family was waiting for the abductors to free Cristina.[23] The Mazzottis had mortgaged their villa, and their friends had collected money to help them pay more than $1 million to the kidnappers. The media covered Cristina's abduction almost daily throughout the month. The *Corriere* alone published a dozen articles, five in the final four days. Italy was therefore following her family's ordeal step-by-step. In a column written by Pierluigi Tagliaferro on 4 August, Cristina's mother asked the media to respect the requested press silence and the police not to intervene in the negotiations until after her daughter's return.[24] Tagliaferro's remarkable depiction of the Mazzottis allows us to picture

Figure 3.1. Cristina Mazzotti, *Corriere della Sera*, 2 September 1975. The author thanks La Fondazione Corriere della Sera for the historical archive material.

The Day Cristina's Body Was Found   75

the predicament faced by the families of the kidnapped, as well as the concern that his own words must have provoked in his readers. Imagining the moment in which the Mazzotti family carefully wrote their appeal to the press, Tagliaferro describes them as "obedient executors of the orders of the *anonima sequestri*," who, terrified, "weigh every word, aware that even one ambiguous adverb can lead the kidnappers to make rash reactions."[25] The family of a kidnapped victim appears to be completely under the control of an invisible power and the life of a hostage hidden in the Italian underworld to depend exclusively on the language used to communicate with her abductors.

In the weeks that followed, the Mazzottis' vulnerability became even more apparent. The kidnappers' silence pushed them to publicly write two more desperate appeals. Their community collected money for authorities to pay anyone with useful information about the case. The Ministry of the Interior offered compensation as well.[26] In a dramatic turn of events, however, on 26 August police discovered Cristina's first hiding place on a farmstead in Piedmont, where she had spent weeks essentially buried inside a hole in the ground. The dimensions were so restrictive that there was little air inside. The kidnappers had given Cristina a short and narrow plastic tube connected to the outside with which to breathe; it was found together with her personal belongings. The police also arrested several individuals involved in the kidnapping. One of them, Libero Ballinari, started to talk. A Swiss citizen who helped abduct Cristina and had been one of her warders, Ballinari was caught while trying to launder his share of the ransom money at a bank in Switzerland. The police made other important discoveries. For instance, they found a large portion of the ransom paid by the Mazzottis in Calabria.[27] It became clear that behind this abduction were both members of the 'Ndrangheta and affiliated criminals working for them in the north. In addition to those already arrested, the police targeted Achille Gaetano, a fugitive from justice and member of the Gaetano clan from Gizzeria, Calabria.[28]

The investigation into Mazzotti's abduction started to overlap with that of the Giuseppe D'Amico kidnapping. Snatched in Rome on 29 June – the night before Cristina was captured – D'Amico spent forty-three days hidden in the caves of Aspromonte. A ship owner from Lazio, he was liberated on 20 August after his brother went to Calabria to pay a ransom of $1 million. It was at this point evident that Calabria was the heart of the *anonima sequestri*. Towards the end of August, after he was released, D'Amico started to work with the police. "We will have him fly over by helicopter because with the Mafia you never know; they could shoot him," Ugo Macera, the police commissioner of Rome

76   Ransom Kidnapping in Italy

and an expert on kidnappings, sent to Calabria by the Minister of the Interior to investigate the case, told the media.[29] This striking declaration by a law enforcement authority demonstrates the territorial power that organized crime held over the region. D'Amico explored the mountains of Aspromonte by helicopter to locate his hiding places. As he later informed the press, however, he was actually looking for Cristina Mazzotti.[30] D'Amico's and Cristina's family's hopes were dashed on the night of 1 September, when, following Ballinari's directions, the police found her body in a garbage dump near Novara.[31] Cristina's uncle, Eolo Mazzotti, would later describe the condition endured by the families subjected to ransom kidnapping:

> The event is in itself unimaginable. You have no experience that can help you in any way. It goes beyond any frame of reference and any type of life you've lived. When I used to read about ransom kidnapping and about the parents who were waiting for the phone call from the intermediary to have reassuring news about the abduction … I asked myself how a father, a mother, waiting for a contact with the kidnappers could sleep, eat, live. My enigma was solved when I was able to directly experience how it was possible not only to maintain your own physiological rhythms but also to consider the phone call as the moment of liberation from the anguish because it is precisely the phone call that puts you, even if indirectly, in contact with your loved one. The call is a moment of relief, of joy … even when the voice says: "Get five billion lire ready … We will cut her ear, we will slit her throat" … Even then you have the sense that the thread has not yet been cut, that the person you care about is not dead yet, and despite everything you hope that nothing bad has been done to her.[32]

If the news about Cristina's death ended her family's hopes, which had persisted in spite of the psychological violence, it also opened up a new grim horizon in Italy.

The Public Response

Two years after the novelist Alberto Moravia published his article on the mutilation of Paul Getty III's ear in the *Corriere* in 1973, Cristina Mazzotti's murder drove him to again take part in the public debate about ransom kidnapping. He did so from the same national platform on 3 September 1975 with an editorial entitled "Reflections on Horror," which explicitly recalled his previous op-ed.[33] As we saw in chapter 2, in 1973 Moravia had claimed that the mindset behind the Getty kidnappers' act of mutilation horrified the country in a way that killing him would not have. This horror made the public aware of a sociological change. Bandits in Italy were no longer opposing the forces of economic power, he had argued, but rather, inspired by the same consumerist and hedonistic ethic, were adopting their methods. The discovery of Cristina's body forced Moravia to adjust his claims. Her young age, her gender, the unbearable conditions of her captivity, the fact that her family had already paid the ransom, and the reason why she was killed – she was probably able to recognize her warders, he speculates – made her ordeal the "perfect horror." He feared that it could cause the public to demand that the death penalty be restored. His reflections in the column are a clear attempt to neutralize this eventuality.

Moravia's article is noteworthy on several levels. First, it reiterates that ransom kidnapping's impact on the public is one of horror. Second, it shows an awareness of organized crime and abductions that he lacked when he wrote his previous article. This awareness is certainly the result of the country's exposure to frequent kidnapping news. Yet it is also the consequence of a new cultural mediation that began to develop in response to this phenomenon. Moravia, like Nascimbeni, recognizes the existence in Italy of a new social model embodied by the figure of the Mafia boss. "Reflections on Horror" questions how this model became available and why someone like Achille Gaetano – responsible for Cristina's abduction – decided to imitate it. Moravia builds his answer on an argument offered to him by a theatrical play he attended in Rome, *A proposito di Liggio* (About Liggio) by Mario Missiroli and Vittorio Sermonti. Arrested in Milan in May 1974, Luciano Liggio was, as we know, one of the most powerful bosses of the Sicilian Mafia active in northern Italy in the early 1970s and the mastermind of several pioneering ransom kidnappings in Lombardy and Piedmont, including those of the manufacturer Pietro Torielli and Luigi Rossi di Montelera (as seen in chapter 1). Missiroli and Sermonti's script reports verbatim the anti-Mafia committee's investigation of Liggio and those involved in his Mafia syndicate. What struck Moravia about this play is the language used during the committee's session: "All those who were interrogated during the session were hiding behind the grotesque dignity of a ridiculous and powerless judicial and bureaucratic language. They were hiding because they did not dare to either punish or propose punishment."[34] These bureaucratic speeches, Moravia notes, function exactly like the sneering masks worn on stage by the characters of *About Liggio* – they grotesquely cover the Italian state's inability to punish powerful criminals. He argues that Missiroli and Sermonti show that the scandal of "the holy acquittals" in Italy was due to the death threats judges received from organized crime. These threats were made possible by political, economic, and social acquiescence with criminals, and their result was the creation of the boss as imitable figure. Through the lens of what Missiroli himself defined as "teatro di realtà" (reality theatre),[35] Moravia's op-ed reflects on a paradox and speaks out against the connection between crime and legal power: criminals had essentially already established the very death penalty he feared civil society could demand in response to Cristina's murder. Impunity was the prize for their efforts. This explains why for Moravia, as Shuster concluded in the *Times* article seen at the beginning of this chapter, "the distant responsibility for the death of Cristina Mazzotti belongs to everyone who permitted the figure of the criminal 'boss' in Italy to become over the years an ideal model to imitate and even, if possible, to develop and perfect."[36] The Mazzotti kidnapping and murder were perceived as a national defeat and brought the country to confront the fact that the violence of organized crime was not only blackmailing the hostages' families. As Missiroli, Sermonti, and Moravia denounced, it was neutralizing the judicial power of the state.

In Moravia's text, horror works as a connection to his earlier public statement on abductions because the Mazzotti murder provoked a shock similar to, if not stronger than, that provoked by the Getty mutilation. Yet the perfect horror that emerges from Moravia's op-ed is the correlate of a perfect criminal model to imitate. As in his first article, Moravia argues that ransom kidnapping prompts Italy to acknowledge an alarming change that was political as well as sociological. However, by considering horror in relation to Cristina's body rather than to a criminal model, we can envision the effects of the violence of kidnapping on Italy's collective imagination and memory. One of the most destabilizing elements of the tragedy was that the date of Cristina's death remained unknown. If the media narrative of the Getty kidnapping began with questions about its authenticity, that of the Mazzotti abduction ended with questions about her death. No one could verify whether she had still been alive when her kidnappers abandoned her in the garbage dump. The discovery of her body added another unbearable element to her story: Cristina was no longer recognizable. As the philosopher Adriana Cavarero argues in her book on violence and horror, dismemberment and decomposition horrify us because the unity of the body, that is, its figure, disappears.[37] The correlate of this unity, states Cavarero, is the singularity and uniqueness of human beings. When Cristina's body was found, the journalist Arnaldo Giuliani first reported the news for the *Corriere*. While praising and tracing the work of the investigators who solved the case, he testified to the discovery of the body that he himself had witnessed: "And here a hand comes to view. Other rubble is moved. A body in decay appears. No official identification, but it is Cristina. Who else could it be?"[38] Even if the witnesses present at this scene knew that the body the police had found was likely Cristina's, they could no longer recognize her. Talking about the heart-wrenching identification that the family had to make, Giuliani adds, "But how can you recognize in a body destroyed by the dirt the same figure of the girl who that night last 30 June left home smiling, happy, with the joy of spending an evening with friends?"[39] The absence of Cristina's likeness from her own body horrified Italy. In a country waiting for her return, this was the loss of someone that everyone knew.

The effects of this horror are reflected in the language of the media, which responded to Cristina's death with a rhetoric typically used to frame traumatic events. The registers that journalists employed to write about the discovery of her body included, for example, diary and self-narrative. In addition to the article cited earlier, Giuliani wrote "The Diary of the Night of Nightmares When the Body Was Found," in which, by using the plural first-person "we," he gives an anguished and personal account of the police's search.[40] He writes, for instance, "We climb down. Our shoes are in the mud. The car's high-beams only point ahead. On the sides, there is a wall of darkness. The air we breathe has a heavy stench that repulses us. 'Where are we?' I ask. 'In a garbage dump.'"[41] Although on occasion Giuliani goes overboard when describing macabre details, this so-called diary testifies to the collective involvement and emotional reactions of those who were present and allows newspaper readers not just to be informed but also to witness. However, journalists' urgency in writing about Cristina's story through self-narratives becomes evident in the aforementioned Biagi article, "Cristina, an Existence Like Many Others."[42] Biagi's editorial sheds light on the Mazzotti abduction as a national trauma and allows us to envision how deeply shattering its impact was on the country's identity. The first notable element is that his article abruptly shifts from the initial shock of the news to a personal account of himself: "The television said it: Cristina Mazzotti is dead. She has been killed. Even the evening news anchor, to whom someone suddenly passed a sheet of paper, seemed frightened. I was alone in my empty house."[43] Biagi immediately tells his readers where he was when he heard the news – a socially common way of talking about traumatic public events. Indeed, disorienting situations require us to locate ourselves.

Yet it is Biagi's use of memory that shows how, with this particular kidnapping and murder, organized crime crossed a limit that was no longer bearable for Italy. He compares its effects to those wrought on

80   Ransom Kidnapping in Italy

the country by World War II and fascism, and he does so by confessing his own reaction to the news:

> When in a country we arrive at such degradation, and abductions become customary, and nothing will ever be known about many of them ... we can even come to believe that the old forms of punishment – the pillory, the amputation of thieves' hands, yes, even the platoon in the square, with the rascals that watch and the old ladies that scream and knit while they wait – are perhaps a refuge. They become a remedy for an upset consciousness, the final attempt and the last defence. Then I remembered that my generation had already lived these scenes, and one man was shot only because he had a beard and looked like a fascist official.[44]

Biagi's first thought is of revenge against the kidnappers – a prevailing public sentiment to which his article gives expression. Like Moravia, Biagi openly fears there would be a push to restore the death penalty. Strikingly, though, the injustice of Cristina's death and the helpless position into which organized crime forced the country reopen his traumatic memories of post-war Italy.

Biagi's use of self-narrative is perhaps partially motivated by the connection he had with the Mazzotti family, who, during Cristina's abduction, asked him to publicly write to her kidnappers – an idea that they together ultimately decided to abandon because it was too risky. However, on several occasions he specified that his "evil thoughts" of revenge were independent from his relationship with the Mazzottis, a family he highly respected and that took a firm position against the death penalty.[45] The significance of the comparison between the social response to the violence of ransom kidnapping and the memory of the aftermath of War World II by someone like Enzo Biagi becomes more evident if we consider that, over his long career, he was known as the journalist who had lived through the 1943 German occupation of Italy and took an active part in the resistance against fascism. Biagi recalls attending the trials of Herbert Kappler and Walter Reder – the German SS functionary and Austrian SS commander, respectively, responsible for two separate civilian massacres in Italy in 1944 – and remembers seeing in them the product of a collective "madness" (in Biagi's words) that had invested Europe. Unlike those responsible for traumatic historical events, Biagi seems to suggest, Cristina's kidnappers acted without being under the pressure of historical forces. The striking implication of his comparison is not, I would argue, its provocative meaning but rather the turmoil it asks us to envision. Biagi's memory of the occupation of Italy in response to the TV news about Cristina's body shows

The Day Cristina's Body Was Found   81

an awareness of the presence of an extraneous power in the country that was capable of exercising any kind of violence. Cristina Mazzotti's death was not just criminal news. It was a national traumatic event that made Italians perceive the phenomenon of ransom kidnapping as a state of emergency for which to suspend the rule of law.

Biagi was not alone in comparing Cristina's kidnappers to the Nazis. Giulio Nascimbeni did so as well in "A Silence and Grief That Ask for Justice," written after he attended Cristina's funeral.[46] Nascimbeni's article is a vivid account that begins with the image of a miles-long line of cars arriving from all over Lombardy to attend the mass in her family's hometown. "To reach Eupilio," writes Nascimbeni, "one had to walk."[47] Thousands of people attended the memorial, and thus most of them had to park in nearby Erba. Nascimbeni describes the streets of Eupilio as being so packed that it was difficult to breathe. Yet it was the crowd's silence that struck the journalist. Nascimbeni portrays this silence not as emptiness but instead as a constant and meaningful presence. It becomes anguish when Elios Mazzotti appears before the public. It signifies the spectral memory of the garbage dump and the state in which Cristina's body was found. More than respect or devotion, the silence becomes a demand for justice for the people looking at the photograph of a smiling Cristina hung on the church's facade – an image everyone could recognize as the same one disseminated by the media. Finally, the silence does not mean that the kidnappers were forgotten by the crowd. Rather, they were looming "like people who came from another side of life, from a dark area that we would never want to identify with the cities, towns and roads we know."[48] The silence of the crowd gathered in Eupilio for Cristina is one of refusal – the silent rejection of heinous violence in a region overwhelmed by Italy's underworld. Nascimbeni closes his article with a comparison of Cristina's kidnappers' violence to that of the Nazis, and he does so through poetry:

> One of De Libero's poems tells the story of a Roman youth that was killed by a German sentinel "because he was laughing." That occurred in September, just like the discovery of Cristina's body and her funeral. Those old lines came back to mind, but more than an epigraph to Cristina, they are for us. The poet says of that September, as of this September, that everyone should carve "the date on his hand."[49]

The abduction and death of Cristina Mazzotti did not simply shake the apathy of the Italians towards ransom kidnappings – as the *New York Times* rightly noted in 1975. The discovery of her body and her funeral shifted the centre of gravity in the Italian imagination of this

82 Ransom Kidnapping in Italy

crime. Framed in public discourse through the memory of the country's occupation during World War II, the narrative of the Mazzotti case depicted ransom kidnapping as historical and unforgettable. The timeless language of poetry and the image of the date carved into the hand that Nascimbeni uses in his article are striking. After giving a detailed account of Cristina's funeral, he freezes this moment in an embodied memory that should be collective because it belongs to everyone. Cristina's story is not something that happened in Italy. It is something that happened *to* Italy. What her kidnappers did to her was perceived as violence against the body of the country as a whole.[50]

From a Sardinian Phenomenon to a National Plague

The day Cristina's body was found, the debate on ransom abductions radically changed. The immediate response to her and her family's tragedy demonstrates the level of identification and emotional participation that the country reached in this particular kidnapping episode. In order to fully recognize the event's impact on the national narrative of the phenomenon, however, we need to shift our gaze from the written pages of the newspapers to the screens of public television. This is the medium that most allows us to immerse ourselves in the atmosphere in which the Italians lived during those years. Unlike newspapers, television offers a visual and acoustic depiction of abduction through which we can identify the objects, symbols, landscapes, and sounds that map the Italian mindset of the time. What is immediately evident from the material available at the Teche Rai (the RAI audiovisual archive) is the impressive number of journalistic broadcasts, enquiries, documentaries, *speciali TG1* and *TG2* (special news programs), in-depth analyses by commentators, and even comedy shows dedicated to ransom kidnapping – perhaps one of the most covered subjects in the history of Italian national public television. I do not refer here to the regular TV news that in the 1970s announced a new abduction almost daily. I am instead pointing to broadcasts that for hours offered their audiences stories and visual mediations of the crime. If ransom kidnapping demonstrates that organized crime was already present throughout Italy in the early 1970s, the public television archive shows that the Italians knew this perfectly well, in contrast with the assumption that the country is discovering the presence of Mafia syndicates in the north only today.[51] This archive also traces a long-standing relationship between television and organized crime. It is noteworthy that when RAI created its first *rotocalco* (a weekly TV news documentary) called *RT* – an early example of investigative journalism in Italy – episode 1 was "Rapporto da Corleone" (Report from Corleone) by journalist Gianni Bisiach, which covered the presence of Mafia in this small Sicilian town.[52] The year was 1962, and the creator of *RT* was Enzo Biagi. Investigative journalism in Italy thus began with reports to the country about the existence of the Mafia. For the first time the word "Mafia" was pronounced on television. Although it only became possible to write the history of this organized crime group after high-profile members of Cosa Nostra – the name of the Sicilian Mafia – started to collaborate with magistrates in the mid-1980s, as historians have noted, its social effects and media accounts were visible and available to the public much earlier. Abductions contributed significantly to this visibility, and not only for the Sicilian Mafia but also – and especially – for the Calabrian 'Ndrangheta.

Up until the kidnapping in Lombardy of Pietro Torielli (1972) – the first of several committed by Cosa Nostra in northern Italy in the first half of the decade – and that in Rome of Paul Getty III by the 'Ndrangheta (1973), ransom kidnapping had been a regional crime that involved Calabria, Sicily (to an extent), and Sardinia in particular. It is important to remember that abduction as an alarming social phenomenon originated in Barbagia, the mountains of Sardinia. In the late 1960s, ransom kidnapping drastically escalated on the island, with dozens of cases in just three years – a fact that, as seen in chapter 1, prompted Italy in 1969 to create a parliamentary committee to investigate crime and banditry in the region. For Italians, therefore, the original kidnappers were known and pictured as Sardinian bandits. The figure of the bandit hidden in Barbagia would long endure in the collective imagination. The bandit's ski mask and the double-barrel rifle became symbols of abductors writ large. Among the earliest RAI national broadcasts that covered ransom kidnapping, we find an April 1968 episode of *TV7* entitled "Il salario del bandito" (The bandit's salary) and a January 1971 episode of *AZ: Un fatto come e perché* (A to Z: The how and why of the facts) entitled "Banditismo in Sardegna" (Banditry in Sardinia), which exemplify the early national narrative of abduction as a Sardinian phenomenon.[53] The fifteen-minute "Bandit's Salary" shot on the island features interviews, aerial images of the mountains, and a voice-over that describes the crime and its figures: the number of banditry groups, ransom and money laundering, and specific cases. The spectator has the impression of being in front of a scenario aesthetically inspired by Westerns, with a deserted landscape, pictures of wanted bandits and their bounties, and a soundtrack composed of a mix of dramatic music and gunshots. Made after the police had killed a bandit, this video gives a clear message to potential kidnappers: the state is strong and will hunt you down. In reality, however, Sardinian investigative procedure allowed families to

84 Ransom Kidnapping in Italy

negotiate with the bandits without the intervention of law enforcement – a strategy that began to be publicly debated.

If *TV7* urged the nation to pay attention to the local problem of banditry in Sardinia, *AZ: Un fatto come e perché* possessed the tools to explain why this problem arose in the first place. Conducted by the journalist Ennio Mastrostefano, the hour-long "Banditry in Sardinia" newscast offers a mediation of kidnapping based both on the Anti-Mafia Parliamentary Committee's then-ongoing study of the island and on journalistic investigations. The broadcast represents an impressive collaboration between RAI and the Italian Parliament that alternates videos shot in Sardinia and in Rome with a live in-studio discussion between Mastrostefano and his guests, who include the president and members of the committee, as well as a Sardinian shepherd. Through the lens of realism and expertise, *AZ* provides spectators documents, data, maps, and footage with which to view kidnapping – a Sardinian phenomenon for which the responsibility and possible solutions were nevertheless national. There is a tangible optimism in RAI linked to the belief that an economic intervention in Barbagia by the state would defeat the rise of banditry. The gaze of the television audience is thus well informed and, most especially, sees the crisis as controllable. Yet by locating abductions in a specific geographically and socially insular place, it is a gaze that keeps the rest of Italy distant and safe. The crime is portrayed as the product of a world that we need to know in order to help but to which we do not belong. This becomes clear in a video in which the journalist Enzo Dell'Aquila describes the events that transpire after an abduction, through the story of an ongoing case in the region.[54] After listening to an interview of the blackmailed family, watching the police helicopters surveying the area, and observing civilians searching for bandits in the mountains, the spectator discovers what happens when the investigations bring no results. In a clip, we follow the car of the family's lawyer driving through Barbagia, while the voice-over explains:

> It is a mandatory itinerary that is carried out for each kidnapping following precise rules. The licence plates of these cars are reported to the bandits. It is an invitation to make contact, to show up and make their demands known. They try to see as many people as possible, to spread word that "the family agrees to negotiate." In Orgosolo, the lawyer Guiso's car stops even in front of the house of Graziano Mesina [the most well-known bandit in Italy]. The woman dressed in black is Graziano's mother. The bandit is in jail, but his friends on the outside are still numerous and can be of help. At this point they become aware of our presence.[55]

The combination of listening to the narrator and seeing villages, streets, faces, and interactions provokes in the spectator the sensation of watching live a typical attempt to make contact with bandits. Yet, while the lawyer and his companion in the video are making themselves visible to Barbagia, we are instead its invisible outsiders. As soon as the two of them realize they are being tailed, the lawyer's companion looks towards the camera, grabs a rock, and firmly gestures for the journalists to leave. Up until this moment the viewers did not know that Dell'Aquila and his crew were filming secretly. This *effet de réel* (effect of reality), in the words of Roland Barthes, makes the spectator aware of their previously unknown voyeurism. Shot undercover, this RAI video attempts to create the illusion of seeing kidnapping as it is – that is, as it unfolds when we are not there. It is striking how close to life in Barbagia RAI gets with this journalistic investigation. The sequence of the lawyer talking to legendary bandit Graziano Mesina's mother, seen in a traditional Sardinian dark dress and veil in front of her house, is exceptional. With "Banditry in Sardinia," ransom kidnapping becomes visible on television, without Italians being exposed to it, and as a phenomenon that the parliamentary committee will soon end.

A few months after Cristina's body was found, *AZ* would depict abduction in a remarkably different way in a February 1976 episode entitled "Sequestro di persona" (Kidnapping).[56] As we have already seen in chapter 2, the 1974 RAI interview conducted with Paul Getty III a few months after his liberation crafted a reassuring image of Italy and portrayed young Getty as unreliable. This video was symptomatic of the anxiety engendered by living in a country where organized crime proved to be a threat for Italian society across the peninsula. For the first time, a hostage had been captured outside of Calabria, hidden in Aspromonte, and mutilated. The otherness of the foreign victim and his family, however, distanced the horror of this kidnapping and its alarming national proportions from its Italian origin and identity. In contrast, the abduction of Cristina Mazzotti raised questions and drove the public to see the phenomenon as an Italian plague. It is true that journalists' first response to her death was to compare her abductors to foreign invaders, a fact that might seem to confirm a shared perception of the Getty and Mazzotti kidnappings as external and other to Italy. However, the kidnappers/invaders comparison resulted from the country's identification with Cristina. The Nazis were not used by journalists as an abstract metaphor with which to depict evil as foreign. Rather, they signified a reaction originating *within* the perceptual frame of the Italian imagination. Shattered by a violence that brought back memories of war, Italy recognized in the Mazzotti abduction and murder the gravity

86 Ransom Kidnapping in Italy

of having organized crime on the country's soil. As the 1976 *AZ* episode allows us to see, within the national narrative of kidnapping, Cristina Mazzotti's name and story functioned as a testimony and set an ethical limit.

No longer a Sardinian crime of national interest, ransom kidnapping was now a phenomenon attributable to Mafia syndicates whose violence and cruelty were afflicting Italians everywhere across the peninsula. Rather than optimistically show a parliamentary committee at work – as it had done just five years prior with "Banditry in Sardinia" – this time RAI aired an interview with the Minister of the Interior, Francesco Cossiga, commander in chief of the police and head of national security. The effects of the Mazzotti abduction and murder on television narratives are immediately recognizable. "Kidnapping" begins with the sequence of a news documentary by the journalist Giuseppe Marrazzo in which we see a countryside in the winter, bare trees, and a man wandering alone. The soundtrack – a piece of Pink Floyd's "Wish You Were Here" – is highly distressing and is suddenly overlapped by a male voice that says, "I will never stop looking, never, I will never stop. I will look for him and I'll find him for sure, dead or alive. And those people will pay for what they did to me. They will definitely pay for the harm they have caused me. I will never stop looking for him. Never."[57] It is the voice of Luigi Riboli, father of Emanuele, who was kidnapped at the age of sixteen – fifteen months before this video was shot – and was never released, even after the ransom was paid. Marrazzo interviews Riboli, whose words, gestures, and emotions fill the screen. The viewer does not know in which region the interview takes place. The initial countryside evokes an interior landscape and individual loneliness more than a specific place and social context. After the tragedy of Cristina Mazzotti, the geography of kidnapping becomes that of the families' grief.

Marrazzo's visual investigation propels us into the heart of the Years of Lead through the testimony and faces of kidnap victims, and especially their families, who are exposed to the audience with extreme close-ups. The second to talk in the documentary is the ten-year-old Mirko Panattoni, snatched in 1973 in Bergamo, Lombardy, when he was seven.[58] The camera scrutinizes his eyes while he recalls his capture and captivity, as if to glimpse the traumatic effects of his ordeal. Most of Marrazzo's work is made up of these close-ups that together create an intimate narrative of abduction that envisions the fear and anguish of defenceless Italians who, following the directions of invisible kidnappers, drive in search of messages and signs of where to leave the ransom or to find their child.[59] The archaic image of abduction as a crime rooted in Barbagia gives way to a modern drama that in Marrazzo's video explodes, together with the Pink Floyd song, in a montage of RAI archival footage of Carabinieri holding a criminal who thrashes, hides his face, and screams (although we cannot hear him); streets full of police and army checkpoints; and photographs of victims abducted in recent years. Strikingly, the first of these is of Paul Getty III taken after his release. No longer treated as a hoax, in 1976 RAI recognizes Getty's ordeal as the national turning point of ransom kidnapping. While the images go by, the voice-over informs us that sixteen people were at that moment being held as hostages, adding: "This crime has become ever more lucrative. There were 38 cases in 1974, 62 in 1975, and 7 in the first two months of 1976."[60] In "Kidnapping," 1970s Italy sounds as if it is under attack by abductors, whose voices can be heard through recordings of phone calls made to blackmail one of the families.[61] In addition to the landline phone, the phone booth – used as a visual background to these recordings – would become an image for the anonymous kidnappers on television. The RAI spectators can no longer safely distance the crime from themselves by localizing before their eyes the origin of kidnapping. Rather, through acoustic perception – epitomized by the ubiquitous phone booth – they imagine the ordeals of those Italians petrified daily by faceless and violent abductors. By hearing the voices of invisible kidnappers, the viewer feels surrounded by and exposed to them. As Maurice Merleau-Ponty argues, the sense of hearing is in fact the one that makes us aware of our body as immersed in the world, that is, visible to it, exposed to it, and therefore vulnerable. Compared to images, these recordings represent for the audience a more three-dimensional experience of abduction. From 1971 to 1976, Italians' understanding of kidnapping went from maps and data to testimony and embodied threats. After the discovery of Cristina's body, *AZ* shifts perspective and, rather than focusing on where kidnapping originates, allows the audience to imagine how far it can go.

In Marrazzo's video, Cristina's murder changes kidnapping from being a drama to being a tragedy. Her story enters in the visual narrative through a photograph that slowly moves from the bottom to the top of the screen, revealing her face and smile and allowing the spectator to recognize her. It is a photo that was disseminated by the press during her captivity. The soundtrack is a low piano note that develops into a dissonant piece. Within the rhythm of the documentary, this sequence creates a sort of *epoché* (suspension), followed by a montage in which we see "the first prison of Cristina Mazzotti" – the captions explain – and "the place where Cristina Mazzotti was found." "What does a murder of this unpredictable and unusual kind leave in the family members, in people?" Marrazzo asks Vittorio Mazzotti, her brother, gently articulating every word. "I would say 'what does it take away' rather than 'what does it leave.' It takes away everything, and nothing else remains," answers Mazzotti, shaking his head slightly.[62] Marrazzo's interview of Mazzotti continues with questions about his parents and about the idea his father had of creating the Cristina Mazzotti Foundation. It is the uncle Eolo Mazzotti, however, who most talks about this initiative. Asked about the ransom that his family paid, he reveals that part of it was tracked down in San Remo, Liguria, but it was subsequently allowed to circulate because the central Bank of Italy in Rome confirmed too late that the banknotes' serial numbers were those of the Mazzotti ransom. Aldo Falivena, the *AZ* host who interviews Minister Cossiga after Marrazzo's documentary, does not accept Cossiga's vague answer about the problem of money laundering in Italy and instead interrupts to ask him to clarify what Cristina's uncle had stated in the video. For journalists – and the rest of Italian society – Cristina's became the name of an undeniable reality that demanded explanation from official institutions. The impact of Cristina's death is visible on the empathic representation of the phenomenon but also on the arguments that it raised. Ransom kidnapping was now known to be national and attributable to Mafia syndicates; the correlate to this new awareness was the media's concern towards law enforcement and politicians. In Falivena's interview of Cossiga, the issue becomes Italian citizens' vulnerability due to the lack of a determined fight against organized crime. Seen through the RAI screen, the state appears to be inadequate to solve the emergency, while the hostages' families seem to have been abandoned amid their ordeals.

Yet what is most noteworthy is the novel way Falivena frames a crime that already had hundreds of victims: "We find ourselves in front of a new kind of crime. The person is degraded to an object. In the hands of whoever kidnapped her the person is a thing, is used as a thing … Why has this kind of crime developed in these past years in our country, and why is it increasing?"[63] In Falivena's first question to Cossiga, it is hard not to recognize the shocking effect of the garbage dump where Cristina's body was found. Reduced to a used thing among other dismissed objects, Cristina suffered an extreme depersonalization that brought the dehumanization of kidnapping beyond a new ethical limit. By defining the human life as sacred, Cossiga emphasizes in his answer the Christian meaning of the term *persona* – a relational and spiritual being irreducible to objectification – to condemn the condition of the kidnap victims. However, he skilfully shifts the interview from an ethical narrative of the hostage kidnapped in Italy to the moralistic analysis of a

The Day Cristina's Body Was Found   89

society exclusively focused on economic values and thus responsible for the criminal phenomenon. Rather than facing the threatening rise of the 'Ndrangheta, Minister Cossiga seems to blame modernity, capitalism, and consumerism. For Falivena, on the contrary, the testimony of Cristina's story offers a new viewpoint from which to question ransom kidnapping from outside the common belief that abduction – he states – was a problem of rich people capable of evading taxes but not the *anonima sequestri*. Strikingly, RAI seems to blame the state for both the spread of the crime and the justifiably indifferent reaction of Italians. According to Falivena, in fact, the state's inability to fight tax evasion generated in Italy a fiscal injustice within civil society that resulted in resentment. Refusing the idea of ransom kidnapping as a means for wealth redistribution and aware of how far the 'Ndrangheta could go without a firm political battle against it, in the following years public television started to produce some of the most powerful journalistic investigations into this Calabrian branch of organized crime, which became known by Italians as the Mafia of abductions.[64]

Broadcasting Kidnapping: The Lead-Up to Aldo Moro's Abduction

In addition to shifting the representation of ransom kidnapping from a Sardinian to a national phenomenon linked to organized crime, and to challenging those politicians in denial of the growth of Italy's Mafias, RAI responded to the murder of Cristina Mazzotti by questioning criminal violence through the eyes of magistrates, lawyers, reporters, victims and their families, and even the kidnappers themselves, as happens in Enzo Biagi's interview with Cristina's warder Libero Ballinari. In 1977 – the year before Aldo Moro's abduction and murder – the number of television mediations of kidnapping multiplied exponentially and incorporated various genres, from documentaries to journalistic analyses to comedy shows. In the documentary "Sequestri: La spirale della violenza" (Kidnapping: The spiral of violence), for example, the director Roberto Malenotti – whose father Maleno was abducted and never liberated – interviews kidnap victims, looking at the crime through the lens of self-narrative.[65] Amid a montage of the victims' oral accounts, Malenotti tells the story of Cristina using authentic material such as footage of her funeral, her family members, the garbage dump, and the helicopters, as well as the recordings of the phone calls between her father and her kidnappers. Together with the recognizable symbols and objects of abduction – such as the ski mask, the landline phone, and the phone booth – the Mazzottis' ordeal becomes in Malenotti's visual narrative evocative of the suffering of all the hostages and their

90 Ransom Kidnapping in Italy

kin. Critical towards the state and its lack of a strong strategy against the crime, Malenotti gives voice to the victims as if to relieve – although it is clearly impossible – the silence of those who never returned home.

Testimony is central in this documentary, as the well-known Jewish Italian novelist Natalia Ginzburg highlights in "Parlano i rapiti" (The kidnapped speak), a review of Malenotti's documentary that she wrote for *Corriere della Sera*.[66] The story that particularly struck Ginzburg is that of Enrico Filippini, who was wrongly arrested for having faked his abduction after he returned home. The survivor's fear of not being believed – which Primo Levi describes in his testimony of Auschwitz – becomes for Filippini a second imprisonment and ordeal. Ginzburg praises television for being a precious medium capable of narrating a story in its entirety in cases like this. She in fact acknowledges that she had only vaguely recalled hearing the news about Filippini's innocence – but had much more clearly recalled the accusations levelled against him – and expresses solidarity with the victim and gratitude towards the director. Ginzburg's perspective is interesting because she writes from the position of a TV viewer of that time who, exposed to daily news about abductions, has a fragmented memory of each kidnapping episode. Aware of Malenotti's personal involvement with the subject, Ginzburg considers his enquiry to be inspired by the words of Cristina Mazzotti's uncle, who at her funeral publicly wished that no one would ever again have to suffer what his family did. Empathy is the key of this documentary, according to Ginzburg, while television becomes a storyteller capable of bringing together facts and voices that would otherwise remain unheard. By broadcasting "Kidnapping: The Spiral of Violence" – a documentary that informs equally about the human cost of abduction and the lack of state resources to combat it, as symbolized by the investigators' useless phones, which only work internally in their offices – RAI sought to convince Italians that they needed to actively participate in the fight against ransom kidnapping because the state was not.

The effects of Cristina's death on television are visible not only from what Italians could watch on RAI but also from what they could not. This becomes clear in the mediation of kidnapping offered by comedy. If testimony and journalistic investigations expose the audience to violence through empathy and awareness, comedy does so through laughter. Yet, while RAI allowed the state to be the object of satire, it protected the victims and their families. Two 1977 comedic sketches provide an example of this policy. The first, "Dove sta Zazà ovvero alto rapimento" (Where is Zazà, or high kidnapping), was part of *Scuola serale per aspiranti italiani* (Night school for

The Day Cristina's Body Was Found   91

aspiring Italians), a variety show in which five comedians pretend to be in a classroom where they learn what Italians think and do. "For homework, through the *sceneggiata* that I will show you now, you will study another aspect of Italian life in recent times: ransom kidnapping," announces the teacher (played by Anna Mazzamauro) to her students and the audience.[67] It is striking to watch kidnapping becoming an aspect of Italian life, but it is even more interesting to see how RAI depicts common beliefs about the phenomenon. The cast performs a *sceneggiata* (a Neapolitan musical comedy that alternates between music and acting) based on the internationally well-known Neapolitan song "Dove sta Zazà" (Where is Zazà). The lyrics – originally written by Raffaele Cutolo in the 1940s – tell the story of Isaia (the narrator), whose girlfriend disappears while they are together at the feast of San Gennaro. The RAI *sceneggiata* offers an original interpretation of Cutolo's song by adapting the story to the news of the time and by using repetition as a structure. In the first scene we see Isaia running to the police station to denounce the abduction of his girlfriend, Zazà. Desperate and crying, he speaks to the police officer, who, laughing, states: "You scared me. You came here to announce a kidnapping, and I thought it was going to be who knows what."[68] Isaia recounts the story of the abduction by singing and acting out Cutolo's lyrics about the feast of San Gennaro. In a second scene, Zazà is tied to a bed and in the hands of her kidnappers: the "carogna" (swine) Aniello Marra, who wears a pinstripe suit typical of a gangster; and a female warder who, although she mimics a Russian accent, recalls Ingrid, the Nazi character in Roberto Rossellini's *Rome Open City*. Zazà is lamenting her condition and worrying that the ransom will not be paid when Isaia and the police officer burst onto the scene and free her. This sequence – Isaia speaking with the officer, the flashback of the capture, and the liberation – is repeated three more times. Zazà is in fact kidnapped three times by the same abductors, who, arrested by the police, are never held in jail. The second time Isaia goes to the police station, the officer tells him that Aniello Marra got out on bail because the crime of kidnapping had been legally reduced to the equivalent of mugging. The third time, Marra is out of prison because he requested and obtained a special leave. When Marra is finally behind bars, Isaia and Zazà hear on the radio that he staged a jailbreak and escaped. Marra tries to abduct Zazà again, but this time Isaia fights him. The *sceneggiata* ends with the police officer getting a promotion for having arrested the kidnappers multiple times over five years, while Marra is now free and celebrating in the French Riviera and the female warder has

92 Ransom Kidnapping in Italy

opened a famous restaurant. Only Isaia is in jail, waiting for his trial for having broken Marra's nose. In the final scene, Isaia – dressed like an inmate – sings:

> It's not a sin if you rob a federal bank, it's not a sin if you're a professional embezzler, if you snatch and kidnap people, if you pocket the cash in Switzerland, if you never pay taxes … but if you're a miserable wretch who tries to get justice for himself with a slap, well then you're caught.[69]

RAI's comedic mediation of kidnapping explicitly criticizes the Italian judicial system and its contradictions. To the widespread belief that the state does not combat tax evasion – as seen in Falivena's interview with Cossiga – RAI adds here the belief that institutional power in fact does not fight against any crime. It is remarkable that kidnapping is seen to be reduced by the law not just to a monetary crime but to the least serious among them – that is, mugging. "Where Is Zazà, or High Kidnapping" uses symbols and places associated with abductions, such as the telephone and the cave in which Zazà is held hostage the second time she is kidnapped. The phone becomes in the *sceneggiata* an object through which to mock the police officer and his pompous but pointless attempt to control the investigation and the negotiations. There are no jokes about the families or the victims. On the contrary, "Where Is Zazà" shows how justice is perceived to be on the side of criminals and against those who, after not receiving any protection, attempt to defend themselves. Through comedy, RAI takes ransom kidnapping seriously and does so by no longer considering the phenomenon external (an element that Zazà's "Russian" warder personifies and parodies) or by accusing an economic model (capitalism) of corrupting long-standing Italian social values. If Italy produces this phenomenon, public television seems to suggest, it is because the country's legal system allows kidnappers to exist and operate.

The second comedic sketch, "Sequestro di persona cara" ("Kidnapping Dear!"), is a two-minute clip by Ettore Scola that is part of *I nuovi mostri* (The new monsters), a feature film composed of fourteen different episodes directed by Dino Risi and Mario Monicelli in addition to Scola that was nominated for an Academy Award for Best Foreign Language Film.[70] In a living room of a house, we see a television crew filming a desperate man (played by Vittorio Gassman) who, sitting on his couch, appeals to the abductors of his beloved wife before an extended microphone. We hear the voice of a TV operator telling the cameraman to shoot some footage of the landline phone; for a moment we watch the man through a TV screen, and then, scanning over newspapers whose

The Day Cristina's Body Was Found   93

titles shout the news of her abduction, we see him crying and imploring the abductors to call:

> I have been here in front of this phone for two endless days and two endless nights to make a heartfelt appeal, to implore the kidnappers to let me know their conditions, everything I need to do. I beg you, call me. My wife is in bad health, she needs assiduous and constant care. So call me, I beg you, at any hour. I have asked and ordered friends, relatives, acquaintances to not call me so that the phone line is always free. So call me, whoever you are, listen to this prayer from a tormented husband. Give me back my wife.[71]

When the troupe leaves, Gassman lifts up his foot to reveal that the telephone cord running underneath has been intentionally cut – by him, as the sketch makes clear by having him point to the sliced wires. When RAI first broadcast *I nuovi mostri*, Scola's episode was censored. Strikingly, it still is; *I nuovi mostri* is available on RAI's website – but without "Kidnapping Dear!" Beyond the obvious gender reading of the sketch – the Italian man who pretends to be a devoted husband while in reality hoping to get rid of his "annoying" wife, who prevents him from expressing his masculinity – there is also a genre limit to consider. Scola is able to capture succinctly the centrality of the object symbolic of the negotiations between families and kidnappers. However, he does so by investing the telephone with a bitter humour that clashes with the anguish with which it was associated in the collective imagination.

"Kidnapping Dear!" is a sarcastic cinematic metanarrative of the journalistic mediation of abduction. Although its context is that of Italian comedy – a genre of which *I nuovi mostri* represents the most cynical and sacrilegious expression – RAI refuses to broadcast a sketch that subverts its own depiction of grief to make people laugh. Scola's choice of turning the television spectators of tragedy into the cinematic spectators of comedy could be seen as a reaction of the genre itself to the spread of ransom kidnapping. Yet his sketch and Gassman's performance would seem more to appropriate the symbol of a violent phenomenon to make a banal and misogynistic joke. By refusing to broadcast this comedic sketch, public television does not censor the satire of news; it censors the satire of victims' testimonies.

The last but not least visible effect of the Mazzottis' ordeal is the radical shift in how newscasts discussed the topic of negotiations between families and kidnappers, as seen in Biagi's 1977 *Proibito* (Forbidden) or Franco Biancacci's 1978 *Storie allo specchio* (Stories at the mirror) – even by means of an audience poll in the latter case. Chapter 4 explores the topic of negotiations, but here it is important to note that while the Getty kidnapping scandalized Italy because the richest man in the world refused to pay his grandson's abductors – and was therefore responsible in the eyes of many for the younger Getty's ear mutilation – the tragedy of Cristina and those who never returned home after their families had paid the ransom troubled public opinion. One of the key debates of Italy's Years of Lead – whether a state should negotiate with terrorists or not – was anticipated by and overlapped with the issue of the negotiations with organized crime and banditry. The question about the state's power to prevent its citizens from paying ransoms to kidnappers would become the object of analysis by legal experts on television and beyond. Even if in different terms than ideological kidnapping, criminal ransom kidnapping was the violence that most meddled in the relationship between the Italian state and its inhabitants, as well as most impacted the rule of law itself. In the 1970s, RAI became the main arena for this debate, which its newscasts continued for over twenty years – that is, far beyond the decade of terrorism.

Conclusion

In "The Quality of Life," an article that Natalia Ginzburg wrote on the Red Brigades for *La Stampa* on 5 May 1978 – four days before Moro's body was found inside the trunk of a red Renault 4 in Rome – the novelist offers an astonishing "non-political" picture of his kidnapping and 1970s Italy.[72] "There exist two ways of looking at the world," she begins in her editorial, "a political way and a non-political way."[73] In this highly politicized historical moment, Ginzburg identifies with the non-political minority and expresses what they feel. If those who look at public events politically see their "origins, reasons, and goal," she explains, those with a non-political gaze have and follow sensations. During the most disorienting days of the Italian Republic, Ginzburg therefore writes according to her body – that is, by giving voice to a perceptional rather than ideological vision of Moro's kidnapping. The non-political people are horrified by the Red Brigades because of their violence and also, she states, because of the "filthy and funereal smell" that comes from their underground schemes that recall to memory "the SS, the extermination camps, and the massacre of the Jews."[74] By using smells, colours, light, and the senses, Ginzburg's embodied language warns readers not to erroneously consider the Red Brigades' abstract rhetoric as "crazed or desperate." On the contrary, this terrorist group possesses – as did the Nazis, although on a different scale – the "devastating and lucid will" to humiliate the "quality of life" in human beings.

The Day Cristina's Body Was Found   95

Outside of any ideological frame, life stands, for Ginzburg, as an ethical measure. To humiliate this immanent quality in the human kind "means to strip both life and death of all real value and worth. It means to make minimal and miserable requests of life, and to give death an empty and dull look."[75] The comparison Ginzburg makes is based not on a conflation of a totalitarian regime and terrorism but rather on the effects of their violence. It is remarkable how in her view violence affects the quality of life not just in its victims but also in the perception of life and death it generates within the human community. Ginzburg urges her contemporaries to defend their own perception as the only possible resistance against the annihilating violence of terrorism and as a necessary starting point from which to imagine, even as a utopia, a better future. Talking about the letters that Moro was writing from his captivity, she notes, in fact, that the pietas they inspire is "dull and desert." Ginzburg, who lived through the years of fascism, depicts the world outside of Moro's hiding place as the most "wretched and miserable scenario that our eyes have ever seen." She offers a highly bleak image of Italy to the readers of *La Stampa* in May 1978.

Yet the striking point of her article is the perspective she uses to narrate her era outside of a political frame. Quality of life is clearly the vantage point from which she both looks at the world around her and recognizes how the Red Brigades were able to exist and operate. Just as Germany prepared far in advance the civic landscape for the Nazis to come and do what they did, Italy did the same leading up to its years of terrorism. Devastating and violent historical moments do not happen suddenly but are instead backed by societies in which the quality of life has already been affected. In response to the pope's public intervention on the matter of Moro's kidnapping, Ginzburg articulates what made terrorist violence possible:

> Non-political people, on the issue of the pope's appeal for Aldo Moro, think that it was a correct appeal, and they do not find it at all strange that he knelt, because it is correct that a pope get down on his knees, and indeed this is a natural posture for a pope. But they wonder why he did not get down on his knees for poor Cristina Mazzotti, during that horrible summer in which nothing more was known of her, or why he does not kneel for the others who have been kidnapped and have not come back, all men being equal before God. They do not find correct the speech he gave the next day, when he emphasized Aldo Moro's high cultural stature, because before God man's public success, his public stature as a human being, is worthless. It seems to us that the death of poor Cristina Mazzotti, her body found in a heap of scraps and rubbish, degraded and humiliated

in everyone the quality of life. It seems to us that then, clearly and right before our eyes, a deserted landscape opened up to which our eyes would later, with horror, become accustomed.[76]

Ginzburg recognizes in ransom kidnapping the violence that in the 1970s afflicted the country to the point of preparing the civic scenario in which the Red Brigades were able to operate. It is not Moro's public stature that justifies the appropriate and belated reaction of the pope. It is "the collective humiliation" that – according to Ginzburg – the Polaroids his kidnappers sent to the media provoked in everyone. By looking at the embodied effects of violence, Ginzburg's perceptual vision of Moro's abduction sees the same humiliation of the quality of life that Italians felt the day Cristina's body was found in a dump. Remarkably, her 1978 non-political article on the Red Brigades demonstrates that – without any ideology or symbols – the 'Ndrangheta had shifted Italy's perception of life and death, shaping the civic horizon of the Years of Lead in which, in Ginzburg's words, "we can't see anything except scraps and waste."

Although in the public memory of the country ransom kidnapping did not reach the status of a historical event as did political kidnapping and, especially, the iconic images of Moro's Polaroids, the effects of Cristina's tragedy on media, the national narrative, and society tell another story. From the day of her abduction, Cristina Mazzotti entered into the imagination of Italians, changing forever their perception of their country. "Before it was we who loved you, now everyone does," reads the memorial card that Enzo Biagi noticed when he went to visit her family.[77] As the daily newspapers showed us, this girl next door embodied an innocence everyone lost. Her abduction made RAI's previous attempts to craft a reassuring image of society and state obsolete and established the ethical limits of television representation. Not only did her story confirm – two years after the Getty abduction – that the real threat was the 'Ndrangheta and not a teenager's hoax, it also compelled Italy to take the kidnapped seriously and to listen to their ordeals. Finally, and most of all, without belonging to the pages of its official history, Cristina's story tapped into Italy's civic and traumatic memories, making the country experience and perceive ransom kidnapping as the most shattering threat after World War II. By looking at the violence of the 1970s through the perspective of Cristina Mazzotti's ordeal – that is, as Ginzburg states, with a non-political gaze – the correlate of the Moro Polaroids becomes the images of a garbage dump that made Italy aware of how far its horrifying criminal underworld could go.

Chapter Four

Troubling the Rule of Law

I thought I was at the centre of the earth in that dirty hole and instead civilization is a few hundred feet away.

Giuseppe Soffiantini[1]

The day after Cristina Mazzotti's body was found in September 1975, the government announced to the country the need for an exceptional intervention due to a state of emergency: "We need to prevent the relatives from ceding to the kidnappers' blackmail," Minister of the Interior Luigi Gui proclaimed to the press.[2] Cristina's death – and the kidnap victims who never returned – proved to Italy that paying ransoms did not assure hostages' liberation. Referring to how relatives of the kidnapped victims should behave, Gui asked the public whether they ought to be "accomplices by force or fear of the criminals, or responsible collaborators protected by the state institutions that fight them?"[3] Gui's rhetorical question clearly suggested the need for a legal ban on negotiating with criminals. Yet the Minister of the Interior – commander in chief of the police and guarantor of national security – invited Italians to actively engage on the issue because, he added, no new reform could happen without their consent. Indeed, the solution the minister was seeking was not just a legal strategy to fight the crime. It entailed, as we shall see, a different idea of the state and its relationship with constituents. Gui's rhetorical question also raises another notable issue. In a moment of crisis, the Minister of the Interior shifted the blame for the violent escalation of ransom kidnapping from the criminals and the state to the families and the victims.

Between 1975 and 1977, the novelist Italo Calvino had a column in *Corriere della Sera* called "The Observatory of Mr. Palomar"; the time frame of this column coincided with the three most decisive years for

98 Ransom Kidnapping in Italy

ransom kidnapping in the 1970s. As seen in chapter 3, from the year 1975 (when Cristina Mazzotti was kidnapped and killed) to 1977 (the year before Aldo Moro shared the same fate), the country felt itself to be under the attack of organized crime and was exposed daily to news about abductions. When the *New York Times Book Review* (1983) asked authors from around the world to comment on the books they were writing at the time, Calvino responded with a presentation of his *Palomar* that reads as a fictional response to Minister Gui's rationale and arguments. Calvino's original plan, he states, was to create a dialogue between two characters:

> I tried to write a dialogue on ransom kidnappings: it was the time in which this plague was starting to become the most profitable industry in our country. Mr. Mohole claimed that only people no one liked and for whom no one would have ever paid the ransom could feel safe; thus, reciprocal malevolence was the only possible foundation for society, while affection and compassion became the tools of the crime, which played on these sentiments. At this point, I reread what I wrote, crumpled up the paper, and threw it away, as I do whenever I suspect that I am writing something that sooner or later I will regret. ... I started writing pieces with only Mr. Palomar, a character in search of harmony in the middle of a world full of torments and screeching.[4]

These are the only lines Calvino wrote as Mr. Mohole, the name of a geological drill that allows one to observe that which is otherwise impossible to reach. As soon as the author gave voice to a character whose gaze could see Italy below the surface in the mid-1970s, what he talked about was ransom kidnapping. Through Mohole, Calvino envisions the experience of being abducted for ransom as that of being suddenly snatched from society and hidden in the interior of the earth – notably using an image that, as seen in the epigraph from Giuseppe Soffiantini, kidnapping victims themselves used to describe their experience.

However, Mohole's argument about ransom payment is shaped in response to the ongoing debate between politicians and legislators that played out in the media, as they pushed for an adequate and updated legal strategy. Though Mohole's bitter irony stopped Calvino from further developing this character in his book, the few lines the writer sketched out from his point of view offer a fictional solution aimed at neutralizing the kidnappers' ransom demands. Only those who no one loves and for whom nobody would pay the ransom will be immune to abduction, explains Mohole. However impractical and absurd, Mohole's "reciprocal malevolence" shows that – by subverting compassion into a tool that supports the crime – ransom kidnapping threatens society at its foundation. If Calvino holds the kidnappers responsible for this subversion, the Italian state ended up criminalizing the victims' families who wished to pay.

Calvino's Mohole recognizes the essential problem inherent to abduction as a systematic plague: this crime troubled Italy's social contract. The latter was threatened not just because malevolence became the sole antidote to the plague – Mohole's thesis – but because ransom kidnapping meddled in the relationship between the state and its citizens. Being kidnapped for ransom meant for the hostages to become victims and criminals at the same time. Subjected to a power other than the law by negotiating for their own liberation – that is, by demanding that the ransom money be paid – they became accessories to the crime in the eyes of the state. This chapter traces the twenty-year-long debate on negotiating, the legal and political consequences of being a hostage, and the country's civic response to this violence. From the analysis of the state's reactions to Cristina Mazzotti's death in 1975, to the 1978 legislative overlapping of ransom and political kidnapping, to the second kidnapping crisis of the late 1980s, and to the anti-kidnapping movement of the 1990s, this chapter demonstrates that for decades the abductions challenged the rule of law in Italy by prompting policies that risked overstepping the constitutional rights of the hostages in the name of defeating domestic banditry and organized crime that the state could not control.

Blaming the Victims

The question Gui posed in 1975 was not completely new. Before the Mazzotti abduction and murder, however, the problem of ransom negotiation was articulated in slightly different terms. Ransom kidnapping started to receive national media attention when it was still a regional phenomenon. In the late 1960s and early 1970s, RAI television broadcasts brought their spectators to Barbagia, Sardinia, to explore the origins of a crime that required state intervention. The question these early journalistic accounts posed concerned the role of the police. Should law enforcement intervene immediately, or should they let the family first initiate the negotiations? This issue was debated, for example, in a 1972 episode of *Sotto Processo* (On trial), a RAI broadcast in which two lawyers defended opposing views on the matter before a judge.[5] After this "trial," the same question was posed to the public at home, and the results were presented by the show's host, Guglielmo Zucconi, in a subsequent episode. The poll was conducted by Doxa – an institute specializing in opinion research and statistics – in 117 cities across the country, with 980 respondents. While 45 per cent answered that in the case of kidnapping it is more correct to prevent private negotiations, 51 per cent were persuaded of the opposite; the remaining 4 per cent were unsure. If the police intervene only after the liberation of the kidnapped, the same Doxa survey asked, would the kidnapping cases rise (49 per cent), fall (21 per cent), or remain the same (18 per cent)? Twelve per cent of respondents were unsure.[6] As the data show, private negotiations prior to police intervention were considered to be more correct, even if the vast majority of the participants believed them to increase the number of abductions. In short, people understood the argument made by the pro-intervention lawyer but agreed with the pro-negotiation lawyer because, Zucconi noted, saving the hostage was the priority. The Getty kidnapping in 1973 – the first abduction by the 'Ndrangheta to shock the nation – cemented these beliefs. Public opinion, as we have seen, faulted Getty's grandfather's initial refusal to pay the ransom and accused him of being responsible for the mutilation of Paul's ear.

After the tragic conclusion of Mazzotti's abduction, Minister Gui proposed a more decisive strategy. His proposal sought to give the state the power to criminalize negotiations tout court. The ultimate goal was to issue a law that, in the case of kidnapping for ransom, would automatically freeze the assets of the hostages, permitting the state to isolate and neutralize the blackmailed families, who would become unable to pay. In addition to having the Ministry of Justice initiate this proposal and the parliament support such a law, Gui needed public opinion on his side. Oronzo Reale, Minister of Justice, agreed with Gui because he believed "the development of the 'kidnap industry'" to be the consequence of a great mistake: that of always surrendering to the criminals' blackmail and paying the ransom.[7] Nevertheless, he expressed concerns about the freezing of assets because of the possible vendetta against the hostage by the kidnappers (for which the state would be responsible) and because it is "a measure taken against the offended person exactly when he most needs help."[8] A new Doxa poll asked Italians if they were in favour of prohibiting private negotiations and, especially, of authorizing the *blocco dei beni* (freezing of assets). Six out of every ten respondents approved, two opposed, and two were undecided. The public therefore agreed with Minister Gui. Yet the matter was complicated and faced, for instance, the opposition of the vast majority of scholars at the International Conference of Criminology hosted by the United Nations in Geneva in September 1975 (when the Doxa conducted its enquiry). The conference participants, who discussed the problem of ransom kidnapping in Italy, considered saving the life of the hostages to be a priority and freezing the assets an ineffective solution compared, for example, to much-needed police reform.[9] However, even without the existence of a national law, in Italy judges in charge of investigating abductions could freeze the victims' assets. Before Cristina's death, no one ever did so. The first was the Deputy Public Prosecutor of Milan, Ferdinando Pomarici, who in March 1976 confiscated the 400 million lire that Renato Alberghini collected to free his father Carlo, kidnapped on 4 February in Trezzano, Lombardy. Although Doxa showed the country to be in favour of the *blocco dei beni*, Pomarici's move provoked a heated media debate among judges, politicians, and citizens. Nevertheless, Pomarici applied this strategy for two consecutive years until he resigned from investigating ransom kidnappings in 1978 after his superior stopped him from confiscating the money collected by a victim's family.[10]

To understand the contrast between what Gui and Pomarici (among others) proposed as a state response to the emergency of ransom kidnapping and the varying opinions of international and national magistrates on this subject, we need to consider two things. First, the Italian criminal code classifies abduction for ransom among crimes against property and not against the person.[11] The monetary intention of the criminal, and not the loss of freedom by the victim, defines the nature of the crime. When in 1976 Pomarici started to confiscate hostages' assets, he could do so on the basis of a possible interpretation of the penal code that required police to intervene before a crime could be completed, in this case by the receipt of the ransom. This gave way to a different line of conduct by public prosecutors, as well as different attitudes by the state towards victims and their families. Pier Luigi Vigna, a magistrate in Florence, went even beyond "the Pomarici line" by arresting kidnapped people's relatives who did not collaborate with the police.[12] The second thing to consider is that in 1974 – that is, between the Getty and the Mazzotti abductions – the Red Brigades reached national notoriety by kidnapping the judge Mario Sossi in Genoa for thirty-five days. Although Sossi was not the BR's first hostage, no one before him had been held for such a long time. "From early 1974," historian Paul Ginsborg observes, "the quality of the Red Brigades' actions changed. From now on they announced 'an attack on the heart of the state.'"[13] Indeed, by snatching Sossi in order to demand the release of prisoners, the BR began to blackmail the state. The remarkable number of abductions for ransom and the rise of the terrorist kidnapping phenomenon prompted Italy to modify its criminal code the very same year (1974). For the first time, a "diversified strategy" (later adopted in other contexts as well) was implemented: on the one hand, punishment was made tougher as a deterrent; on the other, a reward mechanism was put in place if the kidnapper collaborated in freeing the hostage without collecting a ransom. This latter conduct resulted in lighter sentences.[14] The amendments of 1974 did not alter the crime itself, however, which was still categorized as an attack on property.

According to Pomarici, these amendments were not enough, and the alarming kidnapping crisis required a draconian intervention that could not wait for an anti-kidnapping law. The first time Pomarici applied the freezing of assets (March 1976), Francesco Cossiga, Minister of the Interior after Gui, immediately approved his decision on television. "It is necessary that the crime does not pay; that is, that the abductor does not collect the fruits of his crime," he announced on a RAI evening newscast.[15] The minister specified that the state could not be considered responsible for the possible killing of kidnap victims, that the state had the prerogative to obstruct crime by any means, and that without the freezing of assets the state would have been helpless in the face of anyone's blackmail. "Remember Cristina Mazzotti," he told the country, warning that paying the ransom did not always free the hostage.[16] Although Pomarici's initiative significantly divided his own office in Milan, provoked the protest of the families involved, and created different attitudes towards kidnap victims within the same country, the *linea dura* (hard line) against ransom kidnappings that he first put in action was backed by politicians and echoed by the media. Pomarici regularly appeared on television, giving numerous interviews to the press explaining and promoting the rationale of the hard line. However, the perspective of ministers and magistrates who saw negotiations as the weak, emotional response of the state was also affected by a double emergency. The very judges who fought against abductions were combatting terrorism as well. The rhetoric that Pomarici used in a 1977 episode of *Proibito*, a RAI broadcast hosted by Enzo Biagi, opens a window onto this intersection: "What is the breaking point? What is the point beyond which, by yielding to blackmail, a civil society is no longer based on the rule of law but rather becomes a state ruled by force where the strongest, the meanest, the fiercest dominate?"[17] For Pomarici, the kidnappings affecting society were endangering the rule of law and threatening to deliver the state into the hands of ruthless criminals. The only solution was to not yield to the kidnappers' demands. In his view, ransom kidnapping was a direct attack on the state, just as much as terrorism was. By blackmailing the families, the kidnappers were in fact blackmailing a state that could not intervene. Making negotiations impossible would have meant in itself a victory for the state against the crime.

Pomarici clearly became the face of a strong state – an image that the government wanted to spotlight. Although his hard line seemed to offer the immediate, logical, and missing solution Italy needed, it also raised many doubts as to its efficacy and even constitutionality, as we shall see. Yet the effect of this attention and popularity was that of moving the civic discourse on ransom kidnapping from its origins – that is, organized crime and banditry – to the families and the victims held responsible for the rampant spread of abductions. Pomarici, in short, completed what Minister Gui initiated. Calvino recognized this effect when he attempted (without blaming the families) to imagine a society free from ransom kidnapping. As his character Mohole hazarded, no one would abduct anyone in a society without relationships. The social dystopia Calvino refused to write shows that the problem of ransom kidnapping coincided with the issue of negotiations. In the mid-1970s, when the novelist was writing for the *Corriere*, the "strong" state was the one whose only tool against organized crime and banditry was to impose law and order over its victimized citizens. Subjected to the violence of unscrupulous kidnappers, especially of the growing 'Ndrangheta, Italian society – from the north to the south – discovered itself both vulnerable and unprotected. The state in fact showed it did not have a strategy against the crime. Those in danger of being abducted bought kidnapping insurance policies from abroad (a phenomenon that Pomarici used to justify the hard line), obtained licences to carry guns, took self-defence classes, or hired bodyguards, and they also wanted their families to leave the country.[18] The singer Carla Bruni, for example, now the wife of Nicolas Sarkozy, former president of France, moved to Paris as a child due to ransom kidnapping in Italy.[19] Former prime minister Silvio Berlusconi recounts that in the mid-1970s he moved his family first to Switzerland and then to Spain after someone tried to kidnap his five-year-old son, Pier Silvio.[20] Yet Berlusconi's story has a more unclear chapter connected to ransom kidnapping. Judges, investigators, and journalists believe that the Mafia boss Vittorio Mangano lived in Berlusconi's Villa San Martino at Arcore, Lombardy, from 1974 to 1976 in order to protect the future media tycoon from kidnappers. Berlusconi hired Mangano as a horse-keeper and denied knowing about his Mafia affiliation.[21] This was Italy at the eve of Aldo Moro's abduction. While during Moro's captivity the negotiations became the sole focus of civic discourse, it was not the first time that the Italians had heard about the *linea dura*. In early 1978, "the Pomarici affair" was indeed all over the news.

The Year 1978

Pomarici's decision in January 1978 to recuse himself from ransom kidnapping cases was depicted by the national press and public television as a crisis within a crisis. Lawyers, magistrates, and attorneys general were asked to express their opinions in the newspapers. Judges like Pier Luigi Vigna in Florence and Ferdinando Imposimato in Rome were among those who adopted and supported the hard line. In a book-length interview with Pomarici, journalist Ottavio Rossani described the freezing of assets as the only possible tool against ransom kidnapping and suggested that its opponents – namely, the *linea morbida* (soft line) – were indifferent to the phenomenon.[22] Although legal experts and journalists had different positions on this subject, everyone agreed with Pomarici's protest against the lack of a univocal state policy to combat the abductions. For example, Maurizio Michelini, journalist for the communist *L'Unità*, stated that even if his newspaper always criticized the *linea dura* because it opposed families and law enforcement instead of dismantling money laundering, the policy had to be the same for every case.[23] The common perception was that not everyone was served equally under the law. The Superior Council of the Judiciary (CSM) decided to intervene and created a special committee to study and discuss the freezing of assets.

On 16 March 1978, however, the Red Brigades kidnapped Moro and killed his escort. The immediate effect of Moro's abduction happened at the legal level. Emergency legislation radically transformed the text of the law on ransom kidnapping just a few days after his capture.[24] The government drafted a decree that introduced a previously missing category of kidnapping for terrorism, thus entirely redefining ransom kidnapping itself and superimposing the two types of abduction. The punishment for both crimes became thirty years of imprisonment or, in the event of the victim's death, imprisonment for life. Moro's abduction thus made the lawmakers increase the punishment for all kidnappers (terrorists and criminals alike) because the life of the hostage became their main concern. However, when the decree was converted into a law, the two types of offence were separated. Terrorist kidnapping, in fact, could not be listed among crimes against property and therefore was categorized with those against the state.[25] Yet the long effect of Moro's abduction was the traumatic one. For the fifty-five days of his captivity, Italy debated whether negotiating with the Red Brigades was the right thing for the state to do. Although the law shifted towards protecting the life of the hostage, the state adopted a hard line and refused any compromise with the terrorists. The result was Moro's execution.

The day after his body was found inside the trunk of a car in Rome, the world praised Italy for having defeated the Red Brigades in a dangerous moment for its democracy. The most remembered kidnapping in Italy was thus depicted as a victory of the state over terrorism.[26]

If the Moro abduction strengthened the ideology of those in favour of the *linea dura*, it did not shape the analysis of the special committee in charge of studying the freezing of assets. Indeed, in December 1978, the CSM declared the *blocco dei beni* "ineffective and even counterproductive" and expressed scepticism about the proposal to make this strategy law or a general praxis.[27] The occasion for this intervention was the intense debate provoked in the media by the abduction of a five-months-pregnant woman in Milan and the freezing of her family's assets. Marcella Boroli Ballestrini spent fifty-four days in the hands of her kidnappers and was liberated after the Borolis secretly paid her ransom.[28] According to the CSM committee, to freeze the assets or confiscate the money collected for the ransom would not prevent the families from accessing funds through different avenues (loans, relatives, friends) and would merely prolong the hostages' captivity. Families would still try to negotiate without contacting law enforcement or marking the bills used for the ransom, which would subsequently circulate freely as clean cash. Moreover, and perhaps more importantly, the committee found aberrant the idea of neutralizing the kidnappers' goals by criminalizing their targets. In contrast, the CSM recommended several changes, such as coordinating the investigation, training magistrates and police officers, and creating special units composed of the three different branches of law enforcement. Yet the main response to the *blocco dei beni* was a counterproposal to modify the law on wiretapping and bank secrecy.[29] In order to fight the kidnappers, the CSM seemed to warn, the solution was to stop not the ransom payment but rather the money laundering. The real fight against banditry and especially organized crime was in preventing them from cleaning the illicit profits they obtained from their offences.

As soon as the CSM made its analysis public, RAI aired two unscheduled episodes of *Storie allo specchio* (Stories at the mirror), a journalistic broadcast hosted by Franco Biancacci, entirely dedicated to ransom kidnapping and the never-ending *linea dura* versus *linea morbida* dilemma.[30] Biancacci, and therefore state-owned television, took a strong position in favour of the hard line. Although Moro's abduction was not the subject of *Storie allo specchio*, its impact on the ideology of anti-negotiation was clear. By means of the media under its control, the government asserted the reason of state before the country. Its spokesperson was once again Pomarici, the only guest present in both episodes. The most remarkable moments, though, were the exchanges that Biancacci had in the second episode with Eolo Mazzotti (Cristina's uncle) and Giovanni Bulgari, the internationally recognized Roman jeweller, kidnapped by the 'Ndrangheta in Rome on 13 March 1975 and liberated a month later after his family paid a high ransom. Their dialogue spotlights the tension between public television and two victims at the peak of the ransom kidnapping crisis, a few months after Moro's death. Invited to embody two victimized and opposing views on the issue of negotiations, these guests shifted the subject and looked at kidnapping from a wider perspective.

In the previous episode Biancacci had played an old 1975 interview in which Bulgari, still visibly marked by his ordeal, was the first person to publicly define kidnapping as *un affare* (a business) and to proclaim that the state should prevent the families from paying. However, Bulgari now refused to be identified as the victim initiator of the *blocco dei beni* and argued that the matter was more complicated. "After four years we keep having ransom kidnappings at the same pace with which we had them four years ago," he stated, using the RAI platform to criticize the state.[31] Expanding Bulgari's argument, Mazzotti pointed out that in Milan between 1972 and 1978 there were eighty-three abductions, of which fifty-one occurred after the hard line was applied in early 1976.[32] Not at all emotional, and therefore dismantling the idea of the victims as incapable of being objective, Bulgari and Mazzotti approached kidnapping through real numbers and facts. Biancacci's comments, on the contrary, were defensive and based on a wounded nationalistic sentiment, as if the real data of the crime that a victim's uncle showed the audience were an attack on Italian identity. The point was not the nature of Italians, Mazzotti replied, but the evidence that the *blocco dei beni* was not the solution. "Debating between the hard and soft lines means offering the possibility to attract attention to a pseudo-problem rather than to the real one," Mazzotti concluded, while Bulgari nodded.[33] Besides the tension that surrounded the matter of ransom kidnapping in Italy in December 1978, what emerges from *Storie allo specchio* is that the different theoretical approaches on how to fight the crime could now base their arguments on experience and data. As the CSM, Mazzotti, and Bulgari argued, freezing the victims' assets did not halt ransom kidnappings. Indeed, 1977 saw a record seventy-five abductions in a single year. Most of them happened in Lombardy – the region where the hard line began.

Before leaving 1978, there is one further thing worth mentioning. As this section has shown, the Moro case became for many the exemplum of how a strong state should act in order to defend democracy and beat terrorism. During his captivity, though, Moro – like the hundreds of hostages before and after him – tried to negotiate with the world outside the universe of his kidnappers, not to help them obtain what they wanted but rather to save his own life. Moro wrote at least ninety-seven messages from his hiding place, among which were letters, wills, and notes to his family, friends, colleagues, and public figures, including the pope. Some of them were published by the press and opened a wide discussion on their authenticity and on his psychological status, as if his requests were dictated either by the terrorists or by his condition as a hostage. In other words, the belief was that it was his emotional and traumatic reaction to his captivity that led him to think that the state should negotiate.

In his work on Moro's *Lettere dalla prigionia* (Prison letters, 2008), the historian Miguel Gotor stresses that as soon as the Italian government realized that the Red Brigades' intention was to put Moro on "trial" in order to extort political secrets from him and "to put at the centre of their action the hostage's word,"[34] the government started to devalue him. That is, it denied with all available means the reliability of Moro's words. The strategy was to neutralize the terrorists' blackmail against the state in public opinion. The government pursued this goal in three ways: by controlling the press, by obtaining medical opinions that guaranteed the hostage lacked lucidity, and by demonstrating that Moro did not possess any sensitive political and military secrets. About this "psychological anti-guerrilla warfare,"[35] and in particular about the exploitable medical diagnosis, Gotor argues that "this plan provided, in a way, the 'freezing' of the hostage's word, just as judicial authorities started to do in those same months with the assets of the abducted in the kidnappings organized by criminals."[36] Gotor's comparison between Moro's frozen words and the frozen assets of ransom kidnapping's victims is remarkable because it sheds light on how the state, in both political and ransom kidnappings, prevents the negotiation with abductors by controlling and neutralizing the helpless hostages.[37] Furthermore, Gotor emphasizes the role that the terrorists' censorship played in Moro's communication with the external world. They decided, for example, which letters were to become public. They also intentionally manipulated his writing and used it both to blackmail the state and, almost more importantly, to make him visible outside his prison in the way they chose to represent him. Aware of both the state's strategy and the BR's censorship, Moro nevertheless tried to negotiate his release.

As we have seen, the freezing of assets started two years before Moro's abduction, and the public had known about the hard line since

1975. What is often omitted in the memory of the Moro case is that Italy was already the country of kidnapping when the BR attacked the heart of the state. The social background to the most shocking historical event of the Italian Republic explains why speculations about Moro's request to negotiate were wrong. In a letter he wrote to his friend and Minister of the Interior Francesco Cossiga, in which he lists the countries that had negotiated in similar situations, Moro mentions the common cases of kidnappings (common as opposed to political) and specifically refers to the section of the penal code that magistrates used to justified the freezing of assets. "The sacrifice of innocents in the name of an abstract principle of legality, when an unquestionable state of necessity should induce one to save them, is inadmissible," Moro states.[38] In his letter to Benigno Zaccagnini, secretary of the Christian Democrats, Moro's position on the hard line before his own abduction becomes even more explicit. After clarifying that he was asking to negotiate "in full lucidity," he strikingly adds, "After all, I had already expressed these ideas to Taviani for the Sossi case and to Gui regarding a disputed law against kidnappings."[39] When in 1975 Minister of the Interior Gui proposed the law on the freezing of assets, Aldo Moro was the prime minister of Italy, and he opposed the idea because it was dangerous for the hostages. The same day the press published his letter to Zaccagnini, on 5 April 1978, Gui confirmed what Moro had written.[40] His ideas on the negotiations were therefore not the consequence of trauma but his opinion on a long-discussed and familiar subject.

The gravity of the ransom kidnapping crisis that hit Italy in the second half of the 1970s reached the Council of Europe, which officially criticized the hard line. On 24 September 1982, the Committee of Ministers of the Council of Europe published their *Recommendation on Measures to Be Taken in Cases of Kidnapping Followed by a Ransom Demand*, the result of a study conducted by a Select Committee of Experts on Violence in Present-Day Society, created by the European Committee on Crime Problems (CDPC) in 1977 – the year that saw a record number of abductions in Italy. The committee focused deliberately on the criminal and not on the political kidnappings; expressed concern about the risk that the crime, particularly present in the peninsula, could represent for the rest of Europe; and recommended a common strategy that endorsed the *linea morbida*.[41] Although Italy did not issue an anti-kidnapping law that contradicted this recommendation, it did not follow the Council of Europe, allowing prosecutors to continue to freeze the assets of hostages and their families.

The 1980s and the Second Ransom Kidnapping Crisis

Though the hard versus soft line debate of the 1970s never ended, over the next decades parts of civil society looked at kidnapping beyond the issue of the negotiations and acted in solidarity with the victims' families. In the late 1980s, indeed, a second kidnapping crisis made it impossible to ignore what Mazzotti and Bulgari had denounced on television in 1978. The real problem of ransom kidnapping was not the emotional and psychological weakness of the blackmailed families, nor was their isolation the solution. The Years of Lead had already ended in Italy when this second crisis emerged, and the intersection of political and ransom kidnapping became less immediate. Pier Luigi Vigna, who substituted Pomarici in the media, continued to compare these two phenomena. "We cannot be firm with acts of terrorism and not with kidnappings. Who is to say whether the ransom of a kidnapping could not be used for acts of terrorism? Why should I have two different approaches?" he stated on the RAI broadcast *Speciale TG1* in February 1990.[42] Italy, however, was no longer the same country it had been during the *anni di piombo* and, in fact, had recently witnessed the longest kidnappings in its history. If in the mid-1980s the number of the abductions dropped, by the end of the decade their length significantly increased. Marco Fiora, Cesare Casella, and Carlo Celadon, as seen in chapter 1, spent 520, 743, and 831 days, respectively, as hostages in Aspromonte. Their ordeals provoked an anti-Mafia civic response that the country had lacked since the Mazzotti abduction.

In his study on terrorism and Mafia in Milan, the sociologist Nando dalla Chiesa, one of the leaders of the anti-Mafia movement in Italy and the son of Carlo Alberto dalla Chiesa—a nationally recognized general who defeated the Red Brigades in Lombardy and was killed by Cosa Nostra in Sicily in 1982—states that the history of the anti-Mafia movement started in the city of Milan, in response to several Mafia killings that took place in Palermo in the early-1980s (including that of his father).[43] The high number of ransom kidnappings in the 1970s, he continues, should have been enough to turn Lombardy and Milan against the Mafia, but in those years "terrorism rapidly conquered a political and mediatic supremacy."[44] A prejudice was also in place, the idea that "what the South expresses is by definition marginal in relation to the history of the North and its elites."[45] While terrorism represented the trajectory that the world was on, in this view, the Mafia and its "agropastoral crimes" was "folkloristic" and linked to the past. However, dalla Chiesa recognizes in the Cristina Mazzotti Foundation the first attempt to create an anti-Mafia organization, which did not have a following because Milan wanted to forget the abductions, considered "painful personal events."

Dalla Chiesa's analysis is remarkable because it shows that in Milan, and Lombardy more broadly, terrorism overshadowed the phenomenon of the Mafia, which was in fact, as previously seen, also critical. It was organized crime that would become the future, and ransom – not political – kidnapping would remain an alarming problem until the 1990s. However, the mobilization provoked by the Mazzotti ordeal included more than a single attempt, came from civil society, and did not go forgotten. The letter Cristina's father wrote in the *Corriere*, the impact of her death on television and journalism, her funeral, intellectuals' comparison of ransom kidnapping with the violence of World War II, the parallel that the writer Natalia Ginzburg made between Cristina and Moro in *La Stampa* in 1978, and the foundation that Cristina's father wanted and her uncle developed made Milan and Italy aware of the presence of the Mafia in the north. This was the event that turned organized crime into a public and collective matter. Even Calabria reacted to it with the organization of the regional council's first anti-Mafia committee and the first written denunciation of the Mafia phenomenon by the Calabrian Episcopal Conference.[46] Ransom kidnapping received a great deal of attention by the media, but after Cristina's death (and with terrorism in the spotlight), the main narrative pivoted towards the families, with the effect of distancing the public from the struggle. But it was perhaps because of its shocking experience with organized crime that Milan, Cristina's hometown, was the first to react to the early 1980s Mafia violence in Sicily.

Scholars agree that an anti-Mafia movement became visible in the country in the 1980s, anticipating the historical and massive protest against political institutions after the judges Falcone and Borsellino were killed by Cosa Nostra in Sicily in 1992 – a milestone for the anti-Mafia struggle. Already in the 1980s large demonstrations and assemblies took place in Lombardy, Sicily, Calabria, and Campania to speak out against the violence of Cosa Nostra, the 'Ndrangheta, and the Camorra.[47] The most active subjects were young people (especially high school students), teachers and principals, women, and members of the Catholic Church. The movement (still present today) had a strong civic pedagogical mission to educate about the principle of *legalità* (legality) – that is, about the value of a society ruled by law and justice rather than overpowered by organized crime and corruption. It was a resistance that strove for an engaged citizenry aware that *omertà* (silence) and oblivion are the Mafia's most powerful weapons.

Memory was (and still is), indeed, the true backbone of the movement and its ethical foundation. To remember the victims means to recognize in their fight a model and in their deaths a structural injustice, rather than a crime news story, and to create a narrative of the past that history often neglects to write. The response provoked by the second ransom kidnapping crisis was also the expression of the emerging anti-Mafia denunciation in post-terrorism Italy. The way the city of Turin would mobilize against the abduction of Marco Fiora and the powerful protest in Calabria by Angela Casella, mother of Cesare, put at the centre of public attention a reality that the question of negotiations had obscured and avoided facing: Aspromonte.

Marco Fiora was kidnapped in Turin, Piedmont, on 2 March 1987 and was liberated in Ciminà Superiore, Calabria, on 2 August 1988. The seven-year-old's captivity was unbearable and cruel. He spent seventeen months in Aspromonte chained to a cot in abandoned houses and caves, without either bathing or walking, and brainwashed by his warders. The physical and psychological marks of his ordeal were immediately evident to everyone who watched the breaking news of his liberation. Marco's was the longest abduction of a child in Italy. His kidnappers demanded an impossible ransom of five billion lire, which his parents, owners of a garage and a bakery, could not pay. Their numerous appeals to the criminals went unheard, and the ransom negotiation turned into a drawn-out ordeal characterized by long intervals of silence. Over 520 days, the Fioras received only four Polaroids of Marco holding a newspaper and a tape recording of his voice as proof that he was alive. Turin did not remain indifferent. A month after Marco was captured, the city's archbishop, Cardinal Anastasio Ballestrero, published an appeal in the local diocesan newspaper and spoke on *TG3*, the regional RAI newscast. The Fiora family's pain "is not a private matter, but it involves the heart of the whole city, especially in this time of Easter preparations," Ballestrero stated in his first public speech on behalf of a kidnap victim.[48] Seconding the archbishop's appeal, Monsignor Franco Peradotto depicted Marco as a true *figura Christi*, calling him "a small crucifix" in a television interview. These entreaties by the Catholic Church went unanswered, as did those that came later that year at Christmas. In December, Turin's mayor, Maria Magnani Noya, also demanded that the kidnappers liberate the child, giving voice to the many requests she was receiving from residents.[49] The president of the Council of Piedmont did the same. At the national level, the singer and television celebrity Adriano Celentano asked for Marco's freedom in his end-of-year monologue on *Fantastico* (Fantastic), the most popular variety show hosted by Rai Uno.

The appeals intensified in February (for Marco's eighth birthday) when Pope John Paul II pleaded for the kidnappers to return the child to his parents, and a Turinese newsvendor, Pietro Tartamella, went on a "sight strike" – that is, he blindfolded himself like a kidnapped hostage for forty days in protest. In response, the abductors sent Tartamella the fourth Polaroid of Marco to deliver to his family. In March (a year after the boy's capture), the mothers of Reggio Calabria wrote a letter of solidarity in which they urged the men of the syndicate to think of their own children and what it would be like for them to be separated from their families for such a long time. Elementary school children also wrote to the abductors, but the mobilization escalated after three suspected kidnappers were arrested in May. At the UNICEF Universal Day of Childhood Convention in Turin, the mayor, the archbishop, Rabbi Roberto Colombo, and a middle school student publicly demanded that the abductors free Marco. The Alpini (Alpine troops), who were holding their national assembly in Turin that month, led their parade with a large banner reading "The Alpini ask you to free Marco," which was applauded by the city and attracted media attention. In Calabria the archbishop of Reggio, Aurelio Sorrentino, begged the kidnappers "on his knees," while in the small town of Scilla young students brought flowers to their classrooms as a gesture of solidarity. These numerous appeals did not have the desired effect, and the Fiora family would be met with silence for months.

The length of Marco's captivity and the certainty that he was hidden somewhere in Aspromonte turned ransom kidnapping into a true civic and political struggle. In July, Mayor Magnani Noya accepted the proposal of the Federcasalinghe (National Housewife Association) to organize a concert that would allow all the Turinesi to express their support for the Fiora family. "A special night organized by women," the *TG3* journalist announced, "in which an appeal will be addressed directly to the women of the syndicate that keeps the child prisoner."[50] The well-known singer and songwriter Pierangelo Bertoli agreed to play, and thousands of people attended the concert. The Federfiori Torino (National Federation of Italian Florists) co-sponsored the event and donated 10,000 roses to the participants – one for each hour that Marco had spent in Aspromonte. Secular and religious authorities spoke on stage, including the mayor and the representatives of the Catholic Diocese, the Valdese Church, and the Israelite community. "We need to be able to repeat the mobilization that defeated terrorism, by fighting organized crime," Mayor Magnani Noya told Turin.[51] "We love you, Marco. Your city stands by you," she added.[52] After sixteen months of his captivity, Marco's city did not just rally against ransom kidnapping; it started to combat organized crime.

The politics that the women of Turin performed for the Fiora family – a politics of relationship, solidarity, and care – stands in stark contrast to the dystopian individualistic society that Calvino imagined in response to the kidnapping narrative of the mid- to late 1970s. Rather than isolating and blaming the victims and their families for the persistence of the abductions, the Federcasalinghe, the Federfiori, and the city hall called for an active and engaged citizenry to speak up against the perpetrators. There were some initial critiques of the women's proposal because its festive nature contrasted with the gravity of the crime and because the abductors could have seen the potential for the family to ask for public donations. Yet the effect of the concert was the opposite. The visibility that the Fiora abduction reached made ransom kidnapping political. A few days after the mobilization in Turin, Rome responded. One hundred eight deputies signed a parliamentary interrogation asking the prime minister, the Minister of the Interior, and the Minister of Justice to intervene. "If it is true that the child is in a sort of free zone in Aspromonte," the deputies argued, "we ask law enforcement to regain control of the situation in that zone."[53] Five days later, on 2 August 1988, Marco Fiora was liberated. His kidnappers, the press reported, left him close to a ranger station in Aspromonte while escaping the law enforcement helicopters searching for hostages. For weeks the media depicted Aspromonte as the "mountain of kidnapping" and as a militarized borderland reminiscent of wartime. To a journalist who asked him why he called the Aspromonte a "free zone" in the parliamentary interrogation that he wrote, the Communist representative Luciano Violante – future president of the Anti-Mafia Parliamentary Committee – said, "Because no serious control of the territory has ever been done. I do not know if this is due to deliberate will, which would be criminal, or just to ineptitude and thoughtlessness. There are areas completely free, left in the hands of organized crime and Mafia. The Aspromonte is one of them."[54] The Fiora abduction clearly shifted the media, civic, and political narratives of ransom kidnapping from the hard line issue to the unsolved matter of Italy's extraterritorialities.

The public response to Marco Fiora's ordeal is indicative of a change in action in the country. After the example of Turin – one that recalls the philosopher Hannah Arendt's observation that "power corresponds to the human ability not just to act but to act in concert"[55] – ransom kidnapping became too visible a crime. After this, other cities mobilized with protests, demonstrations, and demands for a more decisive state intervention. This visibility – the reason why the 'Ndrangheta's committee decided to stop kidnapping in the early 1990s – is the opposite of *omertà* and is a power that Mafia fears. This became clear with

114   Ransom Kidnapping in Italy

the Casella abduction. Cesare Casella was eighteen years old when on 18 January 1988 he was snatched from his car in Pavia, Lombardy. He spent two years and twelve days chained in Aspromonte and made it back home on 30 January 1990. When Marco Fiora was liberated in 1988, Cesare had already been a hostage for seven months. That summer, Pope John Paul II implored Cesare's kidnappers to free him at the request of Monsignor Giovanni Volta, bishop of Pavia. In mid-September, the press announced that Cesare's high school had organized a march of solidarity that was supposed to end at the cathedral with a mass celebrated by the bishop himself. Pavia, like Turin, was starting to fight back. Strikingly, Cesare's abductors sent a threatening letter to the Casella family to stop the "publicity of his kidnapping."[56] This letter confirms that the 'Ndrangheta feared the democratic and civic agency that could make abduction too visible a crime. As a result, the march was cancelled. However, this forced *omertà* did not last, and two months later 5,000 students marched on the streets of Pavia demanding Cesare's liberation.[57] The Casella abduction would become especially visible thanks to his mother, Angela, whose unique efforts to get her son back would mobilize the region of Calabria and earn her the epithet *madre coraggio* (mother courage).[58]

Speaking Out from Aspromonte

During Cesare's lengthy captivity, Angela Casella went to Aspromonte twice (October 1988 and June 1989). The first time was because the kidnappers had not liberated Cesare after his family paid a ransom of one billion lire. She spent three days in the villages of the Locride (the Ionic side of Aspromonte), where she gave local priests an appeal to the abductors to read during Sunday mass. The Casellas believed the Catholic Church to have more authority to speak up than did political institutions because priests, unlike politicians, had nothing to lose. Strikingly, the newspaper of their hometown, Pavia, funded the trip. Church and media became the family's only means of reaching the kidnappers. Yet it was Angela Casella's second journey that affected the history of ransom kidnapping. In the months that followed her first trip, the abductors asked the family for an additional three billion lire, which they were ready to pay in April 1989, when the magistrate and the prosecutor in charge of the case ordered the confiscation of their assets. The decision was criticized by the press, which now depicted the hard line as ineffective and tried to reopen the 1970s debate. However, Luigi Casella, Cesare's father, did not want to contest the magistracy's ruling and instead went to Calabria to offer the kidnappers –

unsuccessfully – the last five hundred million lire he had borrowed. In response, the abductors asked for two billion. With their assets frozen and Cesare in the hands of his persecutors for more than five hundred days, Angela Casella decided to return to Calabria. Before leaving her hometown, she took a strong position against the state by returning to the mayor her family's ballots for the upcoming European elections and inviting her fellow citizens to boycott the vote as well.

Angela Casella's second journey did not just give visibility to her son's kidnapping. It put Aspromonte in the spotlight. Followed by journalists, and therefore the country, *madre coraggio* spent nearly ten days travelling from one small town to another, mapping a territory whose names became newly familiar to every Italian. Her headquarters was the little town of Locri, but her destinations included San Luca, Platì, Ciminà, the Sanctuary of Our Lady of Polsi, and Zervò, all 'Ndrangheta strongholds. Each of the main national newspapers published up to seven articles a day about her trip, while television shot the distant and unreachable places that the collective imagination had often framed as foreign. What made Angela Casella's approach to Aspromonte remarkable was her ability to reach the local people, especially the women – the true target of her journey. Convinced that the 'Ndrangheta represented only a small percentage of the people of Calabria, Casella appealed to the solidarity of those individuals not involved in business or public life, whose interests were less impacted by organized crime, and who could empathize with her maternal desperation. Angela Casella's journey was a thoughtful and strategic political action. Her simple but highly symbolic gestures were able to create bridges and safe, sharable spaces where her story could intersect with those of the many Calabrian women and young people who showed up in the Locride's town squares. Mothers and children of Mafia victims, ex-hostages, students, priests and bishops, the Women Against the Mafia Association, but also local politicians responded to her call, which began in Locri with Angela asking the people to sign a "notebook of solidarity," as she called it. She repeated this ritual in every village she visited, as well as other symbolic actions, such as chaining herself to a telephone booth; sleeping in a tent in a public square; standing next to signs with messages to her son, the kidnappers, or the state; and speaking at mass (figure 4.1). Her intention was to start a hunger strike and remain in the Locride until her son was freed, but politicians, magistrates, and law enforcement urged her to leave for security reasons.

The effects of her journey surpassed Angela's expectations. She became the leader of a protest that went beyond Cesare's kidnapping and showed the Locride itself to be a hostage of the 'Ndrangheta. After

Figure 4.1. Angela Casella in Calabria, 1989. Photo supplied by Agenzia ANSA.

her first day in Locri, indeed, the city council resigned in a sign of solidarity and in protest against the state. Forty-two mayors followed the example and created a special committee to organize the revolt. The solidarity that Angela Casella stirred gave agency to the families of kidnap victims, to the civil society that decided to be on her side, and to local political institutions. In the eyes of public opinion, this unusual alliance against organized crime emphasized the absence of Rome in Aspromonte. The leaders of the Anti-Mafia Parliamentary Committee and the high commissioner for the Fight Against the Mafia rushed to Calabria to negotiate with the mayors and Angela. Politicians and police chiefs from the capital reacted with a mix of solidarity and criticism. "I do not believe that the Minister of the Interior, when he says that the state did its duty to the fullest, can refer to us, that is, to the sad events that concern my son," Angela Casella said in response to Minister Antonio Gava's comments about her journey, "unless he wants to admit that he represents a defeated state."[59] Prime Minister Ciriaco De Mita lamented on television the unusual way the Casella family handled the kidnapping and criticized Angela's provocative request that the state either pay her son's ransom or intervene in Aspromonte. He also stated that spotlighting the area could have been dangerous for Cesare and that her emotional journey was overshadowing the excellent job done by law enforcement over the years. The chief of the national Criminalpol (special police corps) went even further and told the press that "appeasing the hostage's relatives" is the most difficult part of investigating ransom kidnappings and that "emotionality is one of the reasons why the Casella kidnapping has been prolonged."[60]

De Mita and Luigi Rossi depicted the Casella family through the same emotional frame that the hard line always used to describe the hostages' families, and they portrayed the state instead as a professional, experienced, and successful champion against ransom kidnapping. Yet their narrative did not convince either the media or the public – which were both on the side of *madre coraggio*. *Corriere della Sera* allowed Angela Casella to write a response in its pages.[61] "I don't want to move anybody, I want to make everybody think," she stated in her article, distancing her journey from emotions.[62] And to the criticism that De Mita levelled at her family because, in his opinion, they paid the ransom too early, she said, "We paid after seven months of captivity. How many days, how many hours, are seven months?" – clearly denouncing the stagnation of the state.[63] She also mentioned her decision to not vote in a "country offended by the violence of criminals and the indifference of politicians," and to those who requested her silence, she responded that shouting out was the only way to ask for the help she received in Calabria from "the maternal solidarity of the women and from a community claiming justice for me and for itself."[64] By speaking up from the Locride, Angela Casella located the families of the hostages in the territories controlled by the 'Ndrangheta, bringing the media and Italian society where the state was absent. In so doing, she crossed an imaginary border to interrupt the impossible negotiations imposed by the abductors and to offer a different perspective from which the *latitante* (shirker) state could not speak and the families' voices could be heard. She turned the vacuum of the state and the silence of the hidden kidnappers into a democratic space for her, her son's, and the local population's civil rights, which had been oppressed by violence and corruption.

The images of Marco Fiora and Angela Casella in Aspromonte became more powerful and convincing than the politicians' narrative of kidnapping. In the photos, videos, and articles to which the country was exposed by the late 1980s, the families and the hostages were seen not as responsible for the phenomenon but as its helpless victims. As a result, civic discourse shifted and started to examine the state's responsibility. Among the issues raised by the media were the delay of anti-kidnapping legislation and the state's inability to control the Aspromonte.[65] Marco Fiora and Cesare Casella were in fact only two of six hostages hidden at the same time in the Calabrian mountains. In an article on Angela Casella's journey, the philosopher Salvatore Veca asked his readers, "Where is the state, where are the institutions to which the exercise of sovereignty was democratically entrusted?"[66] The civic action of an individual, Angela Casella, contrasted with the undeniable absence of the state and forced everyone to recognize that "there are physical spaces in this nation in which the monopoly of legitimate violence is not in force, zones in some way extraterritorial, internal borders with other powers, enemy and foreign."[67] *Madre coraggio*'s trip shed light on the extraterritorial control of organized crime. The natural impenetrability of Aspromonte – however real a barrier – could no longer be accepted as an explanation for the kidnapping industry, and a call for responsibility replaced a fatalistic approach. This became evident in Veca's article when, referring to the well-known Bertolt Brecht quote from the *Life of Galileo* (and in so doing connecting Angela's epithet to Brecht's *Mother Courage and Her Children*), he stated: "If a country that needs heroines is unfortunate, the misfortune is not a sort of destiny or a natural calamity. It rather evokes collective responsibilities, it involves institutional plans, and, in the end, people's actions and lack thereof; first and foremost of those who should provide the basic public good of security, on which the minimum content of any association or collective agency that we are used to call 'State' is based."[68] Those who spoke out with Angela Casella in Aspromonte showed that the reason why Italy needed a heroine (and held an international record for ransom kidnapping) was neither fate nor nature but the weakness of the state against the violence and territorial power of organized crime.

The 1990s Anti-Kidnapping Movement

After 743 days of captivity in Aspromonte, and seven months after his mother's journey through the Locride, Cesare Casella was freed on 30 January 1990.[69] The same day the papers covered the news of his liberation, 31 January 1990, Carlo Celadon spent his third birthday in a row in the hands of his persecutors and a new abduction was announced – that of Patrizia Tacchella, a seven-year-old girl from Stallavena di Grezzana, a village in the province of Verona, Veneto. Patrizia spent two and a half months with her warders in a small villa in Liguria until the Carabinieri liberated her on 18 April. Her kidnappers were three businessmen from Piedmont responsible, it turned out, for three previous abductions of children in their region. The media called them "the white-collar gang," an example of how this crime was sometimes imitated by non-professional abductors willing to do anything for financial gain. Before Patrizia was freed, however, her abduction was still believed to be linked to the 'Ndrangheta and provoked a grassroots mobilization that turned the protests of the late 1980s into an anti-kidnapping movement of the 1990s aimed at eliminating the violence of abductions from the country. A few days after her capture, two thousand children and their parents pleaded for her liberation in Piazza Brà, Verona, in a colourful and massive demonstration in which the ex-hostage Cesare Casella was able to participate by speaking over the phone to the square. But it was Patrizia's village that brought the civic struggle against ransom kidnapping to a new level.

The people of Stallavena spontaneously created a committee called Perché Patrizia sia l'ultima (Let Patrizia be the last one), which became particularly visible thanks to an original initiative organized by the local priest.[70] The committee distributed postcards with a photo of Patrizia, an appeal to free her, and the names of the hostages still missing in Aspromonte, which households could mail to the president of the Republic, Francesco Cossiga.[71] Stallavena quickly sent 10,000 copies, but other cities in the Veneto and all over the country started to request them as well. Acclaimed RAI journalist Michele Santoro dedicated an episode of his popular broadcast *Samarcanda* to Patrizia's kidnapping.[72] He introduced the subject by saying that he and his team had always stood on the families' side and then discussed with his guests the freezing of assets that the magistrate of Verona had just adopted with the Tacchellas. For the first time, indeed, a magistrate had applied the new decree issued by the government after the Casella kidnapping. The state's response to *madre coraggio*'s action in the Locride was in fact to make the hard line a national strategy. Yet *Samarcanda*'s real news ended up being Stallavena's people and its committee – with whom Santoro spoke live – and, especially, the postcard project. While Patrizia was held captive, one and a half million Italians requested and sent postcards to President Cossiga.[73] After the examples of Turin and Angela Casella, the hostages' hometowns and families found effective ways to speak up and awaken the part of society willing to fight back. Although the state tried to show strength by making the freezing of assets a decree, the power to shape the kidnapping narrative now belonged to community and civil rights organizers.

The striking novelty of the 1990s was that the hometowns of the kidnapped victims united and their protests went from being a local to a national movement. This was clear on 28 April 1990, when thousands of people marched on Via dei Fori Imperiali in Rome to demand that political powers end the abductions (figure 4.2).

Figure 4.2. "La marcia dei rapiti" in Rome, *L'Unità*, 29 April 1990. Courtesy of *L'Unità News*.

The idea for the demonstration started a few weeks prior, when the Stallavena committee Perché Patrizia sia l'ultima went to Roggiano Gravina, Calabria, to ratify a "twinning" of the two towns and an alliance against ransom kidnapping. Although Patrizia was liberated before the date of the demonstration, the committee remained its principal organizer. One thousand five hundred people from all over the north, but especially from Stallavena and Arzignano, Veneto, departed from Verona on a special night train that the *ferrovie dello stato* (public rail) provided, even though they were then on strike. Five hundred people arrived in Rome from Calabria by bus, and still others came from different regions. The march was completely silent, but its visibility was deafening. Hundreds of signs, banners, and symbols sent clear messages to the political institutions: "Politici, liberate Carlo" (Politicians, free Carlo), "la Calabria chiede: lo stato dov'è?" (Calabria asks: where is the state?), "la libertà è un diritto" (freedom is a right), "Carlo: lo stato ti ha dimenticato, Arzignano no" (Carlo: the state forgot you, Arzignano did not), "al terrorismo mafioso lo stato risponde con l'omertà" (to Mafia terrorism the state responds with silence), "Gava, da che parte stai?" (Gava, which side are you on?), and "perché Patrizia sia l'ultima." The most notable signs, though, were the five banners with the names of the hostages still in the hands of their kidnappers and the dates of their respective captures. "Carlo Celadon, 25 gennaio 1988" (Carlo Celadon, 25 January 1988) read the sign that people from his hometown of Arzignano held that morning – over two years since the day he had been abducted.

The impressive visual effect of the march produced a new narrative. The now-free Cesare Casella and Patrizia Tacchella's father together led the march with other ex-hostages and families. Next to them were the mayors of the victims' hometowns, wearing their official sashes and holding their towns' banners. Although rooted in the Italian local *comuni* (city halls), the language of the protest reflected the awareness of the imminent geopolitical change that the country was about to experience. While in Italy the media continued to announce new abductions, the Berlin Wall fell (1989) and in 1990 Europe began the process that would lead to the creation of the European Union (1993). "We are going to enter Europe with a shameful record," read the large banner held by Carlo Celadon's friends.[74] The march participants – many of them students – went to Rome to denounce the shame of entering the union with the plague of ransom kidnapping and organized crime still unsolved. Strikingly, it was their European identity that offered the young people from the Veneto and Calabria a perspective from which to perceive the crime as a national stigma and to demand a solution.

Conclusion

A week after the march in Rome, and 831 days after his capture, Carlo Celadon was liberated on 5 May 1990.[75] The press and his incredulous father described him as like a concentration camp survivor. Carlo could barely walk, weighed only about ninety pounds, and was visibly disoriented. He later told journalists that his kidnappers gave him a stick with which to beat the rats and snakes that arrived when his cave filled with rainwater. Seventeen years had passed since the first hostage was kidnapped outside of Calabria and hidden in Aspromonte, but images of Carlo in 1990 were no less shocking than Paul Getty's ear mutilation in 1973. While the country had changed, its most horrific crime remained the same. Yet in nearly two decades, the narrative of kidnapping had shifted from focusing on the reason of state argument to the voices of the blackmailed families. The state's response to Angela Casella's journey in 1989 was not only the freezing of assets decree, which would become law in March 1991. While *madre coraggio* was still in the Locride, the state drastically increased the presence of law enforcement in the region and created a special anti-kidnapping force. "The state police force in Calabria went from 2,115 units in 1987 to 4,032 on 1 January 1993," reads the report on the abductions in the region written by the Anti-Mafia Parliamentary Committee.[76] Although it is commonly believed in Italy that the abductions for ransom ended because the state finally adopted the hard line used against terrorism in the 1978 political kidnapping of Moro, the motives that brought this long phenomenon to an end were multiple and more complex (as mentioned in chapter 1). The result of an endless media debate on negotiating, this common belief is also the consequence of a lack of memory. The activism of a civic movement made ransom kidnapping the very thing that the anonymous abductors did not want it to be – a visible crime. "After the noise ... the mother of that guy ... the one that went to Locri and chained herself in San Luca,"[77] state witness Nicola Femia said in his 2017 testimony, explaining why the 'Ndrangheta had called the meeting that halted the abductions. The police control that arrived in Aspromonte during the Casella kidnapping risked interfering with the business that had become for the 'Ndrangheta astonishingly lucrative: international drug trafficking.

However, the last abductions in modern Italy were linked to Sardinian banditry. Even if the number of cases dropped compared to those of the 1970s, in the 1980s and 1990s Sardinian bandits continued to kidnap both on the island and in central Italy (especially in Tuscany and Lazio). In 1983, for example, Anna Bulgari – the second member of the renowned Roman family to be kidnapped for ransom – and her seventeen-year-old son Giorgio Calissoni were captured and hidden in the mountains of Lazio for thirty-five days.[78] Despite the recent recommendation issued by the Council of Europe, the magistrate in charge of this case ordered that the Bulgari family's assets be frozen. In response, the bandits cut off Giorgio's ear, news that was widely covered by the media. Other abductions would capture public attention for the continual cruelty of the bandits. Giulio De Angelis, a contractor from Rome and the father of the popular racing driver Elio, was abducted in the summer of 1988 in Costa Smeralda (Sardinia) and kept in captivity for 142 days. He, too, suffered an ear mutilation. Two more examples are the kidnappings of Dante Belardinelli, captured in Settignano (Tuscany) in 1989, and Giuseppe Soffiantini, captured in Manerbio (Lombardy) in 1997. The next chapter will explore the memoirs of their ordeals, but it is important to remember here that, hidden in the forests of Tuscany by Sardinian bandits, Belardinelli and Soffiantini (each of whom suffered partial mutilation to both ears) represented two opposing views on the "strong" state. A close friend of Pier Luigi Vigna, the magistrate supporter of the *linea dura* since the Pomarici affair, Belardinelli was liberated by the police after sixty-four days of captivity and became a public voice in favour of the hard line. In contrast, Soffiantini, kidnapped years after the freezing of assets became law, spent 237 days in the hands of his abductors and was liberated because the magistrate in charge of his case asked permission for a "controlled payment" – that is, the family was allowed the exact figure demanded by the kidnappers. The Soffiantini kidnapping was analysed by the Anti-Mafia Parliamentary Committee, which only in 1998 created for the first time a special subcommittee to study the phenomenon of ransom kidnapping in the country. Under scrutiny was the effectiveness of the 1991 freezing of assets law. Based on the Soffiantini case, the committee asked to modify the text of the law in which the controlled payment was limited to being an investigative tool, wanting instead to make it a means of saving the hostage's life. In short, as a result of its study, the committee offered a different interpretation of and a new proposal for the *blocco dei beni*. By allowing the magistrate to control the ransom payment needed to save the hostage, the state would have prevented the possibility of the kidnappers changing the amount requested (the family could not have access to more money than the ransom negotiated with the abductors); the creation by the family of a parallel, secret, and dangerous negotiation with the criminals (a sort of black market for the hostage's liberation);

and the reduction of ransom kidnapping to a private matter between the abductors and the family (the *linea dura*'s main issue). The committee also asked to move ransom kidnapping from the property crimes section to the personal crimes of the penal code.

Yet it was a 1992 abduction in Sardinia that marked the narrative of kidnapping like never before, bringing together the horror of the 1970s with the solidarity of the late 1980s – the two key terms through which Italy framed its main ransom kidnapping crises. On 15 January, a seven-year-old boy, Farouk Kassam, was kidnapped from his parents' villa in Costa Smeralda and brought to Supramonte in Barbagia. Along with the 1979 kidnapping of Fabrizio De André and Dori Ghezzi, the popular musicians who spent months hidden in the same area, Farouk's became the most well-known Sardinian case in Italy. Wrongly believed to be part of Prince Karim Aga Khan's family – the well-off Ismaelites' religious leader and co-founder of Costa Smeralda in the early 1960s – Farouk was kept in Barbagia for six months.[79] After more than 150 days of captivity, his kidnappers cut off his ear and sent it to his family, whose assets had been frozen by law. The grim violence against a helpless child shocked the country, which was already living through the traumatizing loss of Giovanni Falcone, the anti-Mafia judge killed on 23 May 1992 in Sicily by a Cosa Nostra bomb.[80] In the days after Falcone's murder, the people of Palermo spontaneously hung white sheets from their balconies and windows with messages of indignation against organized crime and the state and in memory of Falcone. The white sheets were Palermo's original way of breaking the *omertà* and became the symbol of the fight against Mafia still used in Italy today. The news of Farouk's ear mutilation came the same week in which national unions were organizing a march that would bring 100,000 people to the streets of the Sicilian capital in one of the largest anti-Mafia protests ever. On the wave of Palermo, Sergio Zavoli, an acclaimed journalist known especially for his pioneering work on terrorism, used the platform of the newspaper *L'Unità* to appeal to the country to hang white sheets for the young Farouk and his parents as well (figure 4.3).[81]

The proposal was welcomed by the directors of public and private television news broadcasts, which in two days spread the word. It was the first time the media encouraged civil society to act in solidarity with a hostage's family and against kidnappers. *L'Unità* gave space to politicians, intellectuals, journalists, and celebrities to publicly support the initiative – including the president of Italy, Eugenio Scalfari. "La solidarietà per Farouk. La protesta per Falcone" (Solidarity for Farouk. Protest for Falcone) read the title of the article about the two upcoming events. It is striking to see a case of ransom kidnapping next to the 1992 Mafia massacre that destabilized the nation like terrorism

Figure 4.3. Appeal for Farouk Kassam, *L'Unità*, 27 June 1992. Courtesy of *L'Unità News*.

126   Ransom Kidnapping in Italy

had done in 1978. Within (and beyond) these two thresholds of the history of violence in modern Italy, the ransom kidnapping phenomenon never stopped. At the moment in which Sicily and the country said "enough," the media called on an engaged citizenry to condemn the horror in Barbagia.

Among the articles published by *L'Unità* was a letter addressed to "Egregio bandito, maestro d'orrore" (Dear bandit, master of horror), in which the film director Ettore Scola wrote to Farouk's kidnapper to inform him about what Italy was about to do against him and his affiliates. "Something is changing in our country," Scola states. "We are finding the capacity to be outraged, we are starting to convince ourselves that individual time and social time are not separated entities, we are starting to consider the offence made against one as a threat levelled on the collective."[82] The dystopic and individualistic society that Calvino foresaw from the late-1970s narrative of kidnapping is not what Italy became. But that something had changed is visible in the fact that the director of "Kidnapping Dear!" (1977), the short film we analysed in chapter 3 in which a husband feigns desperation over his wife's kidnapping, can no longer approach ransom kidnapping with a sarcastic gaze. Scola's previous dark humour became, in the face of a mutilated young hostage, indignation in 1992. The legacy of Falcone, Palermo, and the recent anti-kidnapping movement is what emerges in Scola's letter and in its audience.

Sardinia and the rest of Italy responded to Zavoli's appeal by hanging thousands of white sheets in many cities and sending messages of solidarity to Farouk Kassam (figure 4.4). It is remarkable that a little boy whose parents and name were neither Italian nor Catholic moved the country to speak out against ransom kidnapping. While two decades earlier RAI television responded to the abduction of a rich American teenager with a video featuring working-class buildings and women hanging laundry as a visual shorthand for a clean and hard-working Italy, this time the media asked the people to express their own agency. A means of breaking the silence that had allowed Sardinian banditry, the 'Ndrangheta, and Cosa Nostra to control their territories through violence, the white sheets became a symbolic and safe space in which private voices could become a collective protest. The Italy that became visible in the 1990s was a country for which ransom kidnapping could no longer be framed as foreign due to the identity of its victim. The time to air the country's dirty laundry in public had come, and the messages on those white sheets hung for Farouk and Falcone silently screamed the awareness of a society wounded by its domestic banditry and organized crime.

IN ITALIA

I candidi lenzuoli appesi domenica sui balconi di tutta Italia simbolo del risveglio delle coscienze Zavoli: «Adesso seguano i fatti»

Il vescovo va a trovare i genitori: «Sono sfiniti, ma hanno speranza» "Cianchino", fantino sardo favorito al Palio di Siena: «Vincerò per lui»

Dopo i teli bianchi, torna l'attesa

L'avvocato dei Kassam: «Un successo importante»

DAL NOSTRO INVIATO
PAOLO BRANCA

■ PORTO CERVO. «Sono sfiniti dall'angoscia, ma hanno anche una grande speranza». Adesso seguano i fatti, chiede il «promotore», Sergio Zavoli. Il giorno dopo la sfida dei lenzuoli commenti e segnali positivi da tutta Italia. Nuovi messaggi di solidarietà ai genitori di Farouk, salutati ieri dal vescovo Meloni, che ha lasciato la diocesi.

«Un successo importante», dice l'avvocato Mariano Delogu, legale dei Kassam. «Il segnale di un risveglio delle coscienze», secondo monsignor Riboldi. «Adesso seguano i fatti, chiede il «promotore», Sergio Zavoli. Il giorno dopo la sfida dei lenzuoli commenti e segnali positivi da tutta Italia. Nuovi messaggi di solidarietà ai genitori di Farouk, salutati ieri dal vescovo Meloni, che ha lasciato la diocesi.

Kassam: «Allah akbar».

A casa Kassam, il vescovo si intrattiene un quarto d'ora. «L'Islam – dice ai cronisti, che lo attendono fuori – è come il cristianesimo, preghiera e speranza...». E dopo aver riferito dello stato d'animo di Fareh Kassam e Marion Blenlot, annuncia con sicurezza: «Anche dopo resteranno comunque in Sardegna».

Il giorno dopo la sfida dei lenzuoli, i commenti e le valutazioni sono assai positivi. L'avvocato Mariano Delogu, legale della famiglia Kassam, non ha dubbi nel valutare personalmente in termini estremamente positivi l'iniziativa promossa da Sergio Zavoli. E aggiunge: «Considero assai importante la risposta che c'è stata non solo in Sardegna, ma anche nel resto del Paese».

Una conferma viene subito dalla Campania: monsignor Antonio Riboldi, vescovo di Acerra, considera tutti quei lenzuoli bianchi apparsi ai balconi e alle finestre del paese, un altro segnale del meraviglioso risveglio di coscienza del nostro popolo. Al punto che il vescovo, allargando il discorso anche alle manifestazioni anti-mafia e anti-camorra – «dovremo ogni tanto chiederci cosa rimane nella nostra coscienza e invece hanno eliminato la parte malata di noi, quella della paura e del disimpegno».

Sulla manifestazione dei teli, torna anche il suo promotore, Sergio Zavoli. Con una valutazione soddisfatta dell'esito dell'iniziativa, ma anche richiamando gli organi dello Stato ai propri doveri. «C'è tanta voglia di bucato nel paese – commenta Zavoli, durante un convegno a Napoli – ma non basta. I teli bianchi infatti non possono fare supplemento di nulla. Spetta ad altri creare le condizioni perché la vita di una società non rinneghi l'uomo come in altri casi di terribile cecità morale. Il gesto di protesta, comunque, è andato a segno. Voleva essere una modesta cosa – osserva ancora Zavoli – ma per fortuna è stato qualcosa di più. E quelli che hanno rifiutato di partecipare? «Forse – ha risposto Zavoli, alla domanda di un giornalista – questo comportamento riguarda solo quelle persone che con malinconica saggezza continuano a lavare i panni sporchi in famiglia». La solidarietà continua ad arrivare, infine, anche dal mondo dello sport. Dopo i ciclisti impegnati domenica in Sardegna nel campionato nazionale su strada, è stata la volta di un fantino famoso di origine sarda, Salvatore Ladu, detto Cianchino, grande favorito per il Palio di Siena. Se ha fatto sapere «Cianchino», ho dedicato a Farouk. E ha aggiunto: «In questo momento a Siena c'è festa, ma per la comunità sarda lo è per il povero bambino pronto ad affrontare l'ordalia di nuovo. Popolino profetizzava una vicenda, così triste ed inspiegabile, spero che possa tornare a casa quanto prima».

Figure 4.4. The white sheets for Farouk, *L'Unità*, 30 June 1992. Courtesy of *L'Unità News*.

Chapter Five

Trauma and Language in the Kidnapping Victim Memoir

In the summer of 1978, in the wake of the assassination of Aldo Moro by the Red Brigades on 9 May, national and international media noticed a spike in publications about terrorism and kidnapping in Italy. In its July review of Italian books, entitled "Terror in the Streets," the *Economist* called these subjects a "gold mine for Italian publishers."[1] A month prior, journalist Sergio Ronchetti similarly described abductions in *La Stampa* as "practically an editorial industry."[2] Ronchetti saw these texts as a lucrative product of "painful news stories" and explained their existence as a consequence of Italy's lack of "authentic writers." In his opinion, the diffusion of literary genres such as autobiography and memoir allowed anyone, from prostitutes to magistrates, to write about their lives. Even the kidnapped and their abductors were now able to become the "reporters of themselves." However, in the case of ransom kidnapping, Ronchetti claimed, publishers did not think through their choices well. These memoirs were published long after the liberation of their authors, whose names were therefore no longer in the spotlight, and after the newspapers had already written everything that was possible to know about their abductions. He wryly suggested that kidnappers should start abducting real writers or poets, which would have earned them more modest ransoms but resulted in better books for publishers.

What emerges from the pages of these late 1970s newspapers and magazines is that ransom kidnapping and terrorism appear alongside one another not merely as news but also as prominent subjects of publishing. Cultural production and prevailing narratives therefore considered both political and criminal violence as representative of that time. Yet, considering that in three decades nearly seven hundred people were kidnapped for ransom in Italy, the number of those who decided to publish their accounts is relatively small, due probably to the fact that victims found it difficult to talk about their ordeals. Nevertheless, between the 1970s and the late 1990s some survivors did write memoirs, including Luigi Rossi di Montelera (1977), Carla Ovazza (1978), Donatella Tesi Mosca (1986), Dante Belardinelli (1990), Cesare Casella (1990), and Giuseppe Soffiantini (1999). These books open a window onto ransom kidnapping that allows us to look at this phenomenon from the perspective of its ex-hostages. Adopting the lens of their testimony does not mean using these texts as documents, facts, or evidence. The accounts of the kidnapped are not archival materials, and their narratives cannot explain the intentionality and circumstances behind the crime. But these are not the right questions to ask the abducted, given that they are not the architects of their abductions. On the contrary, kidnapping is for them an unexpected event that irrupts in their lives and interrupts the flow of time. What we shall instead recognize and investigate is the agency of the victims' accounts. Why did they decide to write their books? What granted them the authority to do so? And is giving an account of their harrowing experience a political action?

Whereas the first part of this chapter investigates the kidnapping memoirs at civic and historical levels and in relation to the media and legal narratives of the time, the second part analyses these written accounts through the lens of trauma and literary studies. It is to the voices of the victims that the remainder of this book now turns. In contrast with Ronchetti's idea that the media already said everything we need to know about this crime, these testimonial narratives bring us beyond the borders dividing territory and extra-territory, visible and invisible, and instead allow us to look at kidnapping from an otherwise impossible proximity. While the country was either following or ignoring the news, debating the negotiations, or protesting against this violent phenomenon, the kidnap victims were enduring unbearable captivities and traumatic relationships with their persecutors. It is thanks to the perceptual frame of their language that we can try to imagine what it meant to be a hostage of ransom kidnapping in modern Italy.

Bearing Witness to Oneself

"I hate and fear a total disappearance, of being without a story and without a body," Giuseppe Soffiantini writes in his memoir *Il mio sequestro* (My kidnapping).[3] The idea of dying in captivity without a narrative that bears witness to his ordeal, or without a cadaver that testifies to the end of his life, is unbearable for a hostage. It means disappearing without memory – that is, completely. Writing to remember is a recurrent expression in the victims' memoirs. Journalists can report the stories of

130   Ransom Kidnapping in Italy

their absences, the reactions of the families, communities, and public, or, after they are released, what happened to them. Journalistic, as well as criminological and jurisprudential, narratives cannot bear witness to their ordeal, however. These other narratives remain external, as we shall see from the kidnap victims' voices.

Among the victims of the 1970s crime wave, Luigi Rossi di Montelera and Carla Ovazza wrote *Racconto di un sequestro* (Account of a kidnapping, 1977) and *Cinque ciliege rosse* (Five red cherries, 1978), respectively. Both books came out more than two years after their authors' ordeals and were among the memoirs that Ronchetti reviewed in *La Stampa*. On 14 November 1973, the twenty-seven-year-old Rossi di Montelera was kidnapped in Piedmont. After four hard months of captivity, which he spent practically buried alive in two different constricted cells, the Revenue Guard Corps freed him on 14 March 1974. He was hidden in a tunnel under a shed in the country, close to a small village in Lombardy called Treviglio. Rossi di Montelera belonged to a well-known family, owners of the famous liquor brand Martini & Rossi. His kidnapping was the second in northern Italy committed by the *corleonesi* Mafia syndicate.[4] Rossi di Montelera was liberated by chance, and his family did not pay any ransom. The Revenue Guard Corps was investigating another recent kidnapping in Lombardy, that of Pietro Torielli Jr., taken in 1972 by the same criminals.[5] Following the kidnappers' tracks, the Revenue Guard Corps searched the shed under which Rossi di Montelera was hidden. When the officers opened the trapdoor of his hiding place, they were shocked to find the hostage sitting in the dark, chained and terrified that they were his persecutors playing a psychological trick on him. Rossi di Montelera remained for hours with his head covered by his jacket. Drawing on his legal background, he asked the lieutenant and the magistrate who found him several juridical questions to ensure they were not his kidnappers. Only later did he agree to exit his cell.

In the preface to his memoir, Rossi di Montelera states that his initial intention was to record an account for legal purposes with which to thereby testify before the law. However, this original plan became a need to describe his lived experience in order to give others "a more precise idea of how a ransom kidnapping occurs" and to communicate the thoughts he had during "a terrible and, at the human level, so unusual experience."[6] He therefore felt an urgency to reach an audience other than the magistrates and to create, for his truth, a space different than the court of law. In his decision to write his account for something beyond a legal audience, we can recognize the Latin-language distinction that the philosopher Giorgio Agamben makes in his book on Primo Levi's testimony between the witness as *testis* – "the person who, in a trial or lawsuit between two rival parties, is in the position of a third party (*terstis*)" – and *superstes*, "a person who has lived through something, who has experienced an event from beginning to end and can therefore bear witness to it."[7] Like Levi, Rossi di Montelera cannot be a "third party" but is instead a survivor who wants to testify to the event he has experienced "from beginning to end."

Rossi di Montelera indirectly indicates a further intention of his book, which is to testify to abduction beyond the limits of media narratives. From just a few passages of his testimony, it is possible to recognize his awareness during his captivity of how the lived experience changed him from being a "news reader" to a "witness" of the phenomenon of kidnapping. "I felt an odd sensation in that moment: I realized, almost as if from the outside, like a spectator, that I was facing that mysterious adventure about which one often reads in the newspapers, of which I had never known the details, and I thought fleetingly: 'Here's how you do a kidnapping,'" Rossi di Montelera writes about the moment of his capture.[8] In this passage, in which he describes realizing that he has become a victim of kidnapping, the reader sees him grow aware of his condition from the outside as though he were a spectator watching the scene unfold. This is the very position he had often held while reading about kidnapping in the newspapers, from which it was not possible to know the "details." In a moment of epiphany, "how one kidnaps" not only becomes real to him but becomes his reality. Journalism therefore allows Rossi di Montelera to recognize from the outside what is happening to him, but a journalistic understanding of kidnapping is surpassed and left on the newspapers' pages as a "mysterious adventure" that he is about to know first-hand. Rossi di Montelera is now inside the scene, and what he feels most is the uncertainty of his future. He therefore leaves the frame of reference provided by journalism and attempts to physically orient himself in order to envision kidnapping through his own perception.

In another section of his memoir, Rossi di Montelera writes that, after being forced to sign the first page of a newspaper to send to his family as proof that he was alive, he could read pieces of articles left in the cell by his abductors. One of these articles gave the news about the political kidnapping of Ettore Amerio, the personnel director of the FIAT factory snatched in Turin on 10 December 1973 by the Red Brigades.[9] "I read in the newspaper that nobody knew anything further about Cavalier Amerio,[10] and that they were developing theories about how the kidnapping took place," Montelera writes. "And it seemed to me that I was able to answer those questions, to be able to explain to everyone what exactly Amerio was thinking, even though I had never seen him in my life."[11]

The hostage here clearly identifies with Amerio, but worthy of note is what he recognizes by reading the news from inside his hiding place. From this internal perspective, he can no longer be an onlooker-reader but instead becomes a witness-reader. Not only does he realize that, as a kidnapped man himself, he can testify to another victim how to resist kidnapping, but he also becomes the voice of the victims, someone who can speak to everyone about an event he had lived from beginning to – if not yet an end – his confined present. In other words, his lived ordeal brings him beyond the reporting and the language of a newspaper, and he now feels the urgency to make visible the otherwise invisible victims by narrating what he has learned through his perceptual frame. The contrast between the discursive knowledge about this crime, which derives primarily from the media, and his personal experience of it is in fact one of the main reasons why Rossi di Montelera chose to write his story after his liberation. "I alert the readers that I am not a writer, but maybe entrusting others with such a personal and intensely lived story would have made it lose the immediacy and fidelity of the facts," he states in the preface.[12] Even if Rossi di Montelera is not a writer, what he lived through confers on him the authority to write his book. A witness in flesh, he becomes, as Agamben would say, an author-survivor. To overcome journalism's inability to reach the level of testimony, Rossi di Montelera drafts his lived account to make visible something that can be seen only from a language that still possesses the immediacy of the experience, a language originating from inside, a language that has been kidnapped.[13]

Unlike Rossi di Montelera, Carla Ovazza decided to testify to her plight while she was still a hostage. "In my cell I always felt the desire, if I were to survive, to recount my experience and describe how and why I was able to 'make it.' I wanted to make those people who would have difficulty imagining it understand the fate of a hostage reduced to being completely unaware of her own destiny and deprived of any defences."[14] Not only this, but her desire to recount her fate to others was also a way of resisting an unimaginable condition, as we shall see. However, a memoir was not the medium that Ovazza originally had in mind to tell her story. It was the French publisher Robert Laffont who invited her to write a book, which came out in France the same year it was published in Italy by Mursia.[15] This book, which Ronchetti in *La Stampa* reduced to the genre of *fumettone* (cartoon), saw a Spanish translation as well, showing an international interest in the testimonial narrative of the Italian kidnapping phenomenon.[16] In a later RAI interview with the journalist Fausta Leoni – a pioneer in giving voice to the trauma of the kidnap victims – Ovazza stated that writing her book became for her a "social duty" because "humanity must be informed about these things." Speaking about the victims who remain silent after their ordeals, she stated that "it is not right because in this way they suffer much more. It is also not right for the social part of life because this is a terrible social plague."[17]

On 26 November 1975, Ovazza was captured in front of her home in Turin. She spent thirty-five days in what she called a "clandestine prison."[18] Her hiding place was an extremely restricted space, which her abductors built inside a farmstead in Martinaia Po, a small village near Cuneo (Piedmont). During her captivity, her warders subjected her to harsh physical deprivations and severe psychological abuses. She was released on 31 December after her family paid the ransom. Her kidnapping was one of the first organized by the 'Ndrangheta settled in Piedmont.[19] When Ovazza realized that she had been kidnapped, she thought there had been a mistake, as hers was a well-off family but not wealthy. She worked at the Bureau International du Travail (BIT), while her husband was an architect. Ovazza even thought she might be victim of a political kidnapping, since she belonged to a Jewish family that "has always been very active in the struggle for the survival of Israel."[20] In her mind, her ordeal could have been an act of revenge against the Israeli community. In reality, her kidnapping was for ransom and performed by a domestic criminal syndicate. The abductors' target was not her immediate family but rather Gianni Agnelli, the owner of FIAT, whose daughter Ovazza's son Alain Elkann had married two months prior. In her cell, Ovazza remembered that the wedding photographs had been published by newspapers and realized those pictures had started the "infernal mechanism" of which she became victim.

"Writing the book was my catharsis; I liberated myself from the nightmares that had never left me since the moment of my liberation. In this way I became the spectator and no longer the actor, and I was able to examine this most sad misadventure," Ovazza later affirmed at a 1978 juridical psychology convention where she was invited to talk about her victimization.[21] Writing her testimony thus allowed her to be no longer inside her kidnapping but rather to look at it from an external perspective. Ovazza here uses the same word, "spectator," with which Rossi di Montelera had indicated his own position during his capture. The spectatorship that journalism cannot provide is made possible through the victims' accounts. Ovazza positions herself as a spectator in relation to her own testimony, meaning that writing gave her a self-reflexivity from which she could analyse her subjugation.

Furthermore, being an author has for Ovazza a greater sociopolitical significance than for Rossi di Montelera. Her intention is not only to better inform readers about this crime but also to raise public opinion up against it. "I rebel against the fact that there is such indifference, that abductions have become part of the nightly news. We have to arouse public opinion, and I believe that it is for this reason that the testimonies of people like me – who have experienced what it means to be victims and want to help those who unfortunately will have to endure the same fate – are what is needed above all,"[22] she declares at the same juridical psychology convention. For Ovazza, testifying is an action against the indifference to a "plague of humanity," which, from her perspective, can no longer be considered at an individual level but must be recognized as a "social plague that concerns everyone."[23] If we compare a passage from her memoir with one from her public comments in 1978, we can see how her personal lived experience made her a voice for the kidnapped more broadly. Ovazza depicts herself in *Cinque ciliege rosse* as "a clump of flesh at the mercy of these unscrupulous beings."[24] The victim is here hidden inside a car, and she does not know if her persecutors are really going to free her as they said they would. Her words are noteworthy for the complete dehumanization they describe. Ovazza vividly testifies to her captured body as no longer having shape. Reduced to mere flesh, she feels absolutely annihilated. In her speech at the convention, her suffered bodily loss marks the victimization of all the kidnapped and reaches a political level. "We cannot allow," she asserts, "that a few people that run a market of human flesh hold in their hands an entire nation that continues to show itself incapable and inept before this shameful crime. For this reason, I have agreed to talk to you today."[25] In front of a specialized audience, Ovazza speaks up to denounce the incapacity of Italian institutions to defeat the crime. Her particular experience cannot be either isolated or confined to the field of victimological studies. Rather, it allows her to define ransom kidnapping as a "a market for human flesh," which, almost undisturbed, subdues the country. A witness to her own ordeal, she feels the duty to testify to it in public in order to fight against a phenomenon that can affect others. In short, writing her book made her the witness-spectator of *every* kidnapping.

Ovazza's unique way of being a witness, compared with that of other victims, is her awareness of the value and power of testimony. As mentioned, Ovazza, unlike Rossi di Montelera, decided to testify to her ordeal when she was still a hostage. She portrays herself as completely unaware of her destiny inside her cell. Unable to see the future, she turned her gaze to the past and relived, in her constricted present, the drama she had lived in 1940, when the Fascist regime's persecution of Jews compelled her and her family to immigrate to the United States.[26]

Like Walter Benjamin's "Angel of History," she thus lived the time of her captivity proceeding backward towards tomorrow and facing the ruins of the past. From this perspective she witnessed the destiny of other Jews who, unlike her family, could not leave the country, including her friend Elena Recanati, whose story Ovazza heard first-hand after the war. In one of the most difficult moments of her plight, two days before her liberation and after having suffered severe threats, Ovazza found herself in an insurmountable abyss when she had a vision of her friend Elena:

> And here, without my noticing, Elena appears clearly before my eyes. I start to talk to her, to talk to this friendly face which in this moment is so close to me. "Elena, you suffered so much at Auschwitz and told me about the tortures to which they subjected you. You had to abandon a very young son, and you always had the strength to fight in order to be able to see him again one day. You suffered from hunger, gangrene, and the most horrendous dysentery. You endured the blows with a unique stoicism; you were abused much more than me, and yet you were able to survive with your extraordinary strength, with your unshakable will ... Elena, help me with your courage, stand by me so that I can find some hope again. You, too, reached the bottom of the abyss, and still you made it! I, too, have to try to recover in order to hug my family again!"[27]

On the edge of the precipice, Ovazza was capable of reaching her friend Elena in a mystical vision that helped her cling to hope. She also recognized, though, how her vision was made possible by the vivid account of her survivor-friend, who in February 1946 wrote her a long and detailed letter about her deportation.[28] Beyond a limit where she was unreachable by anyone else, she could endure her abduction through the power of Elena's words. By repeating those words to her friend's face imagined before her, Ovazza became the voice of a victim's testimony and witnessed in the narration of Elena's harsh past the courage she needed to overcome her unbearable present. Furthermore, mirroring her friend meant for the hostage to be aware of herself as a potential testifier to her kidnapping. This identity gave her both the strength to resist and a sense of duty to testify for other abducted persons.

Although Ronchetti labelled Rossi di Montelera and Ovazza as "reporters of themselves," as if they were useless writers of already-written news stories, in their publications they both position themselves as authors of testimonial narratives which, unlike media, legal, and victimological discourses of the crime, give access to kidnapping through an incarnate and traumatized self. Trauma, perception, and language

136   Ransom Kidnapping in Italy

are indeed at the centre of their texts, which, together with Donatella Tesi Mosca's *Sindrome da sequestro* (Kidnapping syndrome, 1986), were written by the hostages before the second abduction crisis of the late 1980s. Tesi, unlike Ovazza and Rossi di Montelera, lived her ordeal as a complete and dramatic loss of identity. On 12 November 1981, two masked individuals captured her while she was driving home outside of Florence. They were two amateurs who came into contact in prison with Sardinian shepherds sentenced for ransom kidnapping. Once outside, they decided to emulate them by becoming abductors as well.[29] Tesi's family was well-to-do but not wealthy, and she never imagined she could be a possible target. She was working as an English teacher, and her husband was a notary. Her gruelling captivity lasted fifty-four days, which she spent hidden in a hole in the ground in a Tuscan forest. The physical deprivations she suffered exposed her to a complete psychological manipulation by her warder. On 5 January 1982, two days after her family paid a ransom of one billion lire, the Carabinieri found her abandoned in her hiding place near the small village of San Donnino in Certaldo (Tuscany). Back home, Tesi remained utterly under her warder's control. Two weeks after her liberation and while he was still a fugitive from justice, he called her and ordered her to help him escape from the police. Terrified, Tesi obeyed and met him. It was a trap. He later used their encounter to insinuate that she had been his accessory since the beginning of the kidnapping. For this reason, she was charged with connivance by the Italian courts (see chapter 6).

The abnormal relationship with her abductor is at the centre of Tesi's memoir. To confess even the most degrading moments of their bond is for the victim a way of being aware of herself and her syndrome. This self-awareness allows her to testify to others about her kidnapping and at different levels. "Above all this story of mine is a scream, a scream of anguish and rebellion by a woman who two years later still has not found her 'identity.' It is a document, a testimony that everyone should read to truly understand the meaning of the word 'Kidnapping,'" reads the preface of her memoir.[30] It is remarkable that Tesi defines her "screamed story" first as a document and then as a testimony. Her book is in fact a documented account. She backs up her words with a specialized language when necessary. Whenever she mentions decisions made by the magistracy, for example, she reports their official documentation written by the court of law or the attorney general of Florence. She also reports, in medical terms, the psychological diagnosis her lawyer used to demonstrate the state of mind she was in when she committed her "crime." If her traumatic lived experience confers authority on her to

Trauma and Language in the Kidnapping Victim Memoir   137

write her memoir, as Rossi di Montelera and Ovazza also state, knowledge gives her the authority to write a credible recounting. Tesi is able to convert her syndrome into the reliable testimony of her ordeal. Outside the psychological context to which it belongs, this term becomes in her writing the *objective* name for the consequences of an abduction she suffered in her own country, whose institutions, given their experience with the phenomenon, must finally be confronted with it.

Tesi's book came out between the two main kidnapping crises that Italy faced. Although Rossi di Montelera and Ovazza published their books when the phenomenon had reached its peak in the late 1970s, they were captured when the debate over the freezing of assets was not yet at the centre of the media narrative and the Pomarici line did not yet exist. Moreover, Turin, the city where they were both kidnapped, never adopted an anti-negotiation policy and instead hosted prominent soft line advocates such as the magistrate Marcello Maddalena. Tesi's kidnapping, in contrast, happened when the crime narrative coincided with the issue of ransom negotiations and in a region, Tuscany, that (together with Lombardy) was a stronghold for the freezing of assets position. The judge in charge of Tesi's case in fact did prevent her husband from paying the ransom, a decision that prolonged her captivity. In a powerful page from her book, Tesi condemns this decision and does so through a letter that she would have wanted to write to the judges while she was buried in the forest:

> By preventing the ransom payment, they were trampling the right to defend my life. This is what I thought and this I would have written. And I would also have written that the freezing of assets can be a valid measure on a moral level, because we should never cut deals with criminals, this is true. But I think that the State had already cut deals with criminals when the regulations on "pentiti" were enforced ... Article 2 of the Constitution guarantees human rights; article 3 further guarantees "the full development of [man's] personality" and recognizes "the right to family as a natural society" ... From this we understand that the right to life is not only natural and universal, but that it is also a guaranteed right in our Italian Constitution ... With what discretional power or constitutional law can judges and State authorities dispose of the life and fate of a person, without having any certainty about the outcome of the means employed?[31]

This poignant letter to the judges opens up a different perspective on the legal debate on kidnapping seen in chapter 4. Tesi's voice is that of an abducted citizen who, from the depths of her experience as a victim, drew upon the Italian Constitution to defy authorities. What her

138   Ransom Kidnapping in Italy

letter forces us to consider is no longer the relation between the state and criminals or between the state and families but the very relation between the state and the victims. According to Tesi, the *linea dura* goes against the Italian Constitution because it endangers the hostages and excludes them from the guarantees of the social contract. In her words, the kidnapped lose their rights as citizens. Tesi's testimonial narrative gives way to a fundamental question: Against whom does the state strengthen its authority through the freezing of assets? Focused on the penal code and on the negotiations, the legal narrative of the crime almost ignores the hostages' constitutional rights. *Sindrome da sequestro* thus testifies to an extreme experience that demands that the state question its justice. In other words, Tesi's written account reaches a civic and political dimension.

Testimonial Narratives of the 1990s

The second wave of kidnappings in the late 1980s had a significant impact on the production of victim testimonial narratives. The media coverage of Angela Casella's trip to Calabria and of the anti-kidnapping mobilization created an audience eager to read the accounts given by the liberated hostages. However, the media shaped not just the readership but the testimonial authorship as well. Indeed, the kidnapping books published in the early 1990s – unlike those written by Rossi di Montelera, Ovazza, and Tesi – were co-written by ex-hostages and journalists. Two of them also inspired the production of films made for television, creating a continuation between the news, the memoir, and the screen. Cesare Casella's *743 giorni lontano da casa* (743 days away from home, 1990) is a clear example.[32] Written in the first person with the help of the journalist Pino Belleri, the book vividly describes Cesare's unimaginable life in the caves where he was hidden and how he was able to resist unbearable and constrictive conditions. This account recalls Paul Getty's long interview published in 1974 by *Rolling Stone,* seen in chapter 2. Cesare, like Paul, expresses his rage against his kidnappers, who treated him like a dog, he states, and he does so with the tone and the language of a teenager who can finally speak out. *743 giorni lontano da casa* is an instant book published by the prominent publisher Rizzoli two months after Casella's liberation – a strategy of which Ronchetti would have approved – and it was meant to reach a wide public. The book cover shows a photo of Cesare with his well-known mother Angela, and a second edition rapidly followed. Rizzoli's editorial plan of echoing the media resonance of kidnapping cases is also recognizable in *Mio figlio Farouk: Anatomia di un sequestro* (My son Farouk: Anatomy of a kidnapping), Fateh Kassam's account of his son Farouk's abduction written by the journalist Marco Corrias.[33] Giuliano Ravizza (owner of the famous clothing brand Annabella), who in 1981 was abducted by the 'Ndrangheta in his hometown of Pavia (the Casellas' city), also told the story of his ordeal in a biography co-written with Roberto Alessi, published the same year Cesare Casella was freed.[34]

A further example of the second-wave kidnapping memoir is Dante Belardinelli's *Storia di un sequestro* (Story of a kidnapping, 1990), a book that, unlike the others, firmly supports the hard line's motivations for a "strong state" and even exhorts Italians "to be ready to brave tears and blood."[35] If the state gives in to blackmail, Belardinelli claims, the "danger to the collective would be extremely high." Compared to Casella's and Kassam's memoirs, Belardinelli's text considers kidnapping more at the individual, political, and existential levels. Moreover, although offering three divergent perspectives, Tesi, Belardinelli, and Soffiantini represent a common thread within the ransom kidnapping testimonial narrative. All three of them were abducted in the region of Tuscany. On 30 May 1989, three bandits captured Belardinelli in Settignano (Florence) as he drove home. A sixty-four-year-old man, he was the owner of a fairly well-known coffee company in Tuscany called Jolly Caffè.[36] His ordeal lasted sixty-four days, and his hiding place was a tent in a Tuscan forest. Belardinelli's abduction, unlike Tesi's, had an authentic Sardinian root and was marked by two dramatic moments. The first happened a few weeks after his capture. His abductors mutilated both of his ears and sent the cartilage to his family in order to stop them from collaborating with the magistracy and the police. The second occurred the night of 29 July, after the magistrate found out that the family was secretly negotiating and ordered the police to stop Belardinelli's sons-in-law, who were driving that night to meet the criminals and pay them five billion lire. Law enforcement confiscated the money and went to the appointment with the bandits. What was supposed to be a ransom payment became instead a firefight between the police and the kidnappers. Two abductors were killed and another two were injured; five police officers were also injured. At this point, Belardinelli's life was in severe danger. On 3 August, however, a special police corps (Nocs) was able to find him in a forest in the province of Grosseto (Tuscany). Belardinelli's liberation became an important success for the Florentine magistracy, which, by defeating Sardinian bandits present in Tuscany, demonstrated its hard line to be stronger than powerful criminals.

Dante Belardinelli is an Italian citizen who religiously bears witness to his kidnapping and to his possible "sacrifice" in the name of the state and his family. As opposed to Tesi, who testifies to her abduction as a traumatic loss of self, Belardinelli conceives of his ordeal as a test. He lived his captivity as an experience that taught him to pray and to rely upon Providence. During his confinement, he remained present to himself through an imaginary dialogue with his deceased mother and brother, who became his "angels." I consider them his witnesses.[37] His mother's words in particular provided a narration that allowed him to continue his existence within himself and ensured him a redeeming future. Inside his tent-cell, she tells him, "Everybody is waiting for you, you know? And you will see them again, be sure of it. It is what the Lord wants. You will become an important testimony of faith for all those who know and who do not know you."[38] Her words oriented him towards a hopeful tomorrow that his condition nevertheless rendered uncertain. In his memoir, this religiousness becomes the meaning of his tribulation. He envisions his kidnapping as an imposed passion from which he is ultimately relieved and to which he must testify. The authority his mother confers on him in this dialogue determines his way of being a testifier. Belardinelli is an author-survivor because of God's will. The religious dimension of his account is the heart of his book (not by chance published by Edizioni Paoline, a Catholic publisher). Unlike the other victims, particularly in contrast with the female victims, when Belardinelli recounts, he does not *witness* himself. That is to say that his memoir reflects not an awareness of his victimization but rather what he ideologically thinks about his kidnapping. My point is certainly not to belie his testimony but instead to understand the narrative register he uses to give an account of his plight.

Belardinelli's book differs in structure from the other memoirs examined here. It is a coauthored book, alternating chapters written in the first person with chapters written by an external narrator, journalist Giovanni Masotti. While the victim testifies to his ordeal, Masotti traces the exhausting negotiation between Belardinelli's family and the bandits. The presence of two narrators does not merely give voice to distinct points of view from which this kidnapping was experienced (the hostage and his family); it also highlights discordant approaches to it. The double viewpoints correspond to the opposing positions the victim and his family each had in relation to the magistracy. "My family members utterly disagreed with Judge Vigna's line, which prevented them from paying," Belardinelli writes in the introduction.[39] In contrast with his family, he fully approves of the freezing of assets ordered by the magistrate. More importantly, the way he disapproves of the negotiation sheds light on a crucial point of the hard line: to pay the ransom does not assure the freedom of the hostages but rather ensures an intolerable financial self-destruction for them and their families. Belardinelli's critique goes even further. He argues that it is an "irresponsible bias," and not emotions, that makes the blackmailed families believe that paying will free their kin. "My denunciation of my family's existent prejudices in the context of my kidnapping is only propositional: it aims to exclude the existence of these sentiments in all the other current cases of kidnapping," Belardinelli claims.[40]

The denouement of his kidnapping made the victim hold the magistrates who saved him in high esteem (Vigna, who resolved his case, was Belardinelli's close friend even before his abduction). He wanted his memoir, published in 1990, a year before the freezing of assets became law, to be a manifesto for the Florentine hard line in which the victim himself proposed that the government adopt its ideology. In his text, however, he confesses that in the most dramatic moment of his ordeal, after the two mutilations his warders simultaneously inflicted on him, he wrote a desperate letter to his kin asking them to pay for his freedom. He even suggested that his kidnappers let him go so that he could find the money they demanded. Even if what he lived through made him surrender to his kidnappers' will, Belardinelli refuses to look at himself from a victimized perspective and rather testifies to himself as a miraculously saved person. Faith is the cement of Belardinelli's beliefs and the lens through which he interprets his liberation. The religious way he testifies to his kidnapping is that authorized by his mother. Her gaze becomes, in his book, the viewpoint from which he witnesses himself.

With his *Il mio sequestro* (My kidnapping), Giuseppe Soffiantini not only overcomes the fear of dying in captivity without a story to bear witness to his end; he also shapes the future memory of his abduction.[41] One of the last in the history of the kidnapping phenomenon, Soffiantini's ordeal, as seen in chapter 4, questioned the 1991 freezing of assets law that put his life in danger. On the evening of 17 June 1997, three masked and armed men suddenly burst into his house in Manerbio, a small town close to Brescia (Lombardy), and snatched him. The owner of a clothing industry successful in and outside of Italy, Soffiantini was sixty-two and had undergone a difficult heart operation. His captivity lasted 237 days, which he spent hidden in a Tuscan forest in the province of Grosseto. He was released on 9 February 1998, after his family paid a ransom of five billion lire. His abductors were Giovanni Farina and Attilio Cubeddu, two outlaw Sardinian bandits who had settled in Tuscany and were considered among the most wanted by the police.[42] The abduction was marked by dramatic events, such as

142 Ransom Kidnapping in Italy

the death of a detective inspector and the partial mutilations of both the hostage's ears.[43]

Unlike other memoirs, Soffiantini's testimony attests to a strong need to separate his identity from that of his warders, to the point that it becomes the subject of his book's dedication: "so that the victims are not confused with the persecutors."[44] He wrote his memoir not to remember his ordeal, he makes clear, but rather to prevent historical memory from inverting the relationship of those involved. Soffiantini, in other words, testified to authenticate his kidnapped voice. In January 1998, in order to raise public opinion against the hard line carried out by the state and magistracy up to then, his persecutors inflicted a second mutilation on him by cutting off part of his right ear.[45] The kidnappers chose to send the "macabre message" to the Tg5 (private television Mediaset newscast) director, Enrico Mentana, and made the hostage write a letter directly to the journalist. As soon as Mentana received the missive, he read its most significant parts on his newscast.[46] In his book, Soffiantini speaks against those who doubt his account of the kidnapping: "So, once and for all, these words are authentic in the fullest sense of the term, as were authentic Aldo Moro's prison letters ... These words are mine alone."[47] Remarkably, the authority to testify before public opinion as to the authenticity of his letter to Tg5 derives from Soffiantini's identification with Aldo Moro.

Comparing himself with Moro, Soffiantini confesses that he is conscious of the differences in their intellectual statures, thus drawing a distinction between the public importance of the DC president's letters and the private usefulness of his own. The matter of authenticity, though, illuminates another fundamental aspect of his memoir. Soffiantini's is the testimony of an Italian citizen who bears witness to his forest-prison on the border of civilization, where nobody could reach him and from where masked criminals – full of hate towards the state – blackmailed his family by using victimized words that belonged to him. Through the messages the hostages write to their kin, even if composed under duress or by dictation, they are authentically communicating with the external world and imploring for help. In Soffiantini's view, the correlate of a state that freezes the assets of blackmailed families is a state that freezes the victims' desperate words. As seen in chapter 4, in his analysis of Moro's letters the historian Miguel Gotor comes to the same conclusion. For Soffiantini, the state refuses to listen to the individual voices of its citizens. He considers the hard line to be absolutely inadequate because, he states, it focuses on "the spectacular defence of an abstract state, not conceived as the sum of all the individuals belonging to it."[48] Soffiantini, in contrast to Belardinelli, perceives the state to be the sum of its individual citizens rather than the totality of its collectivity:

> The State, the strong State, with valid ethical motivations, is founded on the protection of human life, not on the spectacularity of actions to be shown off on television news. "The surgery was a success, but the patient died." Citizens rejoice when they see the hostage freed ... and smiling together with his family ... To snatch a person from the national community to which he belongs is a deep wound for the State. This wound sutures itself only with the restitution of the free life to the family and national community. Otherwise the State has lost, clamorously lost. No judge, *carabiniere*, or minister can sleep easy when he has sent a gang of kidnappers to jail but has attended the State funeral of the dead hostage. It is a wound that does not close.[49]

Soffiantini shifts the concept of the "strong state," as we found it in Belardinelli's testimony, from being a guarantor of the collective safety to a safeguard of single citizens. In his words, the kidnapped person is a concrete fragment of the state in which all citizens are entirely present. To sacrifice the hostage means therefore to sacrifice society as a whole. From this perspective ransom kidnapping becomes political. Finally, the passage echoes the identification the victim had with Moro. If the ideologists of the hard line look at the DC president's case as the victory of the reason of state against the Red Brigades, in his memoir Soffiantini considers Moro's sacrifice as its defeat. An authentic author-survivor, he attributes his release to the suspension of the freezing of assets required by the public prosecutor's office of Brescia, which, adopting the soft line, saved his life.

Being a Hostage

The first noteworthy element of the kidnapping victim memoir is that it is written exclusively after the abducted are released. While held hostage, the kidnapped are generally not allowed to read or write. Therefore, we cannot frame these texts as prison writings or diaries, even if they share some elements with those two genres, such as the pressure of a totalizing authority under which the imprisoned self writes or, in certain cases, a chronological reconstruction of time. Being a prisoner and being a hostage are not the same thing. We find an illuminating distinction between these two conditions in Guy Delisle's graphic memoir *Hostage* (2017), in which the Canadian cartoonist illustrates and recounts in first person the ransom kidnapping of Christophe André, a

144   Ransom Kidnapping in Italy

French administrator for Doctors Without Borders abducted in 1997 by Chechens in the Caucasus. Two weeks into his capture, André is lying on a mattress on the ground in a dark and empty room, his wrist handcuffed to a radiator:

> Being a hostage is worse than being in prison. In prison, at least you know why you're locked up. There's a reason. Whether it's right or wrong, at least there's a reason. But being a hostage is just bad luck. Wrong place, wrong time. In prison, you know when you'll get out, the exact date ... You can count down the days you've got left to go. Here, all I can do is count the days that have passed without knowing when it'll be over.[50]

Delisle places these words in a series of cartoons that move the reader's eyes from the hostage's body, to a corner of the ceiling that he is staring at, to a light bulb that is always turned off, back to his body, and finally to a door whose handle's "click clack" interrupts his thoughts. The memoirs of the kidnapped, even without Delisle's oppressive and detailed monochromatic cartoons, give the reader the same claustrophobic sensation of being closed inside a hiding place where nothing happens and time does not pass. For more than four hundred pages, Delisle envisions the hostage's timeless condition by illustrating the restrictive space, his minimal movements, and especially his never-ending thoughts.[51] The narratives of kidnapping memoirs more broadly put us in the mind of the abducted as well. Any small noise or word that the hostages perceive or a meal that they receive is a way out from their imagination that brings both them and us back to the emptiness of their captivity. The reader endures with the victims the impossibility of projecting oneself into the future, which comes from waiting without knowing when (and almost if) the release will take place.

Nevertheless, unlike André, the hostages of Italian ransom kidnapping cannot define their condition as "bad luck," unless we consider living in Italy between the late 1960s and the late 1990s as being in a "wrong place, wrong time." This is to say that being a hostage of abduction in Italy has never been an accidental condition. It was instead the consequence of a systematic criminal phenomenon that for years blackmailed the citizens of the country. One could retort that these were only privileged citizens, who for the first time lived the socio-economic reality of the peninsula and therefore its "history." However, the approach that looks at ransom kidnapping as a phenomenon linked to social class struggle does not take into consideration the fact that the victims were not always affluent and that behind the abductions were criminal organizations. Conversely, in their accounts the abducted speak out as individual members of a state in which this crime was able to succeed. If in relation to their kidnappers the hostages, like André, find no reasons that give sense to their condition – money, in fact, just objectifies them – then in relation to the state the hostages demand justice. As seen earlier, with their stories the kidnapped give voice to all the victims of abduction in Italy, and the memory of their personal experience reaches the level of a sociopolitical testimony.

Another central element of the kidnapping memoir, absent in Delisle's *Hostage*, is the relationship the abducted develop with their warders. Unable to understand the language of his kidnappers, André wasn't exposed to what the hostages depict as the most devastating aspect of their captivity.[52] Psychiatrists recognize that, unlike in prisons or in concentration camps, the victims of abductions forge a personal relationship with their enemies due to the loneliness of their experience. The isolation of captivity and the negotiation with the external world are two distinctive conditions of ransom kidnapping that create a unique bond between hostages and their persecutors. They both want the same thing – for the captivity to end as a result of the kidnapped person's families' collaboration – but they are inside an imbalanced and violent relationship, in which the victim occupies an extremely psychologically and bodily vulnerable position. The next part of the chapter analyses how the total isolation of the kidnapped, both communicative and perceptual, brings the victims to depend emotionally on their persecutors for survival. It is to the dangerous closeness to their kidnappers that the abducted testify. Writing their memoirs, as we shall see, becomes a way through which to liberate themselves from the hostage/warder bond and to tell the external world what being kidnapped means.

The Isolation of Captivity

For the kidnapped, one of the most intolerable aspects of their segregation is silence. "I am not a hero. I'm a normal person who fell into abnormal circumstances. The fight is entirely inside that deaf cube of solitary abnormality."[53] In Soffiantini's words, resisting the condition of being captured means overcoming the artificial absence of any possibility of being heard. If the hiding place deprives the victims of their visibility (as we shall see in chapter 6), it also denies their audibility. Making the hostages inaudible, the cell, the cave, and the holes in the ground prevent their reciprocal communication with the world. Forced by their persecutors to not produce any noise that could attract outside attention, the victims are deprived of the possibility of hearing normally as well. The lack of acoustic perception – active (listening) and

146   Ransom Kidnapping in Italy

passive (being audible) – disorients the hostages in both time and space, as Carla Ovazza notes:

> It's necessary for me to pay a lot of attention in order to not lose my sense of time during this never-ending night and to try to maintain some contact with the world of reality, the world of the "others." I try to catch all the sounds in order to situate myself in space. But the silence is absolute. No radio, no human voice ... The hours pass slowly, and I realize how difficult it is to count them when you no longer have any point of reference with the outside, when nothing interrupts the silence, when you can neither read nor speak and you can no longer see the sun go down.[54]

Like Soffiantini, Ovazza here pictures the total separation of her hiding place from the world as a result of an absolute silence that prevents her from both locating herself in space and measuring the passing of time. Without any interruptions that hearing would provoke, she is overwhelmed by an unlimited no-place and no-time. In such a condition, prison, night, and silence become the same.

In complete acoustic isolation, the ego of the kidnapped person has no external points of reference capable of delimiting the corrosive power of temporal and spatial emptiness. If, according to Sigmund Freud, "the ego is first and foremost a bodily ego," meaning that it is derived from bodily sensations and is therefore a mental projection of the surface of the body, during the time of captivity the ego finds itself deprived of its sources.[55] For this reason, the victims experience a sort of vacuous eternity. As Ovazza states, it is the impossibility of reading and talking that particularly prevents hostages from perceiving the passing of time. In her words, the lack of language perception corresponds at an acoustic level to the lack of sun perception at the visual level. Linguistic silence thus obscures her ego. Without mediating their selves through written or spoken words from the outside world, the abducted cannot, to put it in Merleau-Pontian terms, *alienate* into language – that is, they cannot experience themselves as audible (or sensible) through language. Being confined is indeed, for the victims, an exclusion from a communicative dimension, in which the other – writer, listener, or speaker – represents a viewpoint *in* language from which the self can reflexively locate itself inside a narration. The split between bodily perception and language thus prevents the ego from experiencing the impression of movement that being situated inside a narration allows. The result of this split is for the victims a sensation of frozen time. Furthermore, as we shall see, the exclusion from a communicative language is for the kidnapped the most anguishing absence of a witness.

Since the captured generally cannot engage in either reading or writing, they often beg for written language from the outside. In some cases, the persecutors allow them to read old magazines and even books. When this happens, the hostages read the same pages over and over to the point of memorizing them. They even read the want ads, and every word becomes a means of being in touch with something external to their minds. For example, Rossi di Montelera is able to read a few newspapers and books. Remarkably, every time he finishes reading them, he starts to mentally translate them into several languages. Translation gives agency to his ego, a sensation of change, of movement, and therefore the perception of passing time. It is also a way of mediating his self from one language to another. Having found in his pocket a pen and a tiny piece of paper, Rossi di Montelera is also able to secretly write a few lines. These written words are for him extremely important during his ordeal. He calls them his "breviario di soccorso" (rescue breviary), which he reads every time he feels desperate:

> On my slip of paper there is a "paragraph" entitled "Death" ... The brief paragraph starts like so: "Death: a necessary event that concludes a transitory life and brings one to dock at the port of arrival, eternal happiness. The trust that the problem here will resolve itself with time, so force yourself to resist: to think every day only of arriving at the evening." Then follow other notes on the subject. I held death near to me for a good deal of time.[56]

This is the only sentence written during his captivity that Rossi di Montelera records in his memoir. The astonishing aspect of the "paragraph" is that the victim remains outside of it. He is never the subject, and the verbs are conjugated either in the third person or in the infinitive. Only when he gives himself a command ("force yourself") does he appear among the words. Nevertheless, this impersonal language is for his ego an external perspective that helps it to resist and to locate death outside of himself. In other words, his breviary is a means of preventing his ego's annihilation.

As we saw with Ovazza, timelessness and spacelessness hang over the victims, whose egos, feeling threatened and in danger, suffer an unbearable distress. This emerges from Donatella Tesi Mosca's memoir as well:

> Where was I? I felt a great weight on me, an enormous load of anguish and the sensation of being alone on the island of my own soul. And beyond this isolation there was a whole world, down there, among those little

lights, that was living indifferently. People that got up in the morning and went to work and went to bed at night unaware of my drama. How was it possible that a few kilometres away there were people not contaminated by this suffering and loneliness of mine? I felt at my back an absolute emptiness, as if nothing I had done or lived still existed and everything had to be reinvented. And this dismayed me enormously.[57]

During her captivity, Tesi internalizes her isolation to the point that it contaminates her self. Not only can she not perceive the passing of time, but she also finds it impossible to imagine that outside in the world time can carry on indifferent to her situation. The timelessness of imprisonment becomes her self's timelessness. At her back she no longer has a story, meaning that what she lived before her abduction is no longer accessible. Hidden nowhere, Tesi finds herself with a frozen ego – that is, without the memory of a lived time, which she now has to reinvent. In order to overcome this total separation from her life, Tesi needs to reach a communicative language:

> I asked if I could write something, a diary for example, but it was brusquely forbidden to me. I was told that there could be no trace of what was going on inside the hole … But I insisted, because I needed to write. I felt incapable of resisting if I was deprived of even the possibility of expressing myself. It was my only way of communicating and being able to remember later. I wanted to write, to remember my family with written words, to prevent everyone that I loved from becoming lost, vanishing. I wanted to resist all that violence by writing everything that was happening to me, to resist every chance of forgetting, because perhaps one day I would overcome what I was suffering but I could never allow myself to forget the evil that was done to me.[58]

Writing represents for Tesi a hold on the outside world that keeps her from being submerged by her captivity. Without the self-reflexivity that the presence of the other (a listener) in a communicative dimension allows – that is, a way of being linguistically visible – Tesi cannot situate her self in a narration. In the lack of this linguistic mediation, the emptiness of her hiding place erodes her ego. In such a condition, she feels that both the past and the future of her story fade from her memory.[59] Like for Ovazza, the split between perception – in Tesi's case passive perception – and language obscures the victim's ego.

The hostages' exclusion from a communicative dimension is thus a rift between their body and language. Completely isolated, generally unable to read or write, the victims desperately require the presence of their warders with whom to speak. "My heart is thumping, I'm afraid to ask him to stay a little while longer to keep me company, but I need to speak, I need to hear speaking and feel near me the presence of a human being, even if he is a bandit, even if I run the risk of him mistreating and hurting me," reads Ovazza's *Cinque ciliege rosse*.[60] Her wish for an interlocutor exceeds the risk and the threat that this bandit represents for her. What the passage highlights, though, is Ovazza's need to experience language as a sentient-sensible subject, to perceive her warder's words and to be perceivable in words by him. Without a dialogue with the perpetrators, the kidnapped cannot inhabit language through an incarnate dialectic; rather, they inhabit it at the mental level. To put it differently, lacking communication, they live their linguistic nature exclusively as an inner dimension and not as a medium with the world: "I felt terribly the need to speak in order to escape from the mental isolation, that is, in order to not go crazy," Tesi writes. "In fact, I thought I would go crazy if I were alone, and that as long as there was someone near me seeing what I was seeing and feeling what I was feeling, I wouldn't go crazy. And my warder let me speak. I unloaded on him my need to communicate."[61] Talking with their kidnappers is the victims' only means of overcoming their minds' isolation, a condition which is extremely frightening because it leads to insanity. As Donatella Tesi Mosca points out in the previous lines, the reciprocal communication with her warder allows her to share a common world with him and thus to be linguistically in touch with something other than her mental space. According to Don Ihde's definition of inner language as "the imaginative correlate of spoken language"[62] by which "I am aware of myself," the spoken presence of the kidnapper is the perceptual correlate for the kidnapped of their own imaginary presence to themselves.[63] In other words, perceiving language is for the victims a way of being present not only imaginatively but also physically. Moreover, in the absence of reciprocity with the world, the hostages live their bodies as merely biological. As Elaine Scarry would say, in such a condition their voice is the last source of "self-extension." Thus, the voice is the self's way of occupying a space larger than the bio-body and its means of transcending "the edges of the body it will die with."[64] Speaking is, according to Scarry, a mode of survival.

As mentioned earlier, the total exclusion from an external language is for the abducted the most anguishing form that the absence of a witness takes. Rossi di Montelera's testimony gives us a perfect example of this absence. He recounts that after his capture, the kidnappers bring him to his hiding place, which is a cell at the end of an underground passage. When they block the entrance, he remains inside this cold and

150 Ransom Kidnapping in Italy

damp room with two persecutors. While one of them tries to convince him that they are in a cave and tells him that he is the boss, the other one does not speak. Rossi di Montelera starts to have a conversation with the boss, who asks him several questions. "I absolutely did not want to get to know him in that moment, so that he could not feel his conscience cleared and to save my dignity as a victim before him," he writes in his memoir.[65] Rossi di Montelera, who has just become a hostage, is capable of protecting himself from his perpetrator. He is in fact still connected to the world outside and therefore present to himself from an external perspective, which allows him to maintain his identity intact. When the boss leaves the hiding place, though, Rossi di Montelera remains alone with the silent warder. The absence of the persecutor with whom he had a conversation becomes dangerous for the hostage. Having spoken with him means Rossi di Montelera knows his voice and therefore is familiar with this extraneous and powerful figure. "What would happen now that I remained by myself with another warder, whose voice I did not even know, and who, having to stay in that place for a long time, would certainly get nervous and could do anything to me without witnesses?"[66] To have the boss next to him represents for the victim the possibility of being updated about the negotiations and receiving information from the outside world. However, his words depict the scene at a different level: leaving the cell, the boss takes language away from the hostage. In the moment he finds himself enclosed with a silent warder, Rossi di Montelera lives in flesh the exclusion from a communicative dimension, the correlate of which is the lack of witnesses. Feeling completely in the hands of his warder,

> it was therefore necessary to test the warder and try to establish with him that minimum of conversation that would keep both of us from going crazy and create a minimum of reciprocal trust. I have always been convinced that a man, bestial as he may be, is unlikely to kill someone with whom he has talked about this and that, unless he is under the effects of alcohol or madness … I asked him if it was the first time that he guarded a kidnapped person … he told me that it gave him a horrible impression, and he begged me not to talk to him about the subject again. I felt on that occasion a trace of humanity, that positive element in each man that I was also searching for in him to reassure myself and build a minimum of security.[67]

It is this need for a dialogue – to which all the kidnap victims testify in their memoirs – that exposes them to their perpetrators. As Judith Herman underlines in *Trauma and Recovery*, "prisoners of conscience," who are trained to deal with the worst possible imprisonment, constantly "seek to maintain a communication with a world outside the one in which they are confined" because they "are well aware of the danger of ordinary human engagement with their captors."[68] Lacking self-reflexivity and terrified, the kidnapped prefer the company of their persecutors to loneliness. In such a condition, not only do they depend on their abductors "for survival and bodily needs," but, as we shall see, they also develop "an emotional dependence upon their captors."[69]

The Trauma of Captivity

At an emotional level, the complete isolation of captivity is for the kidnapped an absolute loneliness that, as a second imprisonment, keeps them trapped in and exposed to what we can call the *inner front* of their abduction – that is, its psychological front. After the initial trauma of being suddenly captured, the kidnapped live the chain of traumatic events that kidnapping imposes – forced deprivation of liberty, physical abuse, change of hiding places, being chained, being threatened with death and mutilation, humiliations, and sensorial deprivation – with a traumatized self, meaning that they endure captivity with a "disorganized system of self-defense" and with a feeling of "intense fear, helplessness, loss of control, and threat of annihilation."[70] Seen from a traumatic perspective, the lack of communication with the outside world is for the captured a complete lack of external holds that leaves them *alone inside* and makes them feel as though their ego is on the edge of a cliff. In his memoir, Rossi di Montelera vividly describes this feeling:

> Once, years ago, while I was climbing the Dolomites, I found myself stuck on the side of the mountain. I was no longer able to go either forward or back, and I was holding myself up on tiny footholds. After a few tries, I slowly felt my strength fail, I let go of my grip, and I fell. The cord held me. The sensation that I was now experiencing was sort of the same: feeling your strength and defences fail you, and there is nothing you can do about it, no foothold to grab onto, and feeling yourself plummet into empty space, into desperation, with a sense of anguish and fear. But while I was falling in the mountain there was the cord that would have stopped me ... here there was no cord. I was alone with myself, and only in myself could I find the strength to overcome this, or, better, to not die.[71]

Among the experiences he had in his life, that of falling while mountain climbing is for Rossi di Montelera the most appropriate

152   Ransom Kidnapping in Italy

image with which to envision his traumatized ego. His is not just a metaphor; rather, the present collapse of his system of self-defence reminds him of a physical sensation he had in the past. Unlike on the mountain, though, Rossi di Montelera is here completely alone and therefore without anything that can save him from falling. What I called the *inner front* of kidnapping is exactly the internal downfall that the hostages seek to resist with all their strength. The exhausting adaptation of the self to the situation and its reaction to trauma are an unbearable source of anguish and the most dangerous threat of annihilation.[72]

In the existing literature, few studies analyse the effects of the trauma of ransom kidnapping. For this reason, researchers have justifiably investigated this specific type of victimization by comparing it to other situations that present conditions similar to those of the kidnap victims. In their "Le dinamiche relazionali nel sequestro di persona" (Relational dynamics in kidnapping), for example, Salvatore Luberto and Antonio Manganelli examine captivity in Italian ransom kidnapping through the lens of works focused on concentration camp survivors, hospitalized people, and prison inmates.[73] According to their study (and others), what distinguishes ransom kidnapping from other traumatic events – that is, what makes its victims' ordeal unique – is the type of relationship the hostages have with their warders. "The 'relationship' is necessary to maintain a sense of one's own identity, even if in the ways allowed by the particular situation," state Luberto and Manganelli, "because the conservation of some relational activity is tied to the possibility of satisfying basic needs and organizing some defences able to contain the possible devastating consequences, also at a personological level, of a prolonged kidnapping."[74] The hostage-perpetrator relationship is thus necessary because the victims need their warders in order to resist an inner disaster. Luberto and Manganelli explore this relationship, departing from analyses of the warder-prisoner relationships in concentration camps. They base their analogy in particular on psychologist Bruno Bettelheim's works *Surviving, and Other Essays* and "Individual and Mass Behavior in Extreme Situations," which explore the experience of concentration camp survivors.[75] Luberto and Manganelli recognize that, like the prisoners Bettelheim observes, kidnap victims activate defence mechanisms that lead them to identify with their persecutors. Yet isolation and loneliness, they note, are the two elements that mark the hostage-warder relationship in the abduction. This emerges from the victims' memoirs as well. Describing her captivity, for example, Ovazza writes, "I can't stand it anymore, I feel sick, and

I desperately call again because this loneliness has become intolerable to me, because I need to pour out my sorrow to another human being, be he friend or foe, as long as he listens, as long as he makes me forget for a few moments the terrible thoughts that torment me."[76] Without the presence of another human being, the inner front of her kidnapping – its psychological dimension – is unbearable for her to the point that it threatens her more than any deprivations she suffers inside the hiding place.

The exposure to traumatic events – from the position of being alone – is therefore recognized by both specialists and the abducted alike not as *a* condition but rather as *the* condition of the kidnap victims. It is in this emotional context that the relationship with their warders becomes necessary. Rudas, Pintor, and Mascia give an enlightening definition of this type of relationship, calling it "solitudine con il nemico" (loneliness with the enemy).[77] The hostages prefer to share this loneliness with a bandit than to remain by themselves:

> One day, though, there was something new that for me was petrifying ... after the usual conversation, the "Veneto" told me that they would leave me alone. I would have more space, more air, and more comforts. For me, loneliness meant something else: I could no longer exchange a word with anybody, and whatever happened I would be alone and bound. At least the warder made up for my inability to move or act. What's worse, I was sure that as long as there was someone with me, I didn't risk being left to die of hunger, abandoned, or killed by gas. From the moment I was left alone, anything could happen. My pleas came to nothing. I was truly terrorized, I begged them not to leave me alone because if anything happened I wouldn't be able to save myself.[78]

When his kidnapper announces to Rossi di Montelera that he will be left alone for the rest of his confinement, he is frightened. This happens a few days after his capture, during which time he is never by himself but rather shares his cell with a warder. If the latter's presence means for the victim salvation from what his persecutors have threatened him with so far, and therefore from external incidents, it also represents a hold on reality that saves him from the inner dimension of captivity. Talking with a warder is in fact a way to remove what he calls the "spettro di questa solitudine"[79] (spectre of this loneliness), which, without the reflexivity that the dialogue with his captor allows, is lived by the victim as a waking nightmare. In other words, for Rossi di Montelera, remaining alone means living his captivity at the mercy of his unconscious.

154   Ransom Kidnapping in Italy

Luberto and Manganelli note that the abducted establish a dual relationship with their persecutors.[80] In his study, Bettelheim recognizes regression to be one of the defence mechanisms brought on by captivity. The dependency on the warders reproduces in concentration camp prisoners a condition they have already lived in their infancy and thus returns them to a stage that precedes the development of their ego.[81] This psychological infantilism – which is an adaptation of the self – makes the prisoners introject values and attitudes that belong to their persecutors. If on the one hand these introjections are a defence mechanism against the soldiers' power, on the other hand, they lead the victims to identify with their warders.[82] In her work *The Ego and the Mechanisms of Defense* (1936), Anna Freud describes this mechanism as "identification with the aggressor" and states that "there are occasions when it combines with other mechanisms to form one of the ego's most potent weapons in its dealing with external objects which arouse its anxiety."[83] Briefly put, for Anna Freud this mechanism allows the attacked person to shift from a passive to an active position. The lack of any possibility of reacting or escaping makes identification with the dreaded aggressor the only safe place for the threatened ego. In the case of prisoners this identification happens at a more impersonal level, whereas in the case of the kidnapped it happens at a personal level. Isolation and loneliness, as Luberto and Manganelli state, encourage the kidnapped to establish a transference relationship with their warders.

In their memoirs, all kidnap victims identify one of their kidnappers as "il buono" (the good one) and see him not as a bandit but rather as a human being. They also recognize in themselves the psychological regression described by the specialists. In her memoir, for example, Tesi writes,

> I felt so desperate, I was in such a situation of dependency in relation to my warder that I was acting like little kids do with adults on whom they depend to survive. I was reduced to being like a two- or three-year-old child who needs her parents for her most basic needs.[84]

Strikingly, Tesi lives her regression not only emotionally but physically as well. Talking about her abductor, she writes, "Suddenly, he seemed to me a very big, tall, and burly man; his feet seemed huge to me, and I had this sensation throughout the kidnapping, this impression of being physically very small and fragile compared to him."[85]

Both Tesi and Soffiantini recount that the first time they encounter their warders after their liberation, they find these men's bodies to be smaller than during captivity. Soffiantini describes seeing his warder in prison:

> Farina is a little fifty-year-old man. He speaks in a low voice, with a Tuscan and not Sardinian inflection. In the forest I imagined him like a half giant, firm, and without inflection. Here, in prison, he is ten years older than what I had thought in my den. I reiterate that I was never allowed to see either my kidnappers or my warders throughout my captivity, for the simple reason that I was hooded, and when they allowed me to take it off, they were wearing masks.[86]

The disproportion with which the victim imagines his captor shows how, inside their hiding places, the hostages live their psychological regression to the point that they embody it. Also indicative is the fetal position they often assume after humiliating situations. However, it is the way in which they respond to their warders' behaviour that most reveals their infantilism:

> One of the things that I feared the most was in fact his silence. When he was silent it meant that he was mad at me, and his silence had to represent for me a punishment ... And he was silent for several hours: he punished me, he punished me with what made me suffer the most, destroying the bridge that I had created with him, between my and his isolation. I slammed into his silence and cried in silence.[87]

In this passage, Tesi's warder is a severe parent that punishes her through his silence. Her crying vividly shows her complete emotional dependence on this sadistic stranger. In his *Victim Responses to Terror*, Martin Symonds considers this type of attachment a "traumatic psychological infantilism," which "compels victims to cling to the very person who is endangering their lives."[88]

The dual relationship Lumberto and Manganelli describe in their study as well as the traumatic infantilism Symonds examines is known in psychiatric literature as Stockholm syndrome, a psychological phenomenon that involves both victim and persecutor and is particularly evident in kidnapping.[89] Judith Herman, for example, not only recognizes that prolonged segregation, lived in isolation and with fear of death, creates a "traumatic bonding" – that is, a "basic unit of survival" – between captor and victim, but she also underlines how this attachment "is the rule rather than the exception."[90] According to Herman, this bond explains the incomprehensible behaviour of some hostages, who, after their release, "defend their persecutors, visit them in prisons and even raise money for their defense."[91] Symonds specifies, though, that it is not enough to consider this syndrome as an identification with a persecutor. It is more likely that this type of bond happens when the hostage is used as means of blackmail: "The suffering of the victim is the leverage used for negotiations with a third party. Hostages, in their psychological traumatized state, never view negotiations for their release as benevolent. The victim would immediately give all for his release, but he interprets and experiences any negotiation as endangering him."[92] Symonds finds ransom kidnapping to be the perfect example of this type of situation: "He then perceives negotiations, especially if protracted, as indifference, hostility, and rejection – non-loving and life-threatening behaviour – by the very people who are negotiating for his release. This reinforces the pathological transference already developed by the prolonged exposure to the terrorist."[93]

Negotiations play a crucial role in the development of Stockholm syndrome because they make the victims feel exposed to danger even more than does being in the hands of their persecutors. Seen from the perspective of the kidnapped, the people that threaten their lives are not the kidnappers but rather whoever has to pay the ransom. The persecutors are instead perceived as those who will free them if they obtain what they want. Abducted and abductors thus have a common goal: the payment of the ransom. For Symonds, it is exactly this connection against the external world that aggravates the psychological transfer, which causes the hostages to blame their saviours. Moreover, for Herman, subduing the victims is the captors' main intention. "Captivity, which brings the victim into prolonged contact with the perpetrator, creates a special type of relationship, one of coercive control," she writes.[94] Thus, the traumatic bond is a tool the kidnappers use to obtain the control they seek. While the psychiatrists offer different interpretations of the traumatic condition in kidnapping, they commonly overlook the link between trauma and language that the kidnap victims' memoirs instead illuminate.

The Language of Ransom Kidnapping

In the survivors' memoirs, the relationship with the warders is at the centre of the kidnap victims' testimony and is undoubtedly the most upsetting component of their ordeal. They find it difficult and at the same time fundamental to make their readers understand the connection they have with their perpetrators and what the latter represent during their captivity. For this reason, their testimonies are a unique window onto the relational dynamics between hostage and captor described by the specialists as loneliness with the enemy, dual relationships, identification with the aggressor, psychological infantilism, traumatic bonds, and Stockholm syndrome. The voices of the kidnapped provide both new elements and a lived perspective on an otherwise unreachable condition for those who remain external to this type of forced relationship. Their viewpoint is thus essential for imagining situations that researchers themselves have found difficult to reproduce in their psychological experiments, given the uncontrollable and dangerous behaviours of the people involved and observed.[95]

In her memoir, for example, Carla Ovazza dramatically testifies to being an instrument of negotiations and to how this position aggravates the traumatic bond she has with her warder. Her testimony clearly depicts her persecutors' awareness of this link and their intentional use of negotiations as a technique of subjugation:

> I don't feel any resentment towards my warders. Is this perhaps the consequence of the conversations we've had? After all, aside from the blows during the trip and the wax poured in my ears, aside from almost unbearable sanitary conditions and the intense cold, they treated me less badly than I feared ... Maybe they really are victims like they told me.[96]

For the reader, the most disturbing aspect of the victims' accounts is the gap between what their words reveal about their ordeal and the way in which, from inside their captivity, they perceive it. Ovazza here recounts the third day of her imprisonment, and even after a number of traumatic events she cannot hate her perpetrators. On the contrary, she feels pity for them. Ovazza's feeling is linked not to the lack of traumatic severity in what she suffers up to this moment of her captivity but rather to her inability to defend herself. After the first three days, her persecutors announce that they will be liberating her. She spends forty-eight hours euphoric only to then discover that the promise is in reality a lie. Her kidnappers blame the police and her family, telling Ovazza that because her kin refused to pay, their boss ordered them to kill her the next morning. Additionally, they sadistically explain to her exactly how they will murder her. Convinced that she is about to die, she spends her "last night" terrified. This, too, has been another of her captors' lies:

> So the miracle came true! I am no longer going to die! It is an indescribable moment, wonderful, it is a return to life. Moved, I cry. I do not ask for explanations or clarifications. I do not try to understand. I feel reborn. The extraordinary announcement of the unhoped-for rebirth had kind of

thrilled me ... Having come so close to death has kind of traumatized me, has upset me, and, swept up by the joy of this rebirth, it takes me a while to realize the fact that nothing positive has been done and to return to the sad reality of this prison, of this wait, of this feeling of complete impotence. In my mind I recall the nightmare hours spent during this unforgettable night. They have been anguished hours, terrible, dominated by terror.[97]

In less than a day, Ovazza's persecutors bring her from feeling free to facing death. She intensely lives these two extremes as real, and her mind is now utterly upset. Aware of the traumatic bond she has established with them, the kidnappers intentionally use negotiations to aggravate it. By announcing her imminent execution and then delaying it, they make her view them as merciful and as those who, unlike the external world, want to save her from death. The kidnappers next start to threaten Ovazza with mutilation in the event that her family does not collaborate. Instead of protecting herself from the relationship with her captors, Ovazza, who at this point desperately needs a hold to resist the collapse of her mind, begs them for company. We can witness the result of her warders' technique:

Without realizing, I grew fond of this unknown individual and don't feel any resentment towards him. Certainly, it is he who passes on the boss's messages, but he had also addressed me with words of compassion and almost a sense of humanity. He always intervened in the moments when I was worse off. If I could not talk to him any longer, the already long days would seem even more unbearable ... He always knows how to tell me those half words that give back to me a ray of hope, he at least made me understand how hard it is for him to carry out the boss's orders ... What a joy, it's him again! Sitting on the bed, I ask him why he hadn't come anymore.[98]

Heavily traumatized at the beginning of her imprisonment, Ovazza spends the time of her captivity in constant need of her abductors' presence. She develops an aggravated Stockholm syndrome, which her words portray in exactly the same manner as the specialists describe it. She in fact establishes a dual relationship with one of her kidnappers, who becomes for her the saviour and the "buono," and she begins to feel affection for him.[99] Ovazza's testimony shows how the victims' self-defence mechanism is an incredibly powerful weapon in the hands of their aware kidnappers.

Soffiantini explicitly refers to Stockholm syndrome three times and even gives a Christian interpretation of it:

I discover that love is an advantage and, in a situation of extreme isolation, of absolute domination by a brute force, it transforms itself into a weapon of hope. Hope like action, not only hope like prayer. Prayer, during a kidnapping, is love that moves, acts, it forces the other to listen to you. And Lord knows how important it is to receive attention from your warders. I believe that in Stockholm syndrome love becomes a secret agent, the victim's ally, which helps turn the game towards his side ... That "turn the other cheek" had always appeared like an allegory, a symbol, a good intention destined to remain so. As if Jesus were suggesting to you, under the table: "I say it, but it's not mandatory to do it" ... Isolation ... changes the nature of love and hate.[100]

Love and prayers are for Soffiantini the substitute for the movement and the power he lacks. He does not perceive the effects of Stockholm syndrome he recognizes in himself as negative. Instead, they become his "weapon of hope." As Anna Freud states about the identification with the aggressor, these same symptoms are a way of shifting from a passive to an active position. Inside his hiding place he tries to transform the syndrome into action by attempting to convert his warder from evil to good. He does this through an intense dialogue he establishes with the warder that makes Soffiantini trust their relationship and believe that he has some small measure of control. However, what is striking about Soffiantini's case is that in 2007 – ten years after his kidnapping and eight years after the first publication of his testimony – Soffiantini published at his own expense a collection of poems written by his abductor Giovanni Farina.[101] While the latter is in prison, Soffiantini decides to meet him and learns of Farina's passion for writing. Remembering the many times he asked permission to write poetry during his own captivity, Soffiantini decides to realize Farina's desire and publishes his book.[102] His is perhaps another attempt to convert his kidnapper and to make his Stockholm syndrome powerful.

The victims' memoirs allow the reader to recognize the connections between the linguistic isolation of the hostages, their traumatized self, and the kidnappers' narratives. Completely isolated, without dialogue with their persecutors, the hostage's self has no mediations and so it is submerged by its traumatized condition. Tesi says,

Because the dark and the solitariness had become intolerable to me, because I needed to speak and to express my anguish to another being, be he friend or foe, as long as he listened to me and comforted me, breaking an unbearable silence and staving off with his words the hallucinations of the night. So I begged him to stay, to always stay next to me, because that isolation would have made me go crazy, and I begged him to talk, to talk

160   Ransom Kidnapping in Italy

about anything, so that I no longer felt alone and abandoned, so that I had a human presence next to me.[103]

Lacking the perception of external words means for Tesi to be closed inside her inner language, "the language of an inner disaster," through which she can no longer narrate herself but rather in which she finds her self prey to hallucinations.[104] By destroying the possibility of mediating their self through an inner speech and, therefore, of being present through an inner linguistic self-reflexivity, trauma internally excludes the victims from a communicative language. Thus, if trauma is, according to the specialists, a psychological infantilism, it is also a *linguistic infantilism*. It in fact brings the hostage to a prelinguistic condition that comes to obscure their self. The impossibility of an internal narration thus completes their linguistic isolation. It is in such a condition that the language of the warders becomes for the hostages the perceptual frame of their captivity and self. By interrupting the silence that surrounds Tesi, the voice of her warder is the only space available for self-reflexivity and so the only hold she has to be present without going mad. In other words, to perceive the perpetrators' voices is a harbour that saves the kidnapped from their most dangerous kidnapper: their traumatized self. The relief that the abductors provoke makes the victims trust them and believe their narrations.[105] As Tesi recalls,

> This dialogue that I had established with him seemed to me a positive thing at the time, since it drew me out of my solitude, which was the thing that I feared most, but it instead turned out to be a negative thing. In truth of fact, by doing this he was gaining an ever-stronger hold over my personality ... While I was allowing him to get a sense of many sides of my character, he would speak about himself a good deal, but he completely distorted reality ... He engaged me in all of these talks in order to move me and fill me with pity, presenting himself before my eyes as better than he was.[106]

Only after her seclusion does Tesi recognize the danger of her warder's spoken language, with which he had portrayed himself as he wished and made her feel what he wanted her to feel. Unaware of her condition during captivity, she is exposed to violent and distressing words through which her warder kidnaps her self. If the hiding places hide the body of the kidnapped, the language of kidnapping hides their self. For this reason, when the victims return to society, they feel invisible in the spoken language of the outside world.

Trauma and Language in the Kidnapping Victim Memoir   161

In contrast with Tesi, Rossi di Montelera realizes as a hostage that the conversations he has with his captor could be a tool used to subdue him. By narrating his life, Rossi di Montelera's kidnapper appears as a human being to him and wins his trust. However, when he starts to talk about the ransom and insists on asking about his family's wealth, Rossi di Montelera stops trusting him and perceives their dialogue as manipulative. Resisting his perpetrator's technique of extortion, though, is incredibly difficult for the hostage: "It was mortifying to doubt whether the trust I had placed in the warder had been betrayed and was actually the result of a horrific plan of psychological blackmail, of an extortion of information, of espionage."[107] In the face of his perpetrator's betrayal, Rossi di Montelera loses something more than a relationship with his abductor: he loses his belief in the presence of humanity in every human being. Mortified by this loss, and without dialogue, Rossi di Montelera falls into a deep and dangerous depression.

Finally, the need for the perpetrators' voice and for a dialogue is essential for the victims. But it is exactly this need that puts them in the condition of being completely exposed to the power of the abductors, who, taking advantage of their vulnerability, brainwash them. In their testimonies, in fact, the kidnapped declare that during their captivity one of the most intolerable contradictions is listening to the abductors who, accusing their families, tried to make them think that everyone had abandoned them – yet still preferring the kidnappers' company to loneliness. If on the one hand, in order to be physically grounded, the victims need to perceive the spoken language of the abductors, on the other hand, that same spoken language sadistically denies and destroys their world and self. To put it differently, the inner language through which, according to Don Ihde, we are aware of our self becomes narrated for the hostages by the persecutors. Immersed in the only narration allowed, and therefore visible only through their warders' perspective, the kidnapped find themselves captured in what Soffiantini defines as the "lingua senza scampo del banditismo" (banditry's escapeless language).[108] For the ex-hostages, writing is a way out from the isolation and the trauma of their captivity.

The Writing of the Return

When Donatella Tesi Mosca returned to her life after fifty-four days of captivity, she realized that she was a survivor because she felt as though she was coming from a reality not perceptible by anybody else except for the hostages who had experienced it. In her memoir, she describes the passage from being abducted to being free as a "leap in intensity,"

162 Ransom Kidnapping in Italy

an expression that pictures her return home as an abrupt jump from her captivity.[109] Without others' perception there is no mediation between the world of freedom and that of her confinement. "It was as if I was coming from another world where one lived dramatically and spoke another language, anguished and violent," she explains.[110] The leap of intensity for Tesi is a gap between the spoken language of the outside world and that of her abduction. Free, she finds herself linguistically isolated. "It seemed to me that almost everybody talked in a superficial way and that every person could barely touch and barely perceive the surface tip of the deep reality from which I had emerged and which I was still carrying inside," she continues,[111] depicting the words she perceives when back in society in a tactile way, as if they only lightly touch the reality she had lived first-hand. Exceeding the perceptual frame of the language spoken on the surface, the underground world of her captivity remains hidden. This language cannot be, for Tesi, the medium through which to overcome the gap between the reality that now surrounds her and the one she carries inside. Impossible to be perceived by others, the world Tesi interiorized keeps her as a hostage with no witnesses. The split between what kidnapped people experience in flesh and the way "normality" speaks prevents Tesi from reconnecting herself to the present, of which she writes, "it passed, and I was not living it because I was far, detached, still turned backwards, inwardly rooted in my days of anguish, still buried in the forest."[112] Without a testimony to express what she lived through, her mind remains interred in the deep reality of her kidnapping. In such a condition she cannot be back-in-the-world, meaning that her self is still bound to the hole in the ground in which she feels buried. Disconnected from the surface, Tesi lives in a frozen time. Although free, she is not liberated.

The lack of mediation between what the kidnapped experienced and the reality to which they return prevents them from reentering a language in which they can be visible to others. They feel trapped in a parallel linguistic dimension that does not allow them to reach a communicative level. "Nobody notices anything, the cars slip away at the same speed, two of them risk crashing, another one passes with the green light. I am like an extra who got the wrong scene and has entered in another film," Soffiantini writes about the very moment of his liberation.[113] After 237 days of captivity, he portrays the way he reencounters society as the crossing of two movies being shot at the same moment: the story of his release and the story of everyday life. While he is at the centre of his dramatic film, he is an "extra" in the film of the world. The impact with the traffic makes the unique experience of his kidnapping relative. Seen from the unaware perspective of the cars, his liberation becomes like any other infinite number of things that happen in a day. Back at home, the film of everyday life cannot contain that of his captivity, and Soffiantini lives the passing of time according to the rhythm of his suffered agony. "I will realize a few months after my liberation that a mark remained, a deep one. It clearly cuts the year into two parts. The four seasons are reduced to two."[114] During the months of the year that correspond to his kidnapping, Soffiantini returns to being a hostage. Captured in his mind, he relives his segregation in the present. The passing of time therefore cannot make his abduction relative. On the contrary, it is his abduction – a traumatic event that cyclically re-happens to him – that interrupts and splits his year into two seasons. Soffiantini repeatedly experiences, to use Tesi's words, a "leap in intensity" between two realities: that of the "season of freedom" in which he feels liberated and that of his abduction.

By writing their memoirs, the kidnap victims thus seek to overcome the "leap in intensity" between the spoken languages of kidnapping and that of the outside world to which they go back. Written after their release, their texts are not the diaries of their captivity (as noted earlier). I rather consider them as a *writing of the return*. If my definition envisions "when" the victims write, it also, and more importantly, signifies that writing means for them to return to their traumatizing captivity with language as their witness (that is, with a perspective they lacked in isolation). In literary criticism, autobiographical accounts and testimonial narratives are often considered "impossible"[115] – in the case of autobiography because it is an illusion to think that the self-author and the self-character coincide.[116] Their temporalities are indeed different, and the self of the text is the result of memory's mediation rather than the subject of the lived experience.[117] Furthermore, the self is not an essence that precedes the text but is instead its result. In other words, the autobiographical self is always literary and therefore fictional. In this view, testimonial narratives are impossible because traumatic memories cannot be contained by language, meaning that trauma exceeds linguistic representations. Critics warn that the non-coincidence of author and character, or trauma and account, corresponds to the way text and reality do not coincide, and caution that language is a medium rather than a mirror. Although the kidnapping memoirs do not claim the opposite – that is, they do not claim that their authors' texts and lived experiences coincide – they nonetheless allow us to shift perspective and open further considerations into the genre of testimony and its possibility.[118]

One element that emerges from the accounts of the kidnap victims' captivity is that for the isolated hostages, language is a perceptual and acoustic space. The visibility of the self in language is not an image, a linguistic representation. The visibility of the self in language is its audibility. Language is an acoustic space that embodies the self because it enables the perceptual reflexivity of hearing/being audible. This is why in the accounts of captivity, silence (the absence of acoustic and language perception) obscures the hostages' self. In the memoirs, therefore, unlike in literary criticism, the linguistic relationship that is at stake is not the one between an essential Self and the pronoun "I" written on the page. The self is for the hostages neither an essence nor a result of a text; it is a presence (or awareness) that language permits and that isolation and trauma forbid. In his "Bearing Witness or the Vicissitudes of Listening," Dori Laub considers "autobiographical accounts of trauma" as a "medium which provides a listener to trauma."[119] He argues that "bearing witness to a trauma is, in fact, a process that includes the listener. For the testimonial process to take place, there needs to be a bonding, the intimate and total presence of an *other* – in the position of one who hears." Laub concludes that "testimonies are not monologues; they cannot take place in solitude. The witnesses are talking *to somebody*: to somebody they have been waiting for for a long time."[120] The readers are listeners for the kidnapped who write the account of their ordeals. They are, in fact, a viewpoint *in* language from which the victimized can narrate their confinement in a communicative dimension that allows for the self-reflexivity they lacked while hostages. Even if the reader is not present in flesh, he or she represents a linguistic perceptual referent that makes the writers feel exposed to the world and therefore visible in language. This is why during her captivity Tesi desperately needed to write in order to be present physically rather than to feel imaginary. Writing as a communication to an *other* who listens is in fact the correlate of inhabiting language in an incarnate dialectic. It means for the victims to locate themselves in a narration as embodied subjects whose reflexivity occurs between their incarnate self and a perceptive language. To use Merleau-Ponty's terms, the reader who listens gives to language the *flesh*, that is, a perspective that enables the victims to experience themselves as audible. In short, this incarnate language allows the self to be three-dimensional (or mediated) again. What I defined as *writing of the return* can also be defined as *writing in flesh*, which is exactly the definition that the Italian novelist, poet, and film director Pier Paolo Pasolini once gave to testimony.[121] The communicative language of the memoirs (their *flesh*) is the medium through which the kidnapped both witness and bear witness to their ordeals. It is indeed the medium that liberates their self from their perpetrators' narrations and provides the perceptual frame to the spoken language of the outside world.

However, in their memoirs, the kidnapped are not only "talking to somebody"; they are also *confessing* their trauma to the reader. That is, the kidnap victims reach the necessary relation that Dori Laub sees in the testimonial narratives of traumatic experiences through the literary means of confession. The "intimate and total presence of the *other*" can indeed be for the abducted victims a space for judgment. The hostages live the relationships with their kidnappers almost as a forced conversion to another order and therefore as a betrayal of their own values, identities, and families, about which they feel guilty. Confession does not only provide a listener to their traumatic bonds; it also provides absolution and forgiveness. Seen through Michel Foucault's lens, for which confession is the effect of a power,[122] the listener who forgives is also the ethical frame that makes the victims feel shame and guilt about their incomprehensible behaviours. The hostages confess to the outside world that they could not meet the expectation of resisting their perpetrators. Yet the kidnap victims' confession is not just the effect of social expectations and judgments on Stockholm syndrome, but it is also, and more importantly, agency.

Culture theorist Susannah Radstone offers a definition of this genre that differs from the emphasis on power given to it by Foucault. Comparing testimony and confession, she writes that "the two modes of discourse are nevertheless discrete: in confession it is the self that is scrutinized and implicated – the self that is the subject and object of confession. Witness testimony's object, on the other hand, is always an event or an other that is external to the witness."[123] Although it is the self that is both the subject and object of confession, Radstone, unlike Foucault, does not see this mode of discourse as an interiorized power's technology used by the subject to individualize themselves according to who they are supposed to be. In other words, confession is not, like it is for Foucault, the illusion of spontaneously saying the truth when it is imposed by a coercive power and social expectation. Compared to testimony, confession is the mode of discourse of the isolated subject. "Confession speaks from isolation and seeks re-entry into the world," Radstone states.[124] Confessing is for the ex-hostages a way of breaking the isolation imposed by their captivity and a means of breaking the power of the traumatic bond with their persecutors that prevents them from being free after liberation. It is by writing in flesh and through confession that the kidnap victims *return* to the world.

In conclusion, the kidnap victims' memoirs lead us to question the impossibility that literary criticism sees in the genre of testimony beyond the issue of the non-coincidence of text and experience. For the ex-hostages the testimonial narrative is possible as a way to overcome the gap between the language of their abduction and the language of the outside world; as a medium to surmount the linguistic and relational isolation imposed by their captivity; as a possibility for their traumatized self to be three-dimensional again in a communicative language; and as a confession that gives them the agency to break the power of the hostage/warder relationship and, in so doing, to reenter the world.

Chapter Six

The Anatomy of Captivity

"At times I found myself on all fours, with my chain tautly stretched and my head inside the tunnel in order to hear better."[1] With this vivid image, Luigi Rossi di Montelera portrays himself inside the hole of his abduction. Captured in a place that is nowhere and completely isolated from the rest of the world, Rossi di Montelera depicts his body like a dog straining at the chain that prevents him from moving around. This physical torsion propels him forward to overhear the abductors' voices and learn where his cell is located. By trying to give a name to the space where his kidnappers placed him, Rossi di Montelera seeks to be a witness. Before hiding their hostages, kidnappers completely disorient them by making them walk for hours around the area of their hiding places, spinning them around, or carrying them inside their cells. Locked up, blindfolded, and deafened by wax plugging their ears, the victims live their confinement as a prolonged dispossession of their bodily senses. In such conditions, their hiding places become like sealed jars that prevent them from being physically *in* the world. This is to say that during captivity, hostages suffer a split between their bodies and the world that interrupts the reciprocal relationship between the two. This split prevents them from locating themselves in a topological space and, therefore, from being able to recognize the unknown territory in which their persecutors have hidden them.

By shifting the analysis of the victims' accounts of captivity from trauma to the body, the final chapter of this book offers a phenomenological approach to confinement different, for example, from that taken by "Uomini rubati: Le vittime del sequestro di persona" (Stolen men: The victims of ransom kidnapping), an important victimological study on Sardinian ransom kidnapping.[2] As a branch of criminology, victimology conceptualizes abduction with respect to its criminal, financial nature. That is, the persecutors reify the kidnapped body into an object to sell. Seen from this angle, the abuse of the victim's body is motivated by the kidnappers' necessary disregard for human value. To justify and legitimize their behaviour, the persecutors dehumanize the hostages in order to not recognize in them the other. I suggest that the memoirs show that the abductors have another fundamental intention – to remain anonymous. This different perspective allows us to connect the victimized body to the hostages' potential to testify to their kidnapping and to negotiate with their families. I focus on the abuse of the body not as the result of the kidnappers' psychological motivations but rather as the paradigm of the anatomy of imprisonment itself. The dehumanization that the kidnapped depict in their testimonies is not only an expropriation of their value as human beings, which Jean-Paul Sartre (whose work serves as an explicit theoretical frame for "Uomini rubati") would call an existential dehumanization, but also a dismantling of their bodily perception and incarnate condition that prevents them from witnessing their ordeals – therefore, an ontological dehumanization.

In their memoirs, the ex-hostages describe themselves in captivity as "beasts." "They bind me like a dog, like any beast that you want to keep captive," writes Carla Ovazza (as we saw in the introduction).[3] If, on the one hand, being like animals in chains means for the hostages to lose the reciprocal relationship between their bodies and the world, on the other hand, it means to live an absolute physical degradation. "After months without being able to wash myself, a layer of dirt forms on my body, with an oiliness similar to that of an animal," Soffiantini states regarding his complete loss of bodily care in captivity.[4] The impossibility of taking care of their bodies marks the abduction of every kidnapped person, and it is suffered by them as an extreme dehumanization. Chained to their cells and, so to speak, to their bodily needs, the victims depend totally on their warders. In her *Sindrome da sequestro* (Kidnapping syndrome), Donatella Tesi Mosca writes that "unfortunately, when someone is kidnapped, the state of dependency is such that he is reduced to a chained dog who, if by chance the owner pets him, gratefully starts to humbly lick their hand."[5] The corporeal decline works as a means of separating the hostages from their familiar worlds. It slowly corrodes any link they have with their loved ones, bringing them to feel absolutely alone and to consider their warders as the only human beings left in a deserted universe. Through the loss of bodily care, the kidnappers physically force their victims to feel abandoned. The dirt that captivity imposes interrupts the reciprocity between the hostages and the world at a relational level. The "oiliness" which covers their bodies, to use Soffiantini's word, keeps them separated from any care they previously received in their lives outside their hiding places. Bodily deprived of

The Anatomy of Captivity 169

any trace of others, the hostages describe this condition as a cancellation of their worlds. Through physical degradation and abandonment, captivity turns the hostages into desperate negotiators of their own kidnapping. It is not just the fear of being killed that pushes the victims to write the letters that the abductors impose; it is the wish to end the unbearable conditions of captivity.

Through the lens of Maurice Merleau-Ponty's ontology of the flesh and Adriana Cavarero's ontology of vulnerability, this chapter analyses the kidnapping memoir as a medium that testifies to abduction as an experience of disembodiment. The kidnappers confine the hostages in disembodying places because these cause a loss of what Merleau-Ponty defines as bodily reflexivity. I argue that the sensorial deprivations imposed on the kidnapped prevent them not only from perceiving the world outside but also from being exposed to (that is, sensible to) the world. Without the reflexivity of perception (its active and passive components), through which one is present to oneself as an embodied subject (sentient-sensible), the victim becomes a disembodied consciousness, meaning that they cannot situate their body in a topological space. The hiding place becomes a no-place in which the kidnapped are made invisible to both the world and themselves. In chapters 2 and 3, Cavarero's perspective allowed us to shift the horror that the novelist Alberto Moravia recognized in Paul Getty's ear mutilation (1973) and in the discovery of Cristina Mazzotti's corpse (1975) from the agency of their kidnappers to the victims' disfigured bodies. The effect of violence, rather than the intention of the perpetrators, is key for understanding the impact of ransom kidnapping on media and public narratives of the time. This chapter uses Cavarero's theoretical tools to frame the victims' narratives of captivity. By reading their ordeals through the lens of what she calls the "criterion of the helpless" – that is, from the phenomenology of vulnerability and passivity – the book ends by shedding light on ransom kidnapping as an ontological crime.

Beyond "Stolen Men"

In the aforementioned "Uomini rubati: Le vittime del sequestro di persona," a study of Sardinian ransom kidnapping, nearly all of the twenty victims analysed (themselves also Sardinian) "showed impatience, distrust, and mistrust towards institutional figures, which at times almost reached a more or less openly hostile tenor."[6] The authors do not consider this negativity towards institutions to be a symptom of Stockholm syndrome, in which the victims would defend their abductors; instead, they see it as the result of a regional viewpoint.[7] Their explanation for

170   Ransom Kidnapping in Italy

one of kidnapping's consequences is rooted not in the nature of the crime itself but rather in the Sardinian identity of its victims. The negative feelings of the abducted derive not from their experience, argue the researchers, but from their cultural and historical background. Given that the same kind of reactions are also present in the accounts of those abducted outside of Sardinia, however, this focus on a Sardinian "historical mistrust" of the state hints at an underlying sociological prejudice that explains away an anger that is instead innate to kidnapping victimization.[8]

In *Racconto di un sequestro* (Account of a kidnapping), Rossi di Montelera notes several times that during his captivity he was frightened of the police to the point of agreeing with his kidnappers about the need to exclude law enforcement from negotiations. He accepted the secrecy imposed in the letters he was forced to write to his family, believing that institutional intervention would endanger his life. He justified this fear with his knowledge about how other kidnappings had ended. When he describes the moment in which a lieutenant of the Revenue Guard Corps was about to liberate him (as seen in the previous chapter), the hostage does not know what is about to happen:

> I heard someone yell, "Is there anybody here?" I jumped. What was it? Was it a trick of the bandits, who wanted to test my "reserve" before releasing me? I didn't answer. They called again, and I remained silent in fear. I was sure that it was a "bad trick." I heard the door's bolt start to pull back, and I sat on the bed as always with the usual jacket on my head. Someone entered and asked me, "Who are you?" It was certainly a horrible trick, a final test in order to see if I was really able to keep silent. If I kept quiet maybe I had a chance of being freed. If I spoke ...[9]

Incapable of imagining his rescue after four months of captivity, Rossi di Montelera saw this scene as a "horrible trick" designed by the kidnappers to test whether he was able to keep silent. He therefore perceived the first contact with the officer as an attempt by the abductors to ascertain whether they had obtained their scope, that is, remained unknown to the external world. Terrified and doubting the lieutenant's every word, Rossi di Montelera did not answer any questions. Torn between the desire to believe the officer and the fear of being fooled, with his face hidden under his jacket, he scanned every document, photo, and receipt that could prove the identity of his liberator. Rossi di Montelera remained blindfolded for hours inside the hole of his captivity, where two other institutional figures – a major general and a judge – tried to convince him to look at them. Situated between abduction and

The Anatomy of Captivity 171

freedom, the victim feared that his liberators were part of a "horrible performance" staged by his kidnappers. Though afraid of being "horribly deceived," he finally unveiled his face.

Rossi di Montelera's account makes visible how dangerous and even physically painful it could be for a victimized voice to break a long-imposed silence. His memoir testifies to the kidnappers' intent to make it impossible for victims to talk about their kidnapping. The kidnapped are therefore not only reified into ransom-able objects, but their lives depend on a secret that, if revealed, exposes them to death. This is why Rossi insisted on hiding himself under his jacket and, later, in a corner of the police station when he had to reveal the details of his kidnapping.

In Tesi's account, *Sindrome da sequestro*, the anonymity imposed by her kidnappers caused her to distrust institutions completely. Consequently, her liberation became as destructive an ordeal as the kidnapping itself. Tesi testifies to secrecy as a powerful and self-subjugating tool, which, if unbroken, prevents the hostages from escaping the will of their abductors even beyond the time of captivity. After she was released, her warder was still a fugitive from justice. Convinced by him that he belonged to the Red Brigades, Tesi believed her kidnapping to have a secret political matrix. Using the BR, he magnified his power in order to control her. Terrified by his threat that the Red Brigades would kill her children if she testified against him, she hid his (fake) political association from law enforcement. Because of this unbroken bond with her victimizer, Tesi returned to her life still under his control. It was while in this state of mind that, two weeks after having been freed, Tesi received a phone call from her kidnapper, who compelled her to help him escape from the police (as seen in chapter 5). Her account of the encounter with him demonstrates how secrecy subdued her:

In those few moments, I completely lost any sense of reality. I was no longer in the middle of the street in the heart of Florence but found myself again in the hole in the forest, again alone in front of my persecutor, the one whom I could not disobey without running the risk of being shattered. Whereas like this, as it was for a long time inside the hole, obedience meant salvation ... By then dominated once more in his hands, I repeated that I had told the police everything he wanted, that I had done like he wanted me to do, that I had not betrayed him, that I had told the police, the television, the newspapers, how he had been good with me, how he had treated me well, and that I had said nothing, as he had always ordered me, about his belonging to the Red Brigades.[10]

Though in her memoir she guiltily confesses to not having told the magistrate about the believed political matrix of her kidnapping, the victim blamed law enforcement for removing the recording device on her home telephone only a few days after her release. Left alone and without any witness, over the phone Tesi felt completely exposed to the will of her persecutor and obeyed him to the point of illegally abetting a crime.

Tesi's fear of the police prevented her from speaking out against her kidnappers or even trusting her husband. This impossibility of testifying held her hostage and allowed her abductor to manipulate her even outside her captivity. After giving himself up, in fact, he convinced the police that she had been his accessory from the start. Finally, five months after her release, during which time she had to defend herself against prosecution and an array of humiliating accusations, Tesi was acquitted of being an accomplice. Looking back at the moment in which she met the magistrate right after the encounter with her warder, she writes, "How much better would it have been if that Thursday afternoon I had trusted the magistrate who was in front of me and confessed everything to him! … And while everyone in the court that afternoon spoke to me with words of sympathy and understanding, I would hide inside of myself that terrible secret and be unable to talk."[11] The striking aspect of Tesi's account is that, as a victimized voice, she could not ask the police to protect her. Through this mistrust she granted the abductor the power to turn justice and public opinion against her and, therefore, the power to control her even in the world outside her kidnapping. "But did they no longer remember what condition my legs were in when I was liberated?" Tesi asks in her memoir, regarding the law enforcement that witnessed her emerging from a hole in the ground. "How could someone think that, in order to escape with a man, I spontaneously put myself underground, in the cold, and in the horrible hygienic and environmental conditions in which I was found? Without taking under consideration that if I had wanted to leave my husband, I already had a patrimony of my own. One only had to think of the villa in my name," she bitterly concludes.[12]

Fear of law enforcement, rage against the magistrates/liberators, and distrust of institutional figures can be attributed to the victimization of the kidnapped rather than to the cultural mindset pointed to by the authors of "Uomini rubati." The hostages' reaction to the police is linked to the terror of testifying about their ordeals. Moreover, the invisibility that the kidnappers want at all costs is what gives structure to captivity itself, which, in order to prevent the hostages from being witnesses of their abduction, dismantles their perception. The split between the captives' bodies and the world interrupts the reciprocal relationship between the two; it does not allow the victims to locate themselves in space and therefore to be able to recognize the unknown territory in which their persecutors hid them. In *Il mio sequestro* (My kidnapping), Soffiantini recounts that after one hundred days of imprisonment, his kidnappers moved him to a different place. As soon as he was able to perceive and identify the trees outside his tent, he overcame the imposed split between his body and the world:

> I'm happy. The kind of happiness that one can have after over one hundred days of captivity. Let me explain myself: the place where I am now guarantees another resistance. I have a wider vision of the forest and this strengthens me ... For a lover of plants like me, that oak forest which is in front of me is an injection of life. I am between a specimen of ilex and an ancient oak ... I immediately identify the topographical and ambient position ... It is like possessing a treasure map. If I live, I'll come back here with my eyes shut.[13]

His ability to situate himself in a recognizable space made Soffiantini feel stronger against his hooded abductors. He could testify. The kidnappers' desire to prevent the hostages from becoming witnesses determines the structure of captivity, which becomes an artificial construction of a no-place where, completely isolated, the kidnapped are forced to live an extreme experience of disembodiment.

Disembodiment

This section offers a new approach to the experience of captivity in kidnapping by framing the victims' testimonial narratives via a phenomenological lens. After first considering the victimological approach to confinement, we will explore the memoirs through Merleau-Ponty's work *The Visible and the Invisible* (1968). What victimology observes in the experience of captivity in kidnapping is the annihilation of the victim's self. The restriction of movement (as a result of which the abducted person is "no longer the author of action, nor a starting point of what happens"[14]), the sensorial semi-deprivation, and the total absence of body care provoke in the victims such a physical decline that it forecasts sickness and death, annulling any sense of future. The abuses inside the hiding place create in the hostage a split between body and intentionality. Because of this split, the kidnapped cannot transcend themselves and, reduced to a thing among things, they are no longer subjects. If the restriction of movement and the absence of bodily care negate for the

174   Ransom Kidnapping in Italy

victims the possibility of projecting the future, what makes them reach the highest level of self-annihilation is being exposed to the gaze of their warders. During captivity the kidnapped are often blindfolded, or their abductors' faces are purposefully covered. Victimologists recognize this condition as among the most painful for victims, who perceive themselves as "a faceless body":

> The blindfolded hostage is made even more helpless and deprived of subjectivity. He is entirely exposed to the gaze of the Other, who watches him and who in turn escapes from the return of this gaze. The gaze of the warder-guard therefore gains an absolute power over the hostage and his body, which remains at his complete mercy. The experience of the reciprocity of the gaze, thus, is annulled, a reciprocity inherent in the binomial see/being seen that here becomes the exclusive benefit of its passive term.[15]

This unilateral gaze petrifies the hostage, who experiences a total loss of freedom and, dispossessed of subjectivity, suffers this state with extreme anguish and as a loss of life.

The memoirs testify to the power that victimologists attribute to the kidnappers' gaze, which becomes absolutely humiliating when watching the victims in their most intimate moments, such as the satisfying of physiological needs. We find a clear example in Tesi's book:

> But how humiliating it was the first time I had to use the pot with him present, even if secluded in the corner. I have to say that this was one of the worst things to endure in the whole kidnapping, this humiliation, this state in which a woman finds herself squatting on the ground like an animal, without any shame or personal dignity.[16]

The privation of dignity Tesi describes in this passage is present in every memoir, but in some cases the warder's gaze reaches an even more intrusive level, which the hostage must bear to survive. This is the case with Soffiantini, who describes a critical bodily moment – a severe haemorrhage – that he was forced to share with his kidnappers:

> I X-ray my body, while I cry at every effort like a dog. It's blood, it's blood, it runs down and doesn't stop. I check – my pants and hands are bloodstained. I want to stop the bleeding without exposing myself. My intimacy is sacred. We have been accustomed to respect the body of others, especially by avoiding having prying eyes. It is also of the utmost respect to not watch the body of a person who suffers. For this reason I hope to solve

The Anatomy of Captivity 175

the haemorrhage in a few minutes and not say anything to my warders ...
The shame of nakedness belongs alike to the human beasts, if they exist,
as much as to the so-called normal beings.[17]

Here the body requires the intervention of the persecutors' gaze. Soffiantini must expose himself to the eyes of his kidnappers and let them take care of him if he's to overcome an otherwise deadly ordeal. The level of dehumanization reaches its peak and the victim has to experience his body merely in its necessity, renouncing all its existential meanings. In the absence of human values, he describes himself and his abductors as a dog and as beasts, respectively. In other words, Soffiantini lived the intrusive gaze as more painful than his physical pain itself. Feeling dispossessed of his body, he tried to maintain continuity with it by projecting his sense of decency onto the kidnappers' gaze. The victim lived the experience of undressing himself in front of his warder as a passage through which the persecutor became the "new owner of [his] bodily existence."[18]

The victimological perspective considers the body an object if the intentionality of the subject is annihilated. From this viewpoint, the kidnapped are subjects only because they are consciousnesses. This assumption that the subject is an intentional consciousness clarifies the victimologists' description of the experience of being watched by the warders. Rudas, Pintor, and Mascia state that "this destabilization of the subjectivity has in itself the sense of the loss of life itself. To die does not surely mean to lose one's own objectivity in the middle of the world – all the dead are there, in the world, around us – but rather to lose every possibility to unfold as subject to others."[19] In this view, without the self – which the abductors' gaze denies – the victim's body becomes a living cadaver among cadavers in the world. Thus, victimologists consider the body not as being in itself but rather as a vehicle for the agency of the self. However, what emerges from these memoirs is a different function of the gaze in kidnapping that remains outside the dialectic "seeing/being seen" emphasized by an existential approach. The lens of Merleau-Ponty's ontology of the flesh and his ideas of *être* and *incarnate* subject elaborated in *Le Visible et l'invisible* (*The Visible and the Invisible*) allow us to conceptualize this gaze and to shift the analysis of the victims' lived experience from the kidnappers' intentions to the perspective of the victimized bodies. The Merleau-Pontian methodology is highly appropriate for this discussion, given that his positions on the gaze derive from a revision of Jean-Paul Sartre's *L'être et le néant* (*Being and Nothingness*), in which the philosopher elaborates the dialectic "seen/being seen" adopted by Rudas, Pintor, and Mascia.

176   Ransom Kidnapping in Italy

His thought will therefore illuminate a different reading of the body in kidnapping.

Let us begin with what Rossi di Montelera writes about the isolation in captivity:

> The sensation that outside one might think that we are dead on the one hand gives us a great desire to live and scream to everyone that we are alive; on the other hand, it makes us feel a bit as though we had one foot in the grave. Thus "life," at least psychologically, is not only an objective fact linked to the person, whose heart beats, but it is also a "social" fact. If someone lives in an absolute physical isolation and isolated from relationships, even only acquaintances, so as to ensure that others no longer have the perception, the knowledge, or the certainty of his existence as a living being, he already feels a bit dead, or at least "dead to others."[20]

Here Rossi di Montelera, in contrast with what we saw before, experiences death not under the persecutors' gaze but rather in the absence of the world's gaze. One could object that it is still a matter of intentionality, given that kidnapping prevents Rossi from revealing himself as a subjectivity to his warders and to everyone else as well. What his words attest to, though, is a loss of life that has nothing to do with the impossibility of being a consciousness in front of others. Rossi di Montelera testifies to himself as a subject who, not exposed to anyone, cannot be in the world. What the kidnapped live in their experience is not only being seen by their persecutors but also being radically devoid of witnesses and, therefore, made invisible to themselves. In other words, by hiding and totally isolating the victim, kidnapping deprives the hostage's body of its intrinsic visibility. Moreover, this shift from the persecutors' gaze to the world's gaze allows us to consider the kidnapped outside the objectifying dialectic "seeing/being seen," and instead inside the incarnate dialectic "seeing/being visible" – incarnate, as we will see, because it is ontologically inscribed in the body itself as sentient-sensible.[21]

Before analysing the victims' lived experiences in light of this dialectic, I wish to focus on the negation of exposition that kidnapping imposes on the abducted. Merleau-Ponty writes of the body, "The body is not simply a thing *seen* in fact (I do not see my back), it is visible by right, it falls under a vision that is both ineluctable and deferred."[22] The visibility of the body exceeds any perceptual vision that objectifies it because it never coincides with its frontal appearance before the eyes of another subject; rather, it remains visible at its back. This deferred vision depends not on the perception of an effective looker but on the body as visible "by right." The kind of invisibility which Rossi di Montelera

The Anatomy of Captivity 177

lives as an experience of death is an absence of exposition and therefore, in Merleau-Pontian terms, of any possible deferred vision. This absence is for the victimized body something more original than the invisibility linked to the lack of frontal perception – an invisibility at 360°, one's body not visible tout court.

We find a vivid example in Soffiantini's memoir. While he was hidden in a forest in the Tuscan hills, a group of hikers walked by his tent. His kidnappers were ready to open fire should someone discover them. Torn between the fear of and the desire of being seen,

> [I hope] that someone within that little group of hikers is particularly capable, able to spot me and stay silent for a while and to call for help once it is safe. I expect what a kidnapped man expects, completely deprived of a semblance of freedom, even more when he hears life passing by. And he lives in a circle of death, without voices and without a contact that makes him certain of still being in the world, really alive in the world of the living.[23]

Soffiantini's perception acts as a mirror that reflects to him the condition of the kidnapped. Perceiving the hikers' voices reminds him of the lack of voices within his captivity. Furthermore, perceiving the presence of people depicts him inside captivity, which is instead the absence of any contact with the external world. That is to say, the proximity of other human beings gives him the perspective from which to envision himself as closed inside a "circle of death." Strikingly, by situating his gaze on the presence of the hikers (presence that is a perceived location), he starts to write in the third person, locating himself inside kidnapping. He therefore becomes the witness of himself thanks to a function of the gaze that is not intentional but is instead linked to what Merleau-Ponty calls the reversibility of the flesh.

To better understand this function of the gaze, we have to briefly clarify the Merleau-Pontian incarnate subject as well as what he calls the "fundamental narcissism of all vision."[24] The phenomenological concept of subjectivity radically differs from the existential-psychological concept of the subject as the organizer of space through his intentionality. The way in which a human being inhabits the world is, in phenomenology, through his body as being *of it* (as of the world). Merleau-Ponty situates the subject in the world neither through his body merely as empirical nor through the representations of his consciousness but rather in that *between* (the body and the world) which he calls the flesh.[25] He argues that in an experience that has not been "worked over" (disposed by thought), we discover not a transcendental ego but a being which is itself *of* the sensible-world, a being that "knows it before knowing it."[26] My hand which touches things is itself a subject to be touched. There is always a "shift," a "spread," which prevents the body from being immanent to it. Being sensible to myself is a way of being present to myself, which does not coincide with an abstraction of my thought. In this intertwining of the body as sentient and sensible, the division of subject and object disappears.[27] I never, at the same instance, experience my hand as touching and touched. The reversibility we found within the two dimensions of the body happens within subject and world as well. What Merleau-Ponty calls the flesh is exactly this reversibility (an "incarnate principle"), which situates the phenomenological subjectivity in the visible, audible, and touchable, without reducing them to objects. What we saw about the "toucher" is reformulated with the "seer" as well:

> There is a fundamental narcissism of all vision. And thus, for the same reason, the vision he exercises, he also undergoes from the things, such that, as many painters have said, I feel myself looked at by things, my activity is equally passivity – which is the second and more profound sense of the narcissism: not to see in the outside, as the others see it, the contour of a body one inhabits, but especially to be seen by the outside, to exist within it, to emigrate into it, to be seduced, captivated, alienated by the phantom, so that the seer and the visible reciprocate one another and we no longer know which sees and which is seen.[28]

In this "narcissism of all vision," perception becomes action and passivity as well. The passive aspect of seeing does not coincide with being objectified by an intentional gaze; it coincides with being visible while seeing. The principle of reversibility, which the ontology of the flesh illuminates, allows the subject to situate himself in the world by looking at himself *from* the outside, not just *in* the outside. If for an intentional consciousness space is nothing but an organized and disposed container of objects, the space correlated to an incarnate gaze is rather "topological (that is, cut out in a total voluminosity which surrounds me, in which I am, which is behind me as well as before me)."[29] The alienation by the blind gaze of things, this possible ecstatic intertwining, allows me to become the witness of my being in the world, that is, the witness of me being exposed – of my body as whole.

As the kidnapping memoirs testify to, the isolation of captivity dismantles the victims' bodies as sentient-sensible and, in doing so, prevents them from witnessing themselves inside it. Brutally chained in the hiding place of their ordeals, the kidnapped are absolutely there without being able to situate themselves inside what they are living. Writing about the moment when he is forced to enter his cell, for instance, Rossi demonstrates how being no longer exposed to the world renders his body no longer sensible:

> The usual bandit lifted me. With my feet, I felt the edges of a hole, a trapdoor, and I felt myself lowered beneath ground level. In that moment I truly felt a swell of terror, unconscious but horrible. When I touched the bottom, I was ordered to keep stooping down until I was on all fours. Then they made me move forward, pulling me by the hands. It was an underground passage, very narrow and sodden. I felt buried, and only in that moment did I have the physical impression of an irremediable loss of liberty, even if only temporary. As long as I was in the open air, on my feet, and hearing noises, I seemed to still have a minimal amount of liberty or, better, life. But that tunnel that I was leaving behind me made me touch with my hands the true meaning of imprisonment for the first time.[30]

Rossi di Montelera moves completely under the persecutors' control. Blindfolded, he testifies to his "burial" according to his sense of touch. The striking aspect of this passage is that here Rossi testifies to the very moment of his body's loss of visibility. The path to his cell takes him not only from being free to being a hostage but also from being exposed to being drastically hidden (figures 6.1 and 6.2). While still outside, even if in his abductors' hands, hearing makes him feel alive.

By moving along the underground path, the victim arrives at the opposite of Merleau-Ponty's "topological space." Behind him Rossi di Montelera does not have the world but instead that dark tunnel he touched. The world is cancelled and with it any possible deferred vision of his own visibility. He has therefore become invisible tout court. Rossi's memoir testifies to a split that is intrinsic to the body itself, namely the split between the body as sentient and as sensible. The hiding place prevents the hostage from experiencing the reversibility of the flesh. Captivity not only dismantles the intentional subject (the organizer of the space) but also dismantles the incarnate subject (exposed to the space). This ontological dehumanization is what I mean by disembodiment.

Inside the cell, perception loses its passive aspect. Confinement, in fact, negates the dialectic body/world. The reversibility between the hostage and the hiding place is between two invisible and therefore impossible reversibilities. There is no reflection. The hiding place occupies that "place between" the victims' bodies and the world, where reflection would happen; it becomes a tangible space so close to them that it almost coincides with them. During captivity, the hole, the cell,

Figure 6.1. Luigi Rossi di Montelera enters his cell with law enforcement to verify that it is the hiding place where he was held captive. Photo supplied by Agenzia ANSA.

Figure 6.2. Luigi Rossi di Montelera's cell. Photo supplied by Agenzia ANSA.

The Anatomy of Captivity   181

or the tent becomes the hostage's body made not sensible. This is clear from another passage of Rossi's memoir:

> That [passing] plane provoked in me a fleeting thought of freedom. There I was under the ground while above my head, above my cell that in this moment opened up, a plane was flying with its many passengers … Life outside was going on the same as always, even if I was under there. And those passengers who were looking out from the windows to admire the Turinese hills did not realize that hundreds or thousands of metres below them there was an underground hideout, but with the entrance open, and I was inside! … I felt a mad desire for freedom.[31]

In a moment in which there is a fissure in his cell, the world can enter and Rossi di Montelera becomes visible to himself. As when Soffiantini heard the hikers walk by his tent, perception acts as a mirror. By perceiving the plane, Rossi can situate himself inside the underground passage, looking at himself from the outside. He becomes a witness. The passive aspect of perception is here allowed, and the victim's body can be in a reversible relationship with the world. By alienating into the plane, the blind gaze of his visibility envisions the condition of his captivity. Becoming one of the passengers, Rossi sees his open cell between him and the gaze of the world. The dialectic of perception returns to his body, its visibility mutilated.

Soffiantini's memoir allows us to consider the victim's isolation from the world not as the opposite of a topological space but rather as its desertification. When Soffiantini hears the hikers pass by his tent, perception acts like a mirror that reflects the lack of voices in his captivity. The sensation of being dead reaches its peak when he hears them depart, leaving him overwhelmed by the reality of his imprisonment:

> The party moves away. They laugh, one of them starts singing. I think I am dead in the world of the living. The dimension of kidnapping hangs over me. Kidnapping is like having a boulder on your eyes, a sudden paralysis. Everything happens like in those nightmares in which someone talks but can't be heard. He sees the others, but everyone passes next to him and can't see him.[32]

It is after the experience of being absolutely separated even when in extreme proximity with the world that he gives this enlightening definition of kidnapping. Soffiantini testifies to his imprisonment as a loss of bodily reflexivity. He portrays himself as sentient but not sensible. Nevertheless, as soon as he stops hearing the voices, he feels blind and paralysed. Disembodied inside his tent, he can no longer reflect himself in the gaze of the world. Soffiantini, in contrast with Montelera, experiences his imprisonment in the open space of a forest. If Montelera's cell became for him a no-place, for Soffiantini the forest becomes another world in which his body is completely transformed and absorbed. "Forest" is the word he uses most in his memoir, and it is his most powerful kidnapper. To overcome his loneliness, he communicates with birds, plants, and even rats. He also perceives his kidnappers as inhabitants of the forest, and he describes their bodies and movements with bestial characteristics. What is astonishing for the reader, as well as for the victim, is that he is talking about a place in Tuscany. The distance between what he describes and normal life in an Italian region in 1997 is absolute. The forest cancels out the civilized world, becoming an immense, unreachable, and desolating desert. If Soffiantini could maintain a reversible relationship with a "natural world," nevertheless his body could not be sentient-sensible in a "historical world." "I ask myself what happened to the whole technological miracle, the scientific identification from afar, the interception through heat detection ... Instead, I remain in a forest of scanty trees, visible almost to the naked eye and yet invisible to all except my warders," he writes.[33] Even if the victim feels totally exposed, the radical absence of other human beings makes him feel invisible. By preventing the hostages from appearing in a historical space, captivity prohibits their bodies from being social-sensible. In other words, the forest becomes the desertification of a topological space.

Like Soffiantini, Donatella Tesi Mosca lived her captivity in a Tuscan forest. Hidden in a hole in the ground, she was chained and not permitted to exit. Her warder was usually, though not always, there with her. To prevent her from escaping in his absence, he convinced her there were two other kidnappers (his "Sardinian bosses" – i.e., men more powerful than him) outside in the forest looking at her. Tesi recounts that one night he did not come back, and she realized that he would never return. She spent two days inside the hole terrified and waiting for him even though she could have undone her chain. When she finally ventured out, being exposed to the world frightened her:

> The impact with that "outside" was for me a trauma. I was no longer used to open air, to the light of day. The outside reality, the forest, the green, the trees all seemed immense and scared me. I quickly went back inside. By then I was like an animal that feels safer inside its burrow. I had regressed to an animal state. Absurdly, I felt more protected inside the pit

The Anatomy of Captivity   183

than outside in the forest. I tried at least ten times to leave the burrow, but I couldn't handle staying outside, looking. I was still afraid of the reality that surrounded me in which were concentrated all of the terrors of my imprisonment ... And what is most incredible is that, once back inside, I would bind myself once more to the chain because if the Sardinians were by chance to arrive they would have to find me like that.[34]

For Tesi, the gaze of the forest became overwhelming. To be visible, in fact, for her meant to be seen by the "Sardinians." The outside, the topological space that surrounded her, was not deserted but filled with the ubiquity of her invisible and imaginary Sardinian warders. Furthermore, Tesi could not look at the forest because perception alienated her into a perspective from which she felt endangered. In other words, her being exposed coincided with her intrinsic bodily vulnerability. This is why secrecy made her incapable of testifying against her kidnapper. The secret was the linguistic correlate of the hole she could not leave in the forest, a place between her body and the gaze of threatening invisible warders (during captivity the imaginary Sardinians, once back in the civil world the imaginary Red Brigades) to which, if she spoke, she exposed herself.

Soffiantini returned into the "historical world" when his kidnappers abandoned him on a country path, which he described as not a real liberation:

I tear off the bandage. The result, at that moment, is almost insignificant. It's dark all around, the evening is cold, it is a country road ... Right now it doesn't yet seem to me that I am free. As long as I am not free from the dark and the little country road, I hang on to the devilish doubt that one of the warders may come out from behind a bush, hit me over the head, and begin once more that macabre dance of the imprisonment in the trunk, of the moves, of the pits and the tents with the eternal briar borders.[35]

In the dark, Soffiantini felt caught between freedom and abduction. He feared that his liberation was, in Rossi di Montelera's words, a "horrible trick." He recalled the moment he first saw lights on the road:

Lights. Breathless, I shout, "Lights" and raise my hands as if they were coming towards me. Not a syllable comes out. I shouted "Lights" as if I were mute. But now I am no longer blinded by the earlier darkness. Now I will look at those lights and I will be in the houses of the world. The little road comes onto a big street full of traffic.[36]

184   Ransom Kidnapping in Italy

From this dangerous position, being sensible (audible) could be a fatal mistake. Capable of seeing, he arrived at the busy road:

> I risk being run over ten times, the horns bore into my back and the head-lights shave my long beard. For the first time after so long, I see my inter-mittent shadow on the asphalt once more. I am tall and big, and my stride is gigantic like that of an ogre. I am proud of my rediscovered body ... imposing as it becomes visible on that piece of road that leads up to the gas station specified by the bandits.[37]

After 237 days of captivity, in which his body was absolutely present as his main concern, Soffiantini here remarkably declares that he has found it again. As soon as the victim enters the civil world, his back becomes visible. No longer used to being exposed, he does not know how to situate himself in traffic. Strikingly, Soffiantini overcomes disembodiment by encountering his shadow. The intermittent deferred vision, which the car lights project on the asphalt, makes him visible to himself. He is no longer in a desert but rather back in Italy. In the "Working Notes" of *The Visible and the Invisible*, Merleau-Ponty writes, "The flesh is a *mirror phenomenon* and the mirror is an extension of my relation with my body," which he also calls the "I–my shadow relation."[38] It is exactly this three-dimensional relation with space that captivity interrupts. Kidnapping deprives the incarnate subject – the witness of the world – of the gaze of his sensibility and, in so doing, dismantles the reflexive structure of his sentient-sensible body. As Rossi di Montelera, Tesi Mosca, and Soffiantini testify to in their memoirs, the structure of captivity in ransom kidnapping depends on the abductors' intent to remain anonymous. Hidden and isolated from the world, the kidnapped literally disappear in a no-space and thus no longer experience their body as sensible. As a result of this disembodiment, the victims suffer the unbearable condition of becoming invisible to themselves.

Turning the Hostage into a Negotiator

"Men do not bleat" goes a saying common among Sardinian shepherds, indicating how much easier it was for them to hide the owner of a flock of sheep and to keep him from speaking than to hide the flock itself.[39] Yet, as seen earlier, the silence that the secret nature of ransom kidnapping imposes on its victims makes captivity an ordeal that dismantles the hostage as witness. However, if on the one hand the linguistic ability of the abducted represents a threat to their persecutors, on the other it becomes the most effective means of communication by which to obtain

The Anatomy of Captivity 185

their aims. In other words, if the kidnappers fear the linguistic capability of the victims as a weapon to be silenced, they also turn it against the families, forcing the hostages to write letters in which they desperately ask their kin to pay the ransom. By imposing and dictating those letters, the warders oblige the abducted to linguistically objectify themselves, naming their price or commanding what must be done to obtain their release. Through physical and psychological abuse, they make the victims write urgent and hopeless messages with which to shock the world outside. The captivity of ransom kidnapping is a violence designed to turn the hostage into a convincing negotiator.

The kidnap victims' memoirs testify that writing the letters is one of the most painful elements of their ordeals. It is indeed extremely difficult for the hostages to address their families using the language of their abusers. They resist because they do not want to shock their kin and instead try to protect them from what they are actually living. Moreover, the ransom for which they are constrained to ask will provoke the financial downfall of their families, causing them to feel as though they are blackmailing their own relations. In her memoir, for example, Ovazza recounts her fears after having written the first letter from her captivity. "What a terrible thing to write such crazy messages, without being able to reflect even for a minute! Threatened by a huge gun, I am forced to write exactly what they demand, without being able to add something of my own, without being able to make them understand that it is certainly not me, of my own free will, that writes these words. What will their reaction be when they receive them? Will they get it?"[40] In this dictated writing, Ovazza becomes visible to the external world as her abductors command. Dispossessed of her own voice, she is situated in an extraneous and violent language, which is the vehicle for the warders' own intentions. In the experience of dictation, the hostage lives a split between her body's gestures and the words produced by these movements. Her body becomes a mute puppet, which the voice of an invisible ventriloquist makes speak. Ovazza worries whether her message will be perceived as spontaneously written because she fears that her loved ones will feel squeezed directly by her.

The hostages also feel a resistance to writing the letters because they do not want to be seen in the humiliating state to which captivity reduces them. When Rossi di Montelera has to compose the first message to his family, he must copy it from an original written by his kidnappers, who tell him to add something of his own but only on the condition that he writes "pitiable" things.[41] "I would have never missed such an opportunity, since it is not pleasant, after several weeks of darkness and silence, to have to write one's parents a cold letter full of conditions," Montelera states. "But I wanted them to be able to distinguish the dictated part from the free one."[42] As in Ovazza's case, even if the letter does not originate with him, Rossi di Montelera still feels the responsibility of writing to his parents. In his memoir, he meticulously describes how he made clear which part of the message he composed and which was instead dictated. "Writing this letter, I had the sensation, which then returned with every other letter, that I was perhaps writing the last message of my life," he continues. "For this reason, it was very important to me to at least write one comforting sentence to my parents, so that if I were killed they would at least know that I was serene, so that my last message was not for them a perennial trauma, doubt, anguish."[43] The possibility the victims have to communicate with the external world is always lived as potentially the last opportunity they have to be part of it. If Montelera's desire is to protect his parents, in his messages he also wants to appear "serene" to himself. There is in the hostage a resistance that is a sort of shame in being exposed as completely defenceless, incapable of reacting or unable to escape from his kidnappers. The awareness that someone who loves him will receive his letters returns to Rossi di Montelera a degree of integrity and dignity.

The purpose of captivity is to radically defeat any resistance on the part of the hostages by creating a situation in which their only reality becomes the physical dependence on their warders. The connection with the world outside in fact allows the kidnapped to resist being the mediators who negotiate with their kin and thereby help their persecutors fleece them. Captivity must therefore neutralize the desire the abducted have to protect their families and, more importantly, must make them feel abandoned. Seen from this perspective, it becomes clear why the kidnappers reduce them to "dogs," as the victims write in their memoirs. The perpetrators erase from the victims' bodies any traces of the care they had received before the abduction in order to prevent them from "physically remembering" their loved ones and from being connected to any relationship they had. For this reason, I describe disembodiment as a "loss of bodily care," which, making the hostage feel abandoned in flesh, affects them at a relational level.

Confinement must also prove to the hostages that there is no way to conclude the negotiations if not in the way the kidnappers want. The abductors' determination has to be absolute and their power total. The victims' bodies become the place in which these intentions are actualized. There is no freedom without collaboration. As the hideout – hole, cave, and forest – is under their control, so are the victimized bodies. To make an analogy between the structure of ransom kidnapping and that of torture, we can perhaps say with Elaine Scarry that what the kidnappers impose on the hostages is "the conversion of real pain into the fiction of power."[44] Finally, hidden in a place completely other, the hostages are manipulated by their warders, who often pretend to be under the dominion of an omnipotent mysterious leader. In so doing, the warders present themselves as victims controlled by a powerful figure as much as the hostages are. The only difference is that they are forced to do an ignoble job. This feigned "innocence" gives them the tool of coercive control over their kidnap victims, who trust them and find themselves in an utterly unbalanced relationship recalling the one infants have with their caretakers. Chapter 5 already considered the hostage/warder relationship from a psychological perspective as a traumatic bond and infantilization. This chapter moves now to explore this relationship at an ontological level.

The *Horrorism* of Captivity

The chain is a source of anguish for the kidnap victims because it materializes the total physical dependence they have on their warders. Being chained means they must carry that dependency, be constantly aware of it. It means to be tied to their own bodies, which can survive only if their abductors keep them alive. In her *Sindrome da sequestro*, Donatella Tesi Mosca writes that "the anguish of dying alone and abandoned by everyone ... of dying alone and chained, from hunger, from thirst ... surpassed all other fears and feelings. In front of [my warder], who often presented himself as a 'friend,' I was helpless, defenceless, in his hands: he fed me, he warmed me up, he protected me, he helped me to survive."[45] Physically forced to fear abandonment, the captured feel abandoned by the world. Tesi uses the word "helpless" (*inerme*) to describe herself in relation to her warder. In her book *Orrorismo* (*Horrorism*), Cavarero employs the same term to name the condition of the victim: "Defenseless and in the power of the other, the helpless person [*inerme*] finds himself substantially in a condition of passivity, undergoing violence he can neither flee from nor defend against. The scene is entirely tilted toward unilateral violence. There is no symmetry, no parity, no reciprocity. As in the exemplary case of the infant, it is the other who is in a position of omnipotence."[46] The hostages of ransom kidnapping find themselves in a position of total passivity, with their body completely exposed to the other. Cavarero's phenomenology of this passivity and her cultural analysis of the mediation of horror in the Western tradition are the tools with which the rest of this chapter frames the accounts of the kidnap victims.

188   Ransom Kidnapping in Italy

Departing from the inadequacy of traditional political discourse to signify contemporary models of violence, Cavarero coins the neologism "horrorism," which shifts the perspective of theory from the perpetrators to the victims. In her reflection, she does not consider the intentionality of the violent actor (the warrior, the soldier, the terrorist) but rather looks at the passivity of those who suffer brutality in the flesh. The victims are no longer merely the objects of violence; instead they become the passive incarnate subjects whose vulnerability grounds Cavarero's theoretical discourse. The victimized body in particular is for the philosopher the physical referent that allows her to recognize in language a linguistic correspondence capable of signifying violence without falling into the gap of abstraction between the words and the lived experience of human beings. The victim's body is therefore the measure of Cavarero's discourse, which she opens by differentiating the spheres of terror and horror. She shows that the etymology of terror recalls the act of trembling, indicating a physical dimension of fear. The body's movement, signified by the word "terror," finds its correlate in flight: "Its sphere of reference is that of a menace to the living being, which tries to escape by fleeing. This menace is directed, substantially, at life itself: it is a threat of violent death. He who is gripped by terror trembles and flees in order to survive, to save himself from a violence that is aiming to kill him."[47]

The physical reaction horror provokes is radically different. Its etymology recalls a bristling sensation, indicated by the Latin verb *horreo* and the Greek *phrisso*: "The area of meaning covered by '*horreo*' and '*phrisso*' denotes primarily a state of paralysis, reinforced by the feeling of growing stiff on the part of someone who is freezing. The movement of flight, however, seems to be excluded ... There is something of the frightful there, but, more than fear, horror has to do with repugnance."[48] If terror alludes to the fear of dying violently, horror refers to the repugnance for a type of violence that exceeds killing. Horror reflects the physical reaction to a violence that, by attacking the body, attacks not the biological life of the subject but rather her incarnate condition – that is, according to the philosopher, her vulnerability. Cavarero continues, "The body is revulsed above all by its own dismemberment, the violence that undoes it and disfigures it. The human being, as an incarnated being, is here offended in the ontological dignity of its being as body, more precisely in its being a singular body."[49] Disfiguring the unity and wholeness of the body, dismembering – as "a violence that labors at slicing" – horrifies.[50] Becoming unwatchable and unrecognizable petrifies human beings, who, reduced to mere flesh, can no longer appear to the world through their uniqueness. With the neologism "horrorism," Cavarero names an ontological crime that dehumanizes the victims and attacks their embodied singularity.

Mutilations and dismembering were shocking realities linked to the abductions executed by banditry and organized crime. Even the randomness of the violence peculiar to horrorism belonged to this crime; the potential targets were not identifiable (the victims did not belong to the same social class, region, or group), and they were captured unexpectedly, an especially traumatizing component of their ordeal. Yet the kidnapping memoir shows that the violence visible in the media narrative was the tip of the iceberg of an entire structure of captivity that we can call horrorism. What Cavarero's distinction between terror and horror shows is that the body does not coincide exclusively with the biology of humans but coincides with their incarnate condition as well. Trembling and freezing are physical reactions to violent attacks against life and vulnerability – that is, against the body as biological and ontological. "As every torturer knows," Cavarero remarks, "the vulnerable is not the same as the killable. The latter stands poised between death and life, the former between the wound and healing care."[51] Although the abductors constantly threaten their hostages with death, they do not want to murder them because they need them alive in order to negotiate with their families. The kidnappers attack the vulnerability of their victims. Tesi's passage recalls what Cavarero writes regarding the condition of the newborn baby, whose "relation to the other is a total consignment of its corporeal singularity in a context that does not allow reciprocity."[52] However, what seems to upset the helpless Tesi is not only being exposed to her warder's violence or wounds; it is also being exposed to his caretaking. She indeed defines herself as helpless in relation to the gestures that help her. The victims' memoirs bear witness to a type of captivity that oscillates between care and wound, a captivity that converts the hostages' vulnerable incarnate condition into a means of power. Although the fear of death is constantly present in the victims, as Tesi writes, the repugnance for the exploitation of their vulnerability is what prevails in their accounts.

The hostage/warder relationship is a scene of violence in which care becomes an ambiguous instrument of coercive control. "Every time they need me, my collaboration, or better, my passivity, then they are kinder. Caring. Friends who are a little contrite, sorry for the suffering that they are 'forced' to inflict on me. When they want me to write a letter to my family, they are even capable of serving hot meals," Belardinelli recounts. "Slowly, I understand their behaviour. After a few minutes, they base their 'favours' on my writing the first letter. With the right content, with the right tone."[53] In a position of total dependency, the victim needs to believe in the attention they receive from their warders, but this attention also determines the victim's mood and hopefulness – indispensable to resisting captivity. If the warders have the power to make the hostages suffer, they are also the only human beings that can alleviate their suffering. That is, exposed to a unilateral violence, the victims are also exposed to a unilateral care. These two attitudes – hostile and friendly – allow the kidnappers to control their relationship to the victim. During their confinement, the kidnapped slowly recognize this mechanism and perceive their captivity as a cruel trick they cannot escape.

If infancy is, in *Horrorism*, the paradigm for the condition of being exposed to potential wounds and necessary care, motherhood is the paradigm for the original relationship of the helpless being to the other. In the hiding place, wound and care are inseparable and are both performed by the warders. The care the hostages receive is gestures that help them but never truly relieve the inflicted wounds. The kidnapped testify to their captivities as a world absolutely other, whose inhabitants – the kidnappers – subvert the meaning of "relationship" to the point that they cancel the symbolic order of the world from which the hostages come. In short, kidnapping subverts the world of the care (familiar) with the world of the elsewhere (extraneous). Inside this unknown space, the hostages often perceive the ambiguous power of their persecutors as an inversion of motherhood. Among the different mechanisms of defence, which the kidnapped activate during their confinement, the memory of their homes plays a central role. The mother in particular – as seen, for example, in the imaginary dialogues that Belardinelli has with his deceased mother – becomes a way of resisting the unthinkable reality they experience. The mother is lived as a sort of insuperable limit against the erasure that captivity imposes.

This becomes clear when the hostages return home. Tesi recounts, for example, "I finally saw my mother again, the tender sensation of feeling like a child in her arms again, of melting down in tears that she dried, in words that I could tell only to her. I looked her in the eye, and I thought with relief that I had made it, that I did not go crazy."[54] Listening to the maternal voice and being able to talk to her mother means for Tesi reconnecting to an embodied language. The mother represents a relationship authentically original rather than perversely primordial, which returns the victims to a symbolic order of care. The correlate of this order is what the victims call "my world" in contrast with "their world." In Ovazza's account, both her parents represent the possible return to life as it was before the kidnapping and confirm that this order resisted against the existence of an extraneous and violent one.

"Here they are, beautiful, wonderful in their emotion, extraordinary in their strength of mind, my two pillars ... I must look horrendous with my shaved head," she writes, "but they pretend that nothing has happened. My dad keeps hugging me and blesses my return: this is the tangible proof that everything will go back to how it was before."[55] In the encounter with her parents, Ovazza feels that she can now be visible in a world in which a reciprocal gaze is possible. Both Tesi and Ovazza see themselves from the perspective of their parents; while the latter sees her horrible shaved head through them, the former recognizes in her mother's eyes that she did not go mad. They therefore witness the wounds that kidnapping inflicted on them from the viewpoint of care. We see another example in Soffiantini's memoir. When liberated, he finally arrives home and, he writes, "in the middle of the garden, motionless, my mother waits. She is almost ninety, a rock. I can't hug her lest I not be able to hear her welcome me: 'I knew you were coming back.' In our dialect she is certain of the things that must happen, written on the stone of the ancient testaments."[56] For Soffiantini, his mother is an undying presence whose words are both familiar and eternal. The way even adult hostages talk about their parents shows how extraneous the world of their kidnappers is for them and how they experience the relationship with their warders as if they were children.

As daughters, the kidnapped women, like the kidnapped men, live captivity as the conversion of the original caregiving relationship into a horrifying world. Yet as mothers, captivity also converts them into potentially horrifying figures. Cavarero's gendered reading of the cultural mediation of horror offers the tools with which to understand why women are subjected to this conversion. In the Western imagination, she observes, horror has a female face (clearly indicative of a cultural misogynistic gaze). The infanticidal mother Medea most exemplifies a crime against the helpless. Yet the philosopher recognizes another mythological figure that especially personifies horror, Medusa: "Separated from the body, the head of the monstrous woman is also split off from the womb ... Medusa is a sterile mother. She doesn't generate horror nor does she explain why horror should be linked to generation. In her severed head, directly, she incarnates it."[57] Cavarero links Medusa and Medea as figures of motherhood – sterile and murderous – who embody a type of violence that not only belongs to the sphere of the wound but also strikes the victims in the sphere of their human need for care. Mothers who personify the most horrifying otherness, they – non-Greek women – also represent a foreign origin of horror to their Greek narrators. They are therefore mothers of the elsewhere, who generate the extraneous.

192   Ransom Kidnapping in Italy

Ovazza and Tesi write that their kidnappers constantly threatened to kill their children if they reported any detail of their captivity to the police. Petrified by the idea of such a possibility, they become victims and instruments of their own horror. Captivity, in short, transforms kidnapped mothers into potential Medeas. The psychological abuses women suffer, and especially the effects they have, cause an even stronger disembodiment than that which men experience. Ovazza, for example, writes that during her capture, her bodily perception gave her the strength to fight against the overwhelming situation:

> It is a matter of a moment. A large cotton ball is pressed against my nose, a cotton ball evidently soaked in chloroform. "My God, help me, give me the strength to resist, do not let me lose consciousness completely." The implacable hand pushes the cotton ball against my face more and more, but ... the noise of the car is still clear in my ears, and I still hear the gasping breath of the bandits. I haven't lost consciousness, so maybe I will still be able to fight and hear them![58]

After having been psychologically abused inside a cell for days by her warders, who have repeatedly threatened to murder her adolescent son, she lives her own body as dangerous:

> Every time they bring me food, they get as close as possible so I can hear the same litany of threats of everything that can happen to me if I report any of the conversations that I've overheard to the police. And they repeat to me all the atrocities that will befall my family members, especially Giorgio [her youngest son], if I ever betray them and expose them to a possible capture. I am happy that I never heard anything. So even if I wanted to, I can never betray them.[59]

Ovazza greatly fears perceiving her abductors, to the point that she confesses to them every time she can hear something even after they have blocked up her ears with wax. As a result, her warder once pushed the wax inside her ears so forcefully that it perforated her eardrums. From the passage, it is clear that women being able to talk about their kidnapping does not mean betraying their kidnappers but rather betraying their children. In order to not expose their children to the consequences threatened by their persecutors, the female hostages break away from their bodies, renouncing the resistance of their bodily perception.

Tesi also testifies to her fear, as a hostage hidden in a hole in an unknown forest, of being able to perceive. "Once something unusual happened. Suddenly in the afternoon silence, we heard strongly and

clearly the voice of a loudspeaker that was yelling: 'Citizens, citizens ...'
I was able to hear just the word 'citizens' because the bandit jumped
on me and plugged my ears, trying to confuse me and not let me hear
anything else," she writes. "Fortunately, I didn't hear anything that
let me identify the place, otherwise I would have been in trouble."[60]
Tesi recounts other similar situations in which she felt relieved when
her warder prevented her from recognizing where she was hidden.
Once, she could hear the voices of children playing: "With my mouth
bound and my eyes wide with terror, I was thinking about my children,
about their voices, about their gestures ... I realized with dismay that
I no longer remembered them: I had strayed too far from the centre of
myself, from my roots," she confesses. "When indeed I returned home
and finally hugged my children again, I did not cry. It was as if I came
from another world: I was 'rootless.'"[61] Captivity radically disembodies
the victims to the point that they feel as though they belong to another
world.

In the weeks after her liberation, Tesi greatly feared talking about
her warder and her kidnapping because she believed her words had
the power to hurt her children. This fear, though, prevented her from
being their mother: "I held them, I kept them close to me, I felt their
presence, but not a word came out of my mouth ... I could not even cry,
as though someone was still holding me far away, chained to another
reality and other sensations, emotions, that were different and more
violent."[62] The consequences of this psychological status, as mentioned,
created a second ordeal for Tesi with the Italian justice system. Regarding the time she drove to illegally meet her kidnapper, who forced her
over the phone to help him escape the police, she asserts:

> It would have been enough for me to stop, park the car in the middle of
> the road, and start screaming: "Help, help me, I am alone, alone, I don't
> know what to do, I am afraid!" But I kept this scream inside of me and
> it completely destroyed me, convinced as I was of doing the best thing,
> of being forced to behave in that way in order to avoid something much
> worse.[63]

Writing about Medusa, Cavarero notes that if the negation of maternity
is visibly pictured by the drastic absence of her body, it is also portrayed
acoustically: "In the severed head, as offense to the corporeal uniqueness of every life, as though it were a citation of the maternity denied
to her, the wail of the baby becomes a howl ... But since we are still
dealing with a visual image, this howl is soundless ... As though the
experience of horror had strangled the cry in (her, our) throat."[64] Like

The Effects of the Testimonial Narrative of Violence

The kidnappers' cruelty reaches its zenith when captivity becomes a type of "violence that labors at slicing." Threatened with bodily mutilation, the hostages live their confinement constantly horrified. Ovazza, for example, writes that her warder considers her body as a weapon for blackmail, and he repeatedly tells her every part he would cut off from her to convince her kin to pay. In a chapter of his memoir entitled "The Mutilations," Belardinelli recounts the moment in which the persecutors cut off part of his ears. The leader of the bandits has accused him of being responsible for his family's insistence on collaborating with the police because the letters he writes are not convincing enough:

> Someone grabs my arms and ties them behind my back. They make me lie down on one side. They uncover my left ear, lifting up my hood on that side … I hear someone asking for a glove, and then a spray on my ear, and then a request for a scalpel. Now comes the cut. A piece of cartilage falls on my face. The blood oozes on my neck. I clench my fists, I do not cry, I do not lament. They disinfect me. A pungent smell. They turn my head and repeat the operation on my right ear. The blood pours down my neck, a cascade. They immortalize the event with four photos: from the left, from the right, twice from the front. A testimony that must be incontrovertible.[65]

Belardinelli's perpetrators mutilate him and make him visible to the outside world as a horrifying image. Immortalized by the photos, the disfigured hostage captures the essence of the ordeal that the kidnapped are forced to suffer, that is, their being at the same time victims and instruments of a crime. Their bodies become the weapon through which the bandits disarm the blackmailed citizens, obliging them to renounce the protection of and collaboration with the police. By looking at the Polaroid of a mutilated Paul Getty in 1973 through his horrified gaze visible in the photo, chapter 2 shifted the narrative of his mutilation from the media to the victim. The horror in Paul's eyes allowed us to empathize with his condition because we recognized in him the passive subject, and not an object, of violence. The kidnapping memoir has the same effect. It allows the reader to empathize with the horrified hostages exploited by shocking images, letters, audio tapes, and even body parts.

The Anatomy of Captivity   195

Belardinelli reports in his book the imaginary dialogue he had with his mother after the inflicted mutilations in which he asks her to pray for him. Like Tesi, he calls the kidnapped hostages *inermi*. However, his repugnance becomes evident after a sadistic episode in which his kidnapper takes a Polaroid photo of him defecating in a metal bucket. "I hear the click of a camera. He takes a snapshot in those conditions and snickers. 'Are you satisfied?' he murmurs. He goes back to the happy group to show off his 'trophy.' I feel repulsion for this behaviour. Outside it is broad daylight, but I go to bed anyway," he writes.[66] The abductor takes the photo after having earlier watched two of his accomplices treating the victim's mutilated ears. During this previous episode, Belardinelli perceived this kidnapper as completely indifferent to his suffering and heard him chuckling while observing the scene. In the memoir, the Polaroid episode not only envisions the hostage as objectified by the sadistic gaze of his warder; it also reflects the warder's leer, which is present on the page from the perspective of Belardinelli's body. Being exposed to the camera makes Belardinelli experience his visibility in a manner that mortifies his self and causes him depression. The use of photography as a "trophy" to which Belardinelli testifies cannot but recall the scandal of the digital pictures of the Abu Ghraib prisoners taken by American soldiers who tortured them, which circulated online in 2004. Although Belardinelli's photo, unlike those of the Abu Ghraib prisoners, did not become public, the account of his disfigured body being mocked in a humiliating circumstance horrifies the reader.

The violent images that the kidnappers send to the families or to the media seek to make them appear powerful and irremovable. Belardinelli calls the photos of his mutilations "incontrovertible testimonies." There is indeed an element of proof in the nature of the mutilated hostage Polaroids (as seen in chapter 2). They satisfy the need to authenticate the kidnap victim's flesh as well as the kidnappers who really possess the hostage (since many scammers contacted families pretending to be the abductors). Yet the Polaroids prove the authenticity of the victims' letters as well. Soffiantini, twice mutilated by his kidnappers, finds it unacceptable that the world outside can consider the hostages' requests inauthentic only because they are dictated by their warders. As seen in chapter 5, the issue of authenticity led him to write his memoir and to identify with Aldo Moro: "I think about Moro, about how he wrote under the unopposed control of the Red Brigades. I feel this control on my skin, and I am able to understand the anguish of those words that were his and not his at the same time, his thoughts and others' dictation. If others could experience for just a few minutes the condition of being kidnapped, many controversies about the letters' authenticity would fall away."[67] This is the second time that

196   Ransom Kidnapping in Italy

Soffiantini mentions Moro in his book. Unlike the other instance, in which the president stands as an authority that guarantees the truthfulness of his memoir against those who doubt his account, in this case Soffiantini identifies with Moro while still captured inside his hiding place. From this position, Soffiantini can bear witness to Aldo Moro and his letters.

"You write at the same time what you think and what is imposed on you, all mixed together, the true and the false in handwriting that is yours but that belongs to the logic of guns and chains," Soffiantini states.[68] The authenticity of the "letters sent from captivity" is a matter not of authorship or agency but of materiality. To not recognize in the physical presence of these written words the bodily gesture that produced them means for Soffiantini to not see the traces left by a language that comes from a squeezed body, as if in addition to the physicality of their handwriting the world outside needs a piece of mutilated flesh to see the hostages. Noting in his book that law enforcement would soon return his letters to him, he says, "I want to touch and read the paper on which I consumed a pain without limits. At the same time, I have a strong anxiety. It almost seems to me that something physical can lead me back to my prison."[69] For the victim, the paper of his messages, the tangibility of their written language, is the medium that makes visible his victimized body. The idea of touching them creates anxiety in Soffiantini because it would be the equivalent of touching the prison from which they came. It would be to have again a perceptual reflexivity with his hiding place and therefore to physically re-experience his captivity. In short, Soffiantini fears the tangible truth of these letters – that is, the horrifying effects of their violence.

The ambiguity of the messages and the issue of their authenticity find a unique mediation in "Hotel Supramonte," a song that musician Fabrizio De André wrote after he and Dori Ghezzi were kidnapped together from their home in Sardinia in 1979 by Sardinian banditry. Scholars often name De André when discussing ransom kidnapping because of his fame and especially because he never criticized his warders in the interviews he gave after his liberation. His attitude towards the painful experience, though, was not the result of a romantic view of banditry, which he condemned. It was rather from the belief that shepherds in Sardinia were being exploited by criminal violence as much as the hostages. In "Hotel Supramonte," referencing the name of the mountain in Barbagia where the two were hidden, De André sings,

E se vai all'Hotel Supramonte e guardi il cielo
Tu vedrai una donna in fiamme e un uomo solo
E una lettera vera di notte, falsa di giorno

[And if you go to the Hotel Supramonte and look at the sky
You will see a woman on fire and a lonely man
And a letter true by night, false by day][70]

Accompanied by the arpeggio of his guitar and through a delicate melody that resembles a lullaby, De André makes visible in one line the painful double nature of the letters from captivity: true for the hostages, false for the world. Turned by captivity into the negotiators of their kidnapping, the hostages cannot be believed. They are not the subjects of the shocking messages to their families. However, as this chapter has argued, the kidnapped victims are the passive and vulnerable subjects of the effects of violence. By testifying to the horror that they lived in flesh behind those letters, their memoirs, unlike other narratives of ransom kidnapping, allow the listener to perceive, and therefore empathize, along with the victims.

Conclusion

While I was writing this conclusion in a public library in the Veneto, a librarian began reading a picture book to a group of elementary school students as part of an event organized to encourage young readers to use libraries. To my great surprise, the story was about a librarian, Costanza Gentilucci, who is kidnapped for ransom by bandits while walking in the forest. *The Librarian and the Robbers* was originally written in 1978 in English by Margaret Mahy and was translated into Italian in 1985 with the title *La bibliotecaria rapita* (The kidnapped librarian) by Salvatore Pinna and Angela Maria Quaquero, notably for the Sardinian Section of the Italian Libraries Association.[1] In the story, the bandit kidnappers hide Gentilucci in a cave, but when they all come down with the measles, they have to quarantine with her. They permit Gentilucci to go to the library to consult a medical manual to find a cure. She returns instead with many books that she reads to her abductors, who are exposed to literature for the first time. The story concludes with the bandits working at the public library as readers to children and Costanza Gentilucci marrying their leader.

This illustrated book likely did not evoke anything for the elementary school students present at the library that day, but the desire in Sardinia to translate Mahy's kidnapping story (which was published in the original English together with another of her stories about pirates) represents a tangible layer of memory stratified in 1980s children's literature, expressing the need at the time to mediate ransom kidnapping through optimism and hope for the youngest members of the population. The story in fact ends with outlaws becoming part of society thanks to education and with the library animated by these free spirits – a romantic interpretation of bandits. Forest and city are unified by the power of books (not by law enforcement), and it is the agency of the hostage that "converts" the persecutors to her world (a reverse Stockholm syndrome). If

Conclusion   199

the book's optimism is motivated by the age of its readers, it is worth noting that this text was published when the numbers of kidnappings had decreased and seven years before bandits mutilated the young Farouk Kassam (1992).

The scary cave that Costanza Gentilucci controls by reading aloud books to her kidnappers – an action that reminds us of the hostages' need to read in order to resist the isolation of captivity, to which the survivors testify in their memoirs – would become even more frightening after the abductions of Marco Fiora from Piedmont (hidden in Calabria, 1987) and Farouk in Sardinia. Niccolò Ammaniti's 2001 novel and Gabriele Salvatores's 2003 cinematographic adaptation, both titled *Io non ho paura* (*I'm Not Scared*), capture this fear by making the scene in which the nine-year-old protagonist, Michele, finds a child his age held hostage in a dark and horrifying cave the most shocking and distressing moment of their well-known dramas.[2] With a choice that recalls neorealism's use of a children's perspective to mediate traumatic historical events, Ammaniti's book tells a story of ransom kidnapping through the eyes of Michele, who discovers that his father, together with the adults of his small village, is involved in the abduction of Filippo, a boy from Milan. Imagination, perhaps more than realism, is the lens through which Michele becomes aware of his surrounding world. Set in a fictionalized place in southern Italy, in the summer of 1978, *Io non ho paura* mentions neither organized crime nor banditry and emphasizes the power of fiction to control fear. Alone at night or when facing difficult obstacles, Michele uses his fantasy to narrate a reality that he cannot understand, creating stories that give him the courage and strength to save Filippo. As in *La bibliotecaria rapita*, in *Io non ho paura* literature is agency. While the book leaves out specific references to historical ransom kidnappers, it includes elements and objects that Italians associate with abduction. In addition to the cave, for example, the pigs that frighten Michele and his friends evoke the gruesome belief that the *anonima sequestri* fed the bodies of the hostages that never returned to these animals – a fear that Donatella Tesi Mosca mentions in her memoir *Sindrome da sequestro* (Kidnapping syndrome).[3]

Today's podcasts, television broadcasts, cinema, and theatre are bringing back the kidnapping stories that this book explores. However, we conclude with another fictional example that perfectly demonstrates how rooted kidnapping is in the Italian imagination: Elena Ferrante's *L'amica geniale* (*My Brilliant Friend*).[4] One of the most successful works of Italian literature on a global scale, *My Brilliant Friend* tells the story of Elena Greco and Raffaella Cerullo (Lenù and Lila), two friends born and raised in a violent neighbourhood in Naples controlled by the Camorra,

200   Ransom Kidnapping in Italy

the Mafia from the Campania region. The first thing we discover in the novel is that Lila (sixty-six years old) cannot be found. It takes the reader four volumes to learn that what happened to Lila is connected to the earlier kidnapping of her three-year-old daughter Tina.

Lila's son Gennaro calls Lenù to ask if she has any news about his mother. When Lenù discovers that her friend has disappeared without a trace, she decides to write about their lives from their childhood in the early 1950s up to 2011. *My Brilliant Friend* is thus a fictional autobiography, which recounts the history of the Italian Republic as seen from the unusual perspective of the relationship between two women.[5] What almost seems missing in the history in much of the series is ransom kidnapping. The stories that develop in each volume as shaped by the personal memories of Lenù, the narrator, evoke the country's public memory. For example, the story of the worker Pasquale Peluso (Lenù and Lila's close friend from their childhood) and his girlfriend Nadia, a student and the daughter of Lenù's professor, refers to the history of the labour and student political movements of the late 1960s and the radicalization in the 1970s of some of their members, who, in the 1970s, joined leftist terroristic groups such as the Nuclei Armati Proletari (Armed Proletarian Cells, NAP), active especially in the south, the Red Brigades, or Prima Linea. The story of Alfonso, another one of Lenù and Lila's childhood friends, who is assassinated by unknown killers because he is queer, alludes to the unsolved murder of the acclaimed writer and film director Pier Paolo Pasolini. The characters and what they embody span from the neo-fascist violence of the late 1960s and 1970s to the feminist movement, the corruption of the political parties in the 1980s, the *tangentopoli* (bribesville) scandal in the early 1990s, and even the rise of Silvio Berlusconi's television empire and its impact on journalism.

Yet it is the trauma of abduction that ultimately shapes Ferrante's novel. Lila's daughter Tina disappears in the middle of the 1980s, that is, in the middle of *My Brilliant Friend*'s fourth and final volume.[6] At this point of the story, Lenù and Lila are living in the same building in their childhood neighbourhood, where they both have returned after years spent apart. Lenù is a successful writer who studied in the best schools, got married and divorced, and has three daughters: Dede and Elsa from her marriage and the three-year-old Imma, whose father is Lenù's lifelong love and ex-lover Nino Sarratore. Lila, who, unlike Lenù, did not receive any education after elementary school, runs a tech company with her partner Enzo. Lila lives with Enzo, their three-year-old daughter Tina, and Gennaro, Lila's teenage son from her previous marriage. The key scene takes place right before lunch on a special day.

Conclusion 201

Lenù is cooking in her kitchen, and her family is downstairs enjoying a street fair and, especially, Nino's long-awaited visit to his daughter Imma. When Lenù joins them in the street, she finds Lila holding Imma (Lenù's daughter) in her arms while talking to Nino. As soon as Lenù asks where Tina is, Lila abruptly realizes that her own daughter is missing. Strikingly, she recognizes what is happening through a flashback she has to a morning in the 1970s when she could not find her son Gennaro and feared that someone had abducted him (a story the reader knows from volume three and a clear foreshadow of her later ordeal). Lila starts to desperately look for her daughter. Nobody on the crowded street seems to know what happened to Tina. The story that becomes a shared belief is that a fast blue truck ran over the girl and dragged her body away. No blood is left on the street, and Tina's body is never found, even after the neighbours search day and night. In reality, Tina is abducted by anonymous kidnappers, who force Lila to live the rest of her life in anguish and with no answers.

Lenù and Lila have opposite perspectives on Tina's abduction. Lenù's explanation is linked to the romance of the novel, which both friends – although at different moments of their lives – have with Nino Sarratore. According to Lenù, Tina disappeared because Lila was distracted since she was talking to Nino. Left by herself, while the adults focused on Imma, Tina was snatched. Lila, on the contrary, thinks that the real target of the kidnappers was Lenù's daughter Imma, as she confesses to her friend ten years later. Just a few weeks before the abduction, the magazine *Panorama* had published a long article on Lenù and her second novel, set in her Neapolitan neighbourhood. In a large photo, *Panorama* showed "Elena Greco with her daughter," but the little girl next to Lenù was actually Lila's daughter Tina. The mystery of Tina's disappearance remains unsolved, but through Lila's gaze Ferrante alludes to the danger and fear of becoming visible and successful in Italy due to kidnapping. Lila's explanation recalls Carla Ovazza's memoir *Cinque ciliege rosse* (Five red cherries) and the account of her captivity when she realizes that she was abducted because of a photo of her son's wedding with Gianni Agnelli's daughter published in the news magazines.[7] Lila's pain of living her life without knowing what happened to her little girl reminds us of Emanuele Riboli's father, Luigi, pictured by Giuseppe Marrazzo's RAI news documentary (1976) wandering alone in a forest, and of the more than eighty families that lived the same tragedy.[8]

In the first decade of the 2000s, Lenù decides to write a short novel based on her relationship with Lila and the story of her lost daughter. Now in her sixties, she publishes *Un'amicizia* (A friendship), which becomes an immediate success. Lenù's fictionalization of Lila's greatest loss and pain is for her friend a point of no return. She first refuses to see Lenù, to answer her phone calls, emails, or letters, and then she disappears. The fact that an abduction is the reason why the most well-known friendship of Italian literature comes to an end is remarkable on several levels. First, kidnapping is clearly at the centre of Ferrante's creative process and what gives structure to her prose in this book series. Second, in a book about memory, in which the characters allude to history and history shapes the characters, kidnapping is the key traumatic event that impacts its protagonists and their relationship. It is not a love triangle that brings to an end the friendship in Ferrante's book but rather an ethical limit that Lila perceives Lenù as having crossed by writing a novel out of her friend's agony. Lila's perspective evokes the same ethical limit that dramatic stories such as the one of Cristina Mazzotti forced Italian public television to face when it came to the choice of broadcasting Ettore Scola's 1977 comedic sketch "Sequestro di persona cara" ("Kidnapping Dear!").[9] Through her character Lila – who in the 1970s had feared that someone abducted her son Gennaro, whose daughter Tina is kidnapped in the mid-1980s, and who in 1995 tells Lenù that she had always protected Imma because she believed her to be the daughter that the kidnappers really wanted – Ferrante acknowledges how abductions haunted the country for decades. Lila seems to recognize better than anyone else that kidnapping was always a present threat while the historical events mentioned by the narrator Lenù, including the Moro affair, were occurring.

The mediation of abduction, or lack thereof, is thus at the core of *My Brilliant Friend*, as it is in the kidnapping memoir. For the victims of ransom kidnapping (as seen in chapter 5), it is not just the traumatic event that is unbearable but also the return to cultural and social frames that lack a language that makes their ordeals visible. Survivors write to mediate what they witnessed. The three literary examples seen in this conclusion show that in Italian fictional memory, abduction is "the evil" that needs to be mediated to children (*La bibliotecaria rapita*), that children have to face in order to know the world and become adults (*Io non ho paura*), and that literature fails to process if its narrative does not see the helpless (*L'amica geniale*). Indeed, Lenù's book *L'amica* and the story she recounts as a narrator picture Lila as responsible for her own pain. The last time Lila sees and talks to Lenù, the narrator Lenù writes: "She muttered, laughing, that evil took unpredictable pathways. You cover it over with churches, convents, books – they seem so important, the books, she said sarcastically, you've devoted your whole life to them – and the evil breaks through the floor and emerges where you don't expect it."[10] Evil exceeds books, Lila warns. Yet with this reflection on the possibilities of literature (and therefore with a metaliterature) and through the end of this friendship, Ferrante, unlike Lenù the narrator, mediates evil (kidnapping) by bringing literature to its limits (Lila disappears) and by making Tina's abduction visible to the reader as an unspeakable and unexpected trauma rather than as Lila's fault. We also find a similar journalistic example of memory's construction of kidnapping as "the evil" in Pablo Trincia and Luca Micheli's podcast *Buio* (Dark), whose episode about the 831-day-long abduction of Carlo Celadon by the 'Ndrangheta is called "Il male" (The evil).[11] Notably, these literary and journalistic frames are indicative of how Italy remembers ransom kidnapping as a violent and cruel peak that mapped a new ethical territory.

Ransom Kidnapping in Italy shows where this memory comes from and how abduction was processed. To deny the presence of organized crime in Lombardy or Piedmont – as politicians did just a few years ago – not only means to negate a current reality.[12] It means to forget the criminal phenomenon that from the 1970s to the 1990s made Italy experience Mafia wounds at the national level and as a national body. Although several criminal syndicates were responsible for the kidnappings, Sardinian banditry, Cosa Nostra, and the 'Ndrangheta were by far the most active abductors. Of these, the *'ndranghetisti* created the kidnapping industry that allowed the Mafia of Calabria to reach the international stage (as seen in chapter 1). The 1970s media coverage of abduction – one of the most covered subjects by national television and press, as shown by the archival materials explored in this book – demonstrates that Italy knew well the danger that the 'Ndrangheta represented all over the peninsula.

Horror, the hard line, solidarity, and testimony are public, political, and civic responses to the violence of ransom kidnapping and criminal syndicates. If each of them corresponds to the diverse moments in the evolution of abduction, they are also expressions of different perspectives on the crime: the body (disfigured), the (strong) state, civic engagement, and the survivors. The 1973 kidnapping and mutilation of Paul Getty III (seen in chapter 2) and the 1975 abduction and murder of Cristina Mazzotti (seen in chapter 3) horrified the country. Through these two kidnappings, the 'Ndrangheta proved how far its violence could go. Novelists such as Moravia and Ginzburg and journalists such as Biagi, Nascimbeni, and Marrazzo, to name just a few, actively shaped the public discourse processing a trauma that, especially when Cristina's body was found in a garbage dump, became a collective wound. The hard line narrative is the one initiated by magistrates and politicians wanting to prevent the hostages' families from paying ransoms to the kidnappers, who thereby would lose the monetary incentive to perpetuate this crime. A long-discussed issue (as seen in chapter 4), the matter of the negotiations was brought to public attention by the kidnapping of Cristina Mazzotti years before that of Aldo Moro. It is therefore an issue that the state first had to face because of the 'Ndrangheta, not the Red Brigades. Moreover, the hard line became the two-decade-long main narrative that shifted the responsibility for the exponential growth of kidnappings from the abductors to their targets. Minister Gui and Judge Pomarici, among others, spread the message on television and in the press that the state was weak because the families of hostages were not allowing magistrates to be strong enough. Although today many Italians believe that the hard line was the solution against ransom kidnapping, this book shows that the regions where this line was applied are those in which the numbers of abductions were the highest. The matter of the negotiation, chapter 4 argues, is less linear than the rationale that its promoters claim and – as the Consiglio Superiore della Magistratura in 1978 and the Council of Europe in 1982 both addressed – touches ethical, constitutional, and even practical aspects that trouble the rule of law.

However, the wave of ransom kidnapping in the late 1980s provoked a public indignation that recalled the one Italy had with the Mazzotti abduction. The main narrative became that of solidarity, and its subject was civic engagement. The 1988 demonstration and concert in Turin to push Marco Fiora's kidnappers to free the child, Angela Casella's 1989 trip to Calabria to mobilize local women, the postcards that Patrizia Tacchella's small town encouraged Italians to send to the president of the republic, the 1990 march in Rome to denounce the state's absence in Aspromonte, and the 1992 white sheets protest for Farouk Kassam inspired by the one for Giovanni Falcone in Palermo are all indicative of a new anti-Mafia sentiment and agency that arose in the country. Finally, as Ferrante's character Lila shows by disappearing, a book about kidnappings cannot ignore the perspective of its victims. The memoirs of the survivors, chapter 5 argues, possess the perceptual frame that other narratives lack, allowing the kidnapped people to bear witness to their ordeal. The agency of their confessional writing, moreover, offers a new perspective on the possibility of testimony as a genre. Seen through the victims' accounts of trauma and disembodiment, the horror of the 1970s kidnapping narrative by intellectuals and journalists becomes "horrorism." As the final chapter of this book concludes, unlike the hard line narrative (and Italian law), the abduction memoir testifies to ransom kidnapping not as a crime against property but rather as an ontological crime, that is, in the lexicon of political philosophy, a crime against humanity.

Italy was the country of ransom kidnapping before and after the Aldo Moro abduction made history. By looking at the media, political, and cultural mediations of this violent phenomenon from the 1970s to the 1990s, this book gives to this history a different frame. Indeed, if terrorists used abductions such as Moro's to attack the heart of the Italian government, organized crime and banditry used them to blackmail civil society and colonize the country's underworld. Today, while banditry has more or less disappeared, the 'Ndrangheta is one of the most powerful criminal organizations in the world. Ransom kidnapping helped make this transformation possible. To remember decades of abductions tells us about more than an "Italian offence." It tells us about a national domestic threat and its power. Italy was (and still is) a country in which the state did not have complete territorial control, nor the monopoly of force, and where the price of its economic development was extremely high for hundreds of its citizens. Confessions of Mafia *pentiti* can reveal the structure of Mafia, its business, or its connections. Yet the memory of ransom kidnapping, this book demonstrates, knows and makes visible the effects of its violence and the collective cost of living in the land of organized crime.

Notes

Introduction

1 "Mi legano come un cane, come una bestia qualsiasi che si voglia tenere prigioniera." Ovazza, *Cinque ciliege rosse*, 17. All translations are my own unless otherwise indicated.

2 Ovazza, "L'esperienza della vittimizzazione," 92.

3 Moro, *Lettere dalla prigionia*.

4 There is a vast bibliography on the Moro abduction. See, among others, Moss, "Kidnapping and Murder of Aldo Moro"; Wagner-Pacifici, *Moro Morality Play*; Drake, *Aldo Moro Murder Case*; Jamieson, *Heart Attacked*; Katz, *Days of Wrath*; Abse, "Moro Affair"; Moss, "From History to Mystery"; and Glynn and Lombardi, *Remembering Aldo Moro*.

5 On the Red Brigades and left-wing terrorism, see, among others, Ginsborg, *History of Contemporary Italy*; Moss, *Politics of Left-Wing Violence*; Jamieson, *Heart Attacked*; Drake, *Revolutionary Mystique and Terrorism*; Meade, *Red Brigades*; Foot, *Italy's Divided Memory*; Glynn, *Women, Terrorism, and Trauma*; and Cento Bull and Cooke, *Ending Terrorism*.

6 See, for example, Tobagi, *Piazza Fontana*; Moss, *Italian Political Violence*; and Della Porta, *Terrorismi in Italia*.

7 In addition to Piazza Fontana, the other major far-right attacks were "Piazza della Loggia," Brescia, May 1974 (8 dead, 94 wounded); the "Italicus" train, August 1974 (12 dead, 105 injured); Bologna station, August 1980 (85 dead, 177 injured); and the "Rapido 904" train, December 1984 (15 dead, 267 injured). See Jamieson, *Heart Attacked*; and Della Porta and Rossi, *Cifre crudeli*.

8 On far-right terrorism see, among others, Cento Bull, *Italian Neofascism*; Tobagi, *Una stella incoronata di buio*; and Dondi, *L'eco del boato*.

9 See, among others, Sciascia, *L'affaire Moro*; Flamigni, *La tela del ragno* and *Rapporto sul caso Moro*; Ventura, *Per una storia del terrorismo italiano*; Gotor, *Il*

208   Notes to pages 5–7

memoriale della repubblica and *L'Italia del Novecento*; Calogero, Fumian, and Sartori, *Terrore rosso*; Santa, *I nemici della Repubblica*; Galfré, *La guerra è finita*; Ceci, *Il terrorismo italiano*; Panvini, *Cattolici e violenza política* and *Ordine nero, guerriglia rossa*; and Turone, *Italia occulta*.

10 Pisano, *Dynamics of Subversion*, 59.
11 Alessandro Pardini, "Relazione sui sequestri di persona a scopo di estorsione," in *Commissione parlamentare sul fenomeno della mafia e altre associazioni criminali* (istituita con legge 1 ottobre 1996, n. 509).
12 Pardini, 34.
13 Pardini, 35.
14 Pardini, 39–40.
15 See, for example, articles in business magazines such as "E ora anche la difesa diventa un fatto personale" or articles on kidnapping insurances such as "Scandalo a Milano."
16 See Berlusconi's interview with Alan Friedman in *My Way*; and Trebay, "French President's Lover."
17 In this book Luberto and Manganelli compare the phenomenon of ransom kidnapping in Italy to the same phenomenon in other European countries. Between 1968 and 1983, there were 561 kidnappings in Italy. Between 1968 and 1972, the number of kidnappings in other European countries were: Germany, 48; France, 42 (between 1974 and 1982); Spain, 142 (all of them between 1980 and 1982); the UK, 232 (between 1979 and 1981); and in the Netherlands, Belgium, Austria, Switzerland, Denmark, Norway, and Sweden the number of kidnappings was insignificant. See Luberto and Manganelli, *I sequestri di persona*, 76–83.
18 Ciconte, "Un delitto italiano."
19 Puzo, *Godfather*; Coppola, *Godfather*; *La piovra*.
20 See Lupo, *History of the Mafia*; Dickie, *Cosa Nostra, Blood Brotherhoods*, and *Mafia Republic*; Paoli, *Mafia Brotherhoods*; Ciconte, *Processo alla 'Ndrangheta* and *Alle origini della nuova 'Ndrangheta*; Sergi and Lavorgna, *'Ndrangheta*; Gratteri and Nicaso, *Fratelli di sangue, Fiumi d'oro*, and *Storia segreta della 'Ndrangheta*.
21 Varese, *Mafias on the Move*; Dalla Chiesa, *Passaggio a Nord*.
22 See, for example, Pickering-Iazzi, *Mafia in Italian Life and Literature* and *Mafia and Outlaw Stories*; Renga, *Unfinished Business, Mafia Movies*, and *Watching Sympathetic Perpetrators*; Dainotto, *Mafia*.
23 Saviano, *Gomorra*. After the publication of his book, Saviano received death threats from the Camorra and has since lived under police escort.
24 Garrone, *Gomorra*; *Gomorra – la serie* (*Gomorrah*).
25 See Dickie, *Cosa Nostra*; and Lupo, *History of the Mafia*.
26 See, among others, Stille, *Excellent Cadavers*; Caselli, *Le due guerre*.

Notes to pages 7–17   209

27 Beccaria and Turone, *Il Boss Luciano Liggio*.
28 Minuti and Veltri, *Lettere a San Luca*. The prominent journalist Corrado Stajano, who wrote the preface to this collection, calls these "letters from racism," denouncing the violent comments present in these texts as motivated by the historical racism demonstrated towards the southern population of the peninsula dating back to the Italian Unification. See Stajano, "Lettere dal razzismo."
29 Biondani, "A Milano la mafia non c'è"; see also Portanova, Rossi, and Stefanoni, *Mafia a Milano*.
30 Journalist Ottavio Rossani calls the expression *anonima sequestri* "a stereotypical definition that does not mean anything if not that authorities are not able to 'enter' in the industrial organization of kidnapping and unmask the connections," in Rossani, *Intervista sui rapimenti*, 19. The word *anonima* was in reality used by the press since the 1960s to talk about the abductions in Sardinia by banditry, which was thought to be controlled by powerful people. In addition to "anonima sequestri," the press also used "anonima rapitori" and "anonima banditi," such as in two articles of the daily *La Stampa*. See "Scoperta l'anonima banditi?" and "Ordine di arresto per il dottor Piras."
31 Cavarero, *Orrorismo*.
32 Merleau-Ponty, *Phenomenology of Perception* and *Visible and the Invisible*.
33 Caruth, *Unclaimed Experience*, 4.
34 Caruth, 5.
35 Alexander, "Toward a Theory of Cultural Trauma."
36 See Tiziano, "I sequestri di persona?"

1. Italy's Extraterritorialities: Tracing the History of Ransom Kidnapping

1 Moravia, "L'orecchio di Getty."
2 See chapter 2.
3 Cagnetta, "Inchiesta su Orgosolo."
4 Alberto Carocci, co-director of *Nuovi Argomenti*, was also denounced. See Cagnetta, *Banditi a Orgosolo*, 32.
5 See Hobsbawm, *Primitive Rebels*, 4; De Seta, *Banditi a Orgosolo*.
6 De Seta's two short documentaries, *Pastori di Orgosolo* and *Un giorno in barbagia*, are now part of the collection *Il mondo perduto*.
7 Cagnetta, *Bandits d'Orgosolo*. The book was also published in Germany as *Die Banditen von Orgosolo: Porträt eines sardischen Dorfes* (Düsseldorf-Wien: Econ, 1964). For the first Italian edition see Franco Cagnetta, *Banditi a Orgosolo* (Florence: Guaraldi, 1975).
8 Moravia, "Nota di Alberto Moravia," 282.
9 Moravia, 281.

210   Notes to pages 17–21

10 See Moravia, "L'orecchio di Getty," "L'ex-Italia delle bande," "Riflessioni davanti all'orrore," "Il complesso di Elettra," and "Pasolini o il mito della cultura contadina."

11 "La società in cui, grazie ad abusi e delitti di vario genere e origine, l'equilibrio si ristabilisce da solo." Moravia, "L'ex-Italia delle bande."

12 "Non è la società moderna e democratica … bensì una società di tipo molto più tradizionale e antico che, negli ultimi tempi, è venuta sempre più affiorando nel nostro paese." Moravia, "L'ex-Italia delle bande."

13 "Ricacciare indietro la società dei sequestri." Moravia, "L'ex-Italia delle bande."

14 Moravia, "Pasolini o il mito della cultura contadina."

15 "Era inutile che io, per esempio, gli dicessi che i mali d'Italia venivano non già dall'industrializzazione e dal consumismo ma dalla putrefazione secolare della sua amata cultura contadina; che quella che lui chiamava criminalità di massa, cioè la mafia, i sequestri, le rapine … era in realtà la criminalità dei contadini malamente e insufficientemente inurbati." Moravia, "Pasolini o il mito della cultura contadina."

16 On the differences between Sardinian crime and Mafia, see Arlacchi, *La mafia imprenditrice*.

17 It is important to mention that during the *anni di piombo* Rome was also the centre of an urban phenomenon of ransom kidnapping whose mastermind was a criminal organization known as the Banda della Magliana. See *Dossier Banda della Magliana*; Imposimato, *I sequestri d'Italia*; and Dickie, *Mafia Republic*.

18 Giuseppe Medici, "Relazione di maggioranza," in *Commissione parlamentare d'inchiesta sui fenomeni di criminalità in Sardegna* (istituita con legge 27 ottobre 1969, n. 755), 19.

19 Medici, 21–38.

20 Rudas and Marongiu, "Il sequestro di persona," 108.

21 Giuseppe Panico and Giuliano Oliva, "Analisi di alcuni aspetti del sequestro di persona," in *Commissione parlamentare d'inchiesta sui fenomeni di criminalità in Sardegna* (istituita con legge 27 ottobre 1969, n. 755), 363. On the same subject, see also Giuseppe Puggioni and Nereide Rudas, "Caratteristiche, tendenzialità e dinamiche dei fenomeni di criminalità in Sardegna," in *Commissione parlamentare d'inchiesta sui fenomeni di criminalità in Sardegna* (istituita con legge 27 ottobre 1969, n. 755), 192, 245–6.

22 On the use of force and the attitude of the state towards Sardinia from after World War II until the first half of the 1970s, see Fiori, *La Società del malessere*; and Pintore, *Sardegna*.

23 Puggioni and Rudas, "Caratteristiche, tendenzialità e dinamiche," 145.

24 For the life of the nomadic shepherds see Cagnetta, *Banditi a Orgosolo*.

Notes to pages 21–7   211

25 The anthropologist Antonio Pigliaru maintains that there exists an unwritten code of law handed down from antiquity in the *barbaricina* culture based upon vendetta. See Pigliaru, *La vendetta barbaricina*.

26 Pardini, "Relazione," 20–1.

27 Pardini, 20.

28 Ciconte, "Un delitto italiano," 190.

29 On banditry and the values celebrated by the *barbaricina* culture, there is an extensive literature, of which I note a few texts beyond those cited in other notes: Marongiu, *Teoria e storia del banditismo sociale* and *Criminalità e banditismo in Sardegna*; Corda, *La legge e la macchia*; and Pigliaru and Lombardi Satriani, *Il banditismo in Sardegna*.

30 Many biographies of Graziano Mesina have been published, including Vergani, *Mesina*; Massaiu, *Mesina perché?*; Mesina, Banda, and Moroni, *Io, Mesina*; and Pisanò, *Lo strano caso del signor Mesina*.

31 On the bandit as a symbol in the *barbaricino* world, see Hobsbawm, *Primitive Rebels* and *Bandits*.

32 Another motivation that led people to *latitanza* regards those who really were guilty. Many criminals forced the inhabitants of their villages to testify on their behalf in order to be absolved due to insufficient evidence.

33 Marongiu and Paribello, "Il sequestro di persona," 116.

34 Marongiu and Paribello, 116–17.

35 See Marongiu and Paribello, who add that "in almost 80 per cent of cases the criminals come from the same district (144 out of 181)." Marongiu and Paribello, 117.

36 Rudas and Marongiu, "Il sequestro di persona," 112.

37 Luberto and Manganelli, *I sequestri di persona*, 38.

38 Pardini, "Relazione," 25–6.

39 In those years Milan was notable not only for the strong presence of Sicilian *mafiosi* but also as a centre for the 'Ndrangheta and international criminal groups, like a Marseillais clan who carried out six kidnappings between 1975 and 1976. In 1977, the Sicilians, Calabrians, and Marseillais acted together in a few kidnappings. See Ciconte, "Un delitto italiano," 198.

40 Dickie, *Mafia Republic*, 172.

41 Pardini, "Relazione," 25.

42 Rossani, *L'industria dei sequestri*, 40.

43 Luberto and Manganelli, *I sequestri di persona*, 45–6.

44 Luberto and Manganelli, 45.

45 Luberto and Manganelli, 17.

46 Luberto and Manganelli, 22.

47 Pardini, "Relazione," 28.

48 On this phenomenon, see Ciconte, *Processo alla 'Ndrangheta*, 160–8.

212 Notes to pages 28–32

49 The kidnapping of the surgeon Renato Caminiti, captured at Villa San Giovanni on 26 August 1970 and released after only two days, was the 'Ndrangheta's first (Pardini, "Relazione," 27). On this kidnapping, see also Gambino, *La mafia in Calabria*, 157–8.

50 On the kidnappings perpetrated by the 'Ndrangheta in Calabria and in other regions in the first half of the 1970s, see Arcà, *Mafia, potere, malgoverno*, 54–64.

51 Pardini, "Relazione," 27–8.

52 Gratteri and Nicaso, *Fratelli di sangue*, 54.

53 Gratteri and Nicaso, 54. Sharo Gambino also spoke about kidnappings as an expression of generational change in the 'Ndrangheta, demonstrating that the crime was motivated by a desire by the new generations to gain wealth. See Gambino, *La mafia in Calabria*, 161.

54 On the kidnapping of Getty, see chapter 2.

55 Macrì, "'Ndrangheta e sequestri di persona," 164.

56 Macrì, 164.

57 These public projects have never been completed.

58 Pardini, "Relazione," 28.

59 On this transformation of the Mafia, which was not limited to the Calabrians, see Arlacchi, *La mafia imprenditrice*.

60 Macrì, "'Ndrangheta e sequestri di persona," 164.

61 Antonio Zagari wrote and published his memoir in 1992. Saverio Morabito gave the account of his life as a boss to the journalists Piero Colaprico and Luca Fazzo, who wrote and published his story in a first-person account. See Zagari, *Ammazzare stanca*; Colaprico and Fazzo, *Manager calibro 9*.

62 Pardini, "Relazione," 28–9.

63 Cesare Casella recounted his kidnapping in a book written in the first person by the journalist Pino Belleri. See Casella, *743 giorni lontano da casa*.

64 Chapter 4 will explore the impact of these three kidnappings on media and the public.

65 For a concise and detailed account of Zagari's and Morabito's revelations, see Pardini, "Relazione," 27.

66 Luciano Violante, "Relazione di minoranza," in *Commissione parlamentare sul fenomeno della mafia e altre associazioni criminali* (istituita con legge 23 marzo 1988, n. 94), 24–5.

67 Ciconte, "Un delitto italiano," 206.

68 Another peculiarity of the 'Ndrangheta matrix that distinguishes it from other matrices was that for the Calabrian *cosche*, kidnapping had a broader strategic function, that is, it acted as "delitto esca" (crime bait-and-switch). If Cosa Nostra rejected extortion kidnapping in order to not attract the forces of order into Sicily, the 'Ndrangheta utilized it in order to focus that attention on a circumscribed territory inside inland Calabria, thereby

Notes to pages 32–4   213

creating for themselves the liberty with which to administer to the illicit trafficking that they conducted on their coasts. See Ciconte, "Un delitto italiano," 201.

69 Gratteri and Nicaso, *Fratelli di sangue*, 54.
70 Gratteri and Nicaso, 64.
71 Marongiu and Paribello, "Il sequestro di persona," 115.
72 On the Catanzaro Trial, see Tobagi, *Piazza Fontana*.
73 The anarchist Giuseppe Pinelli was wrongly suspected and detained by the police not long after the bombing. He died on 15 December 1969 by falling from the window of the police station in Milan where he had been held beyond the time consented by the law.
74 Amodei and Bosio, *Il processo*.
75 The trial was postponed twice: in 1976 after the murder of Francesco Coco, attorney general of Genoa, and in 1977 because of the assassination of Fulvio Croce, president of the Turin Bar Association.
76 After 134 defections, Adelaide Aglietta, secretary of the Radical Party, agreed to be a jury member. The trial started 9 March 1978. The following day, the Maresciallo Rosario Belardi was killed. The BR claimed responsibility for his murder at the trial, as they did later for the death of Aldo Moro and his bodyguards. In a 2018 article, the politician and former magistrate Luciano Violante remembers these events, writing, "Turin's courthouse was used as the sounding board for the murders" by the BR. See Luciano Violante, "Torino, 40 anni."
77 "Cadaveri eccellenti" (illustrious corpses) was originally, in Alexander Stille's words, "a term used in Sicily to distinguish the assassination of prominent government officials from the hundreds of common criminals and ordinary citizens killed in the course of routine mafia business." Stille, *Excellent Cadavers*, 6.
78 The Caccia murder has recently received scholarly attention in Italy. The thirtieth anniversary of his death in 2013 and the 2015 arrest of Rocco Schirripa, one of the two assassins, have awoken interest in an otherwise erased story. On the wave of the Operazione Minotauro (Minotaur Operation) – a five-year-long maxi-investigation and trial of the 'Ndrangheta in Piedmont that ended in June 2011 with more than 150 arrested – law enforcement started to investigate Schirripa, who, found guilty of killing Caccia, was sentenced to life in prison on 19 February 2020, that is, almost four decades after the fact. On Caccia's assassination, see Tranfaglia and De Palma, *Il giudice dimenticato*; and Bellone, *Tutti i nemici del Procuratore*. On Schirripa's trial, see Elisa Sola, "Dalla droga ai riti della 'Ndrangheta"; Ciccorello and Pecorelli, "Bruno Caccia"; F.Q., "Bruno Caccia" and "Omicidio Caccia."

214   Notes to pages 34–5

79 PrRC, Procura della Repubblica di Reggio Calabria, 1995: 5754. Cited in Paoli, "Broken Bonds," n101.
80 See Sergi, *La "Santa" violenta*. See also the documentary by Oliva and Fierro, *La Santa*.
81 On the 'Ndrangheta's relationship with Freemasonry, see, for example, Paoli, *Mafia Brotherhoods*, 114–17; and Dickie, *Craft*.
82 See, for example, Gratteri and Nicaso, *Storia segreta della 'Ndrangheta*, 135–8.
83 Grasso, "Era odiato dalla mafia"; Grasso, "Il magistrato ucciso"; Martinelli, "Forse il giudice Ferlaino fu eliminato"; Feltri, "Orribile sospetto."
84 Scopelliti escaped from Palmi's jail in Calabria in February 1975, while Scriva escaped from Civitavecchia's jail in Lazio in April 1975. Scriva previously asked Ferlaino to be transferred to Calabria, but the judge denied his request. See Guidi, "È stato un evaso?"; Grasso, "Un detenuto."
85 By the time the court delivered the sentence in 1980, Scopelliti was no longer alive, whereas Scriva and Giacobbe, even if acquitted, remained in prison for other crimes. Scopelliti was accused of Erika Ratti's kidnapping (1978) and under trial when he died. The journalist Ottavio Rossani tells Scopelliti's story in a fascinating article in which he details the boss's accomplishments and virtues as if he were a celebrity. Rossani, "Emigrò a Milano." On Scopelliti and kidnapping, see also "Da piccolo contrabbandiere."
86 "Il 'boss' Antonio Giacobbe."
87 Gerardo Gambardella, "Assassinato a colpi di lupara"; Grasso, "L'uccisione di Ferlaino."
88 "Commissione di magistrati a Catanzaro."
89 Guidi, "Calabria"; Madeo, "Si indaga sulla magistratura," 1–2; Madeo, "La regione Calabria"; "Reggio Calabria."
90 The official reason the investigation did not take place is not clear. However, the news that such an investigation was planned by the CSM opened a large debate in the media and beyond. The Procuratore Generale della Corte d'Appello di Catanzaro, Donato Massimo Bartolomei, took a firm position against what he considered a false accusation against the magistracy in Calabria and particularly against an article published by the national magazine *Panorama*, which, in his opinion, cast a shadow on the integrity of the legal system in his region; see "Catanzaro: Protesta per un articolo su presunti rapporti giudici-mafia." Moreover, as a reaction to the parliamentary discussion about the justice system of Calabria, Bartolomei invoked the intervention of the army in the region to solve the problem of "banditry" – neglecting to

Notes to pages 36–7 215

use the term 'Ndrangheta; see "Il PG chiede l'intervento dell'esercito." Another episode connected to the same debate is the accusation that the Onorevole Salvatore Frasca moved against Bartolomei and other judges at the conference "Mafia, Stato e Società," sponsored by the region in 1976; Frasca was later sentenced for defamation. See Franz, "Condannato ex deputato." For the doubts about the magistracy in Calabria as an effect of the investigation, see Madeo, "Il giudice contagiato"; Madeo, "Chi finge che la mafia non esista"; Ciuni, "Inquietanti domande"; Madeo, "Gruppo liquida tutto."

91 Historians Tranfaglia and De Palma criticized the media for having quickly forgotten Caccia's murder as soon as it became clear that it was not a terrorist act. According to these scholars, this is a clear indication of how journalism in 1983 was still inexperienced at covering organized crime. See Tranfaglia and De Palma, *Il giudice dimenticato*, 75–8.

92 Tranfaglia and De Palma's *Il giudice dimenticato* and Bellone's *Tutti i nemici del Procuratore* both detail the secret service's investigation, which resembles a detective story. Francesco Miano secretly recorded in jail the conversations he had with Belfiore, who indirectly confessed his guilt. Belfiore was arrested soon after Caccia's murder for abetting the assassination of Carlo Sanna, a Sardinian involved in the *Calabresi's* businesses. Miano, instead, had been incarcerated a few months earlier for drug dealing. Both bosses ended up being in the same prison, where Miano received a recorder device from a secret service agent.

93 Placido Barresi, Belfiore's brother-in-law, was also prosecuted but was acquitted due to a lack of evidence.

94 Bellone emphasizes the judges' moral responsibilities for the Caccia murder and dedicates an entire section to the judge Luigi Moschella, whose collaboration with the Calabresi was largely proved. Historically connected for having been the initial prosecutors of red terrorism, Moschella and Caccia became, respectively, the anti-hero of the Turin courthouse and a role model for young colleagues. However, Bellone's severe critique is especially addressed to the High Council of the Judiciary, which did not take a firm position against Moschella's and other magistrates' malfeasance. Bellone, *Tutti i nemici del Procuratore*.

95 In addition to being the mastermind of Cristina Mazzotti's kidnapping, Antonio Giacobbe is considered to have been responsible for the Ferlaino murder, and another criminal involved in her abduction, Demetrio Latella, is suspected to be Bruno Caccia's missing killer. Latella, a Calabrian known as Luciano, in 2008 confessed to be guilty of abducting Cristina. His fingerprint coincided with the one found in 1975 on the car where the girl was with her friends when she was snatched. Because the Mazzotti case was already closed, Latella did not go to jail. The

216   Notes to pages 37–44

Caccia family and their lawyer, Fabio Repici, believe that in 1983 Latella worked as a hitman for Angelo Epaminonda, the well-known boss of the homonymous Mafia clan active in Milan and involved in the casinos' money laundering with Belfiore and his clan. Epaminonda, according to the Caccias, could be the other mastermind of their father's murder. On Latella as kidnapper, see Corvi, "La famiglia Mazzotti," 11; and Corvi, "Omicidio Mazzotti," 19. On Caccia's family's request to investigate Latella, see Ciccarello, "Omicidio di Bruno Caccia."

96 See chapter 6.
97 See chapter 4.
98 Pisano, *Dynamics of Subversion*, 57.
99 Dickie, *Mafia Republic*, 166.
100 See chapter 2.

2. The Kidnapping of the Golden Hippy

1 See introduction.
2 The two Polaroids first appeared in the news on 19 March and 21 April 1978, respectively.
3 See Bianchi and Perna, *Le polaroid di Moro*.
4 The media spread Getty's remark all over the world. It now appears in *The New Yale Book of Quotations*, ed. Fred R. Shapiro (New Haven, CT: Yale University Press, 2006), 319, which attributes it to the *Minneapolis Star*, 27 July 1973.
5 Belpoliti, *Da quella prigione*.
6 See in particular the chapter "La foto" in Belpoliti, *Da quella prigione*, 24–51.
7 In his *The Camera Does the Rest*, Peter Buse states that the technology of the Polaroid camera inspired a kidnapping subgenre in both literature and film. See chapter 2, "Intimate, One of a Kind," 70–2.
8 After the release of *All the Money in the World*, the Italian journalist and film director Vito Bruschini published a novel inspired by the Getty kidnapping. Bruschini, *Rapimento e riscatto*.
9 Scarpa, *All the Money in the World*; Pearson, *Painfully Rich*. The 2017 edition of Pearson's book changed the title to *All the Money in the World: The Outrageous Fortune and Misfortune of the Heirs of J. Paul Getty*.
10 Maddaus, "'All the Money in the World' Angers Family"; and Waxman, "True Story."
11 See Miller, "Getty Family Threatens Lawsuit"; see also Sulcas, "The 'Trust' Equation"; McDonell-Parry, "John Paul Getty III"; Mackenzie, "Tragic True Story"; Miller, "Did Paul Getty Help Stage His Kidnapping?"
12 Eszterhas, "J. Paul Getty III."
13 Eszterhas, "J. Paul Getty III."

Notes to pages 45–53   217

14 "Intervista del 1974 a cura di Scarano a Paul Getty III."
15 "Intervista del 1974 a cura di Scarano a Paul Getty III."
16 The granddaughter of the billionaire publisher William Randolph
    Hearst, Patricia Hearst, was kidnapped by the American terrorist group
    Symbionese Liberation Army on 4 February 1974. She was arrested and
    then pardoned after a controversial trial and almost two years spent in
    prison. Hearst gave an account of her ordeal in a memoir co-written with
    Alvin Moscow, *Every Secret Thing*. On her case, see also Graebner, *Patty's
    Got a Gun*; and Toobin, *American Heiress*.
17 "Intervista del 1974 a cura di Scarano a Paul Getty III."
18 "Intervista del 1974 a cura di Scarano a Paul Getty III."
19 Ghislanzoni, "I soldi trovati sono quelli del riscatto."
20 In addition to the aforementioned article, see also Ghislanzoni, "Come
    in Calabria è scattata"; Menghini, "Il confronto si terrà"; "Paul Getty III
    'Sono pronto a tornare a Roma'"; Giuliani, "Nel casolare"; Menghini,
    "Arriveremo anche ai capi della gang"; Menghini, "Sale a cinque"; Giuliani,
    "Il vero 'giallo' comincia adesso"; Ghislanzoni, "Le oscure attività."
21 Barilà, "Il superlatitante Saverio Mammoliti."
22 "Vuol dire che invece di avere un rapimento a settimana, come stava
    avvenendo in questi ultimi tempi, ne avremo uno al giorno." In "Taviani:
    La magistratura."
23 Barilà, "Arrestato per droga."
24 "Anche la giustizia sa distinguere tra boss e semplici gregari." In
    Martinelli, "Il presunto ideatore."
25 Martinelli, "Resta il dubbio."
26 Martinelli, "Paul Getty non simulò il sequestro."
27 "Sequestro Getty."
28 "È una pietra miliare nello sviluppo dell'attività criminosa della mafia
    reggina." In De Simone, "La drammatica evoluzione."
29 See Gratteri and Nicaso, *Storia segreta della 'Ndrangheta*. See also Gratteri
    and Nicaso, *Fiumi d'oro* and *Fratelli di sangue*; Ciconte, *Processo alla
    'Ndrangheta*; Fontana and Serarcangeli, *L'Italia dei sequestri*; and Rossani,
    L'industria dei sequestri.
30 Minoli, "Il rapimento di Paul Getty."
31 1976 Lagonegro interview in Minoli, "Il rapimento di Paul Getty."
32 Martinelli, "Faccia a faccia coi rapitori."
33 "1973: Anno di grandi sequestri," 5.
34 "Paul Getty III aveva progettato il finto rapimento"; "Mi farò rapire," 4;
    Ghislanzoni, "Il giovane Getty," 10.
35 "Gli amici dicevano spesso a Paul," 1.
36 "Rapito il nipote di Paul Getty?," *L'Unità*, 5; "Getty: Fuga, sequestro o
    scherzo," 4; "Anche la madre dubita," 10.

218　Notes to pages 53–9

37 "Il giovane Paul Getty scomparso," 1.
38 "Il nipote dell'uomo più ricco del mondo ha 17 anni e appartiene alla sinistra sovversiva." In "Il giovane Paul Getty scomparso."
39 "Paul Getty III in una curiosa posa da foto-modello" and "Paul Getty III in una recente foto da 'bravo ragazzo.'" The three articles are: "Il silenzio dei rapitori"; "L'hippy d'oro"; and "Petrolio, miliardi e gialli insoluti," 4.
40 "Drammatica invocazione," 4.
41 "Forse visto in Corsica," 1.
42 "Paul si è fatto rapire," 1; "È a bordo d'un panfilo," 4; "Paul interprete di se stesso," 5.
43 "Rapimento autentico o simulato?," 4; "Due tesi a confronto," 5.
44 "'Troppo svogliati' gli strani rapitori," 5.
45 "Un attico di sei stanze arredate in sfarzoso stile americano." "Continua il silenzio dei rapitori," 4.
46 "Avvolta in una elegante vestaglia di seta" and "gli occhi cerchiati dall'angoscia per la notte insonne." "Continua il silenzio dei rapitori," 4.
47 "Seno libero" and "gambe affusolate." "Un messaggio di Paul alla madre," 4.
48 "Gail Harris ha vissuto questa vicenda con molto coraggio e con molto autocontrollo, senza perdere mai la calma e suscitando per questo, fra il pubblico italiano, una sorta di diffidenza. E nemmeno ora è cambiata, dopo che tutto è finito nel migliore dei modi e quando si pensava che potesse finalmente abbandonarsi ai suoi sentimenti di madre e di donna." Pandolfo, "'Quando mi hanno tagliato l'orecchio,'" 5.
49 "Da buon italiano." Pandolfo, 5.
50 "Ti manderemo un dito di Paul," 4; Di Dio, "'Se Paul voleva denaro bastava,'" 5.
51 Del Re, "Senza Famiglia," 1.
52 Trivelli, "È suo o non è suo?," 5.
53 "Fotocronaca di un'avventura notturna," 5.
54 "Errori madornali [come] quelli di uno straniero che … abbia ben poco tempo dedicato allo studio." "Il grido di Paul," 4.
55 Passarelli, "Come 'taglia' un orecchio," 6.
56 On this subject see Rossani, *L'industria dei sequestri*; Montalbano, "Ransom Kidnapping."
57 "Sembra ispirare un raccapriccio maggiore dei tanti cadaveri di cui, ieri come oggi, sono piene le storie dei sequestri." Moravia, "L'orecchio di Getty," 1.
58 "Un atto di disperata barbarie"; "rivela l'esistenza di un piano, sia pure atroce, cioè la presenza di un elemento positivo, la ragione, applicato al delitto." Moravia, 1.
59 "Coscienza sociologica." Moravia, 1.

Notes to pages 59–68   219

60 "I banditi di un tempo erano, essenzialmente, 'diversi'; quelli di oggi, altrettanto essenzialmente, sono invece 'simili.' Il che equivale a dire che l'etica del consumo, del profitto, dell'edonismo a tutti i costi non poteva alla fine non estendersi anche al delitto." Moravia, 1.

61 "È dunque la somiglianza del metodo che spaventa, non la diversità. Spaventa perché contiene una critica, un dubbio, un sospetto sulla validità del metodo stesso. Così si spiega che all'orrore dell'opinione pubblica per la crudeltà dei banditi si aggiunge una oscura e inquieta riprovazione per il nonno che afferma di non voler pagare il riscatto." Moravia, 1.

62 Pansa, "Disarmati di fronte," 1; Alberoni, "Come nel Medioevo," 1.

63 Bevilacqua, "Questa è la storia di Paul Getty III," 3.

64 "Se l'intento delle Brigate Rosse era quello di fotografare un ostaggio (e nella prima foto lo è), lo sguardo di Moro in questa seconda istantanea annulla ogni intenzione, e ci raggiunge. Cosa ci vuole dire? Niente di più che un'affermazione di presenza, il suo *ci sono*. Forse è per questo *esserci* comunicato dal suo sguardo dissimmetrico che la fotografia continua a significare. Buca lo spessore della storia, quella Storia che chi ha scattato l'immagine credeva di scrivere, o riscrivere, con un atto di forza. Di tutto l'accumulo di dolore, sofferenze e folli disegni che sottendono e che seguono questo atto, l'unica cosa che mi pare ancora significativa è lo sguardo di Aldo Moro." Belpoliti, *Da quella prigione*, 43.

65 Linfield, *Cruel Radiance*, 24.

66 Linfield, 30.

67 Cavarero, *Horrorism*, 12.

68 Linfield, *Cruel Radiance*, 22.

69 "E se è vero che il nonno non paga per 'scoraggiare il ricatto in linea di principio' e servire in tal modo la civiltà, ebbene la sua cieca determinazione di puritano pareggia (non diciamo che supera) la nefandezza dei rapitori." Laurenzi, "Crudeltà e avarizia," 11.

3. The Day Cristina's Body Was Found

1 Shuster, "Italians' Apathy Over Kidnappings."

2 Shuster, "Italians' Apathy Over Kidnappings."

3 Cristina's story recently inspired the play *5 centimetri d'aria*, a collaboration between the Teatro piccolo di Milano and the University of Milan. Rampoldi, Dalla Chiesa, and Ornati, *5 centimetri d'aria*. On Cristina's story see Pickering-Iazzi, *Dead Silent*.

4 Giuliani, "'Chi è Cristina?'"

5 In her excellent work on child abduction in the United States, historian Paula S. Fass states that "our definition of the crime (even, indeed, the courts' definition) has been historically derived." Fass, *Kidnapped*, 9.

220   Notes to pages 68–71

6 For the analysis of the press, I focus in particular on the numerous articles published by the main national newspaper, *Corriere della Sera*, which was also the newspaper of Milan – the Mazzottis' hometown.

7 Biagi, "Cristina, un'esistenza come tante," 3.

8 "La strategia del sequestro di persona ha un copione fisso che non si apre a molte varianti. In casa Mazzotti si vive accanto al telefono. Ormai da ore. Ma il tacere angoscioso della suoneria fa parte della crudele regola del gioco: tenere sulla corda i familiari dell'ostaggio al limite estremo della resistenza nervosa." Giuliani, "'Chi è Cristina?,'" 7.

9 Giuliani, "Rompono il silenzio," 9.

10 "Insanabile piaga dei rapimenti." "Accanto al grande colpo (che oggi si chiama Giuseppe D'Amico, l'armatore romano, come ieri si chiamò Getty Junior o Alemagna o Rossi di Montelera o Bulgari), si assiste a una serie sempre più fitta di colpi minori." Nascimbeni, "Dai riscatti-miliardo al sottofatturato dei sequestri," 1. Luigi Rossi di Montelera, Daniele Alemagna, and Gianni Bulgari were kidnapped in 1973, 1974, and early 1975, respectively. Daniele Alemagna was seven years old, and his abduction lasted a few days. Their families owned very important Italian brands such as the vermouth label Martini & Rossi, the sweets company Alemagna, and the luxury brand Bulgari, renowned for jewellery, watches, and perfumes, among other things.

11 Nascimbeni, "Dai riscatti-miliardo al sottofatturato dei sequestri."

12 "Più indifesa, esposta a un procedimento di ipotetica decimazione." Nascimbeni, "Dai riscatti-miliardo al sottofatturato dei sequestri."

13 Hobbes, *Leviathan*.

14 "Odissea disumana." "Giorno dopo giorno, notte dopo notte, ad aspettare che squilli il telefono, che venga almeno un segno di pietà, che la tenace speranza abbia un conforto." Nascimbeni, "Dai riscatti-miliardo al sottofatturato dei sequestri."

15 "Quella del lavoro, dello studio, della vita quotidiana di una famiglia, sotto l'incognita di un silenzio che è come uno spettro." Nascimbeni, "Dai riscatti-miliardo al sottofatturato dei sequestri."

16 "Al presidente della Repubblica. I seguenti cittadini, preoccupati per il dilagare della criminalità, in particolare per quanto riguarda i sequestri di persona a scopo di estorsione, collegati verosimilmente con la concentrazione nella regione di numerosi soggiornanti coattivi, chiede il suo alto intervento affinché promuova attraverso le forme costituzionali provvedimenti capaci di affrontare risolutamente questo grave problema. I sottoscritti si fanno altresì interpreti dell'angoscia e del dolore di quei familiari di rapiti che sono nella materiale impossibilità di accedere alle assurde pretese dei delinquenti, per richiedere l'urgenza del suo intervento

Notes to pages 71–6   221

al fine di evitare ad altri la triste e distruttiva esperienza." P.E, "'Pagate altrimenti mi ammazzano,'" 7.

17 Stajano, *Il disordine*, 115–34. Published first in Borghese, *Un paese in tribunale.*

18 Mazzotti, "Vi parlo dei rapimenti," 1–2.

19 "Con parole quasi pacate e di grande civiltà il tema generale della violenza e dei sequestri." Mazzotti, "Vi parlo dei rapimenti."

20 "Alla difesa di una vittima innocente, al senso della famiglia, ai sentimenti." Mazzotti, "Vi parlo dei rapimenti."

21 "Contro questa sciagurata prospettiva chi vuole difendere le istituzioni democratiche e lo stato di diritto, e con esse la propria sicurezza, deve sapere prendere posizione perché il fenomeno dilagante della criminalità può trovare soltanto nella coscienza morale e nell'impegno democratico il deterrente più distruttivo per una sconfitta totale e definitiva." Mazzotti, "Vi parlo dei rapimenti."

22 One of the most active anti-Mafia associations in Italy today is Libera, created by Don Ciotti in 1994 (https://www.libera.it/). For a history of the anti-Mafia movement see, among others, Santino, *Storia del movimento antimafia*; and Jamieson, *Antimafia*. For the relationship between anti-Mafia and new media see Pickering-Iazzi, *Italian Antimafia.*

23 Tagliaferro, "La famiglia ha pagato un miliardo," 5.

24 Tagliaferro, "Cristina è ancora in mano ai rapitori," 5.

25 "Obbedienti esecutori degli ordini dell'anonima sequestri." "Soppesano ogni parola, consapevoli che anche un solo avverbio ambiguo può indurre i rapitori a reazioni inconsulte." Tagliaferro, "Cristina è ancora in mano ai rapitori."

26 "Cento milioni a chi darà notizie di Cristina Mazzotti," 6.

27 Munzi, "Filmati i volti degli 'esattori,'" 6.

28 Munzi, "Ancora nascosto sull'Aspromonte," 1.

29 "Lo facciamo volare in elicottero perché con la mafia non si sa mai: potrebbero sparargli addosso." Munzi, "Filmati i volti degli 'esattori,'" 6.

30 Munzi, "Sarebbe nascosto sull'Aspromonte," 7.

31 On the investigations, see Chirico and Magro, *Dimenticati*, 67–80; Fontana and Serarcangeli, *L'Italia dei sequestri*, 114–17; and Rossani, *L'industria dei sequestri*, 67–76. See also Cesa, *Cristina Mazzotti.*

32 "L'avvenimento è di per sé inimmaginabile. Non hai riscontri di esperienza che ti possano in qualche modo aiutare. Esce da qualsiasi schema, da qualsiasi tipo di vita vissuta. Quando io, prima, leggevo dei sequestri di persona e dei genitori che attendevano la telefonata dell'intermediario per avere notizie rassicuranti sul sequestro … mi chiedevo come un padre, una madre, in attesa del contatto con i rapitori, potessero dormire, mangiare, vivere. Il mio enigma si è sciolto quando ho potuto direttamente sperimentare come fosse possibile non soltanto

222   Notes to pages 76–80

mantenere i propri ritmi fisiologici, ma considerare la telefonata come il momento della liberazione dall'angoscia perché è proprio la telefonata, che ti mette, sia pure indirettamente, a contatto con la persona cara. La telefonata è un momento di sollievo, di gioia … anche quando la voce dice: – Preparate cinque miliardi – … – Le tagliamo l'orecchio, le tagliamo la gola – … – perfino allora hai il senso che il filo non è ancora interrotto, che la persona amata non è morta e malgrado tutto speri che non le sia stato fatto niente di male." Stajano, *Il disordine*, 122, 128.

33 Moravia, "Riflessioni davanti all'orrore," 1.

34 "Tutti coloro che venivano interrogati durante la seduta si nascondevano dietro la grottesca dignità di un ridicolo e imponente linguaggio giudiziario e burocratico. Si nascondevano perché non osavano né punire né proporre una punizione." Moravia, "Riflessioni davanti all'orrore."

35 Augias, "Novità in cartellone."

36 "A nostro avviso, la lontana responsabilità della morte di Cristina Mazzotti risale a tutti coloro che hanno permesso che la figura del boss criminale diventasse in Italia in questi anni un modello ideale da imitare e, perfino, se possibile, da sviluppare e perfezionare." Moravia, "Riflessioni davanti all'orrore." Cited in Shuster, "Italians' Apathy Over Kidnappings."

37 Cavarero, *Orrorismo*.

38 "Ed ecco affiora una mano. Si spostano altri detriti. E compare un corpo in disfacimento. Nessun riconoscimento ufficiale: ma è Cristina. Chi altri potrebbe essere?" Giuliani, "Trovato il corpo di Cristina," 1–2.

39 "Ma come si può riconoscere in un corpo disfatto dalla terra la stessa figura di ragazza che quella sera del 30 giugno scorso uscì da casa sorridente, allegra, con la gioia di una serata da passare con gli amici." Giuliani, "Trovato il corpo di Cristina."

40 Giuliani, "Il diario della notte degli incubi quando il corpo venne ritrovato," 2.

41 "Scendiamo. Scarpe nel fango. Gli abbaglianti illuminano solo in avanti. Ai fianchi abbiamo una parete d'oscurità. Nell'aria si respira un tanfo greve, che respinge. 'Dove siamo?' chiedo … 'in un discarico di rifiuti.'" Giuliani, "Il diario."

42 Biagi, "Cristina, un'esistenza come tante," 2.

43 "L'ha detto la televisione: Cristina Mazzotti è morta. È stata uccisa. Anche lo speaker dell'ultimo telegiornale, al quale hanno passato all'improvviso un foglio, sembrava sgomento. Ero solo nella casa vuota." Biagi, "Cristina, un'esistenza come tante."

44 "Quando in un paese si arriva a tanta degradazione, e i rapimenti entrano nella consuetudine, e di molti non si saprà mai più nulla … si arriva persino a credere che le antiche punizioni, la gogna, le mani tagliate ai ladri, sì anche il plotone in piazza, coi monelli che guardano e le vecchie

Notes to pages 80–6   223

che gridano e fanno nell'attesa la maglia, sono forse un riparo, diventano per la coscienza sconvolta, un rimedio, l'ultimo tentativo e l'ultima difesa. Poi mi sono ricordato che la mia generazione ha già vissuto queste scene, e uno venne fucilato soltanto perché aveva la barba e assomigliava a un gerarca fascista." Biagi, "Cristina, un'esistenza come tante."

45 Durand, "Gli zii di Cristina," 8.

46 Nascimbeni, "Un silenzio," 1.

47 "Per raggiungere Eupilio bisognava andare a piedi." Nascimbeni, "Un silenzio."

48 "Come gente venuta da un altro versante della vita, da una zona buia che non vorremmo mai identificare con le città, i paesi e le strade che conosciamo." Nascimbeni, "Un silenzio."

49 "In una poesia di De Libero è raccontata la storia di un ragazzo romano ucciso da una sentinella tedesca 'perché rideva.' Quel fatto avvenne di settembre come il ritrovamento e il funerale di Cristina. I vecchi versi sono tornati alla memoria. Ma più che come un'epigrafe a Cristina, essi sono per noi. Dice il poeta che di quel settembre, come di questo settembre, ognuno si deve incidere 'la data sulla mano.'" Nascimbeni, "Un silenzio."

50 A few months after Cristina's corpse was found, her father passed away. To Italians, he died of a broken heart, adding a tragic epilogue to an already tragic story.

51 On this subject, see Dalla Chiesa, *Passaggio a Nord*.

52 Bisiach, "Rapporto da Corleone."

53 *TV7* was a *rotocalco* created by RAI right after the end of *RT*, which existed for only one season. While *RT* was a biweekly broadcast, *TV7* was aired weekly. *AZ: Un fatto come e perché* was created in 1969.

54 The case is that of Assunta Calamida Gardu, the first woman ever snatched in Sardinia, who was abducted on 29 September 1970 and released after eighteen days.

55 "È un itinerario obbligato che viene eseguito a ogni sequestro seguendo regole precise. Le targhe di queste auto vengono segnalate ai banditi. È un invito a prendere contatto a farsi vivi a far conoscere le loro richieste. Si cerca di vedere quanta più gente possibile, di passare parola "la famiglia è disposta a trattare." Ad Orgosolo l'auto dell'avvocato Guiso si ferma anche dinanzi alla casa di Graziano Mesina [the most well-known bandit in Italy]. La donna in nero è la madre di Graziano. Il bandito è in carcere ma i suoi amici fuori sono ancora numerosi possono essere di aiuto. A questo punto si accorgono della nostra presenza." Dell'Aquila, "Banditismo in Sardegna."

56 Falivena and Locatelli, *AZ: Un fatto come e perché*.

57 "Non smetterò mai di fare le mie ricerche, mai, non mi fermerò mai. Lo cercherò, vivo o morto lo troverò senz'altro. E pagheranno quelli, quello

224   Notes to pages 86–91

che mi han fatto. Il male che hanno fatto a me lo pagheranno senz'altro. Non smetterò mai di cercarlo. Mai." Marrazzo, "Sequestro di persona."

58 Mirko Panattoni was kidnapped 23 May 1973 and was released 7 June 1973 after his father paid a ransom of 300 million lire.

59 In addition to Panattoni, the kidnapped victims are Emanuele Riboli (Lombardy), Francesco Cribari (Calabria), Giuseppe Valenza (Calabria), Carla Ovazza (Piedmont), Vincenzino Guida (Campania), Cristina Mazzotti (Lombardy), and Luigi Rossi di Montelera (Piedmont).

60 "Questo crimine è divenuto sempre più pagante. 38 casi nel '74, 62 nel '75 e 7 nei primi due mesi del '76." Marrazzo, "Sequestro di persona."

61 Francesco Cribari's kidnappers with his uncle Luigi Cribari.

62 "Un delitto di questo genere imprevedibile, insolito, che cosa lascia dentro, nei familiari, nelle persone?" "Io direi che cosa porta via più che cosa lascia. Porta via tutto, non rimane più niente." Marrazzo, "Sequestro di persona."

63 "Ci troviamo di fronte a un nuovo tipo di crimine. La persona è degradata a oggetto. Nelle mani di chi la sequestra la persona è una cosa, è adoperata come una cosa ... come mai questo tipo di crimine si è sviluppato negli ultimi anni nel nostro paese ed è in aumento?" Falivena and Locatelli, *AZ: Un fatto come e perché*.

64 A few examples of broadcasts produced by RAI on the 'Ndrangheta are the 1977 "Mafia Calabrese" (Calabrian Mafia) and "Gente di San Luca" (People of San Luca), the 1978 *Tg2 Dossier* "Gli intoccabili di Taurianova" (The untouchable from Taurianova), and the 1981 *Tg2 Dossier* "Tutti gli uomini della fibbia" (All the men of the buckle). These news documentaries are now available on the RAI website as part of a collection entitled 'Ndrangheta S.p.A., which brings together different investigations into Calabrian Mafia made by the national TV over time. The title RAI picked is noteworthy. S.p.A. is an acronym for Società per azioni (joint stock company), which often appeared on the label that the press gave to the criminal syndicates dedicated to ransom kidnapping: Anonima Sequestri S.p.A. (Anonymous Kidnapping Joint Stock Company). For RAI, the connection between the 'Ndrangheta and the crime with which they made their fortune is still visible in this title.

65 Malenotti, "Sequestri: La spirale della violenza." The film producer Maleno Malenotti was kidnapped in Tuscany in 1976; he never returned home even after his family paid the ransom.

66 Ginzburg, "Parlano i rapiti."

67 "Per i compiti a casa attraverso la sceneggiata che adesso vi mostrerò studierete un altro aspetto della vita italiana degli ultimi tempi: i sequestri di persona." Verde, *Scuola serale*.

68 "Mi ha spaventato. Viene ad annunciare un sequestro di persona e io chissà cosa credevo." Verde, *Scuola serale*.

Notes to pages 92–6   225

69 "Chi rapina la banca di stato non è peccato, chi per arte si da al peculato non è peccato, chi sequestra e rapisce la gente chi in Svizzera intasca il contante, chi di tasse non paga mai niente ... ma se un misero con la sventola vuole farsi giustizia da sé, beccato lo è." Verde, *Scuola serale*.

70 The English title of *I nuovi mostri* is *Viva l'Italia!*, which emphasizes the film's sarcastic approach to Italian identity and attitude. The literal translation of Scola's episode "Sequestro di persona cara" is "Kidnapping of a dear person," while "Kidnapping Dear!" is the English version.

71 "Io sono qui davanti a questo telefono, da due giorni interminabili e due notti interminabili, per rivolgere un appello implorante, una supplica ai rapitori, perché mi facciano sapere le loro condizioni, tutto quello che devo fare. Vi prego telefonatemi. Mia moglie non ha molta salute. Ha bisogno di cure assidue costanti. Quindi telefonatemi, vi prego, a qualunque ora. Io ho pregato, ho ordinato a amici, parenti, conoscenti di non telefonarmi mai in modo che il telefono sia sempre libero. Quindi chiamatemi. Chiunque voi siate ascoltate questa preghiera di un marito straziato. Restituitemi mia moglie." Scola, "Sequestro di persona cara."

72 Ginzburg, "La qualità della vita."

73 "Esistono due maniere di guardare il mondo, una maniera politica e una maniera non politica." Ginzburg, "La qualità della vita."

74 "Un odore immondo e funerario, che ricorda le Esse Esse, i campi di sterminio nazisti e le stragi degli ebrei." Ginzburg, "La qualità della vita."

75 "Significa rivolgere alla vita delle richieste minime e miserabili, e rivolgere alla morte uno sguardo spento e vuoto." Ginzburg, "La qualità della vita."

76 "I non politici, riguardo all'appello del Papa per Aldo Moro, pensano che sia stato un giusto appello, e non trovano affatto strano che si sia messo in ginocchio, perché un papa è giusto che si metta in ginocchio, e anzi questa è in un papa un'attitudine naturale. Si chiedono però perché non si sia messo in ginocchio per la povera Cristina Mazzotti, in quell'orrenda estate in cui non se ne sapeva più nulla, o perché non si metta in ginocchio per gli altri che sono stati rapiti e non tornano, essendo gli uomini tutti uguali dinanzi a Dio. Non trovano niente giusto il discorso del giorno dopo, quando egli ha dato rilievo all'alta statura culturale di Aldo Moro, perché dinanzi a Dio non vale nulla l'esito pubblico, la pubblica statura dell'uomo. Ci sembra che la fine della povera Cristina Mazzotti, il suo corpo ritrovato in un cumulo di rottami e rifiuti, abbia degradato e umiliato in tutti la qualità della vita. Ci sembra che si sia spalancato allora, dinanzi ai nostri occhi, in modo chiaro, lo scenario deserto al quale i nostri occhi si sarebbero più tardi, con orrore, avvezzati." Ginzburg, "La qualità della vita."

77 "Prima ti amavamo noi, ora ti amano tutti." Biagi, "Una sera di pioggia."

226   Notes to pages 97–101

4. Troubling the Rule of Law

1 "Pensavo di essere al centro della terra, in quella buca sporca e invece la civiltà è a poche centinaia di metri." Soffiantini, *Il mio sequestro*, 40.
2 Ghislanzoni, "Gui," 1.
3 "Favoreggiatori per forza o per timore dei malviventi, o collaboratori responsabili e protetti dagli organi dello Stato che li combattono?" Ghislanzoni, 1.
4 "Provai a scrivere un dialogo sui sequestri di persona: era l'epoca in cui questa peste cominciava a diventare nel nostro paese l'industria più redditizia. Il signor Mohole sosteneva che solo le persone antipatiche a tutti, per le quali era evidente che nessuno avrebbe mai pagato il riscatto, potevano sentirsi al sicuro; dunque la malevolenza reciproca era l'unico fondamento possibile per la società, mentre l'affetto e la compassione diventavano il sostegno del crimine, che proprio su questi sentimenti faceva leva. Arrivato a questo punto rilessi quel che avevo scritto, appallottolai il foglio e lo gettai, come faccio ogni volta che ho il sospetto di star scrivendo qualcosa di cui prima o poi potrei pentirmi … Mi misi a scrivere dei pezzetti con il solo signor Palomar, personaggio in cerca d'un'armonia in mezzo a un mondo tutto dilaniamenti e stridori." Calvino, *Palomar*, vi.
5 Zucconi, "Il sequestro di persona."
6 Zucconi, *Sotto Processo*, episode 6.
7 Fumo, "Reale commenta la tesi Gui."
8 Fumo, "Reale commenta la tesi Gui." Among the different political parties, the one whose members unanimously opposed Gui's view was the Socialist Party.
9 Scabello, "Obiezioni e dubbi," 9; and Nascimbeni, "Perché proprio l'Italia è il paese dei rapimenti?," 1–2.
10 The Zambeletti family collected the money to free their father Ludovico, owner of a pharmaceutical company, who was kidnapped in November 1977. Apparently, the Procuratore della Repubblica di Milano, Mario Gresti, stopped Pomarici from confiscating their money because a politician asked him to do so. The Zambeletti were a powerful family, and Pomarici denounced the disparity with which Gresti approached this case compared to the previous one. Michelini, "Pomarici"; and Solazzo, "Il procuratore Gresti," 6.
11 The earliest legal debate on the problems connected to this crime goes back to the drafting of the Zanardelli Code (1889) – the first Italian legal code. The focus of this twenty-year-long debate can be best summarized by the question that guided the lawmakers' process: Is ransom kidnapping a crime against person or against property? Although many believed

Notes to pages 101–5   227

abduction for ransom to affect personal liberty, Article 410 of the criminal code deemed it a property crime. The law regarded ransom kidnapping as an attack on the state's authority rather than on the individual, thus conceiving the state itself as the protector of property rather than of individual freedom. The same position was confirmed by the Rocco Code of 1930, and therefore by the Fascist State, which placed Article 630 (robbery or ransom kidnapping) among crimes against property, where it is still found in today's code. For a detailed analysis of the legislative process on ransom kidnapping, see Brunelli, *Il sequestro di persona*.

12 Peruzzi, "Hanno pagato per Banchini," 6.
13 Ginsborg, *History of Contemporary Italy*, 363.
14 Established under Article 605 of the criminal code, which regulates non-ransom kidnapping.
15 "Occorre che il reato non sia pagante; cioè che il rapitore non incassi il frutto del crimine." "Cossiga è d'accordo sul provvedimento Pomarici," 1.
16 "Cossiga è d'accordo sul provvedimento Pomarici," 1.
17 Biagi, *Proibito*.
18 P.T., "Scandalo a Milano," 31; "E ora anche la difesa diventa un fatto personale," 38–42.
19 Trebay, "French President's Lover."
20 See Berlusconi's interview with Alan Friedman in *My Way*.
21 Berlusconi fired Mangano after he organized the abduction of one of his guests. See Stille, *Sack of Rome*; Sisti and Gomez, *L'intoccabile*; Foot, *Archipelago*, 240.
22 Rossani, *Intervista sui rapimenti*. For a juridical opinion in favour of the *linea morbida* see Maddalena, "I sequestri di persona"; for one in favour of the *linea dura* see Vigna, "Il sequestro di persona."
23 Michelini, "Pomarici."
24 Brunelli, *Il sequestro di persona a scopo di estorsione*, 99–119; Montalbano, "Un'emergenza lunga trent'anni."
25 On why ransom kidnapping remained a crime against property, see Dalia and Conso, *La legislazione dell'emergenza*, 45–6.
26 Historian Paul Ginsborg states that "the crisis of Italian terrorism, as is generally recognized, dates from the death of Moro. With hindsight, it would thus seem correct to argue that those who advocated intransigence were in the right. Had Moro not been killed but exchanged for one or more imprisoned terrorists, the Red Brigades would have appeared both invulnerable and willing to compromise, with the result that their appeal would almost certainly have widened." Ginsborg, *History of Contemporary Italy*, 385.
27 Martinelli, "Il Consiglio della magistratura," 7.

228   Notes to pages 105–9

28 The daughter of the president of De Agostini, a very well-known geographical institute in Novara, Piedmont, Marcella Boroli Ballestrini was kidnapped on 9 October and was liberated on 3 December after her family paid one billion six hundred million lire unbeknownst to law enforcement. See Nava, "Per un miliardo e 600 milioni," 1.

29 Martinelli summarized the committee's report in his article "Il Consiglio della magistratura," 7.

30 Biancacci and Levi, *Storie allo specchio*. The two episodes were aired on 6 and 13 December 1978.

31 Biancacci and Levi, 13 December 1978.

32 Biancacci and Levi, 13 December 1978.

33 "Far dibattere fra la linea morbida o dura significa offrire proprio la possibilità di attirare l'attenzione su uno pseudo problema anziché sul problema reale." Biancacci and Levi, 13 December 1978.

34 Gotor, "La possibilità dell'uso del discorso," 205.

35 Gotor, 206.

36 "Questo disegno prevedeva, in un certo senso, il 'congelamento' della parola del prigioniero, proprio come l'autorità giudiziaria, in quegli stessi mesi, aveva iniziato a fare con i beni dei rapiti, nei sequestri organizzati dalla criminalità comune." Gotor, 209.

37 For an analysis of ransom kidnapping from an economic perspective, see Rossi, *Teoria dei giochi*.

38 "Il sacrificio degli innocenti in nome di un astratto principio di legalità, mentre un indiscutibile stato di necessità dovrebbe indurre a salvarli, è inamissibile." Moro, *Lettere*, 8.

39 "Del resto queste idee già espressi a Taviani per il caso Sossi ed a Gui a propsito di una contestata legge contro i rapimenti." Moro, 14.

40 Moro, 15n9.

41 "a. The freezing of the victim's assets or those of his family is one method that has been applied by certain prosecutors in Italy in order to prevent the ransom from being paid and thus leave the authorities a free hand. The Committee was convinced that this kind of measure was likely: i. to aggravate the situation of the victim and his family unnecessarily. The family would then be faced with a fresh dilemma – whether to comply with the decision of the authorities or to disregard it and collect the means to pay the ransom; ii. to encourage a kidnapped person's family not to inform the authorities at once that a kidnapping had occurred; iii. to make the authorities morally responsible for the victim's death." Council of Europe, "Committee of Ministers Recommendation," 678–9.

42 "Non si può essere fermi per i fatti di terrorismo e non fermi per i sequestri. E chi mi dice che una somma di sequestro può essere destinata

Notes to pages 109–14   229

a fatti di terrorismo? Perché dovrei tenere due diversi atteggiamenti?" Sposini and Scaccia, "Quei giorni di Cesare."

43 Dalla Chiesa, "Lotte civili a Milano."

44 Dalla Chiesa, "Lotte civili a Milano."

45 Dalla Chiesa, "Lotte civili a Milano."

46 Madeo, "La regione Calabria"; Madeo, "I vescovi calabresi."

47 Jamieson, *Antimafia*; Fava, *I disarmati*; Santino, *Storia del movimento antimafia*; Dalla Chiesa, *Milano-Palermo la nuova resistenza* and *Manifesto dell'antimafia*; Pickering-Iazzi, *Italian Antimafia*. See also Ravveduto, "'Voi siete la schifezza di Napoli'"; Sorgonà, "Società e 'ndrangheta"; Blando, "L'antimafia come risorsa politica"; Gavini, "L'utopia palermitana"; and Moge, "La Sicile."

48 *TG3* Piemonte, 9 April 1987.

49 Maria Magnani Noya was the first female mayor of Turin (1987–90). She was previously a member of the Italian Parliament and in 1990 served in the European Parliament, of which she was elected vice president in 1992.

50 *TGR* Piemonte edizione serale.

51 "Dobbiamo saper ripetere la mobilitazione che ha sconfitto il terrorismo, opponendoci alla criminalità organizzata." Rovera, "Sequestro Fiora," 6.

52 "Marco, ti vogliamo bene. La tua città è stretta attorno a te." Rovera, 6.

53 "Se è vero che il bambino si trova in una specie di zona franca dell'Aspromonte, chiediamo alle forze dell'ordine di riprendere in quella zona il controllo della situazione." The initiators were Luciano Violante (vice president of the Parliamentary Communist Group), Bianca Guidetti Serra (Proletarian Democracy Group), and Gianni Wilmer Ronzani (Communist Group). Besides sharing the same political views, the three deputies were connected to Turin and therefore aware of what the city had done for the Fiora family. They lately became active anti-Mafia parliamentary members. Violante, especially, served as president of the Anti-Mafia Parliamentary Committee (1992–4) and wrote several books on the subject. It is worth mentioning that Serra was a very well-known figure in Turin. Among Primo Levi's closest friends (he sent to her the news about his deportation to Auschwitz), in 1943 she became an active partisan and fought in the resistance against fascism.

54 "Perché non è mai stato fatto nessun controllo serio del territorio. Non so se ci sia una volontà deliberata il che sarebbe criminale o c'è soltanto incapacità e incoscienza. Ci sono delle aree completamente libere, lasciate in mano alla malavita organizzata e alla mafia. L'Aspromonte è una di queste." *TGR* Piemonte.

55 Arendt, *On Violence*, 44.

56 Repossi, "'Basta pubblicità,'" 37.

230 Notes to pages 114–19

57 "Cinquemila studenti," 37.

58 On Angela Casella see Siebert, *Secret of Life and Death*; and Sergi, *La "Santa" Violenta*.

59 "Non credo che il ministro dell'Interno, quando dice che lo Stato ha fatto per intero il proprio dovere possa riferirsi a noi, cioè alla triste vicenda che riguarda mio figlio … a meno che non voglia ammettere di rappresentare uno stato sconfitto." Barillà, "Una mamma sfida la 'Ndrangheta," 7.

60 "Tenere buoni i familiari dell'ostaggio"; "l'emotività è una delle ragioni per le quali il sequestro Casella si prolunga." Nese, "Mai mostrarsi disperati," 11.

61 Casella, "Non capisco De Mita," 1, 9.

62 "Non voglio far commuovere nessuno, voglio far ragionare tutti." Casella, 9.

63 "Noi abbiamo pagato dopo sette mesi di prigionia. Di quanti giorni, di quante ore sono fatti sette mesi?" Casella, "Non capisco De Mita." In an interview, Luigi Casella said that when his family collected one billion lire for the ransom, they had to pay 535 million lire in taxes to the Italian state. See Biglia, "È ancora braccio di ferro."

64 Biglia, "È ancora braccio di ferro."

65 The anti-kidnapping law would have allowed magistrates to financially investigate the abductions with the same tools used by the existing Rognoni–La Torre anti-mafia law (1983), which grants access to bank information and therefore tackles the money laundering.

66 "Dov'è lo stato, dove le istituzioni cui è stato democraticamente delegato e affidato l'esercizio della sovranità?" Veca, "Lo stato debole."

67 "Vi sono spazi fisici in questa nazione in cui non vige il monopolio della violenza legittima, zone in qualche modo extraterritoriali, frontiere interne con altri poteri, nemici e stranieri." Veca, "Lo stato debole."

68 "Se sfortunato è il paese che ha bisogno di eroine, la sfortuna non è una sorta di destino o calamità naturale. Essa evoca responsabilità collettive, chiama in causa il disegno delle istituzioni e, alla fin fine, le azioni e le non azioni di persone; in primo luogo, di chi dovrebbe fornire il bene pubblico elementare della sicurezza, su cui si basa il contenuto minimo di qualsiasi associazione o agenzia collettiva che usiamo chiamare 'Stato.'" Veca, "Lo stato debole."

69 Cesare Casella gives an account of his ordeal in the book *743 giorni lontano da casa*.

70 Don Battista Tacchella, cousin of Patrizia's father.

71 The other names on the postcard were Carlo Celadon, Andrea Cortellezzi, Mirella Silocchi, and Vincenzo Medici.

72 Santoro, *Samarcanda*.

Notes to pages 119–31   231

73 "Mr. President, I am appealing to your moral and civic authority for the political institutions to take all the initiatives, and the legal and judicial measures, necessary to defeat the shameful plague of ransom kidnapping." R.I., "A Cossiga dieci mila cartoline."

74 "Entriamo in Europa con un primato vergognoso."

75 Carlo Celadon has recently talked about his ordeal in an Italian podcast series. See Trincia and Micheli, "Il male."

76 *Commissione parlamentare sul fenomeno della mafia e altre associazioni criminali* (istituita con legge 1 ottobre 1996, n. 509).

77 Tiziano, "I sequestri di persona?"

78 Gianni Bulgari was snatched by the 'Ndrangheta in 1975.

79 Farouk's father, Fateh Kassam, wrote the memoir *Mio figlio Farouk.*

80 "Orrore, ucciso Falcone" (Horror, Falcone killed) read the *Corriere della Sera* page that gave the news.

81 Zavoli, *La notte della Repubblica*, Rai 2. Zavoli also published a book with the same title in 1992.

82 "Qualcosa nel nostro paese sta cambiando," Scola states, "si sta trovando la capacità di indignarsi, ci si va convincendo che tempo individuale e tempo sociale non sono entità separate, si prende a considerare l'offesa fatta a uno come minaccia imposta alla collettività." Scola, "Egregio bandito."

5. Trauma and Language in the Kidnapping Victim Memoir

1 "Italian Books: Terror in the Streets," 99.

2 Ronchetti, "Dopo le tristi memorie," 4.

3 "Odio e temo una scomparsa totale, senza storia e senza corpo." Soffiantini, *Il mio sequestro*, 104.

4 See Pardini, "Relazione," 25; and Beccaria and Turone, *Il Boss*, 85–108.

5 See Pardini, "Relazione," 25; and Beccaria and Turone, *Il Boss*, 19–83.

6 "Un'idea più precisa di come si svolge un sequestro di persona"; "un'esperienza allucinante e umanamente così particolare." Rossi di Montelera, *Racconto di un sequestro*, 7.

7 Agamben, *Quel che resta di Auschwitz.* English translation: Agamben, *Remnants of Auschwitz*, 17.

8 "Provavo una strana sensazione in quel momento: mi rendevo conto, quasi dal di fuori, come uno spettatore, di trovarmi di fronte a quell'avventura misteriosa di cui si legge spesso sui giornali, ma di cui non avevo mai conosciuto i particolari, e pensai fugacemente: 'Ecco come si fa un rapimento.'" Rossi di Montelera, *Racconto di un sequestro*, 11.

9 On his kidnapping, see Rossani, *L'industria dei sequestri*; and Fontana and Serarcangeli, *L'Italia dei sequestri*, 65.

232   Notes to pages 131–4

10 *Cavalier* (Order of Merit for Labour) is an official Italian title.
11 "Leggevo sul giornale che nessuno sapeva più nulla del cav. Amerio,
    e si facevano varie supposizioni sulle modalità del rapimento, e a me
    pareva di poter rispondere a quegli interrogativi, di poter spiegare
    a tutti esattamente cosa stava pensando il cav. Amerio, che non
    avevo mai visto in vita mia." Rossi di Montelera, *Racconto di un
    sequestro*, 82–3.
12 "Avverto i lettori che non sono uno scrittore: ma forse affidare ad altri un
    racconto così personale e intensamente vissuto gli avrebbe fatto perdere
    l'immediatezza e la fedeltà dei fatti." Rossi di Montelera, 7.
13 On the impossibility of journalism to reach the level of testimony,
    see Shoshana Felman's interesting chapter "Camus' *The Plague*, or A
    Monument to Witnessing" in Felman and Laub, *Testimony*, 93. Felman
    analyses Camus' *The Plague* as a literary witness to the Holocaust and
    emphasizes his considerations of journalistic narration as incapable of
    bearing witness to the victims.
14 "Nella mia cella avevo sempre provato il desiderio, se mai fossi
    sopravvissuta, di raccontare la mia esperienza e di descrivere come
    e perché ero riuscita 'a farcela.' Volevo far capire, a chi difficilmente
    avrebbe potuto immaginarselo, la sorte di un ostaggio ridotto ad un essere
    completamente ignaro del proprio destino e privato di qualsiasi difesa."
    Ovazza, *Cinque ciliege rosse*, 5.
15 Ovazza, *L'interminable nuit*.
16 Ovazza, *Diario de un secuestro*.
17 Leoni and Mastrostefano, "Memorandum Sequestri." On the duty to
    testify, see Margalit, *Ethics of Memory*.
18 "Prigione clandestina." Ovazza, *Cinque ciliege rosse*, 5.
19 See Sciarrone, "La diffusione in aree non continue: Il caso del Piemonte,"
    in *Mafie vecchie, mafie nuove*, 213; and Varese, *Mafias on the Move*, 31–64.
20 Ovazza, *Cinque ciliege rosse*, 12.
21 "Scrivere il libro è stata la mia catarsi; mi sono liberata dagli incubi che
    non mi avevano mai lasciato dal momento della mia liberazione. Sono
    così diventata spettatrice e non più attrice, ed ho potuto fare un esame
    molto esatto di questa tristissima avventura." Ovazza, "L'esperienza della
    vittimizzazione," 87.
22 "Mi ribello contro il fatto che ci sia un tale assenteismo, che i rapimenti
    siano diventati fatti di cronaca. Bisogna svegliare l'opinione pubblica e
    credo che più che altro per questo servano le testimonianze di persone
    come me che hanno provato cosa vuol dire essere vittime e che vogliono
    aiutare quelli che purtroppo dovranno ancora subire la stessa sorte."
    Ovazza, 92.
23 "Una piaga sociale che riguarda tutti." Ovazza, 92.

Notes to pages 134–7   233

24 "Ormai sono un fagotto di carne in balia di questi esseri senza scrupoli."
Ovazza, *Cinque ciliege rosse*, 133.

25 "Non si può permettere che poche persone che fanno mercato di
carne umana tengano in pugno una nazione intera che continua ad
ergersi incapace ed inetta di fronte a questo vergognoso delitto. Per
questo ho accettato di parlarvi oggi." Ovazza, "L'esperienza della
vittimizzazione," 92.

26 On the Ovazzas' story under fascism, see Stille, "The Ovazzas," in
Benevolence and Betrayal.

27 "Ed ecco, senza accorgermene, Elena si presenta lucidissima di fronte ai
miei occhi. Mi metto a parlarle, a parlare a questo viso amico che in questo
momento mi è tanto vicino. 'Elena, tu hai sofferto tanto ad Auschwitz
e mi hai raccontato le torture a cui ti avevano sottoposto. Avevi dovuto
abbandonare un figlio piccolissimo ed avevi sempre avuto la forza di
lottare per poterlo rivedere un giorno. Soffrivi la fame, la cancrena, la
dissenteria più spaventosa. Avevi sopportato le botte con uno stoicismo
unico; eri stata maltrattata molto più di me, eppure eri riuscita a farcela
con la tua forza straordinaria, con la tua volontà incrollabile … Elena,
aiutami con il tuo coraggio, stammi vicina perché io possa ritrovare un
po' di speranza. Anche tu eri arrivata al fondo del baratro, eppure ce l'hai
fatta! Anch'io devo cercare di riprendermi per poter riabbracciare i miei!'"
Ovazza, *Cinque ciliege rosse*, 125–6.

28 I am extremely grateful to Guido Foa, Elena Recanati's grandson, for
sharing this information with me.

29 The official "Report About Ransom Kidnapping" highlights, among the
characteristics of these ordinary kidnappers, their "scanty professionalism
in the conduct of every stage of the kidnapping with the consequent
danger, for the hostage, of losing his/her life." Tesi's belongs to the few
examples of this type of kidnapping presented by the official report. See
Pardini, "Relazione," 16.

30 "Sopra a tutto questo mio racconto è un grido, un grido di angoscia e
di ribellione da parte di una donna che a distanza di due anni non ha
ancora ritrovato la sua 'identità.' È un documento, una testimonianza che
ognuno dovrebbe leggere per capire veramente il significato della parola
'Sequestro.'" Tesi, *Sindrome da sequestro*, 10.

31 "Impedendo il pagamento del riscatto, stavano calpestando il diritto alla
difesa della mia vita. Questo pensavo e questo avrei scritto. Ed avrei scritto
anche che il blocco dei beni può essere una misura valida sul piano morale
perché con i delinquenti non si dovrebbe mai scendere a patti, è vero; ma a
me sembra che lo Stato sia già sceso a patti con i delinquenti quando sono
state attuate le norme sui 'pentiti' … La Costituzione nell'art.2 garantisce i
diritti inviolabili dell'uomo, nell'art.3 garantisce inoltre 'il pieno sviluppo

234   Notes to pages 138–42

della sua personalità' e riconosce 'i diritti della famiglia come società naturale' ... Da ciò si deduce che il diritto alla vita non è solo un diritto naturale e universale ma è un diritto garantito dalla nostra Costituzione Italiana ... Con quale potere discrezionale la Magistratura, o meglio quale norma costituzionale autorizza i poteri pubblici a disporre della vita e della sorte di una persona, senza avere nessuna garanzia sul risultato dei mezzi usati?" Tesi, 94–5.

32 Casella, *743 giorni lontano da casa*. Roberto Malenotti's film for television *Liberate mio figlio* (1992) was inspired by the Casella kidnapping. Malenotti's father was also kidnapped in the 1970s and never returned (see chapter 3).

33 Kassam and Corrias, *Mio figlio Farouk*. A different example of the kidnapping memoir in Sardinia is Gianni Murgia's *Sona ca ti sonu e ... continuo a bussare: Autobiografia di un sequestro* (1997), in which Murgia denounces the absence of the state on the island and the inefficiency of both the police and the judiciary.

34 Ravizza and Alessi, *Dentro una vita*.

35 "Essere pronti anche a sfidare 'lacrime e sangue.'" Belardinelli and Masotti, *Storia di un sequestro*, 19. Belardinelli's memoir inspired the film for television *Doppio agguato*, directed by Renato de Maria, produced by Mediaset, and aired by Canale 5 in October 2003.

36 For more biographic details see Fontana and Serarcangeli, *L'Italia dei sequestri*, 160–6.

37 Specialists recognize the creation of an imaginary dialogue to be a defence mechanism of the ego, which, in captivity, tries to escape an unsustainable situation. See Herman, *Trauma and Recovery*, 87–8.

38 "Ti aspettano tutti, sai? E tu li rivedrai, siine certo. È il Signore che lo vuole. Tu diverrai una testimonianza importante di fede per tutti coloro che ti conoscono e non." Belardinelli and Masotti, *Storia di un sequestro*, 83.

39 "Non erano affatto d'accordo i miei familiari con la linea del giudice Vigna che impediva di pagare." Belardinelli and Masotti, 21.

40 "La denuncia dell'esistenza dei pregiudizi dei miei familiari nel contesto del mio sequestro è solo propositiva: vuole escludere l'esistenza di questi sentimenti in tutti gli altri casi di sequestro in atto." Belardinelli and Masotti, 22.

41 Soffiantini's kidnapping inspired the film for television *Il sequestro Soffiantini*, directed by Riccardo Milani.

42 On Giovanni Farina, see his profile as reported in the official sentence for Soffiantini's case, in Ricci, *La Sardegna dei sequestri*, 451. On Attilio Cubeddo, see Colarieti, "Caccia al bandito Curbeddu."

43 Mario Almerighi, the magistrate that enquired into the inspector Donatoni's assassination, wrote the book *Mistero di Stato*. See also Veltri, *Sequestri*.

44 "Perché le vittime non siano confuse con i carnefici." Soffiantini, *Il mio sequestro*, 130.

Notes to pages 142–4   235

45 The hostage's first mutilation was announced by the media but denied by the Soffiantinis' lawyer, pushed by the investigators. Not receiving the attention that they sought, the kidnappers cut the victim's other ear.

46 In his memoir, Soffiantini recalls a letter that Enrico Mentana wrote him after his liberation in which he says that he would have given the news about his mutilation even if the magistracy had forbidden him.

47 "Allora, una volta per tutte, queste parole sono autentiche nel senso pieno del termine, così come erano autentiche le lettere dal carcere di Aldo Moro ... Queste parole sono soltanto mie." Soffiantini refers here to the controversial debate that the grey zone of his kidnapping raised. Someone accused him of having paid his kidnappers an extra ransom by giving them checks he had at home when they captured him or even after his liberation. Creating suspicion about this latter version was Soffiantini's trip to Australia where he visited Farina (his warder), who, a few months after the kidnapping, was captured in that country in possession of fake documents. Soffiantini perceives these calumnies as a way of making him appear as his kidnappers' accomplice against the law – that is, as an attempt to overlap the victim and his persecutors before public opinion. See Soffiantini, *Il mio sequestro*, 195.

48 "La difesa spettacolare di uno Stato astratto, non concepito come la somma di tutti gli individui appartenenti a quello Stato." Soffiantini, 196.

49 "Lo Stato, lo Stato forte, con valide motivazioni etiche, si fonda sulla salvaguardia della vita dell'uomo, non sulla spettacolarità delle azioni da presentare in prima serata ai telegiornali. 'L'operazione è riuscita, ma il paziente è morto.' I cittadini gioiscono quando vedono l'ostaggio libero ... e sorridente insieme alla sua famiglia ... Portare via una persona alla comunità nazionale a cui appartiene è una ferita profonda per lo Stato. Essa si sutura soltanto con la restituzione della vita libera alla comunità familiare e nazionale. Diversamente lo Stato ha perso, clamorosamente perso. Nessun giudice, nessun carabiniere, nessun ministro può dormire sonni tranquilli, quando ha messo in galera una banda di rapitori e ha partecipato alle esequie di Stato dell'ostaggio morto. È una ferita che non si chiude." Soffiantini, 146.

50 Delisle, *Hostage*, 104.

51 Brian Keenan, an Irish professor who was kidnapped in Beirut in 1985 by Shi'ite militiamen and kept in captivity for five years, gives a vivid description of the hostage condition: "My first hours, then days and then weeks I found myself constantly having to deal with the slow hallucination into which I had been dropped. I had been removed from a known reality. The four concrete walls of my shoe-box-sized cell formed my only vista. Beyond these I could see nothing, only my imagination gave me images, some beautiful, some disturbing and unendurably ever-present. The vast landscape of the mind unfolds on its own. A times I felt the compensations of this gift and at other times cursed my

236 Notes to pages 145–8

imagination that it could bring me sensations so contorted, so strange and so incoherent that I screamed; not out of fear but out of the rage and frustration of having to deal with these flashing pictures of which I could make little or no sense." Keenan, *Evil Cradling*, 32.

52 We also find a description of this in Keenan's memoir: "Exaggerating this distorted sensitivity were the voices of my captors in a disembodied language which I didn't understand but could hear being spoken, being whispered, being shouted beyond the walls of my cell." Keenan, 32.

53 "Non sono un eroe. Sono una persona normale, capitata in una vicenda anormale. La sfida è dentro, tutta dentro quel cubo sordo di solitaria anormalità." Soffiantini, *Il mio sequestro*, 27.

54 "Bisogna che faccia molta attenzione a non perdere la nozione del tempo, in questa notte che non finisce mai e per cercare di mantenere un contatto col mondo della realtà, il mondo degli 'altri.' Cerco di captare tutti i rumori, per situarmi nello spazio. Ma il silenzio è assoluto. Né una radio, né una voce umana … Ho paura soprattutto di essere così sola … Le ore passano lentamente e mi rendo conto di quanto sia difficile contarle quando non si ha più nessun riferimento con l'esterno, quando niente interrompe il silenzio, quando non si può né leggere né parlare e non si può vedere il sole tramontare." Ovazza, *Cinque ciliegie rosse*, 27.

55 S. Freud, *Ego and the Id*, 20.

56 "Sul mio foglietto c'è un 'paragrafo' intitolato 'morte' … il paragrafetto inizia così: 'Morte: evento necessario, che conclude una vita transitoria e fa approdare al porto d'arrivo, la felicità eterna. Fiducia che il problema qui col tempo si risolve, quindi impormi di resistere: ogni giorno pensare solo ad arrivare a sera.' Poi seguono altri appunti sull'argomento; la morte me la son tenuta vicina per un bel po' di tempo." Rossi di Montelera, *Racconto di un sequestro*, 88.

57 "Dove ero? Mi sentivo addosso un gran peso, un enorme carico di angoscia e la sensazione di essere sola sull'isola della mia anima. E al di là di questo isolamento c'era tutto un mondo, laggiù, in mezzo a quelle piccole luci, che viveva indifferente. Gente che si alzava la mattina e andava a lavorare, e andava a letto la sera inconsapevole del mio dramma. Com'era possibile che a pochi chilometri esistessero persone non contaminate da questa mia sofferenza e solitudine? Sentivo alle mie spalle il vuoto assoluto, come se non esistesse più nulla di ciò che avevo fatto o vissuto e tutto fosse da reinventare. E questo mi dava un enorme sgomento." Tesi, *Sindrome da sequestro*, 46.

58 "Chiesi se potevo scrivere qualcosa, un diario per esempio, ma mi fu proibito in malo modo. Mi fu detto che non dovevano rimanere tracce di quanto succedeva nella buca … Ma insistevo, perché avevo bisogno di

scrivere. Mi sentivo incapace di resistere, se privata anche della possibilità di esprimermi. Era il mio solo modo per comunicare e per potere poi ricordare. Volevo scrivere, ricordare i miei cari con le parole scritte, per impedire a tutti coloro che amavo di perdersi, di svanire. Desideravo oppormi a quella violenza scrivendo tutto quanto mi succedeva, oppormi ad ogni possibilità di dimenticare, perché quello che stavo soffrendo un giorno l'avrei forse potuto superare, ma non avrei mai dovuto dimenticare il male che mi era stato fatto." Tesi, 38–9.

59 For the connection between traumatic disembodiment and lack of memory, see the chapter titled "Spatial Orientation" in Connerton, *Spirit of Mourning*. Connerton writes, "The art of memory relies, most fundamentally, not on a stable system of places, but on a stable system of places in the body" (101). In the case of Tesi, a traumatic disembodiment and a lack of language perception cause the absence of time and therefore the impossibility of remembering.

60 "Il cuore mi batte, ho paura di chiedergli di rimanere un po' a tenermi compagnia, ma ho bisogno di parlare, ho bisogno di sentir parlare e di sentire vicino a me la presenza di un essere umano, anche se è un bandito, anche se corro il rischio che mi maltratti e mi faccia del male." Ovazza, *Cinque ciliegie rosse*, 28.

61 "Sentivo enormemente il bisogno di parlare per uscire dall'isolamento mentale, e cioè per non impazzire. Infatti pensavo che sarei impazzita se fossi stata sola, e che fino a che c'era qualcuno vicino a me, che vedeva quello che vedevo io e sentiva quello che sentivo io, non sarei impazzita. E il mio carceriere mi faceva parlare. Scaricavo su di lui il mio bisogno di comunicazione." Tesi, *Sindrome da sequestro*, 45.

62 Ihde, *Sense and Significance*, 38.

63 I am here paraphrasing Ihde, who writes in his book, "If I am present to myself in terms of inner language, the imaginative correlate of auditory perception, why should not the other be most manifestly present to me through spoken language? His spoken presence is the perceptual correlate of my own presence to myself through imagination," Ihde, 39.

64 Scarry, *Body in Pain*, 33.

65 "Non volevo assolutamente familiarizzare con lui in quel momento, perché non potesse sentirsi scaricata la coscienza, e per salvar la mia dignità di vittima nei suoi confronti." Rossi di Montelera, *Racconto di un sequestro*, 15.

66 "Cosa sarebbe successo ora che rimanevo solo con un guardiano di cui non conoscevo neppur la voce, che dovendo restare a lungo in quel posto si sarebbe certamente innervosito e avrebbe potuto farmi qualunque cosa senza testimoni?" Rossi di Montelera, 16.

238   Notes to pages 150–2

67 "Era quindi necessario saggiare il guardiano e cercare di stabilire con lui quel minimo di conversazione che evitasse a entrambi di impazzire e che creasse un minimo di reciproca fiducia. Io sono sempre stato convinto che un uomo, per quanto bestiale sia, difficilmente può uccidere qualcuno con cui ha conversato del più e del meno, salvo che sia sotto l'effetto dell'alcool o della pazzia … gli chiesi se era la prima volta che custodiva un rapito … mi disse che faceva un'impressione orribile, e mi pregò di non parlargli più dell'argomento. Sentii in quell'occasione un fondo di umanità, quell'elemento positivo di ogni uomo che cercavo di scovare anche in lui per rassicurarmi e per costruirmi un minimo di sicurezza." Rossi di Montelera, 17–18.

68 Herman, *Trauma and Recovery*, 81.

69 Herman, 81–2.

70 Herman, 33–4. In her passage, Herman quotes Andreasen, "Posttraumatic Stress Disorder."

71 "Una volta, anni fa, mentre scalavo una delle Torri del Sella, nelle Dolomiti, mi trovai incordato in parete; non riuscivo più ad andare né avanti né indietro, e mi tenevo ad appigli veramente minimi. Dopo un po' di tentativi mi sentii lentamente venir meno le forze, mollai la presa e precipitai: mi tenne la corda. La sensazione che provavo ora era un po' dello stesso genere: sentire che le forze, le difese vengono meno, che non c'è nulla da fare, nessun appiglio da aggrapparsi; e ci si sente piombare nel vuoto, nella disperazione, con un senso di angoscia e di sgomento. Ma mentre precipitando in montagna c'era la corda che mi avrebbe trattenuto … qui non c'era nessuna corda: ero solo con me stesso, e solo in me potevo trovar le forze per vincere, o meglio per non morire." Rossi di Montelera, *Racconto di un sequestro*, 61–2.

72 Jan Philipp Reemtsma, a prominent German intellectual and heir to a great fortune who was abducted for ransom in Germany in 1996, eloquently describes the experience of his captured self in his memoir *Im Keller* (*In the Cellar*).

73 Luberto and Manganelli, *I sequestri di persona*, 51–63. The psychiatrists Angela Favaro, Daniela Degortes, Giovanni Colombo, and Paolo Santonastaso, whose research is based on interviews with twenty-four victims of Sardinian kidnapping between 1967 and 1997, examine their material through studies that consider the hostage-taking linked to acts of terrorism or war. See "Effects of Trauma"; see also, by the same authors, Degortes et al., "Il sequestro di persona come evento traumatico." Finally, in their "Uomini rubati: Le vittime del sequestro di persona" (Stolen men: The victims of ransom kidnapping), Nereide Rudas, Giampaolo Pintor, and Irene Mascia do not compare the results of their investigation of Sardinian victims with the few studies available on the same subject but rather explain why ransom kidnapping belongs to those traumatic

Notes to pages 152–4   239

experiences that, according to the American Psychiatric Association, cause posttraumatic stress disorder (PTSD). See "Uomini rubati."

74 "La 'relazione' è necessaria per il mantenimento del senso della propria identità, se pure nei modi consentiti dalla particolare situazione ... perché alla conservazione di una qualche attività relazionale è legata la possibilità di soddisfare bisogni fondamentali e di strutturare una qualche difesa atta ad arginare le possibili conseguenze disastrose, anche sul piano personologico, di un sequestro prolungato." Luberto and Manganelli, *I sequestri di persona*, 53.

75 Bettelheim, *Surviving, and Other Essays* and "Individual and Mass Behavior."

76 "Non ne posso più, mi sento male e chiamo di nuovo disperatamente, perché la solitudine mi è diventata insopportabile, perché ho bisogno di sfogare il mio dolore con un altro essere umano, nemico o amico che sia, purché mi stia a sentire, purché per qualche istante mi faccia dimenticare i pensieri allucinanti che mi tormentano." Ovazza, *Cinque ciliege rosse*, 55.

77 Rudas, Pintor, and Mascia, "Uomini rubati," 161.

78 "Un giorno però ci fu una novità, per me agghiacciante ... dopo la solita conversazione il 'veneto' mi preannunciò che mi avrebbero lasciato solo. Avrei avuto più spazio, più aria, più comodità. Per me la solitudine voleva dire invece ben altro: non avrei più potuto scambiare una parola con nessuno, qualunque cosa fosse accaduta sarei stato solo e per giunta legato. Almeno il guardiano suppliva alla mia impossibilità di muovermi e di agire. Inoltre, cosa ben peggiore, ero certo che finché c'era qualcuno con me non correvo rischi di esser lasciato morir di fame, abbandonato o ucciso col gas. Dal momento in cui fossi rimasto solo invece poteva succedere qualunque cosa. Le mie implorazioni non servirono a nulla. Ero veramente terrorizzato, li scongiuravo di non lasciarmi solo perché qualsiasi cosa fosse accaduta non mi sarei potuto salvare." Rossi di Montelera, *Racconto di un sequestro*, 45–6.

79 Rossi di Montelera, 49.

80 As Herman points out in her study on captivity, the more frightened an isolated victim is, "the more she is tempted to cling to the one relationship that is permitted: the relationship with the perpetrator. In the absence of any other human connection, she will try to find the humanity in her captor." See Herman, *Trauma and Recovery*, 81.

81 Luberto and Manganelli, *I sequestri di persona*, 55–6.

82 Luberto and Manganelli, 56.

83 A. Freud, *Ego and the Mechanism of Defense*, 109–10.

84 "Mi sentivo così disperata, ero in una tale situazione di dipendenza nei confronti del mio carceriere, che facevo come fanno i bambini piccoli con i grandi, da cui dipendono per sopravvivere. Ero ridotta come una bambina di due o tre anni che ha bisogno del genitore per ogni sua minima necessità." Tesi, *Sindrome da sequestro*, 45.

240   Notes to pages 154–6

85 "Mi sembrava improvvisamente molto grande, un uomo alto e ben piantato; i suoi piedi mi sembravano enormi e questa sensazione la conservai per tutto il sequestro, questa impressione di essere fisicamente molto piccola e fragile nei suoi confronti." Tesi, 26.

86 "Farina è un omino di circa cinquant'anni, parla a bassa voce, inflessione toscana e non sarda. Nel bosco io l'ho immaginato come un mezzo gigante, modi decisi, senza inflessione. Qui, in prigione, ha dieci anni più di quelli che gli ho dato nel covo. Preciso, ancora, che non ho mai potuto vedere né i miei sequestratori né i miei carcerieri durante tutta la prigionia, per il semplice fatto che ero incappucciato, e quando mi consentivano di togliere il cappuccio loro portavano la maschera." Soffiantini, *Il mio sequestro*, 117.

87 "Una delle cose che temevo di più era infatti il suo silenzio. Quando stava zitto voleva dire che era arrabbiato con me, e il suo silenzio doveva rappresentare per me una punizione … E stette in silenzio per diverse ore: mi puniva, mi puniva per mezzo di ciò che più mi faceva soffrire, distruggendo il ponte che avevo creato verso di lui, tra il mio e il suo isolamento. Cozzavo contro il suo silenzio e piangevo in silenzio." Tesi, *Sindrome da sequestro*, 45–6.

88 Symonds, "Victim Responses to Terror," 134.

89 "The phenomenon has received little attention in the literature. No study has examined the frequency of the occurrence of Stockholm syndrome among hostages or kidnap victims, although clinical observations tend to suggest that the duration of captivity and the isolation foster its development." Favaro et al., "Effects of Trauma," 976.

90 Herman, *Trauma and Recovery*, 82.

91 Herman, 82. It is important to note that not all researchers agree on the presence and dynamics of this phenomenon. In contrast with Herman's position, Rudas, Pintor, and Mascia do not consider Stockholm syndrome to be a rule; rather, they emphasize how this psychological bond is determined by the victims' lack of "self-maturity." Among the Sardinian kidnapped they had examined, they claim to find that only one shows evidence of Stockholm syndrome. This victim is a woman who was seventeen at the time of her kidnapping, and her identity, they state, was perhaps not developed and sure. The researchers' conclusion is that if at the moment of their abduction the captured have already a "good maturity of the Self," the trauma does not "affect their psychological balance." Rudas, Pintor, and Mascia, "Uomini rubati," 168.

92 Writes Symonds: "The Stockholm syndrome has often been viewed as the hostage's identification with the terrorist. I think the concept doesn't adequately explain hostage behaviour. I have found it more useful to view hostage behaviour as an attempt to relate to an individual who has first captured the hostage by an act of terror and then used the victim as an instrument to obtain an objective from a third party." Symonds, "Victim Responses to Terror," 134.

Notes to pages 156–9   241

93 Symonds, 134.
94 Herman, *Trauma and Recovery*, 74.
95 On these experiments, see for example the famous Zimbardo, *Psychological Power and Pathology of Imprisonment.*
96 "Non provo nessun risentimento per i miei carcerieri. Sarà la conseguenza delle conversazioni che abbiamo avuto? In fondo, a parte le botte del viaggio e l'operazione cera alle orecchie, a parte le condizioni igieniche quasi insopportabili ed il freddo intenso, mi hanno trattata meno peggio di quello che temevo ... Forse sono veramente delle vittime come mi hanno raccontato." Ovazza, *Cinque ciliege rosse*, 45.
97 "Allora il miracolo si è avverato! Non muoio più! È un attimo indescrivibile, meraviglioso, è il ritorno alla vita. Piango commossa. Non chiedo spiegazioni, né precisazioni. Non cerco di capire. Mi sento rinascere. Lo straordinario annuncio dell'insperata rinascita mi ha come elettrizzata ... Il fatto di aver sfiorato la morte così da vicino mi ha come traumatizzata, mi ha sconvolto e, presa dalla gioia di questa rinascita, mi ci vuole un po' di tempo per riprendere coscienza del fatto che non è stato ancora fatto nulla di positivo e per tornare alla triste realtà di questa prigione, di quest'attesa, di questo sentimento di completa impotenza. Con la mente ripenso alle ore di incubo trascorse durante questa notte indimenticabile. Sono state ore angosciose, tremende, dominate dal terrore." Ovazza, 64.
98 "Senza accorgermene, mi sono affezionata a questo essere sconosciuto e non provo per lui alcun rancore. Certo, è lui che mi trasmette i messaggi del capo, ma mi ha anche rivolto parole di pietà e quasi con un senso di umanità, è sempre intervenuto nei momenti in cui stavo peggio. Se non potessi più parlargli, le giornate che sono già tanto lunghe mi parrebbero ancora più insopportabili ... Lui sa sempre dirmi quelle mezze parole che mi ridanno un filo di speranza, lui, se non altro, mi ha fatto capire in tutti i modi quanto gli sia duro eseguire gli ordini del capo ... Che gioia, è di nuovo lui! Seduta sul letto gli chiedo come mai non è più venuto." Ovazza, 82–3.
99 Ovazza, 46.
100 "Scopro che l'amore è una convenienza e in una situazione di estremo isolamento, di dominio assoluto da parte di una forza brutale, esso si trasforma in un'arma di speranza. Speranza come azione, non solo speranza come preghiera. La preghiera, durante un sequestro, è l'amore che si muove, che agisce, costringe l'altro ad ascoltarti. E Dio solo sa quanto sia importante ricevere attenzione da parte dei carcerieri. Credo che nella Sindrome di Stoccolma, l'amore diventi un agente segreto, l'alleato della vittima, che contribuisce a piegare la partita dalla sua parte ... Quel 'porgere l'altra guancia' è sempre apparso un'allegoria,

242   Notes to pages 159–62

un simbolo, una buona intenzione destinata a rimanere tale. Come se Gesù ti suggerisse, sottobanco: 'Io lo dico, ma non è obbligo farlo' … L'isolamento … cambia la natura dell'amore e dell'odio." Soffiantini, *Il mio sequestro*, 55–6.

101 Farina, *Giuseppe Soffiantini pubblica*.

102 Del Frate, "Le poesie del mio rapitore."

103 "Perché il buio e la solitudine mi erano diventati intollerabili, perché avevo bisogno di parlare e di esprimere la mia angoscia ad un altro essere, nemico o amico che fosse, purché mi ascoltasse e mi confortasse rompendo un silenzio insopportabile e allontanando con le sue parole tutte le allucinazioni della notte. Allora lo pregavo di restare, di restare sempre accanto a me, perché quell'isolamento mi avrebbe fatto impazzire e lo pregavo di parlare, di parlare di qualsiasi cosa, perché non mi sentissi più così sola e abbandonata, perché avessi una presenza umana accanto a me." Tesi, *Sindrome da sequestro*, 168–9.

104 The lack of self-reflexivity in the inner language of the kidnapped recalls Blanchot's *Writing of the Disaster*. In his work, trauma makes the subject external to language; that is, the traumatized self cannot inhabit words and therefore cannot experience a linguistic self-reflexivity. See Blanchot, *L'écriture du désastre*.

105 See Leys, *Trauma*.

106 "Questo dialogo che avevo stabilito con lui mi sembrava allora una cosa positiva, perché mi toglieva dalla solitudine che era ciò che temevo di più, ma poi invece è risultato un fatto negativo. Infatti così facendo lui si impadroniva sempre più della mia personalità … Mentre io gli facevo intuire tanti lati del mio carattere, lui di se stesso parlava molto, ma ne falsava completamente la realtà … Tutti questi discorsi me li faceva, mostrandosi ai miei occhi migliore di quello che era, per impietosirmi e commuovermi." Tesi, *Sindrome da sequestro*, 47.

107 "Era mortificante il dubbio che la fiducia riposta nel guardiano fosse tradita, fosse anzi il risultato di un mostruoso programma di ricatto psicologico, di carpimento di notizie, di spionaggio." Rossi di Montelera, *Racconto di un sequestro*, 34–5.

108 Soffiantini, *Il mio sequestro*, 156.

109 "Un salto di intensità." Tesi, *Sindrome da sequestro*, 154.

110 "Venivo come da un altro mondo dove si viveva drammaticamente e si parlava un altro linguaggio, angoscioso e violento." Tesi, 154.

111 "Mi sembrava che quasi tutti parlassero in modo superficiale e che ogni persona potesse sfiorare appena e appena percepire un lembo in superficie della realtà profonda da cui ero uscita e che ancora mi portavo dentro." Tesi, 154.

Notes to pages 162–8 243

112 "Mentre il presente scorreva ed io non lo vivevo perché ero lontana, distaccata, ancora rivolta indietro, interiormente radicata ai miei giorni di angoscia, ancora sepolta nel bosco." Tesi, 154.

113 "Nessuno si accorge di niente, le macchine scivolano via alla stessa velocità, due rischiano il tamponamento, un'altra passa col verde. Sono come una comparsa che ha sbagliato scena, è entrata in un altro film." Soffiantini, *Il mio sequestro*, 221–2.

114 "Mi accorgerò, alcuni mesi dopo la mia liberazione, che un segno è rimasto, profondo. Taglia nettamente l'anno in due parti. Le stagioni da quattro si riducono a due." Soffiantini, 220.

115 For an analysis of the limits of autobiography and its literary debate, see, for example, Gilmore, *Limits of Autobiography*.

116 In the canonical *On Autobiography*, Philippe Lejeune writes that "in order for there to be autobiography (and personal literature in general), the *author*, *narrator*, and the *protagonist* must be identical." Lejeune, *On Autobiography*, 5. This "autobiographical pact," together with the notion of the autonomy and independence of the autobiographical self, elaborated by critics like Georges Gusdorf, is what Lacanian, poststructuralist, and feminist literary criticisms came to define as impossible.

117 For the matter of the self in autobiography, see, among others, Eakin, *How Our Lives Becomes Stories*.

118 For a different consideration of autobiography, especially connected to trauma, and the healing that it makes possible see, for example, Henke, *Shattered Subjects*.

119 Felman and Laub, *Testimony*, 70.

120 Felman and Laub, 70–1.

121 On Pier Paolo Pasolini's concept of testimony as "writing in flesh" in his *Petrolio*, see Montalbano, "Pier Paolo Pasolini e Maurice Merleau-Ponty."

122 See Foucault, *History of Sexuality*.

123 Radstone, "Cultures," 169.

124 Radstone, 175.

6. The Anatomy of Captivity

1 "Mi ritrovavo a volte a quattro gambe, con la catena allungata al massimo e la testa dentro il cunicolo, per sentir meglio." Rossi di Montelera, *Racconto di un sequestro*, 109–10.

2 Rudas, Pintor, and Mascia, "Uomini rubati."

3 "Si, mi legano come un cane, come una bestia qualsiasi che si voglia tenere prigioniera." Ovazza, *Cinque ciliege rosse*, 17.

244   Notes to pages 168–73

4 "Dopo mesi senza potermi lavare, si forma sul mio corpo uno strato di sporco, di untuosità simile a quello di un animale." Soffiantini, *Il mio sequestro*, 179.

5 "Purtroppo, quando si è sequestrati, lo stato di dipendenza è tale che si è ridotti come cani a catena che se per caso il padrone li accarezza, per gratitudine si mettono a leccargli umilmente la mano." Tesi, *Sindrome da sequestro*, 167.

6 Rudas, Pintor, and Mascia, "Uomini rubati," 170.

7 Rudas, Pintor, and Mascia, 170.

8 See Symonds, "Victim Responses to Terror," 129–36.

9 "Sentii gridare: 'c'è qualcuno qui dentro?' Trasalii davvero. Di che cosa si trattava? Era uno scherzo dei banditi, che volevano saggiare la mia 'riservatezza' prima di liberarmi? Non risposi nulla. Chiamarono ancora, e io tacevo nel terrore. Ero sicuro che si trattava di un 'brutto scherzo.' Sentii incominciare a tirare il chiavistello dello sportello, e mi misi sul letto come sempre con la solita giacca sulla testa. Qualcuno entrò e mi chiese 'chi è lei?' Era certamente uno scherzo orribile, una prova finale per vedere se ero davvero capace di tacere; se tacevo avevo forse la speranza di essere liberato, se parlavo … " Rossi di Montelera, *Racconto di un sequestro*, 151.

10 "In quei pochi istanti persi completamente il senso della realtà: non ero più in mezzo ad una strada in piena Firenze, ma mi trovavo di nuovo nella buca del bosco, di nuovo sola di fronte al mio persecutore, colui a cui non potevo disubbidire senza correre il pericolo di essere distrutta, mentre così, come era stato per tanto tempo dentro alla buca, l'ubbidienza significava salvezza … Ormai di nuovo succube nelle sue mani, gli ripetei che avevo detto tutto quello che voleva lui alla Polizia, che avevo fatto come aveva voluto lui, che non lo avevo tradito, che avevo detto alla Polizia, alla televisione, ai giornali, come era stato buono con me, come mi aveva trattata bene, e che avevo taciuto, come sempre mi aveva ordinato, la sua appartenenza alle BR." Tesi, *Sindrome da sequestro*, 176–7.

11 "Quanto sarebbe stato meglio se quel giovedì pomeriggio avessi avuto fiducia nel Magistrato che mi stava di fronte e gli avessi confessato tutto! … E mentre tutti in tribunale quel pomeriggio mi rivolgevano parole di simpatia e comprensione, io nascondevo dentro di me quel segreto terribile e non potevo parlare." Tesi, 172.

12 "Ma non se lo ricordavano più in che stato avevo le gambe quando ero stata liberata? … Ma come si poteva pensare che io, per scappare con un uomo, mi fossi spontaneamente messa sotto terra al freddo e al gelo in quelle orribili condizioni igieniche e ambientali in cui ero stata trovata? Senza contare che se avessi voluto lasciare mio marito, qualche cosa di mio possedevo, bastava pensare alla villa che era intestata a me." Tesi, 186.

13 "Sono contento. Di una contentezza che si può avere dopo oltre cento giorni di prigionia. Mi spiego: il posto in cui mi trovo ora, garantisce un'altra resistenza. Ho una visione più ampia del bosco e ciò mi conforta … per un amante delle piante come me, quel bosco di querce che mi

Notes to pages 173–6 245

sta davanti è un'iniezione di vita. Sono tra un esemplare di leccio e una quercia antica ... realizzo immediatamente la posizione topografica e ambientale ... È come possedere la mappa del tesoro. Se vivo, qui ci torno. A occhi chiusi." Soffiantini, *Il mio sequestro*, 97.

14 "Non è più autore di azioni, né punto di partenza di ciò che accade." Rudas, Pintor, and Mascia, "Uomini rubati," 182.

15 "Il prigioniero bendato è reso ancora più inerme e spogliato di soggettività, è interamente esposto allo sguardo dell'Altro, che lo sorveglia e che a sua volta si sottrae alla restituzione di questo sguardo. Lo sguardo del carceriere-guardiano acquista quindi un potere assoluto sull'ostaggio e sul suo corpo, che permane in sua completa balia. Viene così annullata l'esperienza della reciprocità dello sguardo, che insita nel binomio guardare-essere guardato, diviene qui a esclusivo vantaggio del suo termine passivo." Rudas, Pintor, and Mascia, 182.

16 "Ma come fu umiliante la prima volta dovermi servire del vaso con lui presente, anche se appartato in un angolo. Devo dire che questa è stata una delle cose peggiori da sopportare in tutto il sequestro, questa umiliazione, questo stato in cui una donna si ritrova ad essere come una bestia accucciata in terra, senza avere alcun pudore o dignità personale." Tesi, *Sindrome da sequestro*, 44.

17 "Faccio la schermografia al mio corpo, mentre come un cane guaisco a ogni sforzo. È sangue, è sangue, scende e non si ferma. Controllo, ho i calzoni e le mani insanguinate. Vorrei tamponare senza espormi. La mia intimità è sacra. Siamo stati abituati a rispettare il corpo degli altri, soprattutto evitando sguardi indiscreti. Il massimo rispetto è anche non osservare il corpo di una persona che soffre. Per questo spero di risolvere l'emorragia in pochi minuti e non dire nulla ai miei carcerieri ... Il pudore della nudità appartiene parimenti alle belve umane, se esistono, come ai cosiddetti normali." Soffiantini, *Il mio sequestro*, 109–10.

18 "Davanti al nuovo padrone della tua esistenza corporea." Soffiantini, 113–14.

19 "Questo destituirsi della soggettività ha in sé il senso della perdita della stessa vita. Morire non vuol dire certo perdere la propria oggettività in mezzo al mondo – tutti i morti sono là, nel mondo, intorno a noi – ma bensì perdere ogni possibilità di rivelarsi come soggetto ad altri." Rudas, Pintor, and Mascia, "Uomini rubati," 183.

20 "La sensazione che fuori si possa pensare che siamo morti dà da un lato una gran voglia di vivere e gridare a tutti che si è vivi, ma d'altro canto ci fa sentire un po' con un piede nella fossa. Infatti la 'vita,' almeno psicologicamente, non è solo un fatto obiettivo connesso alla persona il cui cuore batte, è anche un fatto 'sociale.' Se uno vive in assoluto isolamento fisico e in un isolamento di rapporti anche solo conoscitivi tale da far sì che gli altri non abbiano più la percezione, la conoscenza o la certezza della sua esistenza come essere vivente, costui si sente già un

246   Notes to pages 176–81

po' morto, per lo meno 'morto agli altri.'" Rossi di Montelera, *Racconto di un sequestro*, 79.

21   Merleau-Ponty, *Visible and the Invisible*, 136.

22   Merleau-Ponty, 137.

23   "Spero che qualcuno di quel gruppetto di gitanti sia particolarmente abile, capace di avvistarmi, di starsene zitto per un po' e di chiamare aiuto, una volta al sicuro. Pretendo quello che pretende un uomo sotto sequestro, completamente privo di una parvenza di libertà, ancora di più quando sente passare vicino la vita. E lui vive in un cerchio di morte, senza voci e senza un contatto che lo renda certo di essere ancora al mondo. Veramente vivo nel mondo dei vivi." Soffiantini, *Il mio sequestro*, 30.

24   Merleau-Ponty, *Visible and the Invisible*, 139.

25   Gambazzi, *L'occhio e il suo inconscio*, 21.

26   Merleau-Ponty, *Visible and the Invisible*, 130.

27   "Either my right hand really passes over to the rank of touched, but then its hold on the world is interrupted; or it retains its hold on the world, but then I do not really touch *it*." Merleau-Ponty, 148.

28   Merleau-Ponty, 139.

29   Merleau-Ponty, 214. In one of the "Working notes" Merleau-Ponty says, "Take topological space as a model of being." Merleau-Ponty, 210.

30   "Il solito bandito mi sollevò di peso. Sentii con i piedi i bordi di un buco, una botola, e mi sentii calare sotto terra. In quel momento ebbi veramente un moto di terrore, inconscio, ma orribile. Quando toccai il fondo, mi fu ordinato di abbassarmi, sempre più, finché fui a quattro gambe. Poi mi fecero avanzare, tirandomi per le mani. Era un cunicolo sotterraneo, bassissimo, fradicio. Mi sentii seppellire, e solo in quel momento ebbi l'impressione fisica della perdita irrimediabile, sia pur temporanea, della libertà. Finché ero all'aria aperta, in piedi, e sentivo dei rumori, mi pareva di avere ancora un minimo di libertà, o meglio di vita; ma quel cunicolo che mi lasciavo alle spalle mi faceva per la prima volta toccar con mano il vero significato della prigionia." Rossi di Montelera, *Racconto di un sequestro*, 12–13.

31   "Quell'aereo mi provocò un fugace pensiero di libertà. Io ero lì sotto terra mentre sopra la mia testa, sopra la mia cella in quel momento aperta volava un aereo con tanti passeggeri … la vita fuori continuava identica a sempre, anche se io ero lì sotto. E quei passeggeri che guardavano fuori dai finestrini per ammirare la collina torinese non si accorgevano che a qualche centinaio o migliaio di metri sotto di loro c'era un rifugio sotterraneo, ma con l'ingresso aperto, e che dentro c'ero io! … Ebbi una voglia folle di libertà." Rossi di Montelera, 47.

32   "La compagnia si allontana. Ridono, qualcuno si è messo a cantare. Credo di essere morto nel mondo dei vivi. La dimensione del sequestro mi sovrasta: il sequestro è un macigno sugli occhi, un'improvvisa paralisi. Tutto accade come in quegli incubi in cui qualcuno parla ma non viene

Notes to pages 182–5   247

sentito. Lui vede gli altri, ma tutti gli passano accanto ma non lo vedono." Soffiantini, *Il mio sequestro*, 30.

33 "Mi chiedo dove sia finito tutto il miracolo tecnologico, l'individuazione scientifica a distanza, l'intercettazione tramite la rivelazione di calore … Invece, io rimango nel bosco degli alberi scarsi, visibile quasi a occhio nudo eppure invisibile a tutti, tranne che ai miei carcerieri." Soffiantini, 105.

34 "L'impatto con quel 'fuori' fu per me un trauma. Non ero più abituata all'aria aperta, alla luce del giorno: la realtà esterna, il bosco, il verde, gli alberi, mi sembravano immensi e mi fecero paura. Ritornai velocemente dentro. Ormai ero come un animale che si sente più sicuro nella sua tana: ero regredita allo stato animale. Infatti, assurdamente dentro alla buca mi sentivo più protetta che fuori nel bosco. Per almeno una decina di volte mi provai ad uscire dalla tana, ma non ce la facevo a restare fuori, a guardare; avevo ancora paura della realtà che mi circondava, nella quale si erano concentrati tutti i terrori della mia prigionia … E quello che è più incredibile è che, una volta dentro, mi legavo di nuovo a catena, perché così mi avrebbero dovuto trovare i sardi se per caso fossero arrivati." Tesi, *Sindrome da sequestro*, 117.

35 "Strappo la benda: il risultato, al momento, è quasi irrilevante. Intorno è scuro, la serata è fredda, la strada è di campagna … Adesso mi sembra di non essere ancora libero: fino a quando non mi libero del buio e della stradina di campagna, tengo di riserva il dubbio diabolico che uno dei carcerieri esca da un cespuglio, mi dia una botta in testa e ricominci la danza macabra della prigionia nel baule, degli spostamenti, delle buche e delle tende con contorno eterno di rovi." Soffiantini, *Il mio sequestro*, 216.

36 "Luci. Rimango senza fiato, grido 'Luci' e alzo le mani come se mi venissero incontro. Non esce una sillaba. Ho gridato 'Luci' come un muto. Ma ora non sono più accecato dallo scuro di prima. Ora mirerò a quelle luci e sarò nelle case del mondo. La stradina finisce addosso ad una grande strada piena di traffico." Soffiantini, 216.

37 "Rischio di finire sotto dieci volte, i clacson si inchiodano nella schiena e i fari radono la barba lunga. Per la prima volta dopo tanto tempo, rivedo la mia ombra intermittente su un asfalto. Sono alto e grosso, la falcata è gigantesca come quella di un orco. Sono fiero del mio corpo ritrovato … imponente così come appare su quel tratto di strada che precede quel distributore indicato dai banditi." Soffiantini, 217.

38 Merleau-Ponty, *Visible and the Invisible*, 255.

39 *Commissione parlamentare sul fenomeno della mafia e altre associazioni criminali* (istituita con legge 1 ottobre 1996, n. 509).

40 "Che cosa tremenda scrivere questi messaggi così pazzeschi, senza poter riflettere neanche un minuto! Sotto la minaccia di un'enorme pistola sono costretta a scrivere esattamente come me lo impongono, senza poter mettere niente di mio, senza poter far loro capire che non sono certamente io, di mia spontanea volontà, che scrivo queste parole. Quale sarà la loro

248　Notes to pages 185–91

reazione quando li riceveranno? Se ne renderanno conto?" Ovazza, *Cinque ciliege rosse*, 16–17.

41 Rossi di Montelera, *Racconto di un sequestro*, 67.

42 "Non avrei mai perso una simile occasione. Non è piacevole, dopo qualche settimana di buio e di silenzio, dover scrivere ai propri genitori una lettera fredda e piena di condizioni. Però volevo che potessero distinguere la parte dettata dalla parte libera." Rossi di Montelera, 67.

43 "Scrivendo questa lettera ebbi la sensazione, ripetuta poi ad ogni altra lettera, di stare forse scrivendo l'ultimo messaggio della mia vita. Per questa ragione mi importava moltissimo poter scrivere almeno una frase rasserenante per i miei genitori, perché almeno sapessero, nel caso che mi avessero ucciso, che ero sereno; perché il mio ultimo messaggio non fosse per loro un perenne trauma, dubbio, angoscia." Rossi di Montelera, 68.

44 Scarry, *Body in Pain*, 27.

45 "L'angoscia di morire sola e abbandonata da tutti … morire sola e incatenata, di fame, di sete … superava qualsiasi altro timore e sentimento. Di fronte a lui che si mostrava spesso 'amico,' io ero inerme, senza difese, nelle sue mani: mi nutriva, mi scaldava, mi proteggeva, mi aiutava a sopravvivere." Tesi, *Sindrome da sequestro*, 194.

46 Cavarero, *Horrorism*, 30.

47 Cavarero, 5.

48 Cavarero, 7.

49 Cavarero, 8.

50 Cavarero, 12.

51 Cavarero, 32.

52 Cavarero, 21.

53 "Ogni volta che hanno bisogno di me, della mia collaborazione, o meglio della mia remissività, allora sono più buoni. Premurosi. Degli amici un po' contriti, dispiaciuti della sofferenza che sono 'costretti' a infliggermi. Quando c'è da scrivere una lettera ai miei familiari come vogliono loro, sono capaci persino di servirmi pasti caldi … Pian piano comprendo il loro atteggiamento. Pochi minuti e condizionano i loro 'favori' al fatto che io scriva la prima lettera. Col contenuto giusto, col tono giusto." Belardinelli and Masotti, *Storia di un sequestro*, 53.

54 "Ritrovavo finalmente mia madre, la sensazione tenera di risentirmi bambina nelle sue braccia, di sciogliermi in lacrime che venivano asciugate, in parole che solo a lei potevo dire. La guardai negli occhi e pensai con sollievo che ce l'avevo fatta, che non ero impazzita." Tesi, *Sindrome da sequestro*, 155.

55 "Eccoli, stupendi, meravigliosi nella loro emozione, straordinari nella loro forza d'animo, i miei due pilastri … Devo essere orrenda con la testa rapata, ma loro fanno finta di niente; papà mi abbraccia ancora a lungo e

Notes to pages 191–3   249

mi dà la sua benedizione: questa è la prova tangibile che tutto riprenderà come prima." Ovazza, *Cinque ciliege rosse*, 140.

56 "In mezzo al giardino, ferma, attende mia madre. Ha quasi novant'anni, una roccia. Non posso stringerla altrimenti non riuscirei ad ascoltare il benvenuto: 'Sapevo che saresti tornato.' Nel nostro dialetto ha la certezza delle cose che debbono accadere, scritte sulla pietra degli antichi testamenti." Soffiantini, *Il mio sequestro*, 228.

57 Cavarero, *Horrorism*, 14–15.

58 "È questione di un attimo. Un grosso batuffolo di cotone mi viene schiacciato contro il naso, un batuffolo evidentemente imbevuto di cloroformio. 'Dio mio, aiutami, dammi la forza di resistere, fai che non perda completamente i sensi.' La mano implacabile spinge sempre di più il batuffolo contro la mia faccia, ma … il rumore dell'automobile è ancora chiaro nelle mie orecchie, e sento ancora il respiro affannoso dei banditi. Allora non ho perso i sensi, allora forse sarò ancora in grado di lottare e di sentirli!" Ovazza, *Cinque ciliege rosse*, 11.

59 "Ogni volta che mi portano da mangiare, si avvicinano il più possibile perché io possa sentire la solita litania delle minacce di tutto quello che potrà succedermi se riferirò alla Polizia delle conversazioni che avrei potuto sentire e mi ripetono tutte le atrocità che succederanno ai miei familiari, soprattutto a Giorgio [suo figlio minore], se mai io dovessi tradirli ed esporli ad un'eventuale cattura. Io sono felice di non aver mai sentito niente. Così anche se lo volessi, non potrò mai tradirli." Ovazza, 116.

60 "Una volta successe un fatto strano. Tutt'ad un tratto nel silenzio del pomeriggio si sentì forte e chiaramente la voce di un altoparlante che urlava: 'Cittadini, cittadini …' Feci in tempo a sentire solo la parola cittadini, perché il bandito mi saltò addosso e mi tappò le orecchie, cercando di frastornarmi e di non farmi sentire altro." "Fortunatamente non udii nulla che mi facesse identificare il luogo, altrimenti sarei stata perduta." Tesi, *Sindrome da sequestro*, 57.

61 "Con la bocca tappata e gli occhi sbarrati dal terrore pensavo ai miei figli, alle loro voci, ai loro gesti … Mi accorsi con sgomento che non me li ricordavo più: troppo mi ero allontanata dal centro di me stessa, dalle mie radici." "Quando infatti ritornai a casa e finalmente riabbracciai i miei figli, non piansi. Era come se venissi da un altro mondo: ero 'sradicata.'" Tesi, 57–8.

62 "Me li stringevo, me li tenevo accanto, sentivo la loro presenza, ma non usciva una parola dalla mia bocca … non riuscivo nemmeno a piangere, come se ancora qualcuno mi tenesse lontana, incatenata ad un'altra realtà e ad altre sensazioni ed emozioni, diverse e più violente." Tesi, 156.

63 "Sarebbe bastato che mi fermassi, che bloccassi la macchina in mezzo alla strada e mi mettessi a gridare: 'Aiuto, aiutatemi, sono sola, sola, non

250 Notes to pages 193–7

so che fare, ho paura!' Ma questo grido me lo tenevo dentro di me e mi straziava tutta, convinta com'ero di agire per il meglio, di essere obbligata a comportarmi così per evitare un male molto peggiore." Tesi, 173.

64 Cavarero, *Horrorism*, 17.

65 "Qualcuno mi afferra le braccia e me le lega dietro alla schiena. Mi fanno adagiare su un lato. Mi scoprono l'orecchio sinistro, sollevandomi il cappuccio da quella parte ... sento chiedere il guanto, poi uno spruzzo sull'orecchio, e ancora la richiesta del bisturi. Ora è il taglio. Un pezzo di cartilagine mi cade sul viso. Il sangue mi cola sul collo. Stringo i pugni, non piango, non mi lamento. Mi disinfettano. Un odore acre. Mi girano la testa e ripetono l'operazione all'orecchio destro. Il sangue scende a rivoli sul collo, una cascata. Immortalano l'evento con quattro foto: da sinistra, da destra, davanti due volte. Una testimonianza che deve essere incontrovertibile." Belardinelli and Masotti, *Storia di un sequestro*, 116–17.

66 "Sento il clic di una macchina fotografica. Mi scatta un'istantanea in quelle condizioni e ridacchia. 'Sei soddisfatto?' mormora. Se ne torna all'allegra brigata, a mostrare il 'trofeo.' Provo disgusto per questo comportamento. Fuori è giorno pieno, ma io mi corico lo stesso." Belardinelli and Masotti, 128.

67 "Penso a Moro, a come scriveva, sotto il dominio incontrastato delle Brigate Rosse. Lo sento sulla mia pelle tutto questo dominio e riesco a comprendere l'angoscia di quelle parole sue e non sue nello stesso tempo, il suo pensiero e la dettatura degli altri. Bisognerebbe provare per pochi minuti la condizione del sequestrato e verrebbero a cadere tante polemiche sull'autenticità o meno delle lettere dal carcere." Soffiantini, *Il mio sequestro*, 59.

68 "Si scrive contemporaneamente quello che si pensa e quello che viene imposto, mescolati l'uno dentro l'altro, il vero e il falso in una scrittura graficamente tua, appartenente però alla logica delle pistole e delle catene." Soffiantini, 59. Talking about the issue of the authenticity of Moro's letters, in his "La possibilità dell'uso del discorso nel cuore del terrore," Gotor quotes these passages from Soffiantini's memoir and states that his words allow us to witness the hostage/warder relationship that Moro himself likely experienced writing his letters: "After [Soffiantini's] words, the product of his own experience, it doesn't seem that anything further needs to be said about the authenticity of Moro's letters" ("Rispetto alle sue parole, figlie dell'esperienza, null'altro sembra necessario aggiungere al riguardo dell'autenticità delle lettere di Moro"). Gotor, "La possibilità dell'uso del discorso," 361–3.

69 "Desidero toccare e leggere la carta su cui ho consumato una sofferenza senza confini. Nello stesso tempo ho una forte apprensione. Mi pare, quasi, che qualcosa di fisico possa ricondurmi alla mia prigione." Soffiantini, *Il mio sequestro*, 62.

70 De André, "Hotel Supramonte."

Conclusion

1 Mahy and Blake, *Great Piratical Rumbustification*; Mahy and Blake, *La bibliotecaria rapita*.
2 Ammaniti, *Io non ho paura*; Salvatores, *Io non ho paura*.
3 Tesi, *Sindrome da sequestro*, 174.
4 Ferrante, *L'amica geniale*.
5 On the work of Elena Ferrante see, among others, De Rogatis, *Elena Ferrante* and "Metamorfosi del tempo"; Pinto, *Elena Ferrante*; Milkova, *Elena Ferrante as World Literature*; Ricciardi, *Finding Ferrante*; Russo Bullaro and Love, *Works of Elena Ferrante*; Santovetti, "Melodrama or Metafiction?"; Gambaro, "Il fascino del regresso"; Falotico, "Elena Ferrante"; Benedetti, "Il linguaggio dell'amicizia"; Donnarumma, "Il melodramma"; Bokopoulus, "We Are Always Us"; Lucamante, "Undoing Feminism"; De Rogatis, Milkova, and Wehling-Giorgi, "Elena Ferrante in a Global Context."
6 Ferrante, *Storia della bambina perduta*.
7 Ovazza, *Cinque ciliege rosse*, 13.
8 Marrazzo, "Sequestro di persona."
9 Scola, "Sequestro di persona cara."
10 Ferrante, *Story of the Lost Child*. "Il male prende vie impreviste. Ci metti sopra le chiese, i conventi, i libri – sembrano così importanti i libri, disse con sarcasmo, tu ci hai dedicato tutta la tua vita – e il male sfonda il pavimento e sbuca dove non te lo aspetti." Ferrante, *Storia della bambina perduta*, 428.
11 Trincia and Micheli, "Il male."
12 Biondani, "A Milano la mafia non c'è"; see also Portanova, Rossi, and Stefanoni, *Mafia a Milano*.

Bibliography

Memoirs

Belardinelli, Dante, and Giovanni Masotti. *Storia di un sequestro: La drammatica vicenda di Dante Belardinelli*. Cinisello Balsamo, Milan: Edizioni Paoline, 1990.

Casella, Cesare. *743 giorni lontano da casa: Quando la vita ricomincia è più bello*. Milan: Rizzoli, 1990.

De André, Fabrizio. "Hotel Supramonte." In *L'indiano*, track 5. Universal Music Publishing Ricordi S.r.l., 1981.

Ovazza, Carla. *Cinque ciliege rosse: Una notte lunga trentacinque giorni*. Milan: Mursia, 1978.

– *Diario de un secuestro*. Translated by Juan Giner. Barcelona: Martínez Roca, 1979.

– *L'interminable nui: Rapt à l'italienne*. Paris: R. Laffont, 1978.

Rossi di Montelera, Luigi. *Racconto di un sequestro*. Turin: Società editrice internazionale, 1977.

Soffiantini, Giuseppe. *Il mio sequestro: La storia mai raccontata di 237 giorni di prigionia*. Milan: Baldini & Castoldi, 1999.

Tesi Mosca, Donatella. *Sindrome da sequestro*. Florence: Vallecchi Editore, 1986.

Parliamentary Documents

Commissione parlamentare d'inchiesta sui fenomeni di criminalità in Sardegna (istituita con legge 27 ottobre 1969, n. 755). Doc. XXIII, N. 3 (Rome, 1972).

Commissione parlamentare sul fenomeno della mafia e altre associazioni criminali (istituita con legge 23 marzo 1988, n. 94). Doc. XXIII, N. 12-bis/1 (Rome, 1990).

254   Bibliography

Commissione parlamentare sul fenomeno della mafia e altre associazioni criminali (istituita con legge 1 ottobre 1996, n. 509). Doc. XXIII, N. 14 (Rome, 1998).

Council of Europe. "Committee of Ministers Recommendation on Measures to Be Taken in Cases of Kidnapping Followed by a Ransom Demand." *International Legal Materials* 22, no. 3 (May 1983): 675–80. https://doi.org/10.1017/s0020782900031442.

Teche Rai (Public Television Archive), Rome and Turin

Amodei, Wanda, and Maria Bosio. *Il processo: Un film dal vero*. RAI, 1977.

Biagi, Enzo. *Proibito*. Teche Rai, 11 July 1977.

Biancacci, Franco, and Guido Levi. *Storie allo specchio*. Teche Rai, 6 and 13 December 1978.

Bisiach, Gianni. "Rapporto da Corleone." In Enzo Biagi, *Rotocalco televisivo*. Teche Rai, 31 March 1962.

Dell'Aquila, Enzo. "Banditismo in Sardegna." In Ennio Mastrostefano and Luigi Locatelli, *AZ: Un fatto come e perché*. Teche Rai, 23 January 1971.

Falivena, Aldo, and Luigi Locatelli. *AZ: Un fatto come e perché*. Teche Rai, 20 February 1976.

"Gente di San Luca." Teche Rai, 1977.

"Gli intoccabili di Taurianova." In *Tg2 Dossier*. Teche Rai, 1978.

"Intervista del 1974 a cura di Scarano a Paul Getty III." *Stasera-L'attesa*. Teche Rai, 1974.

Leoni, Fausta, and Ennio Mastrostefano. "Memorandum Sequestri." *TG2 Dossier*. Teche Rai, 8 April 1983.

"Mafia Calabrese." Teche Rai, 1977.

Marrazzo, Giuseppe. "Sequestro di persona." In Aldo Falivena and Luigi Locatelli, *AZ: Un fatto come e perché*. Teche Rai, 20 February 1976.

Minoli, Giovanni. "Il rapimento di Paul Getty: Il sequestro del nipote dell'uomo più ricco del mondo." In *RAI: La storia siamo noi*. Rome, 2003.

'Ndrangheta S.p.A. *Rai Play*. https://www.raiplay.it/programmi/ndranghetaspa.

Santoro, Michele. *Samarcanda*. Teche Rai, 1990.

Sposini, Lamberto, and Pino Scaccia. "Quei giorni di Cesare." *Speciale TG1*. Teche Rai, 3 February 1990.

TG3 Piemonte. Teche Rai, Turin, 9 April 1987.

TGR Piemonte. Teche Rai, Turin, 2 August 1988.

TGR Piemonte edizione serale. Teche Rai, Turin, 21 July 1988.

Verde, Dino. *Scuola serale per aspiranti italiani*. Teche Rai, 10 September 1977.

Zavoli, Sergio. *La notte della Repubblica*. Rai 2, Teche Rai, December 1989–April 1990.

Zucconi, Guglielmo. "Il sequestro di persona." *Sotto Processo*. Teche Rai, 12 December 1972.

– *Sotto Processo*. Episode 6. Teche Rai, December 1972.

Newspapers

"1973: Anno di grandi sequestri." *L'Unità*, 25 November 1973.

Alberoni, Francesco. "Come nel Medioevo." *Corriere della Sera*, 16 December 1973.

"Anche la madre dubita che Paul sia stato rapito." *Corriere della Sera*, 23 August 1973.

Augias, Corrado. "Novità in cartellone: Il teatro-bugia." *La Repubblica*, 24 September 1991.

Barilà, Giuseppe. "Arrestato per droga 'Momo' Piromalli già coinvolto nell'Anonima-sequestri." *Corriere della Sera*, 23 October 1975.

– "Il superlatitante Saverio Mammoliti si sposa indisturbato in Calabria." *Corriere della Sera*, 1 September 1975.

– "Una mamma sfida la 'Ndrangheta." *Corriere della Sera*, 12 June 1989.

Bevilacqua, Alberto. "Questa è la storia di Paul Getty III." *Corriere della Sera*, 21 November 1973.

Biagi, Enzo. "Cristina, un'esistenza come tante." *Corriere della Sera*, 3 September 1975.

– "Una sera di pioggia con i genitori di Cristina." *Corriere della Sera*, 14 September 1975.

Biglia, Andrea. "È ancora braccio di ferro tra il padre e la polizia." *Corriere della Sera*, 19 June 1989.

Biondani, Paolo. "A Milano la mafia non c'è." *L'Espresso*, 22 January 2010.

Casella, Angela. "Non capisco De Mita: Lo Stato ha sbagliato; Ora invoco solo pietà." *Corriere della Sera*, 17 June 1989.

"Catanzaro: Protesta per un articolo su presunti rapporti giudici-mafia." *La Stampa*, 13 December 1975.

"Cento milioni a chi darà notizie di Cristina Mazzotti." *Corriere della Sera*, 26 August 1975.

Ciccarello, Elena. "Omicidio di Bruno Caccia, una pista 30 anni dopo: I familiari 'Nuovo processo.'" *Il Fatto Quotidiano*, 16 March 2014.

Ciccarello, Elena, and Davide Pecorelli. "Bruno Caccia, al via il processo al presunto killer del procuratore di Torino: Davigo tra i possibili testimoni." *Il Fatto Quotidiano*, 6 July 2016.

"Cinquemila studenti in corteo a Pavia 'Liberate Cesare Casella.'" *Corriere della Sera*, 6 November 1988.

Ciuni, Roberto. "Inquietanti domande dei politici sulla magistratura calabrese." *Corriere della Sera*, 11 September 1977.

"Commissione di magistrati a Catanzaro." *Corriere della Sera*, 22 July 1975.

"Continua il silenzio dei rapitori." *Il Tempo*, 14 July 1973.

Corvi, Luigi. "La famiglia Mazzotti: 'Giustizia finalmente.'" *Corriere della Sera* (Edizione Milano), 10 June 2008.

– "Omicidio Mazzotti, impronta inchioda ex boss: Dopo 33 anni caccia ad altri tre rapitori." *Corriere della Sera*, 10 June 2008.

256   Bibliography

"Cossiga è d'accordo sul provvedimento Pomarici." *Corriere della Sera*,
20 March 1976.

"Da piccolo contrabbandiere di 'bionde' a uomo di rispetto della
'Ndrangheta." *Corriere della Sera*, 6 July 1978.

Del Frate, Claudio. "Le poesie del mio rapitore, un riscatto." *Corriere della Sera*,
6 December 2007.

Del Re, Giancarlo. "Senza famiglia." *Il Messaggero*, 12 November 1973.

De Simone, Cesare. "La drammatica evoluzione scandita in 43 cartelle."
Corriere della Sera, 10 January 1984.

Di Dio, Giuseppe. "'Se Paul voleva denaro bastava che lo chiedesse.'"
Il Messaggero, 22 July 1973.

"Drammatica invocazione alla mamma." *Il Tempo*, 19 July 1973.

"Due tesi a confronto sul rapimento del giovane: Rapimento si. Rapimento
no." *Il Messaggero*, 23 July 1973.

Durand, Mino. "Gli zii di Cristina: 'Niente pena di morte ma nessuno dovrà
più soffrire come noi.'" *Corriere della Sera*, 4 September 1975.

"È a bordo d'un panfilo e prepara il film da girare con il riscatto." *Il Tempo*,
23 July 1973.

"E ora anche la difesa diventa un fatto personale." *Espansione*, no. 98 (March
1978): 38–42.

Eszterhas, Joe. "J. Paul Getty III: Exclusive 1974 Interview with Kidnapped Oil
Heir." *Rolling Stone*, May 1974.

Feltri, Vittorio. "Orribile sospetto: Il giudice Ferlaino fu assassinato perché
aveva scoperto in Calabria chi aveva ordinato di rapire Cristina." *Corriere
d'Informazione*, 18 September 1975.

"Forse visto in Corsica a bordo di uno yacht." *Il Tempo*, 15 July 1973.

"Fotocronaca di un'avventura notturna." *Il Tempo*, 23 November 1973.

F.Q. "Bruno Caccia, confermato l'ergastolo per Rocco Schirripa: La figlia
del magistrato ucciso; 'Cercare gli altri colpevoli.'" *Il Fatto Quotidiano*,
14 February 2019.

– "Omicidio Caccia, la Cassazione conferma l'ergastolo." *Corriere della Sera*,
19 February 2020.

Franz, Pierluigi. "Condannato ex deputato: Diffamò cinque magistrati."
Corriere della Sera, 24 October 1983.

Fumo, Lamberto. "Reale commenta la tesi Gui per una legge antisequestri."
La Stampa, 9 September 1975.

Gambardella, Gerardo. "Assassinato a colpi di lupara il magistrato che
processò i novanta mafiosi palermitani." *La Stampa*, 4 July 1975.

"Getty: Fuga, sequestro o scherzo." *Corriere della Sera*, 22 August 1973.

Ghislanzoni, Giancarlo. "Come in Calabria è scattata la trappola per gli
accusati del rapimento di Paul Getty." *Corriere della Sera*, 17 January
1974.

Bibliography 257

- "Gui: Occorre impedire ai parenti di cedere al ricatto dei rapitori." *Corriere della Sera*, 3 September 1975.
- "Il giovane Getty disse a un'amica 'un falso sequestro renderebbe molto.'" *Corriere della Sera*, 15 July 1973.
- "I soldi trovati sono quelli del riscatto: Accusati i banditi dal cervello elettronico." *Corriere della Sera*, 18 January 1974.
- "Le oscure attività degli arrestati." *Corriere della Sera*, 19 January 1974.

Ginzburg, Natalia. "La qualità della vita." *La Stampa*, 5 May 1978.

- "Parlano i rapiti." *Corriere della Sera*, 8 July 1977.

Giuliani, Arnaldo. "'Chi è Cristina? Sei tu? Bene, vieni con noi': Così è stata rapita la figlia dell'industriale." *Corriere della Sera*, 2 July 1975.
- "Il diario della notte degli incubi quando il corpo venne ritrovato." *Corriere della Sera*, 3 September 1975.
- "Il vero 'giallo' comincia adesso con la caccia agli organizzatori." *Corriere della Sera*, 19 January 1974.
- "Nel casolare di uno dei calabresi le tracce di una lunga prigionia." *Corriere della Sera*, 18 January 1974.
- "Rompono il silenzio gli amici della studentessa rapita: 'Il padre di Cristina è pronto a tutto, ma non è ricco.'" *Corriere della Sera*, 5 July 1975.
- "Trovato il corpo di Cristina." *Corriere della Sera*, 2 September 1975.

"Gli amici dicevano spesso a Paul: Perché non ti fai rapire?" *Il Messaggero*, 15 July 1973.

Grasso, Sebastiano. "Era odiato dalla mafia il magistrato ucciso a colpi di lupara a Catanzaro." *Corriere della Sera*, 5 July 1975.
- "Il magistrato ucciso stava per scoprire le menti occulte dei rapimenti in Calabria." *Corriere della Sera*, 6 July 1975.
- "L'uccisione di Ferlaino doveva impaurire i giudici che processeranno trentadue imputati di rapimenti." *Corriere della Sera*, 8 July 1975.
- "Un detenuto evaso tre volte dal carcere avrebbe ucciso il magistrato Ferlaino." *Corriere della Sera*, 7 July 1975.

Guidi, Guido. "Calabria: La magistratura è messa sotto inchiesta." *La Stampa*, 13 November 1975.
- "È stato un evaso a uccidere l'avvocato generale di Catanzaro?" *La Stampa*, 7 July 1975.

"Il 'boss' Antonio Giacobbe fece uccidere un magistrato che indagava sui sequestri?" *La Stampa*, 19 October 1975.

"Il giovane Paul Getty scomparso da 14 giorni: Forse è stato rapito." *Il Tempo*, 13 July 1973.

"Il grido di Paul." *Il Tempo*, 25 November 1973.

"Il PG chiede l'intervento dell'esercito in Calabria per la lotta al banditismo." *La Stampa*, 10 October 1976.

"Il silenzio dei rapitori." *Il Tempo*, 14 July 1973.

258 Bibliography

"Italian Books: Terror in the Streets." *Economist*, 1 July 1978.

Laurenzi, Carlo. "Crudeltà e avarizia." *Corriere della Sera*, 13 November 1973.

"L'hippy d'oro." *Il Tempo*, 14 July 1973.

Mackenzie, Jillian. "The Tragic True Story of John Paul Getty III's Kidnapping: The Saga Is the Subject of the New Show *Trust*." *Town & Country*, 26 March 2018.

Maddaus, Gene. "'All the Money in the World' Angers Family of Getty Kidnappers." *Variety*, 22 December 2017.

Madeo, Alfonso. "Chi finge che la mafia non esista." *Corriere della Sera*, 23 December 1975.

– "Gruppo liquida tutto." *Corriere della Sera*, 11 January 1978.

– "Il giudice contagiato dalla mafia." *Corriere della Sera*, 21 December 1975.

– "I vescovi calabresi 'Combattere la mafia.'" *Corriere della Sera*, 6 December 1975.

– "La regione Calabria si prepara ad affrontare il fenomeno mafia." *Corriere della Sera*, 24 November 1975.

– "Si indaga sulla magistratura in Calabria." *Corriere della Sera*, 14 November 1975.

Martinelli, Roberto. "Faccia a faccia coi rapitori: Paul Getty non ha voluto guardarli." *Corriere della Sera*, 13 May 1976.

– "Forse il giudice Ferlaino fu eliminato perché sapeva troppo sulla mafia dei rapitori." *Corriere della Sera*, 6 September 1975.

– "Il Consiglio della magistratura dice: 'Non serve bloccare i beni del rapito.'" *Corriere della Sera*, 7 December 1978.

– "Il presunto ideatore del sequestro Getty 'Non so niente, la polizia mi perseguita.'" *Corriere della Sera*, 20 May 1976.

– "Paul Getty non simulò il sequestro ma i suoi rapitori restano ignoti." *Corriere della Sera*, 1 November 1976.

– "Resta il dubbio che Paul Getty abbia simulato il rapimento per spillare 1700 milioni al nonno." *Corriere della Sera*, 21 May 1976.

Mazzotti, Elios. "Vi parlo dei rapimenti dopo il sequestro di mia figlia." *Corriere della Sera*, 17 July 1975.

McDonell-Parry, Amelia. "John Paul Getty III: The True Story Behind 'Trust.'" *Rolling Stone*, 20 March 2018.

Menghini, Paolo. "Arriveremo anche ai capi della gang." *Corriere della Sera*, 18 January 1974.

– "Il confronto si terrà a Lagonegro." *Corriere della Sera*, 17 January 1974.

– "Sale a cinque il numero delle persone accusate di aver rapito il giovane Paul Getty." *Corriere della Sera*, 19 January 1974.

Michelini, Maurizio. "Pomarici: 'Non uguale per tutti la linea dura dei sequestri.'" *L'Unità*, 24 January 1978.

"Mi farò rapire e sarò a posto." *Il Tempo*, 15 July 1973.

Miller, Julie. "Did Paul Getty Help Stage His Kidnapping, as *Trust* Suggests?" *Vanity Fair*, 8 April 2018.
– "Getty Family Threatens Lawsuit Over *Trust*, FX's 'False and Misleading' Kidnapping Drama." *Vanity Fair*, 19 March 2018.
Moravia, Alberto. "Il complesso di Elettra." *Corriere della Sera*, 5 October 1975.
– "L'ex-Italia delle bande e dei sequestri." *Corriere della Sera*, 26 May 1974.
– "L'orecchio di Getty e l'industria del sequestro." *Corriere della Sera*, 25 November 1973.
– "Pasolini o il mito della cultura contadina." *Corriere della Sera*, 14 November 1976.
– "Riflessioni davanti all'orrore." *Corriere della Sera*, 3 September 1975.
Munzi, Ulderico. "Ancora nascosto sull'Aspromonte l'uomo che sa tutto di Cristina." *Corriere della Sera*, 31 August 1975.
– "Filmati i volti degli 'esattori' che incassarono l'ultima rata del riscatto di Cristina Mazzotti." *Corriere della Sera*, 29 August 1975.
– "Sarebbe nascosto sull'Aspromonte l'uomo che conosce la sorte di Cristina Mazzotti." *Corriere della Sera*, 31 August 1975.
Nascimbeni, Giulio. "Dai riscatti-miliardo al sottofatturato dei sequestri." *Corriere della Sera*, 11 July 1975.
– "Perché proprio l'Italia è il paese dei rapimenti?" *Corriere della Sera*, 18 September 1975.
– "Un silenzio e un dolore che chiedono giustizia." *Corriere della Sera*, 5 September 1975.
Nava, Massimo. "Per un miliardo e 600 milioni libera la donna incinta: 'Sento che il bambino vivrà.'" *Corriere della Sera*, 4 December 1978.
Nese, Marco. "Mai mostrarsi disperati: La 'ndrangheta non si commuove." *Corriere della Sera*, 15 June 1989.
"Ordine di arresto per il dottor Piras: Sarebbe il capo dell'anonima rapitori." *La Stampa*, 20 October 1967.
Pandolfo, Mario. "'Quando mi hanno tagliato l'orecchio ero sveglio: Ho creduto di morire.'" *Il Messaggero*, 16 December 1973.
Pansa, Giampaolo. "Disarmati di fronte all'industria del sequestro." *Corriere della Sera*, 18 November 1973.
Passarelli, Alfredo. "Come 'taglia' un orecchio il truccatore Noschese." *Il Tempo*, 23 November 1973.
"Paul Getty III aveva progettato il finto rapimento." *Il Tempo*, 15 July 1973.
"Paul Getty III 'Sono pronto a tornare a Roma.'" *Corriere della Sera*, 18 January 1974.
"Paul interprete di se stesso in un film sul suo rapimento." *Il Tempo*, 28 July 1973.
"Paul si è fatto rapire per finanziare un film coi milioni del riscatto." *Il Tempo*, 23 July 1973.

P.E. "'Pagate altrimenti mi ammazzano.'" *Corriere della Sera*, 13 July 1975.

Peruzzi, Giuseppe. "Hanno pagato per Banchini un riscatto di 400 milioni." *Corriere della Sera*, 14 July 1976.

"Petrolio, miliardi e gialli insoluti nella storia dei Getty." *Il Tempo*, 14 July 1973.

P.T. "Scandalo a Milano: La quinta Colonna delle 'polizze nere.'" *Il Settimanale* 5, no. 12 (22 March 1978): 31–2.

"Rapimento autentico o simulato?" *Il Tempo*, 23 July 1973.

"Rapito il nipote di Paul Getty? 'È uno scherzo.'" *L'Unità*, 14 July 1973.

"Reggio Calabria: Restano impuniti metà dei delitti." *La Stampa*, 1 September 1982.

Repossi, Sandro. "'Basta pubblicità sul sequestro se volete rivedere Cesare libero.'" *Corriere della Sera*, 20 September 1988.

R.I. "A Cossiga dieci mila cartoline per Patrizia." *Corriere della Sera*, 20 February 1990.

Ronchetti, Sergio. "Dopo le tristi memorie del rapito leggiamo le memorie del carceriere." *La Stampa*, 10 June 1978.

Rossani, Ottavio. "Emigrò a Milano per entrare nell' 'anonima.'" *Corriere dell'Informazione*, 6 July 1978.

Rovera, Beppe. "Sequestro Fiora: Il concerto riapre la speranza." *Corriere della Sera*, 24 July 1988.

Scabello, Sandro. "Obiezioni e dubbi dei criminologi sulla proposta di legge anti-sequestri." *Corriere della Sera*, 6 September 1975.

Scola, Ettore. "Egregio bandito, maestro d'orrore." *L'Unità*, 28 June 1992.

"Scoperta l'anonima banditi? Orgosolo: Due 'fermi' per il ratto del medico." *La Stampa*, 14 October 1967.

"Sequestro Getty: In appello pene ridotte." *Corriere della Sera*, 23 December 1977.

Shuster, Alvin. "Italians' Apathy Over Kidnappings Is Shaken by Girl's Murder." *New York Times*, 12 September 1975.

Sola, Elisa. "Dalla droga ai riti della 'ndrangheta: Ecco chi è Rocco Schirripa." *Corriere della Sera*, 22 December 2015.

Solazzo, Adriano. "Il procuratore Gresti cerca di indurre Pomarici a far rientrare le dimissioni." *Corriere della Sera*, 24 January 1978.

Stajano, Corrado. "Lettere dal razzismo." *La Repubblica*, 5 May 1990.

Sulcas, Roslyn "The 'Trust' Equation: Wealth and Power Equals Misery." *New York Times*, 18 March 2018.

Tagliaferro, Pierluigi. "Cristina è ancora in mano ai rapitori e la mamma implora: 'Non parlatene.'" *Corriere della Sera*, 4 August 1975.

– "La famiglia ha pagato un miliardo e attende la liberazione di Cristina." *Corriere della Sera*, 3 August 1975.

"Taviani: La magistratura è troppo tenera con i banditi." *Corriere della Sera*, 16 November 1974.

"Ti manderemo un dito di Paul se vuoi essere certa che è vivo." *Il Tempo*, 19 July 1973.

Tiziano, Francesco. "I sequestri di persona? Affari per 'ndrine e servizi." *La Gazzetta del Sud*, 20 October 2017.

Trebay, Guy. "The French President's Lover." *New York Times*, 13 January 2008.

Trivelli, Pietro M. "È suo o non è suo? Di un vivo o di un morto?" *Il Messaggero*, 12 November 1973.

"'Troppo svogliati' gli strani rapitori di Paul." *Il Messaggero*, 18 August 1973.

"Un messaggio di Paul alla madre: Alle 18 hanno telefonato i rapitori." *Il Tempo*, 18 July 1973.

Veca, Salvatore. "Lo stato debole ha bisogno di un'eroina." *Corriere della Sera*, 13 June 1989.

Violante, Luciano. "Torino, 40 anni fa iniziava il processo alle Br che segnò l'inizio della fine." *Corriere della Sera*, 9 March 2018.

Waxman, Olivia B. "The True Story of the Kidnapping Behind 'All the Money in the World.'" *Time*, 25 December 2017.

Film and Media

Beaufoy, Simon. *Trust*. Cloud Eight Films; Decibel Films; Snicket Films; FXP: 2018.

Coppola, Francis Ford, dir. *The Godfather*. 1972.

De Maria, Renato, dir. *Doppio agguato*. Taodue: 2003.

De Seta, Vittorio, dir. *Banditi a Orgosolo*. 1961.

– *Pastori di Orgosolo* (1958), *Un giorno in barbagia* (1958). In *Il mondo perduto: I cortometraggi di Vittorio De Seta*. Milan: Feltrinelli, 2008.

Friedman, Alan. *My Way: Berlusconi in His Own Words*. Directed by Antongiulio Panizzi. 2016.

Garrone, Matteo, dir. *Gomorra*. Rai Cinema: 2008.

Gomorra – la serie (*Gomorrah*). Created by Roberto Saviano. Italy: Sky, 2014–present.

La piovra. Italy: RAI, 1984–2001.

Malenotti, Roberto, dir. *Liberate mio figlio*. 1992.

Milani, Riccardo, dir. *Il sequestro Soffiantini*. Taodue Film–Mediaset, 2002.

Oliva, Ruben H., and Enrico Fierro. *La Santa: Viaggio nella 'Ndrangheta sconosciuta*. Milan: Rizzoli, 2007.

Salvatores, Gabriele, dir. *Io non ho paura*. Niccolò Ammaniti and Francesca Marciano, screenwriters. 2003.

Scarpa, David, screenwriter. *All the Money in the World*. London, 2017.

Scola, Ettore, dir. "Sequestro di persona cara." Episode of *I nuovi mostri*. Produced by Pio Angeletti and Adriano De Micheli. 1977.

Scott, Ridley, dir. *All the Money in the World*. TriStar Pictures, 2017.
Trincia, Pablo, and Luca Micheli. "Il male." In *Buio*, podcast. 21 November 2019.

Books and Articles

Abse, Tobias. "The Moro Affair: Interpretations and Consequences." In Gundle and Rinaldi, *Assassinations and Murder in Modern Italy*, 89–100.
Agamben, Giorgio. *Quel che resta di Auschwitz: L'archivio e il testimone*. Turin: Einaudi, 1998.
– *Remnants of Auschwitz: The Witness and the Archive*. Translated by Daniel Heller-Roazen. New York: Zone Books, 2002.
Alexander, David, and Susan Klein. "Kidnapping and Hostage-Taking: A Review of Effects, Coping and Resilience." *Journal of the Royal Society of Medicine* 102, no. 1 (2009): 16–21. https://doi.org/10.1258/jrsm.2008.080347.
Alexander, Jeffrey C. "Toward a Theory of Cultural Trauma." In *Cultural Trauma and Collective Identity*, edited by Jeffrey C. Alexander, Ron Eyerman, Bernhard Giesen, Neil J. Smelser, and Piotr Sztompka, 1–30. Berkeley: University of California Press, 2004.
Almerighi, Mario. *Mistero di Stato: La strana morte dell'ispettore Donatoni*. Rome: Aliberti, 2010.
Amanniti, Niccolò. *Io non ho paura*. Turin: Einaudi, 2001.
Andreasen, Nancy C. "Posttraumatic Stress Disorder." In *Comprehensive Textbook of Psychiatry*, 4th ed., edited by Harold Kaplan and Benjamin J. Sadock, 918–24. Baltimore: Williams and Wilkins, 1985.
Arcà, Francesco. *Mafia, potere, malgoverno*. Rome: Newton Compton, 1979.
Arendt, Hannah. *On Violence*. New York: Harvest Books, 1969.
Arlacchi, Pino. *La mafia imprenditrice: Dalla Calabria al centro dell'inferno*. Milan: Il Saggiatore, 2007.
– *Perché non c'è la mafia in Sardegna: Le radici di un'anarchia ordinata*. Cagliari: AM&D Edizioni, 2007.
Baliani, Marco. *Body of State: The Moro Affair, A Nation Divided*. Translated by Nicoletta Marini-Maio and Ellen V. Nerenberg. Madison, NJ: Fairleigh Dickinson University Press, 2011.
– *Corpo di stato: Il delitto Moro*. Milan: Rizzoli, 2003.
Ballinari, Libero. *Carceriere fuorilegge*. Edited by Claudio Castellacci. Milan: SugarCo, 1978.
Barbieri, Cristina, and Vittorio Mete. "Kidnappings by the 'Ndrangheta: Characteristics, Institutional Countermeasures and Turning Points." *Modern Italy* 26, no. 4 (2021): 425–44. https://doi.org/10.1017/mit.2021.34.
Beccaria, Antonella, and Giuliano Turone. *Il Boss Luciano Liggio: Da Corleone a Milano, una storia di mafia e complicità*. Rome: Castelvecchi Editore, 2018.

Bellone, Paola. *Tutti i nemici del Procuratore: L'omicidio di Bruno Caccia*. Bari: Editori Laterza, 2017.

Belpoliti, Marco. *Da quella prigione: Moro, Warhol e le Brigate Rosse*. Parma: Guanda, 2012.

Benedetti, Laura. "Il linguaggio dell'amicizia e della città: *L'amica geniale* di Elena Ferrante tra continuità e cambiamento." *Quaderni d'Italianistica* 33, no. 2 (2012): 171–87. https://doi.org/10.33137/q.i..v33i2.19423.

Bettelheim, Bruno. "Individual and Mass Behavior in Extreme Situations." *Journal of Abnormal and Social Psychology* 38, no. 4 (1943): 417–52. https://doi.org/10.1037/h0061208.

– *Surviving, and Other Essays*. New York: Knopf, 1979.

Bianchi, Sergio, and Raffaella Perna. *Le polaroid di Moro*. Rome: DeriveApprodi, 2012.

Blanchot, Maurice. *L'écriture du désastre*. Paris: Gallimard, 1980.

– *The Writing of the Disaster*. Translated by Ann Smock. Lincoln: University of Nebraska Press, 1995.

Blando, Antonino. "L'antimafia come risorsa politica." *Laboratoire italien* 22 (2019). https://doi.org/10.4000/laboratoireitalien.2893.

Bokopoulus, Natalie. "We Are Always Us: The Boundaries of Elena Ferrante." *Michigan Quarterly Review* 55, no. 3 (Summer 2016): 396–419.

Bolacchi, Giulio. "Il sequestro come fatto sociale." *Quaderni Bolotanesi*, no. 22 (1996): 75–101.

Borghese, Giovanna. *Un paese in tribunale: Italia 1980–1983*. Milan: Mondadori, 1983.

Brecht, Bertolt. *Life of Galileo*. Translated by John Willett. New York: Penguin Classics, 2008.

– *Mother Courage and Her Children*. Translated by Eric Bentley. New York: Grove Press, 1991.

Brunelli, David. *Il sequesto di persona a scopo di estorsione*. Padua: CEDAM, 1995.

Bruschini, Vito. *Rapimento e riscatto: Il romanzo del sequestro di John Paul Getty III, erede dell'uomo più ricco del mondo*. Rome: Newton Compton, 2017.

Buse, Peter. *The Camera Does the Rest: How Polaroid Changed Photography*. Chicago: University of Chicago Press, 2016.

Cagnetta, Franco. *Banditi a Orgosolo*. Nuoro: Ilisso, 2002.

– *Bandits d'Orgosolo*. Paris: Buchet Chastel, 1963.

– *Die Banditen von Orgosolo*. Düsseldorf: Econ-Verlag, 1964.

– "Inchiesta su Orgosolo." *Nuovi Argomenti* 10 (September–October 1954).

Calogero, Pietro, Carlo Fumian, and Michele Sartori. *Terrore Rosso: Dall'autonomia al partito armato*. Rome: Editori Laterza, 2010.

Calvino, Italo. *Palomar*. Milan: Mondadori, 1994.

Camus, Albert. *La Peste*. Paris: Gallimard, 1947.

264   Bibliography

- *The Plague*. New York: Knopf, 1948.
Caruth, Cathy. *Unclaimed Experience: Trauma, Narrative, and History*. Baltimore: Johns Hopkins University Press, 1996.
Casalunga, Luigi. *Anonima sequestri sarda: L'archivio dei crimini (1960–1997)*. Genoa: Fratelli Frilli, 2007.
Caselli, Gian Carlo. *Le due guerre: Perché l'Italia ha sconfitto il terrorismo e non la mafia*. Milan: Melampo Editore, 2009.
Cassitta, Giampaolo. *La zona grigia: Cronaca di un sequestro di persona*. Cagliari: Condaghes, 2005.
Cavarero, Adriana. *Horrorism: Naming Contemporary Violence*. Translated by William McCuaig. New York: Columbia University Press, 2009.
- *Orrorismo: Ovvero della violenza sull'inerme*. Milan: Feltrinelli, 2007.
Ceci, Giovanni Mario. *Il terrorismo italiano: Storia di un dibattito*. Rome: Carocci Editore, 2013.
Cento Bull, Anna. *Italian Neofascism: The Strategy of Tension and the Politics of Nonreconciliation*. New York: Berghahn Books, 2007.
Cento Bull, Anna, and Philip Cooke. *Ending Terrorism in Italy*. New York: Routledge, 2013.
Cesa, Alfredo. *Cristina Mazzotti: Sequestro S.P.A.* Como: Editrice Victoria, 1977.
Chirico, Danilo, and Alessio Magro. *Dimenticati: Vittime della 'ndrangheta* Rome: Castelvecchi, 2010.
Ciconte, Enzo. *Alle origini della nuova 'ndrangheta: Il 1980*. Soveria Mannelli: Rubettino Editore, 2020.
- *Processo alla 'Ndrangheta*. Bari: Editori Laterza, 1996.
- "Un delitto italiano: Il sequestro di persona." In *Storia d'Italia, Annali 12: La criminalità*, edited by Luciano Violante, 185–215. Turin: Einaudi, 1997.
Colaprico, Piero, and Luca Fazzo. *Manager calibro 9: Vent'anni di malavita a Milano nel racconto del pentito Saverio Morabito*. Milan: Garzanti, 1995.
Colarieti, Fabrizio. "Caccia al bandito Curbeddu." *Il Punto*, 9 December 2010.
Collin, Richard, and Gordon L. Freedman. *Winter of Fire: The Abduction of General Dozier and the Downfall of the Red Brigades*. New York: Dutton, 1990.
Connerton, Paul. *The Spirit of Mourning: History, Memory, and the Body*. Cambridge: Cambridge University Press, 2011.
Corda, Elettrio. *La legge e la macchia: Il banditismo sardo dal Settecento ai giorni nostri*. Milan: Rusconi Immagini, 1985.
Dainotto, Roberto Maria. *The Mafia: A Cultural History*. London: Reaktion Books, 2015.
Dalia, Andrea Antonio, and Giovanni Conso. *La legislazione dell'emergenza: I sequestri di persona a scopo di estorsione, terrorismo od eversione*. Milan: Giuffrè, 1982.
dalla Chiesa, Nando. "Lotte civili a Milano, tra terrorismo e mafia (1968–1993)." *Laboratoire italien* 22 (2019). https://doi.org/10.4000/laboratoireitalien.2645.

– *Manifesto dell'antimafia*. Turin: Einaudi, 2014.
– *Milano-Palermo la nuova resistenza*. Milan: Dalai Editore, 1993.
– *Passaggio a Nord: La colonizzazione mafiosa*. Turin: Edizioni Gruppo Adele, 2016.
Degortes, Daniela, Giovanni Colombo, Paolo Santonastaso, and Angela Favaro. "Il sequestro di persona come evento traumatico: Interviste cliniche ad un gruppo di vittime e revisione della letteratura." *Rivista di psichiatria* 38, no. 2 (2003): 71–7.
Delisle, Guy. *Hostage*. Translated by Helge Dascher. New York: Drawn and Quarterly, 2017.
Della Porta, Donatella, ed. *Terrorismi in Italia*. Bologna: Il Mulino, 1984.
Della Porta, Donatella, and Maurizio Rossi. *Cifre crudeli: Bilancio dei terrorismi italiani*. Bologna: Istituto di studi e ricerche "Carlo Cattaneo," 1984.
De Rogatis, Tiziana. *Elena Ferrante: Parole chiave*. Rome: Edizioni e/o, 2018.
– "Metamorfosi del tempo: Il ciclo dell'*Amica geniale*." *Allegoria* 73 (2016): 123–37.
De Rogatis, Tiziana, Stiliana Milkova, and Katrin Wehling-Giorgi, eds. "Elena Ferrante in a Global Context." Special issue, *Modern Language Notes* 136, no. 1 (January 2021).
Dickie, John. *Blood Brotherhoods: A History of Italy's Three Mafias*. New York: Public Affairs, 2011.
– *Cosa Nostra: A History of the Sicilian Mafia*. London: Hodder & Stoughton, 2004.
– *The Craft: How the Freemasons Made the Modern World*. London: Hodder & Stoughton, 2020.
– *Mafia Republic: Italy's Criminal Curse: Cosa Nostra, 'Ndrangheta and Camorra from 1946 to the Present*. London: Hodder & Stoughton, 2013.
Dickie, John, John Foot, and Frank Snowden, eds. *Disastro! Disaster in Italy since 1860: Culture, Politics and Society*. New York: Palgrave Macmillan, 2002.
Dogliani, Patrizia, and Marie-Anne Matard-Bonucci, eds. *Democrazia insicura: Violenze, repressioni e Stato di diritto nella storia della Repubblica (1945–1995)*. Rome: Donzelli, 2017.
Dondi, Mirco. *L'eco del boato: Storia della strategia della tensione 1965–1974*. Bari: Editori Laterza, 2015.
Donnarumma, Raffaele. "Il melodramma, l'anti-melodramma, la Storia: Sull'*Amica geniale* di Elena Ferrante." *Allegoria* 73 (2016): 138–47.
Dossier Banda della Magliana. Milan: Kaos Edizioni, 2009.
Drake, Richard. *The Aldo Moro Murder Case*. Cambridge, MA: Harvard University Press, 1995.
– *The Revolutionary Mystique and Terrorism in Contemporary Italy*. Bloomington: Indiana University Press, 2021.
Eakin, Paul John. *How Our Lives Becomes Stories: Making Selves*. Ithaca, NY: Cornell University Press, 1999.
Falletti, Francescantonio. *Nel mirino della 'ndrangheta*. Rome: Koinè, 2007.

266 Bibliography

Falotico, Caterina. "Elena Ferrante: Il cilco dell'*Amica geniale* tra autobiografia, storia e metaletteratura." *Forum Italico* 49, no. 1 (May 2015): 92–118. https://doi.org/10.1177/0014585815578573.

Farina, Giovanni. *Giuseppe Soffiantini pubblica alcune poesie di Giovanni Farina: Poesie*. Edited by Elisabetta Conti. Brescia: La Compagnia della Stampa, 2007.

Fass, Paula S. *Kidnapped: Child Abduction in America*. New York: Oxford University Press, 1997.

Fava, Claudio. *I disarmati: Storia dell'antimafia; I reduci e i complici*. Milan: Sperling & Kupfer, 2009.

Favaro, Angela, Daniela Degortes, Giovanni Colombo, and Paolo Santonastaso. "The Effects of Trauma among Kidnap Victims in Sardinia, Italy." *Psychological Medicine* 30, no. 4 (July 2000): 975–80. https://doi.org/10.1017/s0033291799001877.

Felman, Shoshana, and Dori Laub. *Testimony: Crises of Witnessing in Literature, Psychoanalysis, and History*. New York: Routledge, 1992.

Ferracuti, Franco, Renato Lazzari, and Marvin E. Wolfgang. *Violence in Sardinia*. Rome: Bulzoni, 1970.

Ferrante, Elena. *L'amica geniale*. Rome: Edizioni e/o, 2011.

– *My Brilliant Friend*. Translated by Ann Goldstein. New York: Europa Editions, 2012.

– *Storia della bambina perduta*. Rome: Edizioni e/o, 2014.

– *The Story of the Lost Child*. Translated by Ann Goldstein. New York: Europa Editions, 2015.

Fiori, Giuseppe. *La Società del malessere*. Bari: Editori Laterza, 1968.

Flamigni, Sergio. *La tela del ragno: Il delitto Moro*. Milan: Kaos Edizioni, 1988.

– *Rapporto sul caso Moro*. Milan: Kaos Edizioni, 2019.

Fontana, Bruno, and Pierpaolo Serarcangeli. *L'Italia dei sequestri: Dal banditismo sardo alla mafia, dalla 'Ndrangheta alle Brigate Rosse, venti anni di storia italiana attraverso i fatti, i nomi, i retroscena della più vergognosa "industria" del nostro Paese*. Rome: Newton Compton, 1991.

Foot, John. *The Archipelago*. London: Bloomsbury, 2018.

– *Italy's Divided Memory*. New York: Palgrave Macmillan, 2009.

Forgacs, David. *Messaggi di sangue*. Bari: Editori Laterza, 2021.

Foucault, Michel. *The History of Sexuality*. New York: Pantheon Books, 1978.

Freud, Anna. *The Ego and the Mechanism of Defense*. New York: International Universities Press, 1974.

Freud, Sigmund. *The Ego and the Id*. Translated by James Strachey. New York: W.W. Norton, 1962.

Galfré, Monica. *La guerra è finita: L'Italia e l'uscita dal terrorismo 1980–1987*. Bari: Editori Laterza, 2014.

Galli, Giorgio. *Piombo rosso: La storia completa della lotta armata in Italia dal 1970 a oggi*. Milan: Baldini & Castoldi, 2004.

Gambaro, Elisa. "Il fascino del regresso: Note su *L'amica geniale* di Elena Ferrante." *Enthymema* 11 (2014): 168–81. https://doi.org/10.13130/2037-2426/4596.

Gambazzi, Paolo. *L'occhio e il suo inconscio*. Milan: Raffaello Cortina Editore, 1999.

Gambino, Sharo. *La mafia in Calabria*. Reggio Calabria: Edizioni Parallelo 38, 1971.

Gastaldi, Sciltian, and David Ward, eds. *Era mio padre: Italian Terrorism of the Anni di Piombo in the Postmemorials of Victims' Relatives*. Oxford: Peter Lang, 2018.

Gavini, Diego. "L'utopia palermitana: I gesuiti nella 'primavera' dell'antimafia." *Laboratoire italien* 22 (2019). https://doi.org/10.4000/laboratoireitalien.2837.

Gilmore, Leigh. *The Limits of Autobiography: Trauma and Testimony*. Ithaca, NY: Cornell University Press, 2001.

Ginsborg, Paul. *A History of Contemporary Italy: Society and Politics 1943–1988*. New York: Palgrave Macmillan, 2003.

Glynn, Ruth. *Women, Terrorism, and Trauma in Italian Culture*. New York: Palgrave Macmillan, 2013.

Glynn, Ruth, and Giancarlo Lombardi, eds. *Remembering Aldo Moro: The Cultural Legacy of the 1978 Kidnapping and Murder*. New York: Modern Humanities Research Association and Routledge, 2012.

Gotor, Miguel. *Il memoriale della repubblica: Gli scritti di Aldo Moro dalla prigionia e l'anatomia del potere italiano*. Turin: Einaudi, 2011.

– *L'Italia del Novecento: Dalla sconfitta di Adua alla vittoria di Amazon*. Turin: Einaudi, 2019.

– "Le possibilità dell'uso del discorso nel cuore del terrore: Della scrittura come agonia." In Moro, *Lettere dalla prigionia*, 185–389.

Graebner, William. *Patty's Got a Gun: Patricia Hearst in 1970s America*. Chicago: University of Chicago Press, 2008.

Gratteri, Nicola, and Antonio Nicaso. *Fiumi d'oro*. Milan: Mondadori, 2017.

– *Fratelli di sangue: Storie, boss e affari della 'ndrangheta, la mafia più potente del mondo*. Milan: Mondadori, 2009.

– *Storia segreta della 'Ndrangheta: Una lunga e oscura vicenda di sangue e potere (1860–2018)*. Milan: Mondadori, 2018.

Gundle, Stephen, and Lucia Rinaldi, eds. *Assassinations and Murder in Modern Italy: Transformations in Society and Culture*. New York: Palgrave Macmillan, 2007.

Hearst, Patricia, and Alvin Moscow. *Every Secret Thing*. London: Doubleday, 1982.

Henke, Suzette A. *Shattered Subjects: Trauma and Testimony in Women's Life-Writing*. New York: Palgrave Macmillan, 1998.

Herman, Judith. *Trauma and Recovery: The Aftermath of Violence from Domestic Abuse to Political Terror*. New York: Basic Books, 1992.

Hobbes, Thomas. *Leviathan*. London, 1651.

268 Bibliography

Hobsbawm, Eric. *Bandits*. New York: Pantheon Books, 1969.

– *Primitive Rebels: Studies in Archaic Forms of Social Movement in the 19th and 20th Centuries*. New York: W.W. Norton, 1965.

Ihde, Don. *Sense and Significance*. Pittsburgh: Duquesne University Press, 1973.

Imposimato, Ferdinando. *I sequestri d'Italia: Le inchieste shock dal caso Moro a Emanuela Orlandi*. Rome: Newton Compton Editori, 2013.

Jamieson, Alison. *Antimafia: Italy's Fight Against Organized Crime*. London: Macmillan, 1999.

– *The Heart Attacked: Terrorism and Conflict in the Italian State*. New York: M. Boyars, 1989.

Kassam, Fateh, and Marco Corrias. *Mio figlio Farouk: Anatomia di un sequestro*. Milan: Rizzoli, 1993.

Katz, Robert. *Days of Wrath: The Public Agony of Aldo Moro*. New York: Granada, 1980.

Keenan, Brian. *An Evil Cradling: The Five-Year Ordeal of a Hostage*. New York: Penguin, 1992.

Klopp, Charles. *Sentences: The Memoirs and Letters of Italian Political Prisoners from Benvenuto Cellini to Aldo Moro*. Toronto: University of Toronto Press, 1999.

Lejeune, Philippe. *On Autobiography*. Translated by Katherine Leary. Minneapolis: University of Minnesota Press, 1989.

Leys, Ruth. *Trauma: A Genealogy*. Chicago: University of Chicago Press, 2000.

Linfield, Susie. *The Cruel Radiance: Photography and Political Violence*. Chicago: University of Chicago Press, 2010.

Luberto, Salvatore, and Antonio Manganelli. *I sequestri di persona a scopo di estorsione: Indagine sulla diffusione del fenomeno in Italia dal 1968 al 1983*. Padua: CEDAM, 1984.

Lucamante, Stefania. "Undoing Feminism: The Neapolitan Novels of Elena Ferrante." *Italica* 95, no. 1 (Spring 2018): 31–49.

Lupo, Salvatore. *History of the Mafia*. Translated by Antony Shugaar. New York: Columbia University Press, 2009.

– *Storia della mafia: Dalle origini ai nostri giorni*. Rome: Donzelli, 2004.

Lussu, Emilio. "Brigantaggio Sardo." In *Il cinghiale del Diavolo*, 76–98. Nuoro: Ilisso, 2004.

Macrì, Carlo. "'Ndrangheta e sequestri di persona: Proposte operative." In Atti del Convegno *Mafia e grande criminalità: Una questione nazionale*. Turin: Consiglio regionale del Piemonte, 1984.

Maddalena, Marcello. "I sequestri di persona." In *Manuale pratico dell'inchiesta penale*, edited by Luciano Violante and Sergio Badellino. Milan: Giuffrè, 1996.

Mahy, Margaret, and Quentin Blake. *The Great Piratical Rumbustification & The Librarian and the Robbers*. London: Dent & Sons, 1978.

– *La bibliotecaria rapita*. Translated by Salvatore Pinna and Angela Maria Quaquero. Milan: Editrice Bibliografica, 1985.

Margalit, Avishai. *The Ethics of Memory*. Cambridge, MA: Harvard University Press, 2002.

Marini-Maio, Nicoletta. "A Spectre Is Haunting Italy: The Double 'Emplotment' of the Moro Affair." In *Terrorism Italian Style: Representation of Political Violence in Contemporary Italian Cinema*, edited by Ruth Glynn, Giancarlo Lombardi, and Alan O'Leary, 157–74. London: IGRS, 2012.

Marongiu, Pietro. *Teoria e storia del banditismo sociale in Sardegna*. Cagliari: Della Torre, 1981.

–, ed. *Criminalità e banditismo in Sardegna: Fra tradizione e innovazione*. Rome: Carocci, 2004.

Marongiu, Pietro, and Francesco Paribello. "Il sequestro di persona a scopo di estorsione." In Marongiu, *Criminalità e banditismo in Sardegna*, 109–32.

Massaiu, Mario. *Mesina perché?* Cagliari: Fossataro, 1976.

Matard-Bonucci, Marie-Anne. *Histoire de la mafia*. Paris: Editions Complexe, 1994.

Matard-Bonucci, Marie-Anne, and Marc Lazar. *L'Italie des années de le plomb: Le terrorisme entre historie et mémorie*. Paris: Autrement, 2010.

Meade, Robert C., Jr. *Red Brigades: The Story of Italian Terrorism*. New York: Palgrave Macmillan, 1990.

Melchionda, Achille. *Paura a Bologna: Storia di cinque rapimenti*. Bologna: Pendragon, 2008.

Merleau-Ponty, Maurice. *Phénomènologie de la perception*. Paris: Gallimard, 1945.

– *The Phenomenology of Perception*. Translated by Colin Smith. London: Routledge, 2010.

– *The Visible and the Invisible*. Translated by Alphonso Lingis. Evanston, IL: Northwestern University Press, 1968.

– *Le Visible et l'invisible*. Paris: Gallimard, 1964.

Mesina, Graziano, Gabriella Banda, and Gabriele Moroni. *Io, Mesina: Dal Supramonte ad Asti: Un ergastolo, nove evasioni, una prigione*. Cosenza: Periferia, 1993.

Milkova, Stiliana. *Elena Ferrante as World Literature*. New York: Bloomsbury, 2021.

Minuti Diego, and Filippo Veltri, eds. *Lettere a San Luca: L'Italia scrive al "paese dei sequestri."* Catanzaro: Abramo Editore, 1990.

Moge, Charlotte. "La Sicile, laboratoire de la mobilisation citoyenne contre la mafia (1982–1992)." *Laboratoire italien* 22 (2019). https://doi.org/10.4000/laboratoireitalien.2753.

Montalbano, Alessandra. "Pier Paolo Pasolini e Maurice Merleau-Ponty allo specchio: Una lettura di Petrolio." In *Pier Paolo Pasolini: In Living Memory*, edited by Ben Lawton and Maura Bergonzoni, 185–204. Washington, DC: New Academia Publishing, 2009.

- "Ransom Kidnapping: The Anonymous Underworld of the Italian Republic." *Modern Italy* 21, no. 1 (February 2016): 35–49. https://doi.org/10.1017/mit.2015.3.
- "Snatched from the World: The Phenomenology of Captivity in Italian Ransom Kidnapping." *Modern Language Notes* 132, no. 1 (2017): 204–22. https://doi.org/10.1353/mln.2017.0010.
- "Un'emergenza lunga trent'anni: Lo Stato e i sequestri di persona a scopo di estorsione." In Dogliani and Matard-Bonucci, *Democrazia insicura*, 155–67.
Moro, Aldo. *Lettere dalla prigionia*, edited by Miguel Gotor. Turin: Einaudi, 2008.
Moss, David. "From History to Mystery: The Parliamentary Inquiries into the Kidnapping and Murder of Aldo Moro, 1979–2001." In Gundle and Rinaldi, *Assassinations and Murder in Modern Italy*, 101–14.
- *Italian Political Violence, 1969–1988: The Making and Unmaking of Meanings*. Geneva: United Nations Research Institute for Social Development, 1993.
- "The Kidnapping and Murder of Aldo Moro." *European Journal of Sociology* 22, no. 2 (December 1981): 265–95. https://doi.org/10.1017/s0003975600003726.
- *The Politics of Left-Wing Violence in Italy, 1969–85*. New York: Palgrave Macmillan, 1989.
Murgia, Gianni. *Sona ca ti sonu e ... continuo a bussare: Autobiografia di un sequestro*. Cagliari: Cuec Editrice, 1997.
Napoleoni, Loretta. *Merchants of Men: How Jihadists and Isis Turned Kidnapping and Refugee Trafficking into a Multi-Billion Dollar Business*. New York: Seven Stories Press, 2016.
Nerenberg, Ellen V. *Murder Made in Italy: Homicide, Media, and Contemporary Italian Culture*. Bloomington: Indiana University Press, 2012.
- *Prison Terms: Representing Confinement During and After Italian Fascism*. Toronto: University of Toronto Press, 2001.
Ovazza, Carla. "L'esperienza della vittimizzazione." In *Dalla parte della vittima*, edited by Guglielmo Gulotta and Marco Vagaggini, 87–92. Milan: Giuffrè, 1980.
Palmeri, S. "Criminalità violenta in Italia: Rapporto sul fenomeno del sequestro di persona – a scopo di estorsione – e sul trasferimento nazionale ed internazionale di capitali di origine criminale." *Quaderni di criminologia clinica* 20, no. 2 (1978): 187–220.
Panvini, Guido. *Cattolici e violenza politica: L'altro album di famiglia del terrorismo italiano*. Venice: Marsilio, 2014.
- *Ordine nero, guerriglia rossa*. Turin: Einaudi, 2009.
Paoli, Letizia. "Broken Bonds: Mafia and Politics in Sicily." In *Menace to Society: Political-Criminal Collaboration Around the World*, edited by Roy Godson, ch. 2. New York: Routledge, 2017.

- *Mafia Brotherhoods: Organized Crime, Italian Style*. Oxford: Oxford University Press, 2003.

Pasolini, Pier Paolo. *Petrolio*. Turin: Einaudi, 1992.

Pearson, John. *All the Money in the World: The Outrageous Fortune and Misfortune of the Heirs of J. Paul Getty*. New York: HarperCollins, 2017.

- *Painfully Rich: The Outrageous Fortune and Misfortune of the Heirs of J. Paul Getty*. New York: St. Martin's Press, 1995.

Pickering-Iazzi, Robin. *Dead Silent: Life Stories of Girls and Women Killed by the Italian Mafias, 1878–2018*. Milwaukee: University of Wisconsin Milwaukee Digital Commons, 2019.

–, ed. *The Italian Antimafia, New Media, and the Culture of Legality*. Toronto: University of Toronto Press, 2017.

- *Mafia and Outlaw Stories from Italian Life and Literature*. Toronto: University of Toronto Press, 2007.

- *The Mafia in Italian Life and Literature: Life Sentences and Their Geographies*. Toronto: University of Toronto Press, 2015.

Pigliaru, Antonio. *La vendetta barbaricina come ordinamento giuridico*. Milan: Giuffrè, 1959.

Pigliaru, Antonio, and Luigi Maria Lombardi Satriani. *Il banditismo in Sardegna: La vendetta barbaricina*. Milan: Giuffrè, 1993.

Pinto, Isabella. *Elena Ferrante: Poetiche e politiche della soggettività*. Milan: Mimesis, 2020.

Pintore, Gianfranco. *Sardegna: Regione o colonia?* Milan: G. Mazzotta, 1974.

Pisanò, Giorgio. *Lo strano caso del signor Mesina*. Cagliari: Demos Editore, 1994.

Pisano, Vittorfranco S. *The Dynamics of Subversion and Violence in Contemporary Italy*. Stanford, CA: Hoover Institution Press, 1987.

Portanova, Mario, Giampiero Rossi, and Franco Stefanoni. *Mafia a Milano: Sessant'anni di affari e delitti*. Milan: Melampo, 2011.

Puzo, Mario. *The Godfather*. New York: Putnam, 1969.

Radstone, Susannah. "Cultures of Confession/Cultures of Testimonies: Turning the Subject Inside Out." In *Modern Confessional Writing: New Critical Essays*, edited by Jo Gill, 166–79. London: Routledge, 2006.

Rampoldi, Marco, Nando dalla Chiesa, and Paola Ornati. *5 centimetri d'aria: Storia di Cristina Mazzotti e dei figli rapiti*. Produced by Rara Produzione. 2015.

Ravizza, Giuliano, and Roberto Alessi. Dentro una vita. Milan: Rusconi, 1990.

Ravveduto, Marcello. "'Voi siete la schifezza di Napoli': La nascita del movimento anticamorra in Campania." *Laboratoire italien* 22 (2019). https://doi.org/10.4000/laboratoireitalien.2929.

Reemtsma, Jan Philipp. *Im Keller*. Hamburg: Hamburger Edition, 1997.

- *In the Cellar*. Translated by Carol Brown Janeway. New York: Knopf, 1999.

272 Bibliography

Renga, Dana. *Mafia Movies: A Reader*. 2nd ed. Toronto: University of Toronto Press, 2019.

– *Unfinished Business: Screening the Italian Mafia in the New Millennium*. Toronto: University of Toronto Press, 2013.

– *Watching Sympathetic Perpetrators on Italian Television: Gomorrah and Beyond*. New York: Palgrave Macmillan, 2019.

Ricci, Giovanni Francesco. *La Sardegna dei sequestri: Dalle gesta di Graziano Mesina al rapimento del piccolo Farouk, dal sequestro di Fabrizio De Andrè e Dori Ghezzi al caso Soffiantini*. Rome: Newton Compton, 2009.

Ricciardi, Alessia. *Finding Ferrante: Authorship and the Politics of World Literature*. New York: Columbia University Press, 2021.

Rossani, Ottavio. *Intervista sui rapimenti: Parla Pomarici; La tragedia italiana da Sossi a Moro*. Milan: Edizioni Elle, 1978.

– *L'industria dei sequestri: Dalla mafia alle Brigate Rosse; La storia, le tecniche, i nomi*. Milan: Longanesi, 1978.

Rossi, Osvaldo Duilio. *Teoria dei giochi, microeconomia e sequestro di persona*. Rome: Aracne, 2007.

Rudas, Nereide. "Fenomenologia dei sequestri di persona." *Minerva psichiatrica* 26, no. 2 (1985): 117–35.

Rudas, Nereide, and Pietro Marongiu. "Il sequestro di persona in Italia." In *Forme di organizzazioni criminali e terrorismo*, edited by Franco Ferracuti, 89–130. Milan: Giuffrè, 1988.

Rudas, Nereide, Giampaolo Pintor, and Irene Mascia. "Uomini rubati: Le vittime del sequestro di persona." In Marongiu, *Criminalità e banditismo in Sardegna*, 137–89.

Russo Bullaro, Grace, and Stephanie V. Love, eds. *The Works of Elena Ferrante: Reconfiguring the Margins*. New York: Palgrave Macmillan: 2016.

Santa, Vladimiro. *I nemici della Repubblica: Storia degli anni di piombo*. Milan: Rizzoli, 2016.

Santino, Umberto. *Storia del movimento antimafia: Dalla lotta di classe all'impegno civile*. Rome: Editori Riuniti, 2000.

Santovetti, Olivia. "Melodrama or Metafiction? Elena Ferrante's Neapolitan Novels." *Modern Language Review* 113, no. 3 (July 2018): 527–45. https://doi.org/10.5699/modelangrevi.113.3.0527.

Sartre, Jean-Paul. *Being and Nothingness: An Essay in Phenomenological Ontology*. Translated by Sarah Richmond. London: Routledge, 2018.

– *L'être et le néant : Essai d'ontologie phénoménologique*. Paris: Gallimard, 1943.

Saviano, Roberto. *Gomorra*. Milan: Mondadori, 2006.

Scaccia, Pino. *Sequestro di persona: Il caso Lombardini e la zona grigia dei rapimenti in Italia*. Rome: Editori Riuniti, 2000.

Scarano, Mimmo, and Maurizio De Luca. *Il mandarino è marcio: Terrorismo e cospirazione nel caso Moro*. Rome: Editori Riuniti, 1985.

Scarry, Elaine. *The Body in Pain: The Making and Unmaking of the World*. New York: Oxford University Press, 1985.

Sciarrone, Rocco. *Mafie vecchie, mafie nuove: Radicamento ed espansione*. Rome: Donzelli, 1998.

Sciascia, Leonardo. *L'affaire Moro*. Milan: Adelphi Edizioni, 2007.

Sergi, Anna, and Anita Lavorgna. *'Ndrangheta: The Glocal Dimensions of the Most Powerful Italian Mafia*. New York: Palgrave Macmillan, 2016.

Sergi, Pantaleone. *La "Santa" Violenta: Storie di 'ndrangheta e di ferocia, di faide, di sequestri, di vittime innocenti*. Cosenza: Periferia, 1991.

Shaw, Peter. *Hole: Kidnapped in Georgia*. Pembrokeshire, UK: Accent Press, 2006.

Siebert, Renate. *Secret of Life and Death: Women and the Mafia*. Translated by Liz Heron. London: Verso, 1996.

Sisti, Leo, and Peter Gomez. *L'intoccabile: Berlusconi e Cosa Nostra*. Milan: Kaos, 1997.

Sorgonà, Gregorio. "Società e 'ndrangheta: Il caso di Reggio Calabria." *Laboratoire italien* 22 (2019). https://doi.org/10.4000/laboratoireitalien.2989.

Sossi, Mario. *Nella prigione delle BR*. Milan: Editoriale Nuova, 1979.

Stajano, Corrado. *Il disordine*. Turin: Einaudi, 1993.

Stille, Alexander. *Benevolence and Betrayal: Five Italian Jewish Families under Fascism*. New York: Picador, 1991.

– *Excellent Cadavers: The Mafia and the Death of the First Italian Republic*. New York: Vintage Books, 1995.

– *The Sack of Rome: How a Beautiful European Country with a Fabled History and a Storied Culture Was Taken Over by a Man Named Silvio Berlusconi*. New York: Penguin, 2006.

Symonds, Martin. "Victim Responses to Terror." *Annals of the New York Academy of Sciences* 347 (June 1980): 129–36. https://doi.org/10.1111/j.1749-6632.1980.tb21262.x.

Terr, Lenore C. "Chowchilla Revisited: The Effects of Psychic Trauma Four Years After a School-Bus Kidnapping." *American Journal of Psychiatry* 140, no. 12 (December 1983): 1543–50. https://doi.org/10.1176/ajp.140.12.1543.

Tobagi, Benedetta. *Piazza Fontana: Il processo impossibile*. Turin: Einaudi, 2019.

– *Una stella incoronata di buio: Storia di una strage impunita*. Turin: Einaudi, 2013.

Toobin, Jeffrey. *American Heiress: The Wild Saga of the Kidnapping, Crimes and Trial of Patty Hearst*. New York: Profile Books, 2016.

Tranfaglia, Nicola, and Teresa de Palma. *Il giudice dimenticato: La storia e i misteri dell'assassinio di Bruno Caccia*. Turin: Edizioni Gruppo Abele, 2013.

Turone, Giuliano. *Italia occulta: Dal delitto Moro alla strage di Bologna; Il triennio maledetto che sconvolse la repubblica (1978–1980)*. Milan: Chiarelettere, 2019.

Varese, Federico. *Mafias on the Move: How Organized Crime Conquers New Territories*. Princeton, NJ: Princeton University Press, 2011.

Veltri, Filippo. *Sequestri: Tra violenze e misteri*. Cosenza: Memoria, 1998.

274 Bibliography

Ventura, Angelo. *Per una storia del terrorismo italiano*. Rome: Donzelli Editore, 2010.

Ventura, Francesco. *Il cinema e il caso Moro*. Recco: Le Mani, 2008.

Vergani, Guido. *Mesina*. Milan: Longanesi, 1968.

Vigna, Pier Luigi. "Il sequestro di persona." *Quaderni della giustizia* 3 (1981): 5–6.

Wagner-Pacifici, Robin Erica. *The Moro Morality Play: Terrorism as Social Drama*. Chicago: University of Chicago Press, 1986.

Waite, Terry. *Taken on Trust*. New York: Harcourt, Brace, 1993.

Ward, David. *Contemporary Italian Narrative and 1970s Terrorism*. New York: Palgrave Macmillan, 2017.

Zagari, Antonio. *Ammazzare stanca: Autobiografia di uno 'ndranghetista pentito*. Cosenza: Periferia, 1992.

Zavoli, Sergio. *La notte della Repubblica*. Milan: Mondadori, 1992.

Zimbardo, Philip G., and United States Committee on the Judiciary. *The Psychological Power and Pathology of Imprisonment*. Washington, DC: American Psychological Association, 1973.

Index

Note: Page numbers in *italics* indicate a figure.

5 centimetri d'aria, 219n3
743 giorni lontano da casa (743 days away from home) (Casella), 128–9, 138, 212n63, 230n69

A proposito di Liggio (About Liggio) (Missiroli and Sermonti), 77–8
Agamben, Giorgio, 130–1, 132
agency: in fiction, 199–200; in memoirs, 128–9, 147, 165–6, 175, 196, 204
Aglietta, Adelaide, 213n76
Agnelli, Gianni, 133, 201
Alberghini, Carlo, 101
Alberghini, Renato, 101
Alberoni, Francesco, 61
Alemagna, Daniele, 220n10
Alessi, Roberto, 139
Alexander, Jeffrey C., 11
alienation, 146
All the Money in the World (Scott), 42–3, 50–1, 58
Amerio, Ettore, 131–2
L'amica geniale (*My Brilliant Friend*) (Ferrante), 199–203, 204
Ammaniti, Niccolò, 199, 202
André, Christophe, 143–4

"Angel of History" (Benjamin), 135
anni di piombo (Years of Lead, 1969–c. 1983), 4, 7, 8, 33–4. *See also* Red Brigades (BR); terrorism and terrorist kidnapping
anonima sequestri (anonymous kidnapping), 8–9, 19, 70
anti-kidnapping movement, 12, 118–21, *120*
anti-Mafia law (1965), 27
anti-Mafia movement: assassinations of Falcone and Borsellino and, 73, 110, 124–6, 204; Casella's kidnapping and, 115–18; Cristina Mazzotti Foundation and, 73; Fiora's kidnapping and, 111–13; Kassam's kidnapping and, 124–6, *125*, *127*, 204; second ransom kidnapping crisis and, 109–13
Anti-Mafia Parliamentary Committee (Commissione parlamentare antimafia): Casella's kidnapping and, 116, 122; on kidnappings by 'Ndrangheta, 31; on kidnappings by Cosa Nostra, 26; on Liggio, 77; on Sardinian

276   Index

Anti-Mafia Parliamentary
  Committee (*continued*)
  banditry, 24, 84–5; on Soffiantini's
  kidnapping, 123; Violante and,
  113, 229n53
antisemitism, 133, 134–5
Arendt, Hannah, 10, 113
Aspromonte: Casella's kidnapping
  and, 12, 30, 111, 114–18, *116*, 122,
  138, 204; D'Amico's kidnapping
  and, 75–6; Fiora's kidnapping
  and, 30–1, 111–13, 117–18; Getty's
  kidnapping and, 43, 65; role in
  ransom kidnapping of, 7–8, 24,
  30–3, 38–9, 54
Austria, 208n17
AZ: Un fatto come e perché (A to Z: The
  how and why of the facts), 83, 84–9

Badalamenti, Tano, 25–6
Ballestrero, Anastasio, 111
Ballinari, Libero, 75, 76, 89, 112
Banda della Magliana, 210n17
Banditi a Orgosolo (*Bandits of
  Orgosolo*) (De Seta), 17
Barbagia, 16–19, 20–4, 38–9, 83–5,
  86–7, 99
Barresi, Placido, 215n93
Barthes, Roland, 85
Bartolomei, Donato Massimo, 214n90
bearing witness, 10–11, 129–38,
  141–3, 204
"Bearing Witness or the Vicissitudes
  of Listening" (Laub), 164–5
Beaufoy, Simon: *Trust* (TV series),
  42–3, 58
Belardi, Rosario, 213n76
Belardinelli, Dante: ear mutilations
  of, 123, 139, 141, 194–5; kidnapping
  of, 123; memoir by, 10–11, 128–9,
  139–41, 142–3, 189–90
Belfiore, Domenico, 36
Belgium, 208n17

Belleri, Pino, 138, 212n63
Belpoliti, Marco, 41, 60–1, 63, 64
Benjamin, Walter, 135
Berlusconi, Pier Silvio, 103
Berlusconi, Silvio, 5–6, 103
Bertoli, Pierangelo, 112
Bettelheim, Bruno, 152, 154
Bevilacqua, Alberto, 61–3
Biagi, Enzo: interview with Ballinari
  and, 89; on Mazzotti's abduction
  and murder, 68–9, 79–81, 96; on
  negotiations, 93; *Proibito*
  (RAI broadcast) and, 102–3; *RT*
  (TV news documentary) and, 83
Biancacci, Franco, 93, 105–6
bibliotecaria rapita, La (*The Librarian
  and the Robbers*) (Mahy), 198–9, 202
Bisiach, Gianni, 82–3
Blanchot, Maurice, 242n104
blocco dei beni (freezing of assets):
  Belardinelli on, 140–1; Casella's
  kidnapping and, 114–15, 122;
  hard versus soft line debate of
  1970s and, 100–8; impact of, 32;
  Soffiantini's kidnapping and,
  123, 141, 142–3; Tesi Mosca's
  kidnapping and, 137–8
bodily reflexivity, 44, 169, 181–4
Bontate, Stefano, 25–6
Boroli Ballestrini, Marcella, 105
Borsellino, Paolo, 7, 20, 73, 110
Brecht, Bertolt, 118
Bruni, Carla, 5–6, 103
Bulgari, Anna, 123
Bulgari, Giovanni, 106
Buscetta, Tommaso, 7, 26
Buse, Peter, 216n7

Caccia, Bruno, 20, 34, 36–7
Cagnetta, Franco, 16–17, 18
Calabria: anti-Mafia movement in,
  110, 112; Ferlaino's murder in,
  20, 34–5, 37, 215n95; Tacchella's

kidnapping and, 121. *See also* Aspromonte; 'Ndrangheta (Calabrian Mafia)

Calì, Giuseppe, 35

Calissoni, Giorgio, 123

Calvino, Italo, 97–9, 103, 113, 126

Camera Does the Rest, The (Buse), 216n7

Caminiti, Renato, 212n49

Camorra (Campanian Mafia), 6–7

Camus, Albert, 232n13

captivity: horrorism of, 16–17, 76–82, 187–94, 203, 204–5 (*see also* ear mutilations); isolation of, 145–51. *See also* trauma

Caruth, Cathy, 10–11

Casella, Angela, 12, 111, 114–18, *116*, 122, 138, 204

Casella, Cesare: anti-kidnapping movement and, 111, 119, 121; interviews and, 230n63; kidnapping of, 30, 109, 111, 113–14; memoir by, 128–9, 138, 212n63, 230n69; negotiations and, 114–18, 122; news coverage of, 117

Casella, Luigi, 114–15

Cassina, Luciano, 25

Catanzaro, 20, 33–4

Catholic Church: Casella's kidnapping and, 114; Fiora's kidnapping and, 111–13

Cavarero, Adriana, 10, 63–4, 78, 169, 187–94

Celadon, Carlo, 30, 109, 118, 121, 122, 230n71, 231n75

Celentano, Adriano, 111

Chace, James Fletcher, 48

children's literature, 198–9

Christian Democratic Party (Democrazia cristiana; DC), 3, 108

Ciconte, Enzo, 6, 28

Cinque ciliege rosse: Una notte lunga trentacinque giorni (Five red cherries: A thirty-five-day-long night) (Ovazza): abduction as disembodiment in, 3, 168; agency in, 128–9; *L'amica geniale* (*My Brilliant Friend*) (Ferrante) and, 201; bearing witness in, 10–11, 130, 132–7; horrorism of captivity in, 190–1, 192, 194; hostage as negotiator in, 185–6; hostage-perpetrator relationship in, 157–8; isolation of captivity in, 145–6, 149; trauma of captivity in, 136–7, 152–3

Ciotti, Luigi, 221n22

Clan dei Calabresi, 36

Clan dei Catanesi, 36

Coco, Francesco, 213n75

Colaprico, Piero, 212n61

collective traumatic experience, 11

Colombo, Giovanni, 238n73

Colombo, Roberto, 112

Commissione parlamentare antimafia. *See* Anti-Mafia Parliamentary Committee

Commissione parlamentare d'inchiesta sui fenomeni di criminalità in Sardegna (1969), 20–2, 83

Committee on Crime Problems (CDPC), 108

confession, 165–6

Connerton, Paul, 237n59

Consiglio Superiore della Magistratura (Superior Council of the Judiciary; CSM), 104, 105, 204

Corleo, Luigi, 25

corleonesi, 7, 19. *See also* Cosa Nostra (Sicilian Mafia)

Coronas, Rinaldo, 50

Corrias, Marco, 138–9

Corriere della Sera: Calvino and, 97–9, 103; on Casella's kidnapping, 117; on Getty's kidnapping, 48, 49,

278 Index

Corriere della Sera (*continued*)
50, 53, 59–60, 61–4, *62*, 76–7; on
Mazzotti's abduction and murder,
68–70, 71–5, *74*, 76–82, 110; petition
to Leone and, 70–1; review of
Malenotti's documentary in, 90
Cortellezzi, Andrea, 230n71
Cosa Nostra (Sicilian Mafia):
assassinations of Falcone and
Borsellino and, 7, 20, 73, 110, 124–6;
Dalla Chiesa and, 109; history of,
6–7; ransom kidnapping by the
corleonesi and, 3, 19, 25–7, 32–3,
38; television and, 83; Torielli's
kidnapping and, 25, 77, 83, 130.
See also Rossi di Montelera, Luigi
Cossiga, Francesco, 86, 88–9, 92, 102,
108, 119
Council of Europe, 108, 123, 204
Cribari, Francesco, 224n59
Cribari, Luigi, 224n59
Criminalpol, 117
"Cristina, un'esistenza come tante"
("Cristina, an Existence Like Many
Others") (Biagi), 68–9, 79–81
Cristina Mazzotti Foundation, 12,
73, 88, 109–10
Croce, Fulvio, 213n75
Cruel Radiance, The (Linfield), 63, 64
Cubeddu, Attilio, 141–2
cultural anthropology, 16–19, 20–3
cultural trauma, 11
Cutolo, Raffaele, 91

Dalla Chiesa, Carlo Alberto, 109
Dalla Chiesa, Nando, 109–10
D'Amico, Giuseppe, 75–6
De André, Fabrizio, 37, 124, 196–7
De Angelis, Elio, 123
De Angelis, Giulio, 123
De Mita, Ciriaco, 116–17
De Seta, Vittorio, 17

De Stefano, Paolo, 28
death penalty, 77, 80
Degortes, Daniela, 238n73
Delisle, Guy, 143–4
Dell'Aquila, Enzo, 84–5
Denmark, 208n17
"diario della notte degli incubi
quando il corpo venne ritrovato,
Il" ("The Diary of the Night of
Nightmares When the Body Was
Found") (Giuliani), 79
Dickie, John, 25–6
"dinamiche relazionali nel sequestro
di persona, Le" (Relational
dynamics in kidnapping) (Luberto
and Manganelli), 152, 154, 155
disembodiment, 3, 167–9, 173–84
divorce, 64
domestic terrorism in Italy. See *anni
di piombo* (Years of Lead)
Doppio agguato (TV film), 234n35
"Dove sta Zazà" (Where is Zazà)
(song), 91
Doxa, 99–100
Drug Enforcement Administration
(DEA), 47–8
drug trafficking, 47–8
Dunaway, Faye, 43

ear mutilations: Belardinelli and, 123,
139, 141, 194–5; Calissoni and, 123;
De Angelis and, 123; Getty and,
16–17, 41, 45, 47, 50–1, 52, 56–65,
62, 68, 100, 169, 194, 203; Kassam
and, 37, 124; Soffiantini and, 123,
141–2, 195; vulnerability and, 189
Economist, 128
Edizioni Paoline, 140
effet de réel (effect of reality), 85
*Ego and the Mechanisms of Defense,
The* (Freud), 154, 159
Elkann, Alain, 133

Eszterhas, Joe, 43–5, 47, 51, 66, 138
L'être et le néant (*Being and Nothingness*)
  (Sartre), 175–6
Every Secret Thing (Hearst and
  Moscow), 217n16
existential dehumanization, 168

Falcone, Giovanni, 7, 20, 73, 110,
  124, 204
Falivena, Aldo, 88–9, 92
Fantastico (Fantastic) (variety show), 111
Farina, Giovanni, 141–2, 159
far-right terrorism, 4, 7, 33–4
Fascist regime, 133, 134–5
Fass, Paula S., 219n5
Favaro, Angela, 238n73
Fazzo, Luca, 212n61
Federcasalinghe (National
  Housewife Association), 112–13
Federfiori Torino (National Federation
  of Italian Florists), 112–13
Felman, Shoshana, 232n13
Femia, Nicola, 122
Ferlaino, Francesco, 20, 34–5, 37,
  215n95
Ferrante, Elena, 199–203, 204
Fight Against the Mafia, 116
Filippini, Enrico, 90
Fiora, Marco: civic engagement
  in Turin and, 12, 111–13, 204;
  kidnapping of, 30–1, 109, 111, 114,
  117–18; Polaroid photography
  and, 111, 112
flesh, 164, 169, 175–84
Foucault, Michel, 165
France, 208n17
Frasca, Salvatore, 214n90
Freud, Anna, 154, 159
Freud, Sigmund, 146

Gaetano, Achille, 75, 77
Galli, Carlo, 67

Gambino, Sharo, 212n53
gambizzazioni (kneecapping), 4
Gassman, Vittorio, 92–3
Gava, Antonio, 116
Germany, 208n17
Getty, Ariadne, 42
Getty, Gail: Getty's kidnapping and,
  43, 52, 53–4, 57; Lagonegro trial
  and, 50; newspaper representation
  of, 55–6, 61, 64, 69
Getty, Paul, II, 43
Getty, Paul, III: anthropological
  gaze on, 16–18, 59–60; debate
  on negotiations and, 65–6, 93–4,
  100; ear mutilation of, 16–17, 41,
  45, 47, 50–1, 52, 56–65, 62, 68,
  100, 169, 194, 203; films and
  television series on, 42–3, 50–1,
  58; hoax hypothesis and, 42–3,
  46–7, 49–50, 51–2, 53–5, 57, 64–5,
  78; investigations and trial and,
  45, 47–50, 64–5; kidnapping as
  collective traumatic experience
  and, 11; lack of empathy for, 46,
  51–2, 64; Mammoliti family and,
  28–30; Moravia on, 16–18, 59–60,
  61, 63–4, 65, 76–7, 169; news
  coverage of, 40–2, 48, 49, 50, 52–8,
  59–60, 61–4, 62, 65, 68–9, 76–7,
  83; overdose and death of, 66;
  Polaroid photographs of, 40–2,
  50, 57–8, 60–4, 62; *Rolling Stone*
  interview and, 43–5, 47, 51, 66,
  138; television interviews and,
  45–7, 51, 55, 65, 85, 87
Getty, Paul, Sr., 41, 58, 65, 69
Getty, Talitha Pol, 43
Ghezzi, Dori, 124, 196
Giacobbe, Antonio, 34
Ginsborg, Paul, 101, 227n26
Ginzburg, Natalia, 90, 94–6, 110
giorno e la storia, Il (RAI broadcast), 51–2

280   Index

Giuliani, Arnaldo, 69, 78–9
Godfather, The (film), 6
Godfather, The (Puzo), 6
Gomorra (Saviano), 6
Gotor, Miguel, 107, 142
Gratteri, Nicola, 28
Gresti, Mario, 226n10
Gui, Luigi, 97, 99, 100–1, 108, 204
Guida, Vincenzino, 224n59
Guidetti Serra, Bianca, 229n53
Gusdorf, Georges, 243n116

Hearst, Patricia, 46
Hearst, William Randolph, 217n16
Herman, Judith, 150–1, 155–6
Hobbes, Thomas, 70
Hobsbawm, Eric, 17
horror and horrorism, 16–17, 76–82,
    187–94, 203, 204–5. *See also* ear
    mutilations
Hostage (Delisle), 143–4
hostage-perpetrator relationship,
    136, 152–61, 186–7, 189–94
"Hotel Supramonte" (song), 196–7

Ihde, Don, 149, 161
Im Keller (*In the Cellar*) (Reemtsma),
    238n72
Imposimato, Ferdinando, 104
"Individual and Mass Behavior in
    Extreme Situations" (Bettelheim),
    152, 154
L'industria dei sequestri (Rossani), 26
inerme (helpless), 10, 63–4
inner front of kidnapping, 151–6
inner language, 149, 159–60
International Conference of
    Criminology (Geneva, 1975), 100–1
Io non ho paura (*I'm Not Scared*)
    (Ammaniti), 199, 202
Io non ho paura (*I'm Not Scared*)
    (Salvatores), 199

isolation of captivity, 145–51
"Italians' Apathy Over Kidnappings
    Is Shaken by Girl's Murder"
    (Shuster), 67, 68

Jacovoni, Giovanni, 53–4
Jagger, Mick, 43
Jews, 133, 134–5
John Paul, II, Pope, 112, 114

Kappler, Herbert, 80
Kassam, Farouk, 37, 124–6, *127*, 204
Kassam, Fateh, 138–9
Keenan, Brian, 234nn51–2
Kennedy, John F., 4
kidnap industry, 38. *See also*
    'Ndrangheta (Calabrian Mafia)

La Barbera brothers, 25–6
Laffont, Robert, 132
Lamanna, Giuseppe, 47, 48, 49–50
language: bearing witness and,
    132, 136–7; horrorism of captivity
    and, 188; hostage as negotiator
    and, 184–7; hostage-perpetrator
    relationship and, 156–61; isolation
    of captivity and, 146–51; writing
    of return and, 161–5
Latella, Demetrio, 215n95
latitanza (abscondence, fugitiveness),
    21, 22–3
Laub, Dori, 164–5
Laurenzi, Carlo, 65
Lauro, Giacomo, 34–5
legalità (legality), 110
Leggio, Luciano, 7. *See also* Liggio,
    Luciano
Lejeune, Philippe, 243n116
Leone, Giovanni, 70–1
Leoni, Fausta, 132–3
*Lettere a San Luca: L'Italia scrive al
    "paese dei sequestri"* (Letters to San

Luca: Italy writes to "the village of ransom kidnappings") (Minuti and Veltri), 7
Lettere dalla prigionia (Prison letters) (Moro), 107–8
Levi, Primo, 90, 130–1, 229n53
Lévi-Strauss, Claude, 17, 18
Libera, 221n22
Librarian and the Robbers, The (Mahy), 198–9, 202
Life of Galileo (Brecht), 118
Liggio, Luciano, 7, 25, 49, 77–8
linea dura (hard line).
    See negotiations
Linfield, Susie, 63, 64
linguistic infantilism, 160
Luberto, Salvatore, 6, 26–7, 152, 154, 155
Luisari, Emanuela, 67

Macera, Ugo, 75–6
Macrì, Antonio, 28
Macrì, Carlo, 29
Maddalena, Marcello, 137
madre coraggio (mother courage), 114–18
Mafia: anti-Mafia law (1965) and, 27; history of, 6–9; in Northern Italy, 27, 109–11, 203; *omertà* (silence) and, 7, 71, 110, 113, 114, 124; television representation of, 82–3, 85–91.
    See also anti-Mafia movement; Cosa Nostra (Sicilian Mafia); 'Ndrangheta (Calabrian Mafia)
Magnani Noya, Maria, 111, 112
Mahy, Margaret, 198–9, 202
Malenotti, Maleno, 89–90
Malenotti, Roberto, 89–90
Mammoliti, Michael, 42
Mammoliti, Saverio, 42, 47–9, 50
Mammoliti family, 28–30. *See also* Getty, Paul, III

Mancuso, Antonio, 47
Manganelli, Antonio, 6, 26–7, 152, 154, 155
Mangano, Vittorio, 103
marcia dei rapiti (Rome, 1990), 12, 119–21, *120*
Marongiu, Pietro, 21, 23
Marrazzo, Giuseppe, 86–8, 201
Marseillais clan, 25
Martinelli, Roberto, 49, 50
Marxism, 72
Mascia, Irene, 153, 167–8, 169–70, 172–3, 175
masculinity, 22, 93
Masonry, 34
Masotti, Giovanni, 140
Mastrostefano, Ennio, 84
Mazzamauro, Anna, 91
Mazzotti, Cristina: abduction and murder of, 34, 67–8, 96; debate on negotiations and, 93–4, 97, 106; discovery of body of, 73–6, *74*, 78–9, 169; investigation and trial, 75–6; kidnapping as collective traumatic experience and, 11; newspaper coverage of, 68–70, 71–82, *74*, 110; petition to Leone and, 70–1; television coverage of, 82–3, 85–90
Mazzotti, Elios, 69, 72–3, 81, 110
Mazzotti, Eolo, 76, 88, 106
Mazzotti, Vittorio, 87–8
Medea, 191–2
Medici, Giuseppe, 20–2
Medici, Vincenzo, 230n71
Medusa, 191, 193–4
memoirs and published testimonies: abduction as disembodiment in, 3, 167–9, 173–84; agency in, 128–9, 147, 165–6, 175, 196; bearing witness in, 10–11, 129–38, 141–3, 204; Belardinelli and, 10–11, 128–9,

memoirs and published testimonies (*continued*)
139–41, 142–3, 189–90; Casella and, 128–9, 138, 212n63, 230n69; effects of, 194–7; fear and distrust of law enforcement in, 169–72; Getty's *Rolling Stone* interview and, 43–5, 47, 51, 66; Getty's television interview and, 45–7, 51, 55, 65, 85, 87; Hearst and, 217n16; horrorism of captivity in, 187–94; *Hostage* (Delisle) and, 143–4; hostage as negotiator in, 184–7; hostage-perpetrator relationship in, 136, 152–61, 189–94; isolation of captivity in, 145–51, 159–60; on liberation, 161–3, 170–2, 183–4, 190–1; Panattoni's television interview and, 86–7; second ransom kidnapping crisis and, 138–45; as sociopolitical testimony, 144–5; trauma of captivity in, 10–11, 135–7, 139–40, 151–6, 163–5; as writing of return, 161–5. See also *Cinque ciliege rosse: Una notte lunga trentacinque giorni*; *mio sequestro, Il*; *Racconto di un sequestro*; *Sindrome da sequestro*
Mentana, Enrico, 142
Merleau-Ponty, Maurice, 10, 87, 146, 164, 169, 173, 175–84
Mesina, Graziano, 22, 85
Messaggero, Il, 41, 52–3, 55, 57, 58, 61
Miano, Francesco, 36, 215n92
Michelini, Maurizio, 104
Milan: Mafia in, 27, 211n39; Piazza Fontana bombing in, 33–4
Ministero dell'Interno (Ministry of the Interior), 5
Mio figlio Farouk: Anatomia di un sequestro (My son Farouk: Anatomy of a kidnapping) (Kassam), 138–9

mio sequestro, Il (My kidnapping) (Soffiantini): abduction as disembodiment in, 168, 173, 174–5, 177, 181–2, 183–4; agency in, 128–9; bearing witness in, 10–11, 129, 141–3; horrorism of captivity in, 191; hostage-perpetrator relationship in, 154–5; isolation of captivity in, 145; on liberation, 162–3, 183–4, 191; religion and faith in, 139–40, 141, 158–9; trauma of captivity in, 154–5
Missiroli, Mario, 77–8
money laundering, 19, 36, 75, 83, 88, 104, 105
Monicelli, Mario, 92
Morabito, Saverio, 30
Moravia, Alberto: anthropological gaze on kidnapping and, 16–18, 37–8, 59–60; on Getty's kidnapping, 16–18, 59–60, 61, 63–4, 65, 76–7, 169; on Mazzotti's abduction and murder, 76–8
Moro, Aldo: debate on negotiations and, 11, 40, 65–6, 103, 104–5, 106–8, 142; Ginzburg on, 94–6, 110; kidnapping and murder of, 3–5, 8; kidnapping as collective traumatic experience and, 11; Polaroid photographs of, 40, *41*, 60, 63, 64; Soffiantini and, 142–3, 195–6
Morrissey, Paul, 43
Moschella, Luigi, 215n94
Moscow, Alvin, 217n16
Mother Courage and Her Children (Brecht), 118
motherhood, 190–3
mutilation. *See* ear mutilations

Nascimbeni, Giulio, 69–70, 72, 77, 81–2
Nazi occupation of Italy (1943–45), 80–2, 85–6, 91, 94–5

'Ndrangheta (Calabrian Mafia): as
anonima sequestri (anonymous
kidnapping), 8–9, 19, 70; anti-
Mafia law (1965) and, 27;
Bulgari's kidnapping and, 106;
Caccia's murder and, 20, 34,
36–7; Caminiti's kidnapping
and, 212n49; Ferlaino's murder
and, 20, 34–5, 37, 215n95;
history of, 6–9; in Piedmont,
133; Polaroid photography and,
41–2; ransom kidnapping as
kidnapping industry and, 3,
7–9, 19, 24–5, 27–39, 54, 203, 205;
Ravizza's kidnapping and, 139;
statistical overview of, 4–6. *See also*
Aspromonte; Getty, Paul, III;
Mazzotti, Cristina; Ovazza, Carla
negotiations: Belardinelli on, 139,
140–1, 142–3; Calvino and, 97–9,
103; Casella's kidnapping and,
114–18, 122; Getty's kidnapping
and, 65–6, 93–4, 100; hard versus
soft line debate of 1970s and,
11, 97–108, 114, 117, 137–8,
203–4; Mazzotti's abduction
and murder and, 93–4, 97, 106;
Moro's kidnapping and, 11, 40,
65–6, 94, 101–2, 103, 104–5, 106–8,
109–10, 142; Soffiantini on, 142–3;
Soffiantini's kidnapping and,
123–4; Stockholm syndrome and,
155; television and, 93–4, 99–100,
102–3, 105–6, 109; Tesi Mosca's
kidnapping and, 137–8
neofascism. *See* far-right terrorism
Netherlands, 208n17
New York Times, 67, 68, 78, 81
New York Times Book Review, 97–9
Nicaso, Antonio, 28
Nicholson, Jack, 43
Norway, 208n17

Nuclei Armati Proletari, 4
Nuovi Argomenti, 16–17
nuovi mostri, I (The new monsters)
(Risi, Scola, and Monicelli), 92–3, 126

omertà (silence), 7, 71, 110, 113, 114, 124
On Autobiography (Lejeune), 243n116
Operazione Minotauro (Minotaur
Operation), 213n78
"L'orecchio di Getty e l'industria del
sequestro" (Getty's ear and the
kidnapping industry) (Moravia),
59–60
organized crime. *See* Mafia
Orrorismo (*Horrorism*) (Cavarero),
63–4, 78, 187–94
Ovazza, Carla: kidnapping of, 133,
224n59; television interview and,
132–3. See also *Cinque ciliege rosse:
Una notte lunga trentacinque giorni*

Palermo, 109, 124, 204
Palomar (Calvino), 97–9
Panattoni, Mirko, 86–7
Pandolfo, Mario, 56
Panorama, 214n90
Pansa, Giampaolo, 61
Paribello, Francesco, 23
"Parlano i rapiti" (The kidnapped
speak) (Ginzburg), 90
Pasolini, Pier Paolo, 18, 60
"Pasolini or the Myth of Peasant
Culture" (Moravia), 18
passivity, 187–8
pastoral kidnapping, 20–4
Pavia, 114, 139
Peradotto, Franco, 111
phenomenology of perception, 10
Piazza Fontana bombing (Milan, 1969),
4, 33–4
Pigliaru, Antonio, 211n25
Pinelli, Giuseppe, 213n73

284 Index

Pinna, Salvatore, 198–9
Pintor, Giampaolo, 153, 167–8, 169–70, 172–3, 175
piovra, La (The Octopus) (TV series), 6
Piromalli, Girolamo, 48–50
Piromalli family, 29
Plague, The (Camus), 232n13
Polanski, Roman, 43
Polaroid photography: Belardinelli's kidnapping and, 195; Fiora and, 111, 112; Getty and, 40–2, 50, 57–8, 60–4, 62, 194; Moro's kidnapping and, 40, 41–2, 60, 63, 64
political kidnapping. *See* terrorism and terrorist kidnapping
Pomarici, Ferdinando, 101–4, 105–6, 109, 204
Prima Linea, 4, 36
Proibito (RAI broadcast), 93, 102–3
Provenzano, Bernardo, 25
psychological infantilism, 154–60, 187
Puzo, Mario, 6

"qualità della vita, La" ("The Quality of Life") (Ginzburg), 94–6, 110
Quaquero, Angela Maria, 198–9

Racconto di un sequestro (Account of a kidnapping) (Rossi di Montelera): abduction as disembodiment in, 167, 176–7, 179–81; agency in, 128–9; bearing witness in, 10–11, 130–2, 133–4, 135, 136–7; hostage as negotiator in, 185–6; hostage-perpetrator relationship in, 161; isolation of captivity in, 147, 149–50; on liberation, 170–1; trauma of captivity in, 136–7, 151–2, 153
Radstone, Susannah, 165
RAI (Italian public television): Catanzaro trial and, 33–4; comedy and satire on, 90–3; debate on

negotiations and, 93–4, 99–100, 102–3, 105–6; Fiora's kidnapping and, 111; Getty's interviews and, 45–7, 51, 55, 65, 85, 87; on Getty's kidnapping, 51–2, 87; on Mazzotti's abduction and murder, 82–3, 85–90; Ovazza's interview and, 132–3; Panattoni's interview and, 86–7; on Riboli's kidnapping, 86, 201; Sardinian banditry and, 83–5, 99; Tacchella's kidnapping and, 119
ransom kidnapping: as crime against property, 101–2; effects of, 9–12; in fiction, 198–202, 204; as modern phenomenon, 18–19, 37–9; Moravia on, 16–18, 59–60, 61, 63–4, 65, 76–7, 169; in other European countries, 208n17; statistical overview of, 4–6. *See also* Cosa Nostra (Sicilian Mafia); memoirs and published testimonies; 'Ndrangheta (Calabrian Mafia); negotiations; Sardinian banditry
Ratti, Erika, 214n85
Ravizza, Giuliano, 139
Reale, Oronzo, 100
Recanati, Elena, 135
Recommendation on Measures to Be Taken in Cases of Kidnapping Followed by a Ransom Demand (Council of Europe), 108
Red Brigades (BR): Amerio's kidnapping and, 131–2; Belardi's murder and, 213n76; Caccia and, 36; Dalla Chiesa and, 109; Ginzburg on, 94–6, 110; *linea dura* ("hard line") and, 65–6; Polaroid photography and, 40, 41–2, 41, 60, 63, 64; Sossi's kidnapping and, 17, 101; Tesi's kidnapper and, 171–2; Turin trial and, 33–4. *See also* Moro, Aldo

Reder, Walter, 80
Reemtsma, Jan Philipp, 238n72
religion, 139–40, 141, 158–9
Repici, Fabio, 215n95
Repubblica, La, 40
Riboli, Emanuele, 86, 224n59
Riboli, Luigi, 86, 201
"Riflessioni davanti all'orrore"
    (Reflections on Horror) (Moravia),
    76–8
Riina, Salvatore, 25
Risi, Dino, 92
Rizzoli, 138–9
Rocco Code (1930), 226n11
Roggiano Gravina, 121
Rognoni–La Torre anti-mafia law
    (1983), 230n65
Rolling Stone, 43–5, 47, 51, 66, 138
Rome: anti-kidnapping movement
    in, 12, 119–21, *120*; Banda della
    Magliana in, 210n17
Rome Open City (Rossellini), 91
Ronchetti, Sergio, 128, 130, 132, 135, 138
Ronzani, Gianni Wilmer, 229n53
Rossani, Ottavio, 26, 104, 209n30,
    214n85
Rossellini, Roberto, 91
Rossi, Luigi, 117
Rossi di Montelera, Luigi:
    kidnapping of, 25, 130, *180*; Liggio
    and, 25, 77; television interviews
    and, 224n59. See also *Racconto di
    un sequestro*
RT (TV news documentary), 82–3
Rudas, Nereide, 21, 153, 167–8,
    169–70, 172–3, 175

Salvatores, Gabriele, 199
Samarcanda (RAI broadcast), 119
Sanna, Carlo, 215n92
Santa (Holy), 34
Santonastaso, Paolo, 238n73

Santoro, Michele, 119
Sardinian banditry: anthropological
    gaze on, 16–19, 20–3; De André
    and Ghezzi's kidnapping and, 37,
    124, 196–7; debate on negotiations
    and, 99; history of, 20–4, 122–4,
    205; ransom kidnapping as
    pastoral kidnapping and, 3,
    8–9, 16–19, 20–3, 37–9; statistical
    overview of, 4–6; television and,
    83–5, 99; victimology on, 153,
    167–8, 169–70, 172–3, 175. *See also*
    Belardinelli, Dante; Soffiantini,
    Giuseppe
Sarkozy, Nicolas, 103
Sartre, Jean-Paul, 168, 175–6
Saviano, Roberto, 6
Scalfari, Eugenio, 124
Scarano, Mimmo, 45–7, 51
Scarpa, David, 42–3
Scarry, Elaine, 149, 186–7
Scelba, Mario, 16
sceneggiata (musical comedy), 91–2
Schirripa, Rocco, 213n78
Scola, Ettore, 92–3, 126
Scopelliti, Antonio, 35
Scott, Ridley: *All the Money in the
    World*, 42–3, 50–1, 58
Scriva, Pino, 35
Scuola serale per aspiranti italiani
    (Night school for aspiring Italians)
    (variety show), 90–2
second Mafia war (1984–91), 32
"Sequestri: La spirale della violenza"
    (Kidnapping: The spiral of
    violence) (Malenotti), 89–90
*sequestri di persona a scopo di
    estorsione, I* (Kidnappings
    for ransom) (Luberto and
    Manganelli), 6, 26–7
"sequestro di Cristina, Il" (Cristina's
    kidnapping) (Stajano), 71–2

"Sequestro di persona cara" ("Kidnapping Dear!") (Scola), 92–3, 126

Sermonti, Vittorio, 77–8

Shuster, Alvin, 67, 68, 78, 81

silence, 145–6. *See also* language

"silenzio e un dolore che chiedono giustizia, Un" ("A Silence and Grief That Ask for Justice") (Nascimbeni), 81–2

Silocchi, Mirella, 230n71

Sindrome da sequestro (Kidnapping syndrome) (Tesi Mosca): abduction as disembodiment in, 168, 174, 182–3; agency in, 128–9; bearing witness in, 10–11, 135–8; horrorism of captivity in, 187, 190–1, 192–4; hostage-perpetrator relationship in, 136, 154–5; isolation of captivity in, 147–8, 159–60; language in, 136–7, 164; on liberation and following events, 161–2, 171–2, 190–1; on pigs, 199; trauma of captivity in, 135–7, 139–40, 154–5

Soffiantini, Giuseppe: Calvino and, 98; ear mutilations of, 123, 141–2, 195; kidnapping of, 123, 141–2; negotiations and, 123–4. See also *mio sequestro, Il*

Sorrentino, Aurelio, 112

Sossi, Mario, 17, 101

Sotto Processo (RAI broadcast), 99–100

Spain, 208n17

Speciale TG1 (RAI broadcast), 109

Spirit of Mourning (Connerton), 237n59

Stajano, Corrado, 71–2, 209n28

Stallavena di Grezzana, 118–21

Stampa, La: on *anonima sequestri* (anonymous kidnapping), 209n30;

on kidnapping memoirs, 128, 130, 132, 135; on Moro's kidnapping, 94–6, 110

Stille, Alexander, 213n77

Stockholm syndrome, 155–9, 165, 169–70

Storia di un sequestro (Story of a kidnapping) (Belardinelli), 10–11, 128–9, 139–41, 142–3, 189–90, 194–5

storia siamo noi, La (RAI broadcast), 51–2, 59

Storie allo specchio (RAI broadcast), 93, 105–6

stragismo (slaughter tactics), 4, 7

strategy of tension, 33–4. *See also* far-right terrorism

subjectivity, 177–9

Superior Council of the Judiciary (Consiglio Superiore della Magistratura; CSM), 104, 105, 204

superstes (survivor as witness), 130–1

Surviving, and Other Essays (Bettelheim), 152, 154

Sweden, 208n17

Switzerland, 208n17

Symbionese Liberation Army, 217n16

Symonds, Martin, 155–6

Tacchella, Imerio, 121

Tacchella, Patrizia, 118–21

Tagliaferro, Pierluigi, 73–5

Tandeddu, Pasquale, 22

Tartamella, Pietro, 112

Taviani, Paolo Emilio, 49

tax evasion, 89, 92

television: Catanzaro trial and, 33–4; comedy and satire on, 90–3; debate on negotiations and, 93–4, 99–100, 102–3, 105–6, 109; Fiora's kidnapping and, 111; Getty's interview and, 45–7, 51, 55, 65, 85, 87; on Getty's kidnapping, 45–7, 51–2, 65, 85, 87; on Mazzotti's abduction and murder, 82–3, 85–90; Ovazza's interview and, 132–3; Panattoni's interview and, 86–7; representation of Mafia in, 82–3, 85–91; Sardinian banditry and, 83–5, 99; on Soffiantini's kidnapping, 142; Tacchella's kidnapping and, 119

Tempo, Il, 40–1, 52–6, 57–8, 61

terrorism and terrorist kidnapping: Hearst's kidnapping and, 46; negotiations and, 11, 40, 65–6, 94, 101–2, 103, 104–5, 106–8, 109–10, 142; publications about, 128. *See also* Red Brigades (BR)

Tesi Mosca, Donatella, 136. See also *Sindrome da sequestro*

testis (witness), 130–1

TG3 (RAI broadcast), 111, 112

Tg5 (Mediaset newscast), 142

topological space, 179

Torielli, Pietro, Jr., 25, 77, 83, 130

trauma: in fiction, 200–3; Mazzotti's abduction and murder as, 79–81; in memoirs, 10–11, 135–7, 139–40, 151–6, 163–5; Nascimbeni on, 70

Trauma and Recovery (Herman), 150–1, 155–6

Tripodo, Mico, 28

Trust (TV series), 42–3, 58

Turin: Caccia's murder in, 20, 34, 36–7; debate on negotiations in, 137; Fiora's kidnapping and, 12, 111–13, 204; Mafia in, 27, 36; trial against BR in, 33–4

Tuscany: Sardinian banditry in, 139, 141–2; Soffiantini's kidnapping

and, 182; Tesi Mosca's kidnapping and, 182–3

TV7, 83–4

Unclaimed Experience: Trauma, Narrative, and History (Caruth), 10–11

L'Unità: debate on negotiations and, 104; on Getty's kidnapping, 61; on Kassam's kidnapping, 124–6, *125, 127*

United Kingdom (UK), 208n17

"Uomini rubati: Le vittime del sequestro di persona" ("Stolen Men: The Victims of Kidnapping") (Rudas, Pintor, and Mascia), 153, 167–8, 169–70, 172–3, 175

Valenza, Giuseppe, 224n59

Variety, 42

Vassallo, Pino, 25

Veca, Salvatore, 118

Verona, 119

"Vi parlo dei rapimenti dopo il sequestro di mia figlia" ("I Am Going to Talk to You About Kidnapping Now That My Daughter Has Been Abducted") (Mazzotti), 72–3

Victim Responses to Terror (Symonds), 155–6

victimology, 9, 153, 167–8, 169–70, 172–5

Vigna, Pier Luigi, 101, 104, 109, 123, 141

Violante, Luciano, 113, 213n76, 229n53

Visible et l'invisible, Le (*The Visible and the Invisible*) (Merleau-Ponty), 173, 175–84

Volta, Giovanni, 114
vulnerability, 169, 183, 188–94. *See also* ear mutilations

Warhol, Andy, 41, 43
Women Against the Mafia Association, 115
Writing of the Disaster (Blanchot), 242n104

Years of Lead. See *anni di piombo* (Years of Lead)

Zaccagnini, Benigno, 108
Zagari, Antonio, 30
Zambeletti, Ludovico, 226n10
Zanardelli Code (1889), 226n11
Zavoli, Sergio, 124–6, *125*
Zucconi, Guglielmo, 99–100

Printed and bound by CPI Group (UK) Ltd, Croydon, CR0 4YY
31/08/2025